Future Armies, Future Challenges

Future Armies, Future Challenges

Land warfare in the information age

Edited by Michael Evans, Alan Ryan and Russell Parkin

ALLEN&UNWIN

In fond memory of Ian MacFarling
Friend, Colleague and Sparring Partner

First published in 2004

Allen & Unwin
83 Alexander Street
Crows Nest NSW 2065
Australia
Phone: (61 2) 8425 0100
Fax: (61 2) 9906 2218
Email: info@allenandunwin.com
Web: www.allenandunwin.com

National Library of Australia
Cataloguing-in-Publication entry:

Future armies, future challenges : land warfare in the
information stage

Bibliography.
Includes index.
ISBN 1 86508 626 6.

1. Military art and science. I. Evans, Michael, 1951 Sept.
27- . II. Parkin, Russell. III. Ryan, Alan, 1963- .

355

Set in 11/13 pt Centaur by Midland Typesetters
Printed by South Wind Production, Singapore

10 9 8 7 6 5 4 3 2 1

Foreword

The October 2001 Chief of Army's Land Warfare Conference on the theme of 'Future Armies, Future Challenges: Land Warfare in the Information Age' was held less than a month after the tragic terrorist attacks of 11 September in the United States. As a result, the subject matter of the conference, the future of land warfare, could not have been more grimly realistic. The deliberations of the conference were undertaken by a group of eminent Australian, American, British, French and Indian defence scholars and military practitioners, and took place against an ominous background of preparation for an international military campaign against the Taliban regime and the al-Qa'ida movement in Afghanistan.

The speedy success of the US-led international coalition in removing the Taliban and destroying al-Qa'ida's presence in Afghanistan demonstrated the continuing value of land forces in the age of cruise missiles and stealth technology. As several of the essays in this book make clear, land power remains fundamental to the success of joint operations. It is worth remembering that one of the most memorable justifications for the role of the soldier in war was made by an eminent American sailor, Rear Admiral J. C. Wylie. In 1967, when pondering the *ultima ratio* of strategy, Wylie wrote, 'the ultimate determinant in war is the man on the scene with the gun. This man is the final power in war. He is in control. He determines who wins.'

The 2001 Conference examined three broad themes, all of which are reflected in these proceedings. The first of these themes was the changing shape of conflict and the growing diversity of operations confronting contemporary armies. Throughout the 1990s, we witnessed this diversity in missions conducted as far apart as the Persian Gulf, Bosnia, Haiti, Somalia, Rwanda, East Timor, Kosovo and, most recently, Afghanistan. The second theme considered at the conference was the character of the future challenges that may face the Australian Army and other land forces around the world. These challenges arise from the combination of the advanced military technology, including weapons of mass destruction, the impact of instant media imagery, and the influence of the forces of globalisation. The last theme considered by speakers and delegates concerned the valuable lessons gleaned from recent operational experiences in missions to Bosnia and East Timor. The accounts of these operational lessons are accompanied in this volume by a stimulating discussion of the looming threat now posed to liberal democracy by the new dynamics of international terrorism.

As many of our old certainties slip away with the 20th century, to be replaced by new frontiers of risk, this book is a timely reminder of the complexities faced by the profession of arms. The book's collection of essays is also a reaffirmation of Liddell Hart's famous advice: 'if you wish for peace, understand war . . . This understanding can only be attained if we study war in a purely scientific spirit, with our minds free from any pro-military or anti-military bias which might impair our judgment—and thereby nullify our deductions.' As the early 21st century emerges as an era that is likely to be the most operationally demanding decade in Australian Army history since the Vietnam War of the 1960s, I commend this excellent study to all those who seek an understanding of the changing character of armed conflict.

Lieutenant General Peter Cosgrove, AC, MC
Chief of Army
Canberra, May 2002

Contents

Tables and figures

Abbreviations

ABCA	American–British–Canadian–Australian armies program
ADF	Australian Defence Force
ADFA	Australian Defence Force Academy
ACSC	Australian Command and Staff College
ACT	Australian Capital Territory
AIF	Australian Imperial Force
AME	aero-medical evacuation
ANZAC	Australian New Zealand Army Corps
AO	area of operations
ASEAN	Association of South East Asian countries
AWACS	Airborne warning and control system
C2	command and control
C3I	command, control, communication and intelligence
C4I	command, control, communication, computers and intelligence
CDF	Chief of the Defence Force (Australia)
CEC	Cooperative Engagement Capability
CINC	Commander-in-Chief
INTERFET	International Force East Timor
IOM	International Organization for Migration
JSTARS	Joint Surveillance and Target Attack System
JTF	Joint Task Force
MEB	Marine Expeditionary Brigade

MOUT	military operations in urban terrain
MTW	Major Theatre War
NATO	North Atlantic Treaty Organization
NCW	network-centric warfare
OODA	observation–orientation–decision–action
PACC	Pacific Armies Chiefs' Conference
PAMS	Pacific Armies Management Seminar
PKF	Peacekeeping Force
QDR	Quadrennial Defense Review (US)
RAF	Royal Air Force
RMA	Revolution in Military Affairs
RNA	Revolution in Naval Affairs
SNO	Senior National Officer
SRSG	Special Representative of the Secretary-General
SSN	Submarine, Nuclear
TCWG	tactical coordination working group
UAV	unmanned aerial vehicle
UK	United Kingdom
UN	United Nations
UNOSOM II	United Nations Operations in Somalia II
UNPROFOR	United Nations Protection Force (Bosnia)
UNTAC	United Nations Transitional Authority Cambodia
UNTAET	United Nations Transitional Administration East Timor
UNHCR	United Nations High Commissioner for Refugees
US	United States
USAF	United States Air Force
USMC	United States Marine Corp

Contributors

Major General Peter Abigail

Major General Peter Abigail was born in Sydney on 6 April 1948 and graduated from the Royal Military College Duntroon in 1969 as an infantry officer into the Royal Australian Regiment. He holds a Bachelor of Commerce (Economics), a Graduate Diploma in Strategic Studies, a Diploma of Military Studies (Arts—Merit) and is a Fellow of the Australian College of Defence and Strategic Studies.

Major General Abigail has held a range of regimental and staff appointments, including: active service in South Vietnam as a platoon commander; aide-de-camp to the Chief of the General Staff; company commander in the 3rd Battalion, the Royal Australian Regiment; exchange instructor at the British School of Infantry, Warminster; Brigade Major 1st Brigade; Staff Officer in the Directorate of Plans (Army Office); Commanding Officer of the 3rd Battalion (Parachute), the Royal Australian Regiment; and Military Assistant to the Chief of the General Staff.

Senior appointments have included Director of Resource Management—Army; Director General Corporate Planning and Management—Army; and Director General Joint Operations and Plans, Headquarters Australian Defence Force. He was Commander 3rd Brigade (Ready Deployment Force) in 1993–94 and during this period commanded Operation Lagoon in Bougainville—the first Australian-led joint and combined peace support operation.

In 1980, he attended the Australian Staff College, Queenscliff. In

1989, he attended the Joint Services Staff College Course 40/89 and in 1995 was a participant in the inaugural course at the Australian College of Defence and Strategic Studies.

He was promoted Major General on 13 December 1996 and assumed the appointment of Assistant Chief of the Defence Force (Policy and Strategic Guidance) on 18 December 1996. Under Defence Reform Program reorganisation, on 1 July 1997, Major General Abigail was appointed Head Strategic Policy and Plans within the Australian Defence Headquarters. On 18 June 1998 he assumed the appointment of Deputy Chief of Army. On 13 June 2000 he assumed his current appointment as Land Commander—Australia.

Major General Abigail was appointed an Officer of the Order of Australia in January 2000.

Dr Graeme Cheeseman

Dr Graeme Cheeseman is a visiting fellow in the School of Politics at the University College, Australian Defence Force Academy. He is a graduate of the Royal Military College, Duntroon, and the University of New South Wales. Prior to entering academe in 1988, he served in the Australian Regular Army, the Australian Department of Defence, and as the defence adviser to the Parliamentary Joint Committee on Foreign Affairs and Defence. Dr Cheeseman has written and lectured on Australian defence and foreign policy and policy making, Australia's military and defence organisations and cultures, and Australian and regional security structures and concerns. His most recent publications include *The Howard Government's Defence White Paper: Policy, Process and Politics*; 'Canada's Post-Cold War Military Blues and its Lessons for Australia', *Pacifica Review*, 13(2): 171–92, June 2001; and 'Responding to "New Times": Securing Australia and Britain in a Post-Cold War Era', *Contemporary Security Policy*, 22(1): 99–128, April 2001. His present research interests are focused around the changing role of military forces, and military forces in global affairs, and the concept of 'cosmopolitan militaries'.

Colonel Richard Cousens

Colonel Richard Cousens is the Director of Defence Studies for the British Army and works for the Directorate of Development and

Doctrine based at Upavon in Wiltshire. Commissioned into the Light Infantry in 1969, he commanded at platoon, company and battalion levels with the 2nd Battalion, The Light Infantry. He also served for three years as a company commander with the 2nd King Edward VII's Own Gurkha Rifles in Brunei and Hong Kong. He has completed seven tours in Northern Ireland. He was a member of the Directing Staff at the British Army Staff College from 1991 to 1993. After two years as a Divisional Colonel at the Staff College, Colonel Cousens was the British Army Liaison Officer to US Army Training and Doctrine Command. He chaired an American–British–Canadian–Australian Armies Program (ABCA) Special Working Party on Digitisation. Prior to his current appointment he was Director of Force Development at HQ Infantry in Warminster. He has been in his current appointment since October 2000. Colonel Cousens has also been awarded the OBE and the US Legion of Merit.

Dr Michael Evans

Dr Michael Evans is Head of the Australian Army's Land Warfare Studies Centre and is a graduate in history and war studies of the universities of Rhodesia, London, and Western Australia. Dr Evans has been a Sir Alfred Beit Fellow in the Department of War Studies at King's College, University of London, and a Visiting Fellow at the University of York in England.

He was a regular officer in the post-civil war Zimbabwe Army where, with the rank of Major, he headed that army's War Studies Program and worked with the British Army in the development of a national land force. He has published a wide range of journal articles and papers on military history and contemporary strategy in Australia, Britain and the United States. His recent publications include, *From Deakin to Dibb: The Army and the Making of Australian Strategy in the 20th Century* (2001) and *Australia and the Revolution in Military Affairs* (2001). He is currently completing a book titled, *Military Theory and 21st Century War: The Legacy of the Past and the Challenge of the Future.*

Lieutenant Colonel Robert Leonhard

Lieutenant Colonel Robert R. Leonhard is the Professor of Military Science and the Commander of the West Virginia University Army

ROTC Mountaineer Battalion. Commissioned as an Infantry officer in 1978, Colonel Leonhard earned a Bachelor of Arts degree in History from Columbus College near Fort Benning, Georgia. In 1989, he earned a Master of Science degree in International Relations from Troy State University. In 1994, he completed a Master of Military Arts and Sciences degree at the United States Army's Command and General Staff College.

Colonel Leonhard's military schooling includes the Infantry Officer Basic and Advanced Courses, Bradley Infantry Fighting Vehicle Commander's Course, Airborne School, French Commando School, Command and General Staff College, and the Advanced Military Studies Program.

Colonel Leonhard volunteered for duty in the Gulf War and served with 4th Battalion (Mechanized), 18th Infantry in the 3rd Armor Division. In 1994, Colonel Leonhard was assigned as the Operations Officer, 1st Battalion (Mechanized), 41st Infantry in the 2nd Armor Division at Fort Hood, Texas. He later served as the Chief of Plans, 4th Infantry Division. From 1996 to 1998, Colonel Leonhard served in the Joint Venture Office, Training and Doctrine Command at Fort Monroe, Virginia. Here he planned and administered Advanced Warfighting Experiments—large-scale futuristic tests in information operations—for the US Army's Force XXI program. Colonel Leonhard's awards and decorations include the Bronze Star, the Meritorious Service Medal with three Oak Leaf Clusters, the Army Commendation Medal and the Combat Infantryman's Badge.

Colonel Leonhard is also the author of numerous articles and several books on modern warfare, including his latest, *The Principles of War for the Information Age* (Presidio Press, 1998.) He also wrote *The Art of Maneuver: Maneuver Warfare Theory and AirLand Battle* (Presidio Press, 1991); and *Fighting by Minutes: Time and the Art of War* (Greenwood Press, 1994). He is currently writing a book on strategy.

Major General Duncan Lewis

Major General Duncan Lewis graduated from the Royal Military College, Duntroon, in 1975. He has seen regimental service in the 6th Battalion of the Royal Australian Regiment and three tours with the Special Air Service Regiment. He served with UNTSO as a military observer during the 1982 Lebanon War, and commanded the Special Air Service Regiment from 1990 to 1992, a role that included the command of the national counter-terrorist Tactical Action Group. For his services as commanding officer he was awarded the Conspicuous Service Cross. He has held appointments on the instructional staff of the Royal Military College, Duntroon, and the Army Command and Staff College.

Major General Lewis has served in staff appointments on the Divisional Headquarters, on the Army Headquarters staff as Director of the Defence Reform Program in Army and as the Director of Strategy and International Engagement. During the INTERFET period he was appointed the ADF spokesman on East Timor. He was the Army Attaché in Jakarta from 1994 to 1996, returning to Jakarta briefly as acting Head Australian Defence Staff in 1998. He was promoted to the rank of Brigadier in January 2000 and appointed Commander Sector West UNTAET, Peacekeeping Force in East Timor, commanding the Australian and New Zealand forces on the East Timor–West Timor border. He was awarded the Distinguished Service Cross for his command in East Timor. He was appointed Commander Special Forces in January 2001. In December 2002 he was promoted to Major General and given command of Special Operations Command. This command is a joint organisation with responsibility for the employment of all Australian Special Forces' units.

Major General Lewis is a graduate of the British Army Staff College, Camberley, and the United States Army War College. He holds a BA from the University of New South Wales and a Graduate Diploma in Defence Studies from Deakin University. He is a graduate of the Australian Defence Force School of Languages, where he studied Indonesian.

Group Captain Ian MacFarling

Group Captain Ian MacFarling joined the Royal Australian Air Force (RAAF) in March 1977. Prior to that he had served twelve years in the Royal New Zealand Air Force, where he flew as a navigator on Canberra B(I) 12 bombers, Sunderland Mk 5 flying boats, Bristol Fighters and P3B Orions. In the RAAF he flew as a Tactical Coordinator on P3B Orions, and his last flying duties were at the Aircraft Research and Development

Unit, where he completed the tour as flight commander (slow speed). He has served with the Defence Science and Technology Organisation, Headquarters Australian Defence Force, the University of New South Wales at the Australian Defence Force Academy, International Policy Division of the Department of Defence, the Joint Services Staff College as a member of the Directing Staff, and as Deputy Director of Studies at the Australian Defence College.

Group Captain Ian MacFarling is a graduate of the RAAF School of Languages, the Indonesian Air Force Command and Staff College, the Asia–Pacific Centre for Security Studies in Honolulu, and the Royal Military College of Science in Shrivenham, England. He was educated at Massey University in New Zealand, the University of Queensland, the Royal Melbourne Institute of Technology, and the University of New South Wales. His doctorate is in political science, with a specific focus on civil–military relations in Indonesia.

Group Captain Ian MacFarling joined the Aerospace Centre in August 1999. He was promoted to Group Captain and appointed Director on 14 December 2000.

Colonel Douglas A. Macgregor

Colonel Douglas Macgregor was commissioned in the US Army in 1976 after one year at the Virginia Military Institute and four years at the US Military Academy. After completing airborne and ranger training, Colonel Macgregor served in a variety of command and staff assignments including command of a Division Cavalry Squadron and one year in the War Plans Division of the Army General Staff. During Operation *Desert Storm*, Colonel Macgregor was awarded the bronze star with 'V' device for valour while leading combat troops in the 2nd Squadron, 2nd Amored Cavalry regiment. He wrote *Breaking the Phalanx* while serving as the Army Fellow at CSIS in Washington, DC. Among his other works is *The Soviet–East German Military Alliance*. Colonel Macgregor holds an MA in comparative politics and a PhD in International Relations from the University of Virginia. He was assigned to the US Army Combined Arms Center at Fort Leavenworth, Kansas, and is currently a Senior Military Fellow in the Institute for National Strategic Studies at the National Defence University in Washington, DC.

Rear Admiral Raja Menon

Rear Admiral Menon attended the Indian National Joint Services Academy and was commissioned into the Navy in 1960. A pioneer of India's submarine arm, he was part of the Commonwealth Submarine Course in 1965. He commissioned two submarines in the former USSR as Commanding Officer and later commanded two frigates, the depot ship and a submarine building in Germany and managed the induction of the first four Kilos. He headed the Indian Navy's Tactics Committee for three years and was part of the Indian delegation for talks with Pakistan and Sri Lanka. In 1994 Rear Admiral Menon retired as the Assistant Chief of Naval Staff (Operations).

Since retiring he has specialised in strategic matters. Some of his publications are: *Maritime Strategy and Continental Wars* (1998); *A Nuclear Strategy For India* (2000); and *The Indian Navy—A Photo Essay*. He is a visiting lecturer at the National Defence College, the Staff College, Higher Command Course and the Foreign Service Training Institute. He also frequently contributes to the weekly *Outlook* and the *Times of India*.

Major Russell Parkin

Major Russell Parkin graduated from the Officer Cadet Training Unit, 2nd Training Group, at Ingleburn in NSW in 1982 and was allocated to the Royal Australian Army Ordnance Corps, Army Reserve. After several regimental postings he graduated from the Reserve Command and Staff College (Junior Course) and was posted to HQ 5 Brigade as the SO3 Supply. In 1989 he began a two-year posting on full-time duty at the Directorate of Supply in Canberra. In October 1990 he joined the Regular Army and began a series of staff and instructional postings at the Army College of TAFE, the RAEME Training Centre, the Army Logistic Training Centre and the Directorate of Army Research and Analysis. In 2000 he attended the Army Command and Staff College, Fort Queenscliff and on completion of the course was posted to the Land Warfare Studies Centre (LWSC), Duntroon as a Research Fellow during 2001–02.

Major Parkin holds a Bachelor of Arts and Diploma of Education (1978), a Master of Defence Studies (1990) and a PhD (1998) from the

University of New South Wales. He has published articles in the Proceedings of the Army History Conference, the New Zealand Army Journal, the RAAF Air Power Studies Centre Papers and the Australian War Memorial publication, *Wartime*. Major Parkin's research interests include Joint Warfare, Coalition Warfare and Political–Military Relations.

Lieutenant Colonel Ralph Peters

Ralph Peters retired from the US Army shortly after his promotion to lieutenant colonel. Risen from the enlisted ranks, he became an intelligence officer and a foreign area specialist for Russia and its borderlands. He has served in infantry units, in the Pentagon, and in the Executive Office of the President. His military career and personal interests have taken him to 50 countries, from the Andean Ridge to South-East Asia, and from the Kremlin negotiations to refugee camps in the Caucasus. A controversial thinker, he has published one book on strategy, *Fighting For The Future: Will America Triumph?*, and numerous influential essays and commentaries on subjects ranging from the nature of violence to the future of conflict. Ralph Peters is also a novelist; several of his eleven books have been bestsellers. He has lectured in the United States, Europe and Asia—to government, academic and business audiences—on a wide range of strategy-related subjects.

As a commentator and essayist, Ralph Peters has contributed to *Newsweek*, *The Wall Street Journal*, *The Washington Post*, *The Los Angeles Times*, *Newsday*, *The Washington Monthly*, *Parameters*, *Strategic Review* and numerous other national and international journals and newspapers.

General Sir Michael Rose

General Sir Michael Rose was born in Quetta, former British India, and later educated at Cheltenham College, the Sorbonne and St Edmund Hall, Oxford, where he studied politics, philosophy and economics. In 1999 he was awarded an Hon. Dlitt by Nottingham University.

General Rose joined the Reserves in 1957 and in 1964 was commissioned as a Regular Officer into the Coldstream Guards. He served in Germany and the Middle East before joining the Special Air Service Regiment in 1968. He attended Staff College, Camberley, and subsequently saw active service in the Middle East and Far East. His service career has included duty in Northern Ireland and the Falkland Islands conflict.

General Rose has attended the Royal College of Defence Studies; he has served as the Commandant of the School of Infantry, and as Director Special Forces. He became Commandant of the Staff College, Camberley, in September 1991, and in April 1993 was appointed Commander of the UK Field Army, United Kingdom Land Forces and Inspector General Territorial Army. He commanded the UN Protection Force Bosnia-Herzegovina Command. In 1997 he was the Kermit Roosevelt Lecturer in the United States.

General Rose was appointed OBE in 1978, CBE in 1986 and KCB in 1994. He was awarded the QGM in 1981 and the DSO in 1995. He was made Commander in the Legion d'Honneur by President Chirac in October 1995. Since leaving the Army in 1997, General Rose has written and lectured extensively on peacekeeping and leadership to a variety of audiences around the world. He is the author of *Fighting for Peace: Lessons from Bosnia* which was first published in 1998.

Dr Alan Ryan

Dr Alan Ryan is a Senior Research Fellow in the Australian Army's Land Warfare Studies Centre (LWSC), Duntroon. He was formerly Assistant Dean in the Colleges of Law and Arts at the University of Notre Dame, Australia. Dr Ryan completed his PhD in the Centre for International Studies at Cambridge University. He has degrees in Law and Arts from the University of Melbourne. He served as an infantry officer in the Australian Army Reserve and on attachment with the British Army. In 2000 and 2002 he conducted operational research with the peacekeeping forces in East Timor.

With Dr Michael Evans, Dr Ryan coedited *The Human Face of Warfare: Fear and Chaos in Battle*, published by Allen & Unwin. Other recent works examine multinational military operations, asymmetric warfare, peacekeeping, Australian Army force structure and the conduct of historical operational analysis in the field. His most recent monograph, published by the LWSC, is titled *Australian Army Cooperation with the Land Forces of the United States: Problems of the Junior Partner*.

Associate Professor Hugh Smith

Associate Professor Hugh Smith is a member of the School of Politics at the University College, Australian Defence Force Academy (ADFA). He first taught at the Royal Military College, Duntroon and transferred to ADFA when it opened in 1986. In 1987 he became Founding Director of the Australian Defence Studies Centre. Hugh Smith teaches undergraduate courses on war and strategy, and postgraduate courses on armed forces and society, and on legal and moral problems of international violence. He has published widely on topics such as women in the military, officer education, reserve forces, conscientious objection and other defence issues. He has also edited books on the military profession, on peacekeeping, and on law and armed forces.

Professor Roger Spiller

Roger J. Spiller grew up in Texas and served in the US Air Force from 1962 to 1965 as an air rescue medic. In 1969 he graduated from South West Texas State University and gained his PhD in US military history from Louisiana State University in 1977.

In 1979 Professor Spiller was a founding member of the US Army's Combat Studies Institute (CSI) and served as Director CSI in 1990–91 and 1993–94. He is currently George C. Marshall Professor of Military History at the US Army Command and General Staff College, Fort Leavenworth, including teaching in the School of Advanced Military Studies. From 1982 to 1985 he was Special Assistant to the Commander in Chief of US Readiness Command in Tampa, Florida, and from 1991 to 1995 he was Special Assistant (and personal historian) to the US Army Chief of Staff.

Professor Spiller is general editor of the three-volume *Dictionary of American Military Biography* and a consultant editor for *American Heritage Magazine*.

Brigadier Dominique Trinquand

Brigadier Dominique Trinquand was born in Koblenz (Germany) in 1953. He graduated from Saint-Cyr Military Academy in 1976 and joined the Armoured Cavalry School in Saumur. He served as platoon leader in a reconnaissance (12 Chasseurs Regiment) in France, and in 1981 he returned to the cavalry school as instructor for two years.

In 1988 he graduated from the War College (Ecole supérieure de Guerre) in Paris and was selected to attend the Staff College course in Camberley (UK). In 1991 he was selected to command the French Battalion in Lebanon.

Brigadier Trinquand has had a number of NATO and UN postings, including serving as Military Assistant to the General commanding UNPROFOR (General Cot) in the former Yugoslavia in 1993–94. In May 1994 he reported to the Joint HQ in Paris, where he was responsible for Peace Support Operations and NATO doctrine. He served in Bosnia in 1995 prior to attending the Centre d'études Diplomatiques et Stratégiques in Paris (Centre for Diplomatic and Strategic Studies) and the Royal College of Defence Studies in London (1999).

In 2000, he was assigned to the Centre for Doctrine and Higher education in Paris, where he is currently heading the office of Command and NATO doctrine.

Introduction

Appointment in Samarra: Western strategic thought and the culture of risk

Dr Michael Evans

The Danish philosopher Soren Kierkegaard once wrote that, while life must be lived forwards, it can only be understood backwards. Nowhere was this great truth more starkly illustrated than on 11 September 2001. On that day, the world's most advanced and powerful country, the United States, was exposed to, and temporarily paralysed by, the most devastating attack in its history. A handful of Islamist extremists armed only with knives, possessed of a fringe ideology of millenarianism, and embracing a medieval mystique of death, gave a new and terrible meaning to the concept of that antiseptic phrase, 'asymmetric warfare'—the term *de jour* for the ancient art of unconventional conflict. Four hijacked passenger airline jets were converted from symbols of the prosperity of a high-technology Western civilisation into unwitting flying missiles of destruction.

The magnificent Twin Towers of the World Trade Center in New York—at once the physical pillars of Western capitalism and the cultural symbols of the dominance of Western civilisation—were literally incinerated. Built from 200 000 tons of steel and 425 000 cubic yards of concrete, the Twin Towers were consumed in an inferno, with the loss of over

2800 lives. The only words possible seemed to be those used to describe an earlier aerial tragedy on American soil: 'Oh, the humanity and all the passengers!' [1] The surreal sight of packed airliners exploding as they crashed into New York's World Trade Center was an unprecedented event, captured in real time by stunned members of the electronic media, horrific and seemingly inexplicable. 'Who would have imagined, only a few months ago,' reflected US Defense Secretary Donald Rumsfeld, 'that terrorists would take commercial airliners, turn them into missiles, and use them to strike the Pentagon and the World Trade Center, killing thousands?'.[2] The title of one of the first serious analyses of 11 September, *How Did This Happen?*, captured the sense of widespread shock in the United States.[3]

Given that the conference on which this book is based was held in Canberra only four weeks after 11 September, it was inevitable that the events of that terrible day would overshadow proceedings. Indeed, in many respects, the conference became a meditation on the meaning of war and conflict in the 21st century. Armies now find themselves in an age in which the tools of globalisation and information technology permit a transnational network to wield a level of destruction previously associated exclusively with states. As the conference's keynote speaker, Ralph Peters, noted, 11 September decisively changed the shape of the strategic landscape. For Peters, 11 September was a vindication of his belief that America's predilection for waging modern war according to a 'Revolution in Military Affairs' based on long-range precision missile strike with minimum risk of casualties, is an illusion. It is in the world of ideas that wars must be won, and not in the world of technology. It is on the ground, in the hills and cities of the underdeveloped world that the West must meet a new and deadly challenge from a world of disenchanted warriors and extremists. Such forces reject Western-style modernity while using its very tools—mass communications, air travel and global interconnectivity—to prosecute an anti-Western agenda.

11 September 2001 marks the date on which the Western world left that indeterminate and uncertain period that many commentators have labelled the 'post-Cold War era'. Although most observers have drawn a comparison between 11 September 2001 and the surprise Japanese attack on Pearl Harbor on 7 December 1941, it may be just as useful to draw an analogy with the way in which the post-World War I decade of 1919–29

ended. For the West, both the post-Cold War era between 1989 and 2001, and the age following the Great War from 1919–29 represented a brief time of hope and prosperity. Both eras, however, were abruptly ended by dramatic events in New York, the great hub of Western capitalism.

The era 1919–29—the prosperous years of the League of Nations, Locarno, jazz and automobiles—was shattered by the Wall Street crash of Black Thursday on 24 October 1929, an event that triggered the Great Depression and accelerated the rise of Adolf Hitler and the Nazis to power in Germany, effectively sowing the seeds of a new world war. Similarly, the optimism of the years from 1989 to 2001—the dot.com era marked by the global supremacy of the West's free-market capitalism and by United States President Bill Clinton's freewheeling motto of 'the economy stupid'—was abruptly shattered by the surreal events of 11 September 2001, a day that the American essayist Gore Vidal has called Dark Tuesday because, according to the Koran, it was on a Tuesday that Allah created darkness.[4]

The economic prosperity and optimism of the post-Cold War decade obscured the rise of ominous strategic trends throughout the 1990s. The rise of transnational threats, the activities of diverse non-state actors, and the dangers of the proliferation of weapons of mass destruction did not receive sufficient attention in official Western strategic planning. In the United States, documents such as *Joint Vision 2020* tended to concentrate on major theatre conflict, a high-technology Gulf War *redux* against rogue states such as North Korea or Iraq, or an emerging peer competitor such as China.[5] As the leading American soldier, General John R. Galvin, once observed, historically the United States has a strong dislike of unconventional conflict and engagement in 'uncomfortable wars'.[6] In 1997, Galvin reflected:

> We [Americans] do not like to think about terrorism as a type of war in which cyberspace becomes a battlefield, or chemical and biological weapons are used. Surrogate wars, general violence, subversive activity, numerous small wars, multiplication of intra-state conflicts, and complex humanitarian emergencies have also intruded on our vision of war.[7]

Not surprisingly, before the September 2001 attacks, the al-Qa'ida leader, the six-foot, seven-inch Saudi millionaire, Osama bin Laden, appeared to be an obscure, even eccentric, opponent. After his al-Qa'ida suicide cadres had wreaked destruction on New York and Washington, however, bin Laden burst into the Western political psyche. For the ever-shallow Western electronic media, he seemed to resemble a sinister mastermind, an Islamist Fu Manchu or Dr No, direct from the pages of the novels of Sax Rohmer and Ian Fleming. For more serious Western strategic analysts, the Saudi dissident emerged as arguably the most dangerous Islamic adversary to confront the West since the Ottoman grand vizir, Kara Mustapha, besieged Vienna in 1683.

That the al-Qa'ida movement could wield the resources to mount an operation as sophisticated as that executed on 11 September demonstrated the West's complacency and the magnitude of the new challenge to the security of advanced democratic societies. In the words of the Australian sociologist, John Carroll:

> The West has been caught asleep on duty by the revolutionary new phenomenon of mastermind terrorism ... We have been outsmarted in our domain of strength—functional rationality. A capacity for brilliant long-range planning, mobilising technical expertise, carried out by clear-minded and self-disciplined individuals, has been the key to our civilization. Yet which of our institutions could match the successful hijacking in unison, of four passenger jets, flown skilfully, three of them proceeding to hit their targets—given the potential for the unforeseen in such an intricate mission, carried out in secrecy without a trial-run under tremendous pressure? [8]

Indeed, it has been pointed out that the accuracy of the attacks on New York demonstrated a degree of precision usually associated only with laser, electro-optical or satellite guidance.[9]

In retrospect, then, it is possible to view the years between 1989 and 2001 as an era in which socioeconomic analysis was seen as more important than innovative strategic thought. As the Cold War geopolitical framework that had been constructed over 40 years of ideological struggle between capitalism and communism crumbled under the impact of events, Western strategic thought became fragmented, and lost both clarity and purpose. The years 1989–91 saw the end of the Cold War, followed by the momentous collapse of Soviet Marxism–Leninism, and the victory of Western liberal democracy and market capitalism. Francis Fukuyama captured the triumph of Western social values with his famous phrase 'the end of history'.[10] For most liberal democracies the 1990s became a time of prosperity, marked by the power of the global market-place and by an array of domestic concerns connected to financial globalism. The West took refuge from the continuing ugly violence of the non-Western world—from what Paul Johnson once called 'Caliban's Kingdoms', whether ethnic violence in Central Europe or civil war and terrorism in Africa and the Middle East—by embracing the antiseptic cruise-missile diplomacy practised by the single remaining superpower, the United States.[11]

The 1990s witnessed a general avoidance of risk in strategic affairs as reflected by the American withdrawal from Somalia in 1993, following a handful of ground troop casualties and by the West's casualty-free air campaign against Yugoslavia over Kosovo in 1999. While there was a sizeable number of observers who warned that the future was not neces-sarily Fukuyama's 'end of history' but rather Samuel Huntington's darker vision of a 'clash of civilisations', there was an unmistakable air of strate-gic complacency in the Western democracies.[12]

Yet just as the optimism and prosperity of the 1920s was shattered by the 24 October 1929 Wall Street crash, so too has the memory of the prosperous 1990s been obliterated by the smouldering rubble of the Twin Towers on 11 September 2001. In 1929, from the epicentre of New York the effects of financial catastrophe blew a wind of change through the international political system. The 1930s brought the Great Depression, accelerated the rise of totalitarian dictatorship in Europe, and began an inexorable march towards war. From the ruins of the Twin Towers we can expect changes over the next decade that may be as dramatic as those of the 1930s.

It is, of course, still too early to state with certainty what long-term policy changes 11 September 2001 heralds. Already, however, we have seen the promulgation of the Bush Doctrine ('either you are with us, or you are with the terrorists'), the rapid destruction of the Taliban regime in Afghanistan, and the growth of a new American assertiveness in world affairs. The indications are that the changes to Western security will be at least as profound and dramatic as those of the years between 1947 and

1954, when the concepts of containment and deterrence were laid down as the basis of the grand strategy of the Cold War.[13]

It is no accident that the second Bush Administration—with its proposals for a new Department of Homeland Security, a new unified military command, and a reordering of the Federal Bureau of Investigation (FBI)—has drawn a direct analogy with the early years of the Cold War. In its own words, the second Bush Administration plans to carry out 'the largest government reorganisation since the Truman Administration created the National Security Council and the Department of Defense'.[14] At least one respected historian of international relations believes that the September 2002 National Security Strategy may amount to the most important reformulation of United States grand strategy since the late 1940s.[15] We may be witnessing the emergence of an American strategy designed to neutralise 'terrorists and tyrants', especially those located in the Middle East. This new strategic approach may foreshadow a neo-Wilsonian attempt to make the world safe for democracy 'because otherwise democracy will not be safe in the world'.[16]

In a broader sense, 11 September 2001 highlights the reality that different modes of war and conflict are now merging under the impact of globalisation and new technologies. As observers such as Eric Hobsbawm and Philip Bobbitt have recently noted, in the 21st century, armed operations are no longer the monopoly of governments or states, while the very distinction between war and peace has become more and more obscure; such obscurity threatens the traditional fabric of the international system.[17] In Hobsbawm's words, 'the material equipment for warfare is now widely available to private bodies, as are the means of financing non-state warfare. In this way, the balance between state and non-state organisations has changed.'[18] Bobbitt has warned that contemporary concepts of strategy tend to exclude non-territorial threats and, as a result, the power of Western states to ensure their security by conventional forces is rapidly waning.[19]

The currents bringing about these changes in the character of war and conflict are not entirely new; it is simply that outdated Cold War modes of strategic thought have tended to persist in the West, despite the demise of the Soviet Marxism–Leninism and its vast military machine. As early as 1976, in a remarkable and prescient essay, the leading American social scientist, Professor Adda Bozeman, sketched the contours of the world that was to emerge in the early 21st century.[20] In the process, she anticipated some of the ideas about war of later theorists and historians such as Samuel Huntington, John Keegan and Martin van Creveld.[21]

The central thrust of Bozeman's thesis was that the West's intellectual approach to understanding modern war was either inadequate or rapidly becoming obsolescent because it had largely neglected to explore what she described as the 'value content' of conflict. The fluidity and high incidence of global violence, and the steady proliferation of various types of war were at odds with the West's mechanistic approach to war based on technology and science. The volatile character of modern armed conflict had created a situation in which Western differentiations between 'international' and 'internal' war and notions of separate spheres of 'war' and 'peace' were becoming increasingly blurred and enmeshed.[22] Bozeman argued that, in 'the closed circuit of [Western] war and peace studies', few Western theorists understood the dynamic ideological and social character of war, in which conflict was governed by values and beliefs, not rooted in the culture of the territorial, democratic nation-state.[23] In a passage that could have been written in the late 1990s, Bozeman stated:

> The term 'international war', then, no longer refers exclusively to violent conflicts between states . . . It now stands also for a broad spectrum of armed belligerence within the state, ranging from sporadic urban guerrilla activities to civil wars, wars of liberation and secession, insurrections and other revolutionary uprisings, many of which are initiated and maintained in [sic] behalf of causes espoused by foreign principals. Moreover, the interpenetration of the domestic and foreign environments effaces altogether the conventionally accepted lines between legitimate and illegitimate force, and puts in question the theoretically established distinctions between war and peace.[24]

Bozeman went on to challenge such pivotal concepts in Western international relations as the nation-state, the unified world society and international law. All three concepts, she argued, needed radical revision if they were to have long-term intellectual use when it came to understanding the future of war and conflict. The ideal of the world in the

West was one of a stable global order based on the survival of the state, the maintenance of the international system, and the avoidance of war. Yet, such an approach was unrealistic since 'we have entered an era in which the interacting, independent units are so disparate that references to an "international order" are invalid'.[25]

Anticipating the debate of the 1980s and 1990s over the universal viability of the Westphalian model of the state, Bozeman warned that the modern state was essentially an Occidental creation, not easily exported into other less-modern cultures. As a result, in the political and military turmoil that gripped much of the non-Western world, the state had 'ceased to be a reliable indicator or measure of such phenomena as international war and internal war'.[26]

In Bozeman's view, the rise of new, interlocking conditions meant that the role of the modern state as a medium for realistic differentiation among types of war, and between conditions of war and peace, was in sharp decline. She was highly critical of the academic and political elites of the United States for failing to meet the intellectual challenge of what she called 'the multifaceted nature of modern warfare'.[27] According to Bozeman, the idea that there were universally valid norms governing the conduct of war suggested that 'the United States has begun to resemble Don Quixote: like the Knight of the Mournful Countenance, it is fighting windmills and losing its bearings in the real world'.[28]

Bozeman suggested that, in order to understand the character of war and armed conflict in a multicultural world, it was necessary to refer to the broader and more permanent ideas of culture, and to accept the world as a 'manifold of civilisations'.[29] She defined culture or civilisation as representing 'all that is fundamental and enduring about the ways of a group; that is to say it comprises those norms, values, institutions and modes of thinking in a given society that survive, change and remain meaningful to successive generations'.[30] The ideas that belong to a civilisation were, in her view, more comprehensive and permanent than those held by relatively recent territorial states. Unlike a state, a civilisation could encompass multiple types of conflicts and political forms while being 'more enduring in time, even as it is usually less precisely defined in space'.[31]

Lastly, Bozeman recommended that a close study of comparative African, Middle East, Indian, South-East Asian and Chinese cultural attitudes towards war was more valuable than a focus on the shifting defence policies in the various imported Occidental forms of the state. Such an approach would allow Western policy-makers to recognise and analyse multiple distinct cultures and political systems that differed in their modes of rational and normative thought and in their value orientations towards war and peace.[32]

At the beginning of the 21st century, Bozeman's ideas about the 'multifaceted nature of warfare' and her 'spectrum of armed belligerence' are highly topical. Her notions of conflict's fluidity and merging forms of international and internal war, and her emphasis on a cultural or civilisational approach in explicating conflict, are among the central problems facing Western policy makers and military professionals. In the wake of 11 September, the West's strategic literature is now replete with assessments of the role of non-state actors in war and, above all, with the changing culture of military conflict. A good example of the prevalence of these trends is the United States' *National Security Strategy* published in September 2002.[33] This document notes the merging of domestic and foreign affairs under the impact of globalisation and acknowledges the rise of non-state threats, notably terrorism.[34] The security strategy states:

> America is threatened less by conquering states than we are by failing ones. We are menaced less by fleets and armies than by catastrophic technologies in the hands of the embittered few. We must defeat these threats to our Nation, allies, and friends.[35]

The document goes on to describe 'the battle for the future of the Muslim world' as a battle for the soul of a civilisation that is essentially a 'struggle of ideas'.[36]

What are the future implications for Western armies under the conditions sketched by Bozeman and given firm shape by the new United States security strategy under the Administration of President George W. Bush? The campaign in Afghanistan demonstrated that land power, the oldest form of statecraft known to organised societies, retains its age-old value. The fashionable belief of the 1990s that wars could be won by air power alone rather than by the application of joint air, land and sea forces was exploded by operations in Afghanistan. In their exhaustive study of the aerial precision revolution, the writers Michael Russell Rip and James M.

Hasik warn that military operations in the aftermath of 11 September are likely to require a return to more traditional uses of force. 'The Clintonian legacy of allowing US soldiers "to kill, but not to die" ', they observe, 'is an approach [to strategy] that will have to be abandoned.'[37] Once again, Western nations are faced with the historic task of putting foot soldiers into the field to preserve the interests of liberal democracy. One is reminded of T. R. Fehrenbach's 1963 warning against replacing 'proud legions' with 'pushbutton war':

> You may fly over a land forever; you may bomb it, atomize it, pulverize it and wipe it clean of life—but if you desire to defend it, protect it, and keep it for civilization, you must do this on the ground, the way the Roman legions did, by putting your young men into the mud.[38]

The contributions in *Future Armies, Future Challenges* affirm the central importance of ground forces to the future of war. While some of the essays reproduced in this volume have been updated since the conference to reflect events such as the US-led campaign in Afghanistan and the fall of the Taliban, most remain largely unchanged. Overall, the essays reflect the desire by the Chief of Army, Lieutenant General Peter Cosgrove, for the conference to try to capture the diversity and complexity of the future strategic environment. As a result, the conference proceedings cut a broad intellectual swathe. The opening essay by Ralph Peters is a vivid and controversial overview of the impact of both inter-civilisational and intra-civilisational violence in shaping international security. Carrying echoes of Samuel Huntington and Norman Cohn, Peters paints a particularly bleak picture of a Middle East Islamic civilisation trapped in an apparently unending cycle of cultural crisis, millenarian politics and apocalyptic terrorism.[39] Douglas Macgregor surveys the meaning of American military transformation in a post-industrial age; Michael Evans examines, from an Australian viewpoint, the role of military theory in an age of globalism; and Colonel Richard Cousens of the British Army assesses the continuing place of the close battle in ground warfare.

Rear Admiral Raja Menon, a former senior officer in the Indian Navy, gives a useful non-Western analysis of the links between maritime strategy and land warfare, while Alan Ryan, of the Australian Army's Land Warfare Studies Centre, focuses on problems of mounting coalitions in the Asia-Pacific region. There are two contributions by leading scholars from the Australian Defence Force Academy: Hugh Smith throws a critical eye over the challenge facing armies in the recruitment of future soldiers; and Graeme Cheeseman looks at alternative ways of organising traditional militaries. The problems posed by the divergent issues of the digitisation of the battlespace, of asymmetry and of urban warfare are respectively analysed by Lieutenant Colonel Robert Leonhard of the US Army; Group Captain Ian MacFarling, Director of the Royal Australian Air Force's Aerospace Centre; and by Roger Spiller, George C. Marshall Professor of Military History at the US Command and General Staff College.

The lessons of recent operational experiences by British, Australian and multinational forces are examined by a group of distinguished uniformed practitioners. The operational challenges of Bosnia and East Timor are the subjects of the respective papers of General Sir Michael Rose, formerly Commander of the UN Protection Force in Bosnia, and of Brigadier Duncan Lewis, Commander of Australia's Special Forces. Major General Peter Abigail, Land Commander, Australia, provides a timely analysis of the preparations under way to ready the Australian Army for the complexity of 21st-century conflict, and Brigadier Dominique Trinquand of the French Army analyses the course of recent multinational operations by French and European forces. Finally, this study contains the transcript of an insightful panel discussion on the spectre of mass-casualty terrorism; Ralph Peters, General Rose, Rear Admiral Menon and Brigadier Lewis participated in the discussion.

The content of this book is therefore varied and eclectic, and contains material of interest to satisfy a wide circle of serving officers, scholars and policy makers. If any single theme emerged from the 2001 conference, it was the need for armies to be able to operate across a full spectrum of operations ranging from counter-terrorism and shaping the battlespace through to managing difficult peace operations to the challenge of waging high-tempo conventional warfare. In early 21st-century conditions, advanced armies must be capable of participating in joint multidimensional operations in highly complex theatres, where the distinctions between conventional and unconventional conflict, political responsibility and military control may be increasingly blurred. Military professionals will have to learn to fuse the traditional roles of combat leaders and technicians of violence with the new roles of soldier–statesmen and soldier–scholars.[40] Such multifaceted demands are likely to require an agility and flexibility of thought and action that will broaden and deepen the concept of Western military professionalism in the future.

The challenges of future war are unlikely to be confined to uniformed professionals. Western policy makers and publics will need to revise their attitudes towards, and knowledge of, the use of force. In particular, Western politicians and electorates will have to summon the moral courage to deploy soldiers, sailors and air personnel in life-threatening missions in the environment of what has been called a postmodern 'risk society'.[41] It is important to note that 'risk', a word that comes from the Portuguese 'to dare', does not mean the same thing as the notion of danger. Risk refers to 'hazards that are actively assessed in relation to future possibilities'.[42] Risk in contemporary Western society describes an attempt to break away from the traditional ideas of fate and destiny in favour of the technical ability to manage future events. In its pursuit of risk management in every aspect of daily living, from stranger danger in child care to pesticide use in food growing, the West has sought to make war an instrumental, rather than an existential, challenge to contemporary life.[43] In postmodern conditions, war is viewed by many as antiseptic and air-delivered by a 'safe military'—a 'virtual' phenomenon—that for the majority of Western citizens, even for some in uniform, is witnessed mainly on television or video screens. Strategy is reduced to mere targeting and the swift delivery of ordnance.[44]

The problem with this approach to war is that it assumes that armed conflict can always be reduced to a simple technological assessment and, above all, be kept at a safe distance from the West's cities and suburbs. Alas, the West's future opponents are unlikely to grant our desire to transform war into a Western spectator sport. Indeed, one of the lessons of the 11 September 2001 attacks may be that a safe military can only mean an unsafe society. It is a pleasant idea to believe that war can be abolished by the applied reason of civilisation, but unfortunately such a belief also runs counter to everything that we know about the course of history. We may wish to distance ourselves from war but, as the Greek philosopher Heraclitus observed over 2500 years ago, war is a form of human fate and is 'the father of all, the king of all'.[45] Nothing in our modern world suggests that it is time to revise this bleak judgment.

Ultimately, the drive by Western elites to risk-manage the shape of war in the future puts one in mind of W. Somerset Maugham's unforgettable fable about the Arab servant who, in the market of Baghdad, encounters the shrouded figure of Death.[46] The latter beckons to him and the servant, terror-stricken, flees home and entreats his master to lend him a fast horse so that he can ride to Samarra in order to escape his fate. The master agrees and, following the servant's departure, goes down to the market himself. Encountering Death, the master states, 'My servant is young and healthy,' and asks, 'Why did you beckon him?', to which Death replies: 'I did not beckon. Mine was a gesture of surprise. I did not expect to see him this afternoon in Baghdad, because he and I have an appointment tonight in Samarra.'[47]

Part I

The changing shape of conflict

The West's future foes: simplification and slaughter

Lieutenant Colonel Ralph Peters

When traditions crack and social orders struggle, men and nations yearn for reassurance. Those that feel the weight of change most painfully do not want to know why they have failed; rather, they want to know who they might blame. No man desires to face his own inadequacy, nor do civilisations blame themselves for their own collapse. Once, men blamed the gods. Now, in the Middle East, they blame America and the West. The difference is hardly one of substance.

The threat of inter-civilisational violence that we face today arises from the massive dimensions of much of humankind's unwillingness— or inability—to accept responsibility for failures wrought at home. This flight into excuses is an ancient phenomenon, but modernity has intensified its effect and dramatically broadened its scale. Now the advent of the postmodern, techno-industrial juggernaut of Western civilisation is pushing the matter toward a culmination. We are witnessing the globalisation, not of democracy, but of blame and self-exonerating simplifications insisting that centuries of bad choices do not count in human failure so much as that distant, satanic America of liberty, justice—and opportunity—for all.

Freedom terrifies the failed, whether we speak of individuals or of entire civilisations. Men cling to what they know, despite the flood of evidence that what they know will only drag them under, and the more traditional the society, the more desperately those myriad hands clutch at the myth of a golden, unmolested past. We have entered the age of global mass delusion, of global accusation, of civilisational rage that cannot bear the burden of its shame. Our times will not be bloodless.

This human aching for simplification and bogeymen to blame has always come to the fore when social organisation proved inadequate, whether it had to do with plague-ridden Greeks who raced to appease their deities, or with plague-ridden Europeans slaughtering Jews to drive out the Black Death. The greatest crisis of the Western order in the past thousand years (and the catalyst of the West's rise), the Protestant Reformation spawned no end of cults as prescriptive as those of today's Islamists. Yet, even then the West had begun to feel its vitality and the cults were soon driven, bloodily, to the periphery. The next greatest crisis, the industrial revolution, with its social and geographical dislocations, drove men with traditional skills and yearnings to despair. The simultaneous emergence of utopian political theories sought to make the world at once intelligible and manageable. However, like all theories, these ideologies only sought to simplify contemporary understanding of change. No matter how complex any theory may appear, mankind is infinitely more inventive, more inspired, and more mischievous than any theoretical approach can accommodate. Marxism and Socialism, then Fascism, National Socialism, Stalinism, and the Japanese imperial religion that responded to modernity with fury—all of these were efforts to simplify an ever more complex world. Seduced and deluded by rhetoric, we misunderstood each of these counter-revolutions: none was about the future. Every single ideology inflicted upon the world, whether nominally of the Right or the Left, was conservative in its unwillingness to accept the sprawling diversity of human possibilities. Beyond the anglophone world and much of Western civilisation, the purpose of many political thinkers has always been to limit human possibility, and to force humankind into a mould congenial to the disaffected intellect.

Even the English-speaking world was not entirely immune to the reductive disease of theory and ideology, although our adaptive structures and our head-start on human liberty bred a population that always viewed the book-bound 'revolutionary' with suspicion. Our culture of argument inoculated us against demagogues—a circumstance of great historical fortune. Nonetheless, a minority of the anglophone population, alarmed at the dislocations of their times, turned to a series of fundamentalist religious 'awakenings', from the latter half of the 18th century, each revival of rigorous faith synchronised with only the slightest delay behind waves of disorienting progress. Blessedly, most of these turns to religion were benign, and some were even beneficial to development, emphasising sobriety and duty. Elsewhere, ideology, with its delicious absolutions and its ready-to-hand villains, swept the most developed states. Imagine how dreadful the 20th century would have been—how much worse—had French intellectuals had the courage of their 'leftist' totalitarian convictions.

In the 20th century, the human passion for simplification—in the degenerate forms of theory and ideology—led to massive slaughters, and it is no accident that the adaptive anglophone states, with their allergy to prescriptive ideologies, were the ultimate victors. The struggle often seemed a near-run thing—and that struggle was spawned by the discontent of states that were, with the exception of Russia, largely historical successes that had been tripped up in their forward march; these states were, even at their lowest points, not without hope. Their sense of failure was trivial compared with that in the Islamic world today. Now we face a phenomenon without historical precedent: an entire civilisation of global reach has failed before our eyes. Certainly, regional cultures and civilisations have failed in the past, and some have disappeared but for scattered ruins. Humankind has never before had to contend with the stubborn non-competitiveness of a billion like-thinking people. As already indicated, conservative Islamism is profoundly prescriptive. Islamists are drawn together by a utopian belief that the 'Golden Age' of Islam can be resurrected, but only by abandoning secular forms of government and institutions in favour of theocracy. That which traditional, conservative Muslims cherish in the matter of social organisation—from the subjugation of women to the behavioural strictures of faith—guarantees economic, cultural and military failure in the modern (to say nothing of the postmodern) era. Given human nature and the failure's inchoate rage, it is no wonder that we are confronted with merciless acts of terror. The miracle is that we have seen so little terrorism to date.

If we list the cardinal factors (out of a complex of thousands, large and small) that enabled the most-developed states, led by the robust, meritocratic civilisation of anglophone nations, to succeed beyond the dreams of even our own parents, we find that each enabling characteristic is anathema to most states with majority Islamic populations—and nowhere more so than in the old Muslim heartlands. We thrive and we compound our successes because of the degree to which we have broken down barriers of privilege, gender, race and religion. Our societies cherish the freedom of information and have developed, over centuries, an innate sense of what is true and false. We are scrupulous bookkeepers (and the recent Enron scandal in the United States demonstrated what happens to those who cheat). We minimise corruption throughout our societies and enjoy the mechanisms for pulling even the mighty down when their misbehaviour becomes evident. We do not rely on bloodlines for protection and have broken the tyranny of the extended family (one of the greatest impediments to human progress). We have learnt an astonishing degree of tolerance (excepting British football hooligans). We value education and have struck a functional balance between extending its benefits equitably and ensuring that the most talented are not stymied. We view work as a virtue in itself and, last but not least, we have learnt the painful art of self-criticism: when things go wrong we sometimes lose our tempers, but soon enough we ask ourselves what went wrong, and then we apply sophisticated skills to fixing the problem.

If you turn each of these points into its negative, you have described Saudi Arabia, Pakistan, Egypt, Sudan and many another state that is little more than a cultural prison. And here we must state firmly: every one of these failures is home-grown. The Crusades are a worse excuse for non-performance than 'The dog ate my homework'. Islam's blows against Europe were far harsher, enduring into the 19th century in the Balkans and on the marches of the Russian Empire. Islam's failure is in no sense the fault of the West. The development of Muslim societies is crippled by their core values, by the lies they tell to each other and to themselves, and by the cruelty with which they have organised their societies.

Of course, it would be better for all of us were the Islamic world to evolve, swiftly, into a success story in which prosperity, tolerance and the rule of law enabled us all to interact to our collective benefit. However, the core Muslim states are not going to develop successfully in our lifetime—and likely not thereafter. We will have to contend with the consequences of failure in a civilisation that, by functional Western standards, is increasingly unbalanced psychologically. This is not good news.

For some states, there may, indeed, be hope. Iran may surprise us, as it slowly flushes extremism from its system. This country's tragedy was that it got what it wanted, and now that what it wanted does not work, it may find a chance to set a healthier direction. Iran may be able to climb back up—although success is far from guaranteed. It is, at least, a country whose culture is older, richer, more robust and much more promising than that of the Arab world. The next decade or so may well see Iran and the United States become strategic partners once again, with both allied with India, Israel and Turkey (where ethnicity trumps religion and history differs) in a disciplinary alliance against the murderous impulses of the region's many failures.

The jury remains out on Malaysia and Indonesia, and the factors involved are so complex and case-specific that they cannot be addressed here even in summary. In the past, Indonesia has made the classic error made by other Muslim states, such as Egypt and Pakistan. Attempts to appease extremists by avoiding extensive crackdowns and by looking the other way in the hope that the problem will remain tolerable have not worked elsewhere—the cancer that is fundamentalist terrorism does not simply go away. In the wake of the Bali bombings, Indonesia has been forced to confront the terrorists in its midst. The future of Islam is up for grabs in Indonesia and Malaysia. We can only hope that the trend continues towards political secularism, not towards religious extremism. However, these possible exceptions only prove the rule. We do not so much face Samuel Huntington's 'clash of civilisations' as bear witness to the crash of one civilisation. This is no equal struggle, and we are going to win. Increasingly, however, the peoples of the old Muslim heartland display a virulent turn of mind: *après nous, le déluge*—with, quite literally, a vengeance.

When people turn to ideologies, the secular movements take on religious overtones and transcendental rhetoric, while reactionary religious 'revivals' focus on secular behaviours and physical destruction. Nazism and Stalinism both evolved into religions with mortal gods (as did, explicitly, the Japanese Greater East Asia Co-prosperity Sphere). Now, fundamentalist Islam focuses not on spiritual content, but on overt behaviours mandated by God—rendering the deity no more than a brutal headmaster—and on earthly retaliation for imagined wrongs. Indeed, what a visitor to any Islamic country comes away with is a haunting sense of how cruelly the local elite has exploited their co-religionists. The blame for this exploitation is often deflected onto the CIA, or onto Hollywood, or onto Zionism—that indispensable enemy of failed, corrupt and degenerate regimes.

Invariably, such ideologically-driven movements, religious or secular, turn apocalyptic in their desperation. In the 20th century such movements have butchered *kulaks* by the millions, imprisoned tens of millions of the 'enemies of the people' in camps and gassed perceived enemies in death factories. Raping and slaughtering their way through the cities of lesser races, they have not been content until they had caused destruction of millenarian proportions, bringing down the walls of Berlin around themselves or the walls of the World Trade Center Towers around us. The impulse is always toward extravagant forms of death, and every ideological movement approaching its zenith adorns itself with macabre rituals. Our petty theories do not explain this deeply human impulse, and many of us refuse to accept this ingrained taste for darkness—despite the evidence served up by the 20th century. Now we see before our eyes clear evidence of a civilisational death-wish among the more extreme Islamists—but suicidal visions require a great deal of foreign company for a grand immolation. It may be wise for us to pay attention.

Elsewhere, I have written of the differences between practical and apocalyptic terrorists. On 11 September 2001, we were shocked so deeply because we had long since grown accustomed to dealing with practical terrorists, those whose goals are political and of this earth (if sometimes grandiose). Such terrorists hijack planes and hold the passengers captives as bargaining chips. We were unprepared to deal with apocalyptic terrorists, whose vision is, ultimately, not of this earth, and whose deepest urge is toward nihilistic destruction—no matter the passing rhetoric about earthly injustice. Apocalyptic terrorists, who cannot be appeased or ever sated, hijack airliners with a very different intent, as America learnt so painfully on 11 September 2001.

Across the past few decades, we have seen a fundamental shift in the tenor of terrorism. The liberation and separatist movements of the 1960s and 1970s that sought to change local orders through violence are still with us. However, they have increasingly yielded pride of place to men possessed by visions of a blood-soaked divinity, men who claim that the finger of god has chosen them for vengeance, men whose rewards are finally not of this earth. The practical terrorist may be willing to sacrifice his life for his cause, but he would rather live to see his dreams made real. The apocalyptic terrorist, in his purest form, yearns for death, for annihilation and cosmic resolution. He is the unhappiest of men, incapable of finding contentment on this earth. Usually, he cannot find a satisfactory relationship with society, no matter his level of privilege—and, with remarkable consistency, he lives in terror of female sexuality. He aches for clear rules amid the chaos of change. Despite his willingness to sacrifice himself (in his case, a selfish impulse), he is finally a man afraid. He longs for a mythic past that he has conjured as a golden age when such as he were accorded their full due, and when those of less rigor were punished appropriately. The apocalyptic terrorist would always rather destroy than build, rather kill than redeem, and, no matter his calls for justice, he could not build a workable regime upon this earth, since humanity would ever disappoint him.

Certainly, the vigour of the apocalyptic terrorist's commitment varies—not all are anxious for martyrdom. But enervated societies and rotten regimes can be up-ended by even a small number of men desperate to die 'for god'. Such men hope to kick-start Armageddon and to bring on the end of days, to borrow from Christian parlance, since apocalyptic terrorism, historically, has produced plenty of Christian killers, and Jewish and Hindu ones, as well. It seems that Islam has simply come up for its turn, although the scale of the problem has no precedent, thanks to the raw numbers of the disaffected and the dualistic nature of modern technologies. Contrary to the media, the problem is not the Muslim masses, but the critical mass of madmen within the huge reactor of society—and that molten core is growing.

No matter how successful and sustained our war against terrorism, we still will suffer more blows. We can, however, reduce the frequency and scale of those attacks dramatically, and that is what we are doing as I write. Still, this is a struggle that will endure beyond our lifetimes, fought in fits and starts. I do not doubt our ultimate success, but we must prepare ourselves for some unpleasant surprises along the way. We must not hesitate to terrorise the terrorists. Only ferocity works against such men. All measures short of resolute and uncompromising violence directed against them amount to slow surrender.

Fortunately—in a perverse sense—we may rely on these apocalyptic terrorists themselves to help us maintain the resolve to exterminate them wherever we find them. Their weakness always lies in their success: they inevitably overreach, exciting outrage and allowing us to discard the super-structures of nonsense that peace imposes on our policies and our militaries. The viciousness of these terrorists reminds us that we must be feared by all those that wish us ill. The attacks of 11 September 2001 provide a classic example: Had the terrorists only struck the Pentagon, much of the world would have cheered, and even some of America's nominal allies would have snickered behind closed doors. However, the graphic monstrosity of the attacks on the World Trade Center Towers brought home to every civilised state the necessity of fighting back with vigour. Without the terrorists' success, America would likely not have mustered the backing for its subsequent successes against them. Even the late-2002 terrorist attack on India's parliament serves as an illustration: savagery in Kashmir was one thing, but attacks against the government in New Delhi quite another, and Pakistan was lucky, indeed, that the United States had a momentary interest in keeping the local peace.

In Peshawar madrassas, Hamburg apartments or Afghani mountain caves, terrorists talk themselves into a fantasy world of greater power than they wield in practice, imagining that their attacks will bring down states, empires and civilisations. But the ambition—the madness—of the apocalyptic terrorist always outstrips practical possibilities in the end. Such men are impatient for death and God, and certainly impatient with the world. Small successes encourage them to great follies. This fact may be small comfort for their victims, but it guarantees that their tactical successes ultimately lead to strategic defeats.

This chapter strikes a pessimistic tone, but only because it has discussed the failing civilisation of Islam. Yet, even Islam sheds some rays of hope, if fewer than we might desire. There will be, at last, a liberal reformation in Islam, perhaps beginning in this very decade (although the process will take longer to mature). That reformation is, however, not going to come in the desolate, bitter Islamic heartlands. It is likeliest to begin in North America and the anglophone world, where the successes of our societies, economies and culture will seduce the children and grandchildren of Muslim immigrants, inspiring them to repair their faith and fit it to modernity, as those of other religions have done before them. The positive pressures exerted by our societies, the vivid examples abounding, and the possibilities that open up to open minds are far likelier to drive humane reforms in the Islamic faith than the delicious resentments and indispensable hatreds of those states where Islam chokes the future to death.

No matter what the situation is in the Muslim world, the West and its allies will do just fine. We are only at the beginning of a century that promises tremendous expansions of our wealth, power and possibility. In this age of multiple, intermingled revolutions—in gender, racial and religious relations in our societies, in technologies, in citizen empowerment, in military reach, in economic vigour and the power of information—we possess the skills to reinforce success, while discarding things that fail along the way. We of the West are creatures of change, while our antagonists resist the very changes that could begin to liberate them. But, then, liberation is really a Western concept, after all; adapted as a slogan by non-Westerners, it rarely led to freedom and opportunity (except for local elites, who stole with unbelievable panache, from Africa to the Middle East to Asia). Freedom, democracy, equitable laws well enforced—we grew these in our backyard gardens, and we cannot yet know how well they will transplant to other cultures. The coming century will decide. That century will belong to those men and women unafraid of change.

Clausewitz's chameleon: military theory and practice in the early 21st century

Michael Evans

Almost all things have been found out, but some have been forgotten.
Aristotle

A s the world enters the 21st century it appears that we are in the midst of revolutionary trends in international security, with the forces of information technology and globalisation seemingly transforming the theory and practice of war. In retrospect, it is now possible to see the decade between the collapse of Soviet communism in August 1991 and the attacks on the Pentagon and the World Trade Center in September 2001 as an era of the unexpected. No-one in the West expected, still less predicted, the fall of the Soviet Union; the Iraqi invasion of Kuwait and the Gulf War; the Asian financial crisis; the Indian and Pakistani nuclear detonations; and, of course, the events of 11 September 2001.

Over the past decade, armed conflict has not remained within the traditional parameters of conventional warfare between rival states. From Somalia to Bosnia to Kosovo, East Timor and Afghanistan, the face of war has assumed bewildering expressions. Under new global security conditions, the postmodern has collided with the pre-modern, the cosmopolitan has confronted the parochial, while the Westphalian state system has been challenged by new sub-state and trans-state forces. Conventional high-tech Western armed forces have had to come to terms with a world of failed states populated by ethnic paramilitaries; of rogue regimes equipped with ballistic missiles and poison gas; and of radical extremists embracing a philosophy of mass-casualty terrorism.

For Western policy-makers and military professionals these are deeply perplexing times; war seems more dynamic and chameleon-like than ever before. There are pressing questions: What is the future of war in conditions of great flux? Can traditional ideas of military power continue to dominate in an age of both globalisation and fragmentation? What is the meaning of Western military supremacy in an era when democratic civilisation—as demonstrated by the events of 11 September 2001—is highly vulnerable to unexpected and unorthodox threats?

This chapter seeks to provide some answers to these questions. The approach adopted reflects a conviction that, while events are always impossible to predict, it is possible to undertake intelligent analysis of trends in order to try to make some interim judgments about the kind of military conditions that might emerge in the near future. Four areas are explored. First, the fragmentation of the international system in the 1990s is analysed in an attempt to demonstrate how new political conditions caused a diffusion of conflict modes, bringing great uncertainty to the world of military analysts. Second, the main theories of war that emerged in the 1990s and the complexity these brought to traditional military thinking are examined. Third, a snapshot is provided of some of the most important challenges facing the West in terms of the theory and practice of military art over the next decade and a half. Finally, some of the likely characteristics of warfare over the next decade are identified and subjected to tentative analysis.

War in the 1990s: The new international system and the diffusion of conflict

In the 1990s there appeared to be a major transition occurring in international relations away from a mainly state-centred system towards one marked by greater forms of interdependence and interconnectedness. This process of interconnectedness was propelled by the dual impact of globalisation and its handmaiden, the information revolution. Together, these two forces appeared to have altered the context within which modern states operated, bringing about an apparent redistribution of power between states, markets and civil society.[1]

From a military perspective, the globalisation occurring over the last decade is perhaps best described as a process in which space and time have been so compressed by technology as to permit distant actions to have local effects and vice versa. The international system that had emerged by the beginning of the 21st century was an interconnected world order in which regional and local military developments had the potential to be of global significance.

Defence analysts quickly discovered that conflict and disorder anywhere in the world could be quickly transmitted everywhere—and invested with crisis—by a pervasive global communications media, symbolised by the Cable News Network (CNN). It was also discovered that globalisation was not a homogenous process, but contained a striking paradox in that it brought about both convergence and divergence. The notion of interconnectedness and a heightened sense of global conscious-ness are paralleled by polarisation and by particularism. As President Clinton said in April 1999, the West finds itself engaged in 'a great battle between the forces of integration and the forces of disintegration; [between] the forces of globalism and the forces of tribalism; [and the forces] of oppression against empowerment'.[2]

In effect, by 2001 the contemporary international security system had bifurcated, that is, it had split between a traditional 20th-century state-centred paradigm and new 21st-century sub-state and trans-state strata. The great change in the early 21st-century international system from that of the last quarter of the 20th century is the transition away from a dominant state-centric structure towards one marked by a greater number of sub-state and trans-state actors.[3] With bifurcation came a reduction in the relative significance of strategic geography, simply because the globalisation of the information era does not appear to allow any state or society to retreat behind physical or moral borders.[4]

It is important to understand clearly what is meant by the relative decline of strategic geography. In no sense does such a statement imply 'the end of geography' in the same sense that Francis Fukuyama famously spoke of 'the end of history'.[5] In terms of logistics, campaign planning and topographical analysis, geography remains fundamental to the art of war, while geopolitics remains an important component of statecraft.[6] Nonetheless, the effect of strategic geography as a primary rationale for defining a nation's defence and national security postures has declined. In many respects, the impact of globalisation on security has led to a shift away from territoriality towards connectedness as perhaps the central change in international security in the first decade of the 21st century. The process of this transformation—in which older forms of linear conflict have been supplemented by new forms of non-linear conflict— has been recognised by both Western and non-Western strategists. For example, the leading American strategic analyst, Philip Bobbitt, has observed, 'national security will cease to be defined in terms of borders alone because both the links among societies as well as the attacks on them exist in psychological and infrastructural dimensions, not on an invaded plain marked by the seizure and holding of territory'.[7] Similarly, two Chinese strategists have pointed out that we are entering an age of unrestricted warfare in which 'there is no territory that cannot be surpassed; there is no means which cannot be used in . . . war; and there is no territory or method which cannot be used in combination'.[8]

The result of globalisation over the past ten years has been the development of an unpredictable and complex pattern of armed conflict. Under conditions of global strategic bifurcation, the old distinctions between civil and international conflict, between internal and external security, and between national and societal security began to erode. It has become clear that, in an era in which various transnational and sub-state forces were greatly empowered by technology, issues such as civil conflict, terrorism and the danger of the proliferation of weapons of mass destruction could no longer be easily quarantined within states or regions. From the early 1990s onward, such issues emerged as global strategic threats precisely because they acted to blur the distinction between internal and external crises. Under new conditions, transnational and sub-state forces threatened not just states, but entire societies and thus the fabric of international stability itself. Consequently, traditional ideas about warfare came under challenge as the political, economic and military dimensions of security merged closer and state-on-state war appeared to have become supplemented by new forms of sub-state and trans-state conflict.[9]

The changing character of conflict and war mirrored the bifurcation of the international security system. The various views expressed about the future of military conflict reflected the post-Cold War fragmentation of international security and the diffusion of contemporary war into a variety of different modes. In the 1990s war became at once modern (reflecting conventional warfare between states); postmodern (reflecting the West's cosmopolitan political values of limited war, peace enforcement and humanitarian military intervention); and pre-modern (reflecting a mix of sub-state and trans-state warfare based on the age-old politics of identity, extremism and particularism).[10] It is important to note that none of these categories represent neatly divided compartments of activity; rather they overlap and interact with each other. The United States Marine Corps' recent doctrine of the 'three block war'—in which troops may be engaged in a conventional firefight, peace operations and humanitarian relief simultaneously in a single area—captures the essence of this complex interaction.[11]

While modern, postmodern and pre-modern forms of war overlap with each other, each mode has distinctive features. Modern war remains symbolised by a classical philosophy of encounter battles on land, air and sea between the armed forces of rival states. This mode of classical warfare can be traced back to the first properly recorded battle in history, when the Egyptians defeated the Hittites in the chariot and infantry battle at Kadesh in 1285 BC.

In the West's public consciousness, modern war is based on high technology and the type of conventional force-on-force warfare that we associate with the two World Wars, Korea and with recent conflict in the Persian Gulf. In contrast, postmodern war is mainly symbolised by the extremes of Western risk-aversion since the stakes seldom involve issues of vital security or national survival. Postmodern war is based on high-tech aerospace power, casualty limitation and cautious exit strategies, such as we saw during the Kosovo conflict of 1999. As the *New York Times* put it, Kosovo was the model of a postmodern conflict, 'a calibrated war, enabled by high-tech weaponry, guided by the flickering light of opinion polls'.[12] However, postmodern conflict based around high-technology aerospace power has created its own antithesis: asymmetric warfare waged against Western society, including a threat from weapons of mass destruction.[13]

For its part, pre-modern war is symbolised by the kind of blood-and-iron fighting that the West now allegedly abhors. Pre-modern war is essentially social rather than technological in character; it is an expression of the existential rather than the instrumental aspect of war.[14] Those who wage such struggles may choose to sport middle-class suits and exploit the spread of advanced technology, but their mentalities are a mixture of the anti-modern, the millenarian and the tribal in outlook. Such radicals embody what Pierre Hassner has called 'the dialectic of the bourgeois and the barbarian'.[15] Pre-modern conflict merges unconventional or, to use the term *de jour*, asymmetric warfare methods with the conventional or semi-conventional military activities of failed states. The pre-modern model of conflict also tends to exploit the rise of non-state actors, cultural-identity politics and ethnopolitical conflict. In many respects, pre-modern war represents a cultural revolt against the philosophy of Western liberal globalism; it is a conscious rejection of the universal values based on cosmopolitan democracy that followed victory in the Cold War. For many pre-modern radicals, the social order offered by globalisation is anathema, since it appears to be a facsimile of the secular, materialistic and trivial world inhabited by Homer Simpson. For millenarian radicals of political Islam such as Osama bin Laden, the West's cults of hedonistic individuality and intellectual relativism fly in the face of societies that define themselves by collective spirituality and timeless cultural traditions.[16]

Pre-modern struggles embrace aspects of sub-state or intra-state civil conflict and ethnic cleansing, ranging from Bosnia to Somalia to East Timor. Unlike the old national liberation insurgents of the Cold War era, pre-modern radicals are more concerned with age-old cultural identity than with a universal class ideology of Marxism; with a strategy of population displacement rather than with winning popular support; and with sectarianism and secession rather than with building inclusive model societies. One of the biggest changes in contemporary military affairs, then, has been the obsolescence of the Cold War political model of unconventional warfare and, as a result, much of the West's counter-insurgency theory.[17]

When distilled to basics, these three overlapping models of modern, postmodern and pre-modern war appear to provide us with two vividly contrasting images of future conflict: one that appears to be mainly symmetric, and one that appears to be largely asymmetric. On one hand, we have the blend of modern and postmodern war seen in the 1991 Gulf War and waged in the air over Kosovo in 1999, to serve as grim metaphors of Western supremacy in any conventional conflict. On another level, however, we are confronted with a strange mixture of pre-modern and postmodern conflict—a world of asymmetric and ethnopolitical warfare—in which machetes and Microsoft merge, and apocalyptic millenarians wearing Reeboks and Raybans dream of acquiring weapons of mass destruction. To use a Hollywood analogy, it is as if the West's space hero, Buck Rogers, is now lined up against assorted road warriors from the devastated society portrayed in the Mad Max films.

Military theory in the 1990s

The fragmentation of war has been mirrored in the world of strategic analysis. In the 1990s, military theory reflected the rapid diffusion of conflict following the end of the bipolar Cold War world. Multiple new theories of armed conflict appeared in the first half of the 1990s. At the beginning of the decade, the American analyst, John Mueller, gave us the 'obsolescence of major war' theory, in which he argued that war in the advanced West was as outmoded as slavery and duelling.[18] The Israeli scholar, Martin van Creveld, followed Mueller by declaring that the Gulf War was a historical freak, a throwback to World War II rather than a vision of 21st-century war. Van Creveld argued that the long era of interstate war—first codified by the Prussian philosopher, Carl von Clausewitz, in the early 19th century—had ended. What he described as Clausewitzian 'trinitarian war'—based on the nexus between people, government and armed forces—was dead, while Western military theory derived from classical warfare had become obsolescent.[19]

The American futurists, Alvin and Heidi Toffler, then gave us the theory of Third Wave, high-technology information warfare that helped initiate the revolution in military affairs (RMA) debate.[20] According to the Tofflers, and the information-age warfare theorists who followed them, the Gulf War provided a glimpse of postmodern war as the realm of high-technology. Precision strike, dominant battlespace knowledge, and stealth platforms would shape future conflict. In the 1990s it was RMA-style ideas that dominated American force planning for a future based on fighting two major theatre wars as enshrined in the Pentagon's blueprint, *Joint Vision 2010*.

In contrast, military writers such as Robert Kaplan, Philip Cerny and Ralph Peters proceeded to give us a vision of future war in which the form of social organisation involved was far more important than the level of technology employed.[21] For Kaplan, the war of the future was the 'coming anarchy' of a Hobbesian world of failed states; for Cerny it was the 'neo-medievalism' of warlordism and violent disintegration; and for Peters it was a struggle by Western forces waged against a world of warrior cultures and paramilitaries from Mogadishu to Grozny. Samuel P. Huntington then published his seminal 1996 study on the coming of a 'clash of civilisations', in which conflict between world cultures and 'fault-line wars' would dominate the geopolitical future.[22] Finally, in 1999 the British analyst, Mary Kaldor, put forward a theory of 'new wars' based on identity politics and the privatisation of violence challenging the new global order.[23]

By the turn of the century, the West was awash in a world of competing ideas about the future of armed conflict. War and conflict had, in effect, unravelled like a splintering rope into a variety of multiple strands. War could be whatever one sought in the cookbook of theory: it could be desert combat in the Gulf; it could be street fighting in Grozny; or it could be somewhere in-between the two. Armed conflict could also be asymmetric or 'fourth-generation warfare' waged by guerrillas and terrorists against the West's conventional military supremacy. War could also be the ominous New Terrorism of nuclear, chemical and biological warfare conducted by rogue regimes and non-state entities, a phenomenon described in August 1998 by former US Secretary of State, Madeleine Albright, as representing 'the war of the future'.[24]

From theory to practice: the challenge of future war

Given the proliferation of military theory and uncertain political conditions, what then are the possible contours of future warfare over the next decade? While accurate prediction of events is impossible, it is possible to speculate cautiously about emerging trends. In September 1999, the bipartisan US (Hart–Rudman) Commission on National Security/ 21st Century stated:

> The future strategic environment will ... be one of considerable turbulence ... The international system will be so fluid and complex that to think intelligently about military issues will mean taking an integrated view of political, social, technological, and economic developments. Only a broad definition of national security is appropriate to such a circumstance. In short we have entered an age in which many of the fundamental assumptions that steered us through the chilly waters of the Cold War require rethinking ... *The very facts of military reality are changing, and that bears serious and concentrated reflection.*[25]

If the Hart–Rudman Commission's judgment about the a change in the facts of military reality is correct—and many, including the author of this chapter, believe that it is—then those concerned with preparing for armed conflict in the early 21st century must expect to confront a range of old, new and hybrid forms of armed conflict. During the Cold War, the West confronted a uni-dimensional threat from Soviet Marxism–Leninism—an adversary whose motives were certain and whose moves were expected. In the new century, such predictable conditions no longer apply. In the words of the present US Secretary for Defence, Donald H. Rumsfeld, new military thinking is now required to arm Western societies 'against the unknown, the uncertain, the unseen, and the unexpected'.[26]

It has become imperative for all concerned with security issues to pay greater attention to the merging of previously discrete forms of war across a spectrum of conflict. The conceptual basis for the study of warfare in the West must now be broadened to include a rigorous study of the inter-action between interstate, sub-state and trans-state conflict, and the diffusion of contemporary military capabilities. We have to recognise that, in an age of interconnectedness, linkage and interdependence seem to pervade all aspects of armed conflict. Military analysts and force structure specialists have to concentrate on the multifunctional use of force in highly complex operations. In addition, military professionals must learn to embrace the challenges of proportion, coercion and dissuasion as well as the older traditions of battlefield destruction. In particular, what the US Hart–Rudman Commission has described as 'the spectrum of symmetrical and asymmetrical threats we anticipate over the next quarter century' must receive increased attention from both military theorists and policy makers.[27] In short, the challenge is to prepare for full-spectrum conflict.

Such a preparation is more difficult to undertake than many defence analysts realise. It is true that the notion of a spectrum of conflict is not a new idea, but for most of the Cold War, an understanding of war in the West was based on generic intellectual categories of conventional (high-intensity) and unconventional (low-intensity) conflict. Most of us engaged in the field of strategic studies thought in terms of separate worlds of conventional inter-state (or high-intensity) and unconventional intra-state (or low-intensity) military activity. Unfortunately, the spectrum of conflict that is emerging in the early 21st century is distinguished by its merging categories, by its multidimensionality and by its unprecedented interaction.[28]

In an era when all security issues are interconnected and when the national security of Western states has become critically dependent on the health of international security, single-scenario strategies and rigid military force structures have become anachronistic. Traditional concepts of deterrence and defence need to be supplemented by new doctrines of security pre-emption, security prevention and expeditionary warfare. Moreover, the clear separation of peace and war needs to be supplemented by an acknowledgment that modes of war have merged. In a new age marked by networks and instant communications, the need is for advanced military forces with a broad range of skills across a spectrum of conflict. These skills may involve preventive deployment, pre-emptive strike, war fighting, peace enforcement, traditional peacekeeping and peace building, and counter-terrorism.[29]

The intellectual challenge facing military professionals is not as Martin van Creveld would have us believe, to consign Carl von Clausewitz and

2000 years of Western military knowledge into the dustbin of history. Rather, the task is to learn how to fight efficiently across the spectrum of conflict. No responsible Western military theorist can accept at face value the thesis of the 'obsolescence of conventional war' or the paradigm of asymmetric warfare as main force-planning or doctrinal determinants. In a dangerous and unpredictable world, military professionals and their political masters must prepare to fight in conditions of a 'high–low mix'. This preparation is still best accomplished by always being ready in the alleyways of war to tame the big wild cats and not simply the vicious little kittens. Advanced militaries must be able to fight Iraq's Republican Guard as well as Taliban and al-Qa'ida militia and terrorists. As every good operational commander knows, in the military art, one can 'trade down' but one can never 'trade up'. Moreover, all the evidence that we have indicates that success in peace support operations requires the kinds of conventional firepower, mobility and force protection that can only be drawn from military establishments that are optimised for conventional warfighting.[30]

Readying ourselves for conventional war does not, however, absolve us from undertaking a major transformation in the way we think about, and conceive of, the use of military force. The most pressing intellectual task facing all of us at the crossroads of the old and new centuries is one of rapid adaptation to new and merging forms of conflict. In the West we have to reconcile how we would *like* to fight with how we might *have* to fight. We have to try to synthesise relevant features from the massive literature on the Gulf War—RMA high-technology classical model of warfare with the changing reality of conflict—both conventional and unconventional—as it presents itself at the beginning of the 21st century. We have to undertake an intellectual exploration of the growing interaction between interstate, sub-state and trans-state conflict, and conduct a rigorous investigation of the phenomenon of merging war forms: internal, international, postmodern, modern and pre-modern.

The merging of modes of armed conflict suggests an era of warfare quite different from that of the recent past. Fighting in the future may involve conventional armies, guerrilla bands, independent and state-directed terrorist groups, specialised anti-terrorist units and private militias. Terrorist attacks might evolve into classic guerrilla warfare and then escalate to conventional conflict. Alternatively, fighting could be conducted on several levels at once. The possibility of continuous, sporadic armed conflict—blurred in time and space, waged on several levels by a large array of national and sub-national forces—means that the reality of war in the first decade of the 21st century transcends a neat division into distinct areas of symmetry and asymmetry.[31]

Indeed, it is arguable that the main reason for much of the intellectual confusion surrounding war at the turn of the century stems from the lack of a conceptual synthesis between the requirements of traditional conventional war and the emerging blend of interstate, trans-state and non-state modes of conflict in the 21st century.[32] It is no accident that the most productive areas of military theory have been those that have attempted to concentrate on the expanding phenomenon of war. The most interesting new approaches have come from those who have endeavoured to examine the growing complexity of conflict, its holistic yet multi-dimensional character and its sociological, as well as technological dynamics. Conceptual progress has come from analytical work into war's connection to society and the state; from assessing the convergence of modes of conflict and the growing requirements to control armed violence in an age of instantaneous media imagery; and in the area of developing multipurpose forces that can wage warfare across a spectrum of conflict.

In short, it is the interactive character of war—Clausewitz's famous chameleon 'that adapts its characteristics to the given case'—that has proven to be the most original avenue for analysis.[33] The immediate future of war lies perhaps in two key areas. The first area lies in the realm of multidimensional theories of war and conflict, which call for multifunc-tional forces for intervention missions. Second, the evolving theory of counter-war or 'mastery of violence' demonstrates a potential to assist military practitioners and policy-makers to understand and deal with armed conflict as a multifaceted phenomenon.

A multidimensional approach to war and conflict

According to the leading Russian theorist, Makhmut Gareev, 21st-century war is becoming 'multi-variant'.[34] Under these circumstances, advanced armed forces need to develop a multidimensional approach to conflict. The most interesting American and British military theory reflects a growing recognition that, in a new age of multiple threats, the discrete categories of conventional and unconventional conflict are becoming blurred, along with corresponding legal and moral restraints.

Much of the West's present drive towards preparing to meet an accelerating convergence of military challenges is shaped by three ideas. First, armed forces must become multifunctional in order to possess the ability to adapt to differing modes of war right along the conflict spectrum. Second, as questions of both national and societal security merge and interpenetrate, it is clear that possessing a reactive operational strategy alone is inadequate as a means of deterrence. Security in the new era of liberal globalism also requires a willingness to undertake intervention and a corresponding need for proactive military forces. Third, if political and technological conditions now permit radical groups and rogue states to use ballistic or biological weapons to inflict mass casualties on democratic societies, then this new challenge must be met by military preemption in ways that have not been seen since the late 19th century.

In other words, those that espouse a doctrine of asymmetric or unconventional warfare aimed at the mass murder of innocent civilians in cities and suburbs must be destroyed wherever and whenever pre-emption is possible. As President George W. Bush stated recently, it is necessary for the West and its allies to act decisively against the new threat emanating from 'the perilous crossroads of radicalism and technology'.[35] In short, a real threat has arisen from the diffusion and proliferation of advanced technology—from standoff missiles to commercial space systems to possible weapons of mass destruction. Preventing such weapons systems from falling into the hands of smaller armies, paramilitaries, militias and other armed groups puts a premium on Western expeditionary warfare.

Two leading American military theorists, Huba Wass de Czege and Richard Hart Sinnreich, have recently given an unequivocal view of the merging of conventional–unconventional conflict:

Clear distinctions between conventional and unconventional conflicts are fading, and any future major conflict is almost certain to see a routine commingling of such operations. Similarly, once useful demarcations between front and rear or between theater and strategic operations will continue to evaporate as the instrumentalities of war become more interdependent and, as is increasingly true of communications and space systems, less easily separable from their civilian and commercial counterparts.[36]

As a result, the future requirement will be for joint forces designed for multidimensional expeditionary-style operations—what the US Army now refers to as 'operational manoeuvre from strategic distance'. Such operations are vital to control theatres where forces might expect to encounter a range of 'high–low' threats and varied forms of conflict. Consequently, the main trends in contemporary Western military theory are towards operations with multinational joint taskforces with a reduced level of headquarters—from corps, division and brigade to force and formation. Future force structure will become more modular and capable of rapid taskforce organisation in order to provide a 'golf bag', or variety, of military capabilities.[37]

In expeditionary warfare, the main need is to reconcile operational versatility with organisational stability. Western forces must be capable of undertaking joint multi-dimensional missions ranging from shaping the environment to air–ground operational manoeuvre through to all-out conventional warfighting. The demands of operational versatility are likely to place a premium on the need for organisational change. The need is for smaller combat formations, such as the combined-arms brigades, to be formed to serve as modular building blocks for forces in the field.[38]

Dealing with multifaceted conflict: counter-war theory and mastery of violence

Recent trends in European–American military theory towards multi-dimensional operations have also been applied to what some European military thinkers now call counter-war theory or 'mastery of violence' as an operational military strategy.[39] In France, the development of counter-war theory reflects the reality that war in the 21st century has become 'a mixture of phenomena'. Some French military thinkers believe that, in contemporary armed conflict, it is now largely impossible to treat war as merely a clash between rival forces. Increasingly, the conventional cannot be separated from the unconventional, and traditional lines of authority between military control and political responsibility are becoming blurred.

A military force may now be required to conduct intervention operations in conditions that correspond to neither classical warfare nor traditional peace-support operations. A counter-war strategy based on the disciplined control of violence may therefore have to be imposed in extremely complex political conditions in which law and order are missing but in which the Law of Armed Conflict must, at all costs, be upheld. As the French military analysts, Brigadier General Loup Francart and Jean-Jacques Patry, observe:

> Military operations are now completely integrated with political, diplomatic, economic and cultural activities. Strategy is no longer simply a matter of defense. The problem is now, more than ever, *to conceive military operations in a political framework.*[40]

General Wesley K. Clark, the American commander who prosecuted NATO's 1999 war against Serbia over Kosovo, has argued in his recent memoir, *Waging Modern War*, that politics in modern war now pervade all of the three normal levels of war, namely tactics, operations and strategy. In the past, politics was mainly a factor at the strategic level where statecraft was required to guide the military instrument. In the early 21st century, however, politics also impinge on the operational and tactical levels of war to the extent that Clark believes that it may now be necessary to think in terms of a 'political level of war'. If General Clark is right, then the implications for future civil–military relations may be profound.[41]

In an age where there is increased integration between military officers, political leaders and a 24-hour electronic media, the goal in using force may not be annihilation or attrition, but calibrated elimination of the enemy's resistance by the careful and proportional use of counter-violence. The possibility of having to use armed force in a surgical manner—with a rapier rather than a broadsword—requires future military thinking and action to be politically sophisticated, legally disciplined and morally correct. These requirements were among the main lessons of the Kosovo conflict. As French military theorists have argued, the aim must be to ensure that the application of force in intervention operations—especially in an age of instant images—can be modulated and shaped by professional militaries in order to accommodate rapidly shifting politics, and flexible operational and strategic objectives.

Some characteristics of warfare in 2015: a tentative analysis

Given the growing complexity of the military art and of the use of force in statecraft in the early part of the new century, what are to be the most likely characteristics of warfare over the next decade? Four basic scenarios can be tentatively envisaged. First, war is likely to remain a chameleon, being able to present itself in interstate, trans-state and non-state modes, or as a combination of these. However, a word of caution is necessary. It would be a serious mistake for any military establishment to dismiss the possibility of interstate conventional war breaking out in future. In some areas of the world such as Western Europe, interstate war may be highly unlikely; however, in much of Asia and the Middle East, interstate conventional war remains a distinct possibility.[42] Nonetheless, in general terms, the merging of modes of armed conflict does suggest an era of warfare in which national, trans-state and sub-state forces may coalesce or confront each other. Moreover, the conventional and the unconventional, the symmetric and the asymmetric may occur almost simultaneously and overlap in time and space.

Second, advanced warfare will be largely joint-service in character. Information-age technologies—especially the dramatic advances in command and control, long-range precision missiles and stealth platforms—have led to an unprecedented compression of time and space in military operations. These developments have, in turn, created a non-linear battlespace based on breadth, depth and height. During the 1990s, the concept of a battlespace replaced the older idea of a linear battlefield that defined armed conflict in the Western tradition from Alexander the Great to the time of World War II and Korea. In essence, the concept of a battlespace has permitted a shift in Western military thought away from the organisation of linear mass towards the idea of a simultaneous and full-dimensional concentration of effects.[43] The idea of concentrating effects is especially significant with regard to the cumulative effect of missile firepower from air, ground and sea.[44]

Third, most Western military experts believe that future operations will favour simultaneous attack in which joint air–ground forces are increasingly likely to be situationally aware, that is, to have an up-to-date view of the battlespace via computer and satellite. Advanced forces are also likely to be networked from 'sensor to shooter', that is, surveillance capabilities will be electronically connected to strike forces. There will probably be fewer troops deployed on the ground, but the individual soldier—sometimes referred to as the 'strategic corporal'—will be able to have a greater impact on events. Greater weapons accuracy and the increased technological ability of soldiers to direct lethal, long-range precision fires—as seen in Afghanistan with ground forces acting as highly effective sensors for air strikes—are likely to become features of war over the next decade.[45]

Fourth, for advanced forces, the dominance of surveillance and strike means that many joint operations are likely to resemble large-scale ambushes. New technology permits the use of deep precision fires and quick manoeuvre throughout an area of operations. If an enemy can be located by stealthy technology and signal intelligence, then traditional movement to contact using forward troops to probe for the enemy's positions will be replaced by well-prepared, deliberate attacks using ambush tactics that exploit rapid positioning of force for maximum effect. However, while precision munitions will help to define future air–ground tactics in long-range or deep attack, they are likely to be of limited use in close operations in which infantry must be employed to finish off adversaries.[46]

In the close battle, armoured forces and artillery are likely to remain extremely useful in applying suppressive fire to support troops in action. In the recent campaign in Afghanistan, American forces put their faith in air cover at the expense of both artillery and tanks. It was soon discovered that, while high-altitude, air-delivered precision munitions are effective against point targets, they are much less useful in area attack. Precision-guided munitions could not destroy stubborn Taliban and al-Qa'ida forces using short-range mortars against advancing American and Australian troops. As a result, the majority of American casualties (28 out of 36) in Operation *Enduring Freedom* came from enemy mortar fire that could have been suppressed had the ground troops been able to respond with direct and indirect fire from their own armour and artillery. The lesson learnt from fierce combat in the complex terrain of Afghanistan's Shah-i-Kot mountains is that, for area suppression, field guns and tanks remain essential in 21st-century warfare.[47] Lessons from Afghanistan were reinforced still further by the events of the 2003 Iraqi War to remove the regime of Saddam Hussein. In ground and joint warfare in Operation *Iraqi Freedom*, combined-arms teams of infantry, armour and artillery appear to have reaffirmed their importance in achieving decision in close combat.[48]

Conclusion

The likely shape of war in the early 21st century essentially reflects the consequences of a bifurcated global system between an older state-centric world on the one hand and new trans-state and sub-state strata on the other hand. The West has entered a period in which classical interstate war has been supplemented by borderless threats from non-state actors operating with the power of modern computers, ease of international travel and, possibly, weapons of mass destruction. These non-state actors can deal lethal blows to any society.

All of these trends, particularly the unholy alliance between new non-state actors and the power of advanced technology, suggest an urgent need for new strategic thinking. The shift towards connectedness and non-linearity, at the relative expense of territoriality and linearity, has become perhaps the central reality of strategy in the first decade of the 21st century. Some international observers believe that the strategic shift from territoriality to connectedness will be revolutionary in its consequences. In the words of Philip Bobbitt:

> We are at a moment in world affairs when the essential ideas that govern statecraft must change. For five centuries it has taken the resources of a state to destroy another state; only states could muster the huge revenues, conscript the vast armies, and equip the divisions required to threaten the survival of other states ... This is no longer true, owing to advances in international telecommunications, rapid computation, and weapons of mass destruction. The change in statecraft that will accompany these developments will be as profound as any that the State has thus far undergone.[49]

The great danger to Western countries is no longer the threat of military invasion of the nation-state, but an assault on the very foundations of our networked society. Western societies are now most vulnerable not so much from external invasion, but from an internal disruption of the connectedness of government, financial and economic institutions that make up critical infrastructures.[50]

It was this great weakness that was identified by al-Qa'ida, with devastating results for the United States on 11 September 2001. Increasingly, national security depends on the protection of a loop of social institutions and the information infrastructures that link them. Unlike the borders of a state, however, it is impossible to protect an entire society solely by homeland defence simply because our reliance on critical infrastructures far exceeds our abilities to protect such systems.

In order to defend Western societies, the nation-state model of war by threat-analysis against defined enemies will have to be eventually supplemented by new modes of strategic thought that concentrate on alleviating the vulnerabilities of modern states to new non-state threats. As the French military analyst, Phillippe Delmas, has warned:

> Today's world is without precedent. It is as different from the Cold War as it is from the Middle Ages so the past offers no basis for comparison . . . Tomorrow's wars will not result from the ambitions of States; rather from their weaknesses.[51]

To meet the military challenges of tomorrow's wars, Western countries will need highly mobile, well-equipped and versatile armed forces capable of multidimensional coalition missions and 'mastery of violence' across a complex spectrum of conflict. We will need new national security apparatuses to coordinate the role of armed forces in threat and vulnerability analysis and to assist in consequence management in the event of traumatic societal attack. In addition, enhanced international intelligence and diplomatic cooperation will be required to ensure that military force is employed with maximum efficiency. Finally, new norms of international law will have to be formulated that allow us, when the enemy can be located, to use force in far-flung and distant military pre-emption operations.[52]

The reality of Western societal vulnerability in conditions of liberal globalism represents a strategic transformation that commands defence experts and politicians to think rigorously about the kinds of war that might lie ahead. We are confronted with a need to find new ways of using force to meet merging modes of war and conflict in an international system that must simultaneously confront both increased integration and fragmentation.

The problems facing policy-makers, strategists and military professionals in the early 21st century have changed dramatically and decisively from those of the 20th century. Military power and capability have expanded outwards to become a spider's web of transnational networks. As a result, preparing for armed conflict is no longer only a matter of simply assembling battlefield strength to destroy defined adversaries, as occurred throughout much of the history of war.

Increasingly, military power is entwined in politics as an instrument that shapes, polices, punishes, signals, warns and contains the strategic environment. The task for strategists is now one of disciplining available military power into a broad security strategy—one that also embraces diplomacy, intelligence analysis and law enforcement—and to do this in a calibrated, judicious and precise manner. In the prophetic words of British strategist, Alastair Buchan, written over 35 years ago, 'the real content of strategy is concerned not merely with war and battles but with the application and maintenance of force so that it contributes most effectively to the advancement of political objectives'.[53] At the dawn of a new century, and of a new and uncertain era in armed conflict, these words are an apt description of the many dangerous challenges that lie ahead in our globalised, yet deeply fragmented, world.

Resurrecting transformation for the post-industrial era

Colonel Douglas A. Macgregor[1]

We must hold our minds alert and receptive to the application of unglimpsed methods and weapons. The next war will be won in the future, not in the past. We must go on, or we will go under.
General of the Army Douglas A. MacArthur,
while serving as Chief of Staff of the United States Army, 1931

Introduction

In 2000 the Bush Administration took office amid high hopes for the fundamental transformation of the Armed Forces. Yet, within months, the problem that transformation was designed to solve—changing a large, expensive industrial-age structure, especially the Army, into a leaner, more strategically agile information-age force—receded as more pressing issues arose. Instead of being transformed, Cold War military structures will remain unchanged for the time being, while morale and quality of life are shored up. Into this policy vacuum, military leaders have tossed an expensive collection of wish lists that tend to one of two extremes: a bigger, faster, better version of some platform already in use, or something out of science fiction with delivery timelines that stretch all the way to 2032.[2] Although these modernisation programs are billed as promoting transformation, they are business as usual.

Fortunately, this is not the whole story. Help may be on the way. The terms of reference for the current Quadrennial Defense Review (QDR) anticipate the emergence of new ground, naval and air forces reorganised for 'more rapidly responsive, scalable, modular task-organised units, capable of independent combat action as well as integration into larger joint and combined operations'[3] sometime after 2006. How the bureaucratic politics of service-centric operational thinking and single-service modernisation will produce this outcome is unclear. This statement also begs the question, why wait until 2006 to build joint warfighting capabilities with today's forces and technologies when the United States needs—and can achieve—these capabilities now in order to protect its global interests? Experience in the private sector demonstrates that successful corporations do not plan to transform in the distant future; they transform constantly, just as the world around them transforms. Military transformation is a process, not an end-state that depends on exotic technologies that may not be available for decades. America can lose its position of military dominance only by standing still and investing in the past.

Rethinking transformation

Transformation—defined as change in the structure of command, control, training, readiness, doctrine, technology and organisation for combat—can produce short-term economies and increased capability well before 2006. Transformation can be phased in now through continuous adaptation, using today's forces and technology with reform and reorganisation that will result in significant improvements in the quality of life and morale, as well as the fighting power of soldiers, sailors, airmen and marines.

The Bush Administration needs a unifying strategic vision for the post-industrial age that can drive transformation. The first step requires recognising that the two major-theatre wars (MTW) capability strategy based on known threats, doctrines and orders of battle no longer applies. The second step requires developing a new strategic formula for the use of American military power that is neither scenario-dependent nor based on service-centric concepts and structures designed to deploy masses of men and *matériel*; the focus must be on critical warfighting capabilities.

Dramatic advances in technology and ten years of experience point the way to a paradigm shift in warfare that will reshape the structure of American military power through the integration of ground, naval and air forces within a joint, network-centric system of warfare. To cope with the new strategic environment, a new operational paradigm based on air, space, missile and information power must emerge long before 2006 to support military operations scaled to meet the requirements of any contingency exactly as envisioned by the Secretary of Defense in the context of the QDR. At the same time, a fresh approach to American military strategy and the employment of American military power is needed—an approach that buttresses the stability of key states around the world, preserves American access to critical bases and infrastructure, and operates to prevent regional crises and conflict rather than react to them.

These points raise a host of questions. What conclusions can be drawn about the direction of the Bush Administration's strategic review process and its impact on transformation? What are the strategic implications of review recommendations? And, finally, how can the Bush Administration move from the implications for change in strategy, structure and joint military operations, derived from the strategic review process, to implementation of real transformation?

These are important questions, but transformation, strategy, joint military operations and, strange as it may seem, readiness, are inextricably intertwined. Otherwise, transformation is reduced to a service-centric, industrial-age quest for a new armoured vehicle, ship or aeroplane that can transform warfare, as the rifled musket and the machine gun are thought to have done. That approach would miss the real promise of the information age—the potential for revolutionary change and transformation through the integration of critical military capabilities across service lines.

Where is transformation headed?

In his speech at The Citadel on 23 September 1999, then-Governor George W. Bush promised to begin an immediate, comprehensive review of the American military—the structure of its forces, the state of its strategy, the priorities of its procurement—conducted by a leadership team under the Secretary of Defense. Bush also noted that he wanted to move beyond marginal improvements to replace existing programs with new technologies and strategies, and exploit the opportunity to skip a generation of technology. Shortly after being appointed Secretary of Defense in early 2001, Donald Rumsfeld used this guidance to create dozens of panels to study a range of security issues. The reviews ended in June 2001, and Administration emphasis on the criticality of joint military operations to transformation are discernible from the results that have been released.

General James P. McCarthy, USAF (Retd), who led a panel on transformation, presented recommendations on 12 June 2001 that highlighted the concept of multi-service early-entry 'Global Joint Response Forces'. According to McCarthy, these forces would combine units from different services as tailorable force modules that train and exercise together, and build on common building blocks: command-and-control systems; intelligence, surveillance and reconnaissance capabilities; space-based assets; and joint logistics capabilities. Though few details on the structure of such a force were provided, McCarthy stressed that the panel was not considering a new force, but how to organise, exercise and train the existing forces, and what capabilities to give them.[4]

RAND analyst David Gompert led the panel on America's conventional forces. He echoed McCarthy's recommendations when he told reporters in a 22 June 2001 briefing that all joint units must be 'ready, rapidly deployable, and employable; tailorable for [a] range of operations; easily integrated and networked; [and] supportable despite distance and dispersion'.[5] When asked about transformation initiatives during testimony in Congress in June, Secretary Rumsfeld listed 'rapidly deployable standing joint forces' as part of a new approach to handling military operations in both the near and long term.[6]

Why is this concept of transformation important? For the first time in recent history, a top-level defence review did not focus on what used to be the outputs of defence planning: carrier battlegroups, fighter wings, army divisions, and marine expeditionary forces. Instead, the defence review posed the vital question: What are the capabilities that a joint force commander needs today and will need in the future? Asking this question in the context of defence planning converted the traditional outputs of defence planning to inputs and equated the results of defence planning with the capabilities provided to a joint taskforce (JTF) pursuing an operational mission. In theory, this approach overturns the unstated World War II-era assumption (despite the Goldwater–Nichols Act of 1986) that developing tactical capabilities and conducting operations remain a purely service function. In this sense, the implications are profound for American defence policy and the administration's subtle advocacy for change. If implemented as outlined by the panel in its published recommendations, JTFs would become the order of the day. Command at the three-star level and above would become joint. Service Title 10 functions would be modified to focus exclusively on organising, training and equipping for specific joint roles and missions versus current service missions.[7] The services would then provide the JTF building blocks or force modules based on the core competencies of each branch.

The recommendations also set the stage for legislation to abolish the World War II mode of relatively independent, sequential missions accomplished by service components under a regional warfighting commander in chief (CINC). This change presumably would lead to the elimination of single-service, three- and four-star headquarters that would no longer be required for the command and control (C2) of joint forces and that would otherwise divert needed personnel and financial resources. Finally, as forces are converted to building-block formations for JTFs, the resulting Armed Forces could adopt a joint rotational readiness base that would make deployments more predictable and that would identify the ground, naval and air forces available at any given time for contingencies. If carried through to its logical end, the new Administration's brand of joint transformation would end the wasteful practice of pouring billions into the services to build sufficient capability to compensate for the hopelessly inefficient single-service mode of employment under a weak and inadequate joint command and control structure. All of these measures could reduce unneeded bureaucratic layers and yield efficiencies that promise significant resource, dollar and personnel savings. However, regardless of the national military strategy, the services will oppose change that does not give their core competencies due appreciation in defence planning and spending.[8] Although the Goldwater–Nichols Act was supposed to address this problem, so many single-service headquarters and control structures survived the process (on the grounds that joint organisations had yet to demonstrate success) that enormous and expensive redundancies remain. Now that the conceptual groundwork has been laid, the issue is how to maintain the current readiness of the Armed Forces to conduct operations while transformation is implemented through changes in organisation, doctrine and technology.

From implications to implementation

As reported in the press, the new national military strategy establishes four objectives: to assure friends and allies, dissuade future adversaries, deter threats and counter coercion, and defeat adversaries if deterrence fails.[9] To these strategic tenets must be added the Administration's reported willingness to scrap the scenario-based two-MTW requirement that has driven US military strategy since the end of the Cold War and to replace it with a one-war-plus policy.

These elegantly formulated tenets of national military strategy provide neither a formula that translates theoretical goals into attainable strategic military objectives nor guidelines for sizing or employing the force. The problem is not difficult to fathom. The absence of Soviet tank armies poised to invade allied territory on short notice complicates matters. Only North Korea fields a force designed to attack on short notice, and this force is rapidly declining in capability and strength. In the meantime, a complex range of threats to American and allied interests is emerging that no single service can address. Accounting for this inability is the fact that future state and nonstate actors will possess not only some form of weapon of mass destruction but also a limited supply of precision-guided munitions, modern air-defence technology, and access to electronic intelligence and satellite imagery provided by third powers.

(This is why theatre and national missile defence must be seen as part of a broader joint transformation strategy.) In sum, a broader range of enemies armed with new mixes of technologies—some industrial-age and some information-age capabilities—will confront the Armed Forces. Adversaries do not require the ability to defeat those forces, only to frustrate their employment in some way.

Whatever strategic framework the administration adopts, it will have certain, unavoidable core features because it must link the raw military capability to dominate the strategic landscape to those areas of the world where economic progress and political stability directly benefit American and allied security. If defence planners stop trying to predict the future, they will be able to identify straightforward requirements for America's military. There are two such requirements that are most significant. First, the Armed Forces must be able to intervene militarily and fight in areas where the United States and its allies have no presence but have either declared strategic interests that are threatened or a considerable political stake in the outcome.

Second, they must also maintain an overseas military presence on land, at sea and in the air in pivotal states or regions to ensure that the United States and its allies can either influence or become involved in crises or fight in conflicts that directly impinge on strategic interests.

This viewpoint means that the United States will selectively use JTFs in war and peace to buttress the stability of key states—primarily around the Eurasian periphery, the Middle East and North Africa—and will operate to prevent regional crises and conflicts rather than react to them. (This regional focus takes into consideration that the rest of the world either is friendly towards the American people or can present no significant resistance to American military power.) In terms of force design and employment, the implications for military transformation of this peripheral strategy are clear. First, JTFs will need highly mobile, rapidly deployable forces-in-being. These forces must be structured for interoperability within an evolving joint framework to incorporate and exploit new technology on a continuous basis. Second, some portion of the ground, naval and air forces will be forward-deployed in key states to preserve American access to critical infrastructure so that the United States can project military power inland. Forward-deployed forces provide tangible evidence of American commitment and a link to the larger strategic power of the United States. In the absence of large forces poised to attack our allies, fewer forces will be needed in a forward-deployed posture than previously. This situation presents the opportunity to reduce, though not eliminate, expensive overseas garrisons.

What military power remains—the bulk of the Armed Forces—must be capable of moving rapidly from widely dispersed staging areas overseas and within the continental United States, deploying into crisis or conflict and initiating offensive operations, all without pausing. Organising these ground, naval and air forces into specialised modules of combat power on rotational readiness so that they can rapidly assemble into joint taskforces is vital.

The 1999 Kosovo crisis illustrates the need for rapidly deployable, ready ground forces to integrate seamlessly into the global strike capabilities that American air, missile, information and space power make possible, both to exploit their potential and to guarantee the safety of the deployed American and allied ground forces. If technology can be exploited to create the conditions for an Inchon-style operation wherever strikes are concentrated, the development of a new structure for readiness and training that is inherently joint is critical. One way to pursue this goal is to treat the forces under service control as a pool of capability packages and place them into a joint rotational readiness structure.

The idea of pooling forces as capability packages is different from the notion of standing JTFs that would permanently control large numbers of forces normally under service command and control. A glance at the military organisation chart during the Cold War explains why. At the top was the body known as the National Command Authorities, below which were the CINCs, then the service component four-star headquarters, then the three-star Army corps, fleets, marine expeditionary and air force headquarters. Below these were the above-the-line forces such as Army divisions and Air Force fighter wings. Today, nothing has changed at the top; however, the bottom layer has contracted, which implies greater sharing of the forces by the same number of higher-echelon headquarters. Clearly, the echelons need to be reduced, but replacing them with standing JTFs that permanently control the shrunken forces at the bottom may not be the answer. For example, the two JTFs or global joint response forces suggested by Gompert would have to be designed for the full range of missions, from an Operation *Desert Storm* to an Operation *Sea Angel*. Such a design seems unworkable and would limit flexibility.

An alternative idea would be to reconfigure existing single-service three- and four-star headquarters as command modules under the control of US Joint Force Command. These modular headquarters could then be assigned to the regional warfighting commands in order to provide the assets from which the CINCs could establish JTF command structures that would enable them to control their forces. The JTFs could be established on the basis of specific mission requirements, albeit much more rapidly and effectively than is the case today. This arrangement also avoids the complicated and unrewarding interservice squabbling associated with the establishment of any one-size-fits-all JTF headquarters.

The approach outlined here preserves today's forces that deploy and fight by creating a larger, predictable pool of ready, available ground, naval and air forces on rotational readiness. These forces can be rapidly deployed to regional commands with a combination of strategic airlift and fast sealift to arrive in strategically pivotal regions 'before the peace is lost'. This approach is vital to the readiness of today's forces while routine joint experimentation and modernisation are conducted. It also promises to reduce personnel tempo, and make deployments and costs more predictable. A possible structure would be cyclical and could comprise a series of six-month-long rotations. These cycles might include an initial training period during which unit and individual training is conducted under service control. Second, a deployment cycle during which units are maintained ready for deployment to joint command and control and become part of the pool that responds to major theatre of war missions, crises, peace support operations, or whatever mission the National Command Authorities assign. Third, a reconstitution cycle during which units return to home station for refitting, modernisation (if required) and leave.

Clearly, this structure also facilitates regular joint training of the forces that are likely to be committed within the readiness windows and makes the commitment of the Armed Forces more comprehensible to the National Command Authorities. Perhaps more important, it allows more humane treatment of the soldiers, sailors, marines and airmen who must deploy on a routine basis.

Transforming concepts and organisation

Secretary Rumsfeld insists that new joint operational concepts are the keys to both transformation and rationalising defence. But what is a joint operational concept, and how does one develop? A joint operational concept involves the integration of service core tactical capabilities on the operational level to achieve unity of purpose and action in the conduct of military operations. American naval aviators in the inter-war period developed new operational concepts when they experimented with the employment of carrier-based aviation to reverse the striking and supporting roles of battleships and aircraft carriers. In fact, American naval tactics evolved throughout World War II, and by 1945 no category of warship, except minesweepers, was employed for the purpose for which it had originally been built.

Studies of European and American forces during the inter-war period suggest a pattern of transformation that is still relevant today. This pattern is characterised by the emergence of a new operational concept. That concept is executed by the adoption of a new doctrine and organisation that increases fighting power. The adoption of doctrine is consolidated with the development of new joint operational architecture that integrates the technologies of ground, naval and air warfare and which is accompanied by a new approach to modernisation, education, training and readiness.

To this pattern must be added the corollaries that information processes are also sources of combat power and should drive organisational design for combat, and that warfighting systems must evolve along with concepts and organisations; the current pace of technological development is so fast that static organisational thinking is impossible. Adaptive structures for the continuous incorporation of new technologies to provide new capabilities are essential.

The current integration of strike and manoeuvre assets linked through nodes and empowered by new terrestrial and space-based communications is the foundation for a new joint operational concept. The idea of linking strike and manoeuvre assets in this way has enormous potential, but how it will work in a purely joint setting is unclear. However, effects-based operations, which originated in the naval and air forces, present an opportunity to demonstrate the integrative nature of joint network-centric warfare in action. The concept of creating effects in order to achieve a specific political–military objective is inherently joint and network-centric; the ground, naval and air forces involved must be interconnected or netted in order to be effective. This concept makes it imperative that all parts of the joint force see the same picture of the battlespace and that whatever one part knows is available to the whole force.[10] To transform how enemy ground forces are attacked in the future, the United States must exploit its unique and unprecedented airborne ground surveillance and precision-targeting capabilities by jointly detecting, tracking and targeting a moving or dispersed enemy with ever-increasing speed and precision throughout a large area. Such a network creates an immensely powerful joint warfighting synergy by enabling a joint commander to orchestrate ground, naval and air forces to achieve effects that complement each other dynamically at the operational and tactical levels of war. The collection, processing, analysis, fusion and dissemination of information must be addressed in a joint operational setting as new technologies compress events in time and space.

New joint operational concepts and structures that integrate diverse service capabilities require a new joint operational architecture to be effective because this architecture breathes life into the concept in two ways. First, such an architecture creates a new set of command relationships that are different from today's single-service warfighting structures. This set of command relationships provides the C2 elements from which CINCs constitute joint taskforces. Second, it drives the services to organise their core capabilities into specialised modules of mission-focused combat power that can be integrated as required into JTFs. The first point requires change on the operational level to supplant the multitude of single-service component commands at home and overseas with joint command and control elements from which JTFs can be constituted. The second point requires change on the tactical level in order to achieve the interoperability essential to joint operations.

The navy and air force face problems when attempting to group forces to become mission-focused capability packages within a joint network-centric framework. Operational thinking in the naval and air forces is converging on ways to exploit jointly the global reconnaissance-strike complex. The Air Force plan to establish ten Air Expeditionary Forces is a critical step in this direction. Air Force strike packages evolve in response to the required mission and target set. The Navy is accustomed to assembling ships into taskforces for specific missions. While new naval platforms are designed and built for strike and manoeuvre operations in the littoral, existing platforms can be equipped and employed differently to provide the capabilities JTF commanders require.

In recent months, the idea of a Marine Expeditionary Brigade (MEB) has re-emerged. It is, in effect, a specialised module of combat power capable of deploying a force of 5000 or more marines quickly and sustaining combat over a wider area than the 2000-man Marine Expeditionary Unit can. The MEB can be scaled to a size that can execute independent missions within JTFs, but without the long deployment timelines for a larger Marine Expeditionary Force—the Marine equivalent of an Army corps.[11]

In sum, scaling and equipping naval and air forces for integration into a plug-and-play joint operational architecture may entail modifications in communications and procedures to facilitate joint interoperability, but these actions will not necessitate dramatic organisational change. For the Army, however, the challenge of integration for joint interoperability has proved thus far insurmountable.

Recent history provides plenty of evidence for why change in the American structure for, and thinking about, warfare is needed now. In contrast to the German attack on France that split the French and British forces by manoeuvre through and around enemy forces to reach the English Channel, Army ground forces in the Gulf War were slowly and deliberately deployed against Iraq's strength, the Republican Guard Corps. The opportunity to exploit the paralysis achieved in the opening days of the air campaign was lost, and the strategic realities of Baghdad's regional influence did not change. During the Kosovo crisis in 1999, the Army and the Air Force were unable to overcome the single-service nature of American warfare. Because they did not face a robust Allied combat force on the ground that was capable of decisive manoeuvre operations, the Yugoslav forces were never compelled to mass and present the target array that the Allied air forces sought.

General George C. Marshall's vision and structure for expanding efficiently from an army of 200 000 to one that would grow to more than 6 million are a legacy of Henry Ford's assembly line and cannot remain the Army organisation for combat or institutional strategy today. The contemporary organisation for combat and concepts of warfare were developed when theatre missile defence, deep-strike operations, JTFs and real-time information sharing did not exist. New missions for today's ground forces that were either unknown or un-anticipated 50 years ago make institutional and organisational change imperative. Without fundamental reorganisation and reform of the Army's warfighting structure, the Army cannot integrate its ground manoeuvre formations around and through massed precision strikes from joint ground, naval and air forces to seize the positional advantage in future war.

Summoning the will to transform the whole Army for the future requires recognising that the most brilliant victories are not those that cost the most blood or are achieved with the crushing weight of numbers but those that are won by surprise, joint strike and manoeuvre to paralyse the enemy. This capability cannot be attained if the Army attempts transformation in isolation from the other services, nor can it transform by re-equipping the old division-based World War II force with new platforms, whether they are wheeled or tracked. When applied to land warfare, joint network-centric warfare demands a 'dispersed mobile warfare' design that differs radically from the traditional army, corps, division and brigade formations of linear warfare. It requires a transformational design with fewer echelons of C2 and a faster decision cycle that employs joint sensors forward with manoeuvre elements in order to provide the coverage needed to exploit the joint potential in the Army's strike formations, as well as the advanced aviation and ground combat platforms in the Army's close-combat formations. Manoeuvre and strike formations are transformed into nodes of joint combat power—deep, close or sustaining—that have the capacity for joint operations on land similar to the operation of ships at sea.

This taxonomy of combat power necessitates the reorganisation of Army forces to become the mission-focused force packages that provide the building blocks for the integration of critical Army capabilities into

JTFs. These capabilities range from theatre missile defence assets and rocket artillery to combat manoeuvre forces and modern attack helicopters. This scheme for land power depends on evolving joint systems and a technical architecture (a set of building codes) for successful aggregation. Reorganising Army forces for integrated joint operations is essential because JTFs without powerful ground forces will not control events in areas of pivotal American strategic interest. Experience shows that missiles and embargoes can punish governments and societies, but only ground forces can reach out and fundamentally change them. Therefore, the question is not whether American dominance in space, in the air and at sea can dramatically influence the conduct of all military operations on land as never before. The real question is whether the Army will be compelled to adjust its thinking, doctrine and structure to exploit the new strategic reality.

Is help really on the way?

In the information age, national military strategy, operational concepts and force designs are all inseparable from the creation of new interdisciplinary teams of armed forces that are capable of both adaptation and rapid joint employment. This interconnection is why development of forces to operate jointly within a new joint network-centric warfighting structure is vital to transformation. It explains why simply recapitalising old warfighting structures will not transform the way that America fights. Old structures and old thinking are linked. As Americans in uniform are witnessing the compression of warfighting operations into a new paradigm of simultaneity, there is a widening gulf between service transformation programs and transformation at the operational level, which must be joint.

The various service transformation programs, if pursued separately, would tinker on the margins of America's military status quo or electrify the horse cavalry, rather than fundamentally reform, reorganise or change national military capability. The thousands of junior officers leaving the Army prematurely provide grim testimony to this fact. They are voting against the status quo with their feet. Only structural and organisational change and new institutional policies will cure this problem.

Without structural and organisational change, thinking is unlikely to change, nor will the substance of the future joint force. Until all of the Armed Forces begin to operate differently with existing assets, the parameters of modernisation will not change, unneeded equipment sets cannot be eliminated, and new requirements will not be identified. The Armed Forces must emulate successful businesses by incorporating some new technologies, rejecting others, adapting practices and structures, narrowing or broadening activities—all in response to changing conditions.

Defence officials cite the transformational power of the German Army's operational concept of *blitzkrieg* as an example for US forces to follow. They note that while only 10–15 per cent of Germany's inter-war military establishment was actually reorganised and re-equipped for this new concept of warfare, the effect was dramatic.[12]

However, the comparison should be extended. The United States is not converting a horse-drawn 19th-century Army into a 20th-century force equipped with combustion engines, aviation technology and FM radios. Also, whereas the Germans were compelled to develop simultaneously new operational concepts, tactics and command structures while fielding entirely new sets of equipment, American ships, aircraft, satellites, tanks, guns and rockets can support transformation now. Finally, German transformation was achieved during the Great Depression, amid political and social turmoil, and in the face of international criticism, whereas the United States is prosperous, stable and the object of international pressure to become more involved militarily in international developments. Given these different circumstances, the United States should take no consolation in the fact that Germany succeeded in transforming only 10–15 per cent of its military, an amount that should not be considered an adequate goal for American efforts. That small portion of Germany's military was ten armoured divisions—roughly the size of the US Army today. Moreover, partial transformation ultimately proved disastrous for Germany. The performance of the transformed force could not compensate for the World War I-style infantry divisions that hampered the German military in Russia.

Winning the battle of ideas

Like Rome after the fall of Carthage, America wields supreme power in the world. But like the victorious Romans, Americans confront new threats and challenges to prosperity and security. America does not hold the patent on innovative ideas or a monopoly on new technology. History demonstrates that an early lead in any one area of military affairs does not convey permanent advantage; Britain introduced the tank in 1916, but Germany exploited it fully.

It is one thing to experiment with a technology or a concept, however, and quite another to displace existing assets or doctrine to make way for the new. Efforts at far-reaching change produce powerful resistance. As Niccolo Machiavelli observed,

> There is nothing more difficult to take in hand, more perilous to conduct, or more uncertain in its success, than to take the lead in the introduction of a new order of things. Because the innovator has for enemies all those who have done well under the old conditions, and lukewarm defenders in those who may do well under the new. (p. 51)

Difficulty is no excuse for inaction, however. Transformation is not an option; it is an imperative.

The difficulty of change on the strategic level is what makes the President's commitment to transformation so important and difficult. Clearly, the Executive Branch cannot make this strategic change alone. Congress must also understand the need and sign on to the policy and plan. The nation's elected representatives are obliged for domestic political reasons to think about people, bases and the defence industry. Many in Congress would, however, welcome the Administration's lead if they believed that true and comprehensive transformation were a top priority and were made participants in the process. Since the early 1990s, Congress has sounded a constant theme urging real change inside the Armed Forces (the Army in particular) during hearings and private sessions with the nation's military leaders because Members of Congress do not view a smaller Cold War force as either prudent or affordable for the times. Members would support Administration efforts if they saw evidence that they were dealing with true and comprehensive transformation and were not being asked to support piecemeal reductions in selected defence programs or preserve today's forces in an obsolete Cold War configuration.

Historic opportunity

America's victory over Spain in 1898 marked the beginning of a new era in world affairs. Overnight, America became a world power. Realising that American national-security institutions had reached block obsolescence, President Theodore Roosevelt instructed Secretary of War Elihu Root to devise a new strategy and structure that would position the United States to play its role in the world as a great power. Then, as now, American military thinking lagged behind the technology of war. Then, as now, new thinking and new organisations were required to propel the nation into the new century.

When the Roosevelt Administration Bill for Army reform and reorganisation came before Congress, many senior officers opposed Root's plan to create an Army General Staff, to convert the 25 000-man Army of cavalry, infantry and artillery regiments to a force of 100 000 troops and six divisions. They asked, 'Why change; after all, we won the Spanish–American War, didn't we?'[13] Despite the opposition to change, Roosevelt skilfully manoeuvred his Bill through Congress, and within two years, Root's successor, Howard Taft, quietly retired the opponents of the Bill. America's military leaders know in principle that obsolete paradigms lead to military disaster. They can cite historical examples of governments and armies that brought catastrophe on their nations by basing their forces and policies on imperfect or delusional models of the world. Now they have the opportunity to demonstrate that they are not prisoners of the past and that they will not repeat those mistakes.

Few historical figures have had Theodore Roosevelt's ability to recognise changes in the strategic landscape, to conceive the measures necessary for military forces to fight and win in the new environment, and to summon the resolve in himself and others to overcome the inevitable resistance to fundamental change. As America's first President of the 20th century, Roosevelt transformed the Army and Navy when there was no immediate threat to American survival. The result was imperfect, but it provided the foundation for American victory in two world wars. The question is: Will the first American President of the 21st century, under similar circumstances, break the deadlock in defence, resurrect transformation and convert today's disjointed armed services into a truly joint force that can guarantee American security and influence for the remainder of this century?

Maritime strategy, land warfare and the revolution in naval affairs

Rear Admiral Raja Menon

India is a challenging country in which to practise maritime strategy; therefore contributing to an Australian book on land warfare is not, perhaps, such an odd thing for an Indian Admiral to do. At the Defence Services Staff College in India where I lecture on maritime strategy once a year, one becomes acutely conscious of the 250 army majors, about half of whom have been shot at in the year preceding their arrival at the college. While it may be easy to get friendly nods from the naval officers present, the overwhelming numbers of army officers—and their questioning stares—makes one steer clear of all dubious theory.

Most formal education and writing on maritime strategy seems to begin with Captain Alfred Thayer Mahan's classic work, *The Influence of Sea Power upon History 1660–1783*.[1] Perhaps not surprisingly, it is difficult to explain to army officers why this great book was written as late as 1890—two thousand years after the principles of land strategy were first discussed by Sun Tzu, or Xenophon, or India's Kautilya. Finding the answer is actually not all that difficult. Travelling the open ocean during the first millennium was much like space exploration in the 1960s. Ships depended solely on coastal navigation marks until the astrolabe and octant enabled a navigator to ascertain latitude in about 1450. It was not until the late 18th century or early 19th century that longitude could be fixed in any precise manner. A recent article on Zheng He's voyage through the Indian Ocean demonstrated the limitations that problems of navigation placed on the development of doctrines of sea power.[2] In a massive feat of coastal navigation, Zheng He made two oceanic trips: one across the Bay of Bengal and the other across the Arabian Sea. These two voyages were made from point to point, along routes already sailed by local mariners with considerable knowledge of fixed routes. When members of my generation were at school, it was taught that Vasco da Gama navigated from Portugal to India. It was only 30 years ago that it became known that an Indian pilot, Ibn Majid, navigated da Gama's ship from Sofala to Calicut along a route that he had already travelled dozens of times.

Open ocean warfare could develop only after navigators had solved the riddle of calculating both their latitude and longitude. Even so, most sea battles occurred along certain latitudes off strategic ports where one fleet attempted to 'hold' a certain latitude. Mahan's book *The Influence of Sea Power on History* analysed eleven wars. Of these, eight were either purely maritime wars (such as the Anglo-Dutch war) or predominantly maritime wars (such as the Anglo-French conflict in the Bay of Bengal). The remaining three were continental wars in which there was a maritime component, such as the war of the Spanish Succession and the Anglo-French alliance against the United Provinces. I concede that all these wars have been brilliantly analysed from the point of view of winning the naval conflict. It is, however, difficult to establish that the sea wars were in all cases coordinated with the conflict on land or, more importantly, that the maritime war led directly to the peace talks.

An anecdote from my own service career might serve to demonstrate the problem of coordinating maritime operations with a land war. The Indo-Pakistan conflict is a longstanding dispute, the long-term causes of which are beyond the scope of this chapter. The immediate political background to the war in 1971 is that Pakistan (which then consisted of two halves) went to the polls in 1970, and East Pakistan's Awami League won the overall majority in the Parliament situated in Islamabad. The losing candidate from West Pakistan, Zulfigar Ali Bhutto, persuaded the Pakistan Army to deny the Awami League the right to form the government. East Pakistan erupted in riots, which were brutally suppressed. Ten million people migrated to India. The international community contributed generously to refugee relief, but India was stuck with a massive refugee problem that continued to grow rapidly. After signing an Indo-Soviet treaty of friendship in mid-1971, the Indian Government decided to go on the offensive in the winter of 1971. A winter offensive was selected because this is when snow blocks the passes in the Himalayas, thus preventing China from intervening on her ally Pakistan's behalf.[3]

Much of the political direction for the war still remains classified, but it is fairly clear that the Indian Army's initial objective was to carve out sufficient territory in East Pakistan to resettle the refugees while fighting a defensive war in the west. These circumstances reflected a classic continental war situation. What should navies do in such a situation? The Indian Navy undertook four main tasks. From April 1971 onwards it blockaded East Pakistan. It trained Bengali irregulars to operate behind the enemy lines in a largely riverine area. It prepared to fight in the west to preserve sea lines of communication, and it built up its forces for an attack on Karachi, the sole West Pakistan port.

The war in December 1971 eventually took its own turn when the army commanders in the East advanced so rapidly as to reach Dacca within eleven days. Once Dacca was reached, the Bengalis declared independence unilaterally, and a new nation was born. The Indian Navy impounded about 40 merchant vessels between April and December 1971, thereby isolating East Pakistan and contributing to the feeling of isolation and abandonment. At the start of the war, carrier aircraft attacked and sank all remaining shipping in East Pakistan, including at least one ship that had been earmarked for those leaders that intended to flee. In retrospect, it was obvious that the strategic centre of gravity of the war was in the Bay of Bengal and that the navy therefore contributed to the political purpose of the war. 'So, what is the complaint?', you may ask. The complaint is this. Ask any student of this war what the Navy did in 1971 and they will say, 'It attacked Karachi'—which is true. In arguably the most dramatic incident of the war, the Indian Navy towed four OSA-class missile boats a thousand miles with a frigate and loosed them on Karachi, sinking a destroyer, a minesweeper and a merchant vessel; and setting the oil complex ablaze.[4] The people, the parliamentarians and the ministry of finance were impressed and a continentally minded people recognised the Navy's role in war, although the people never understood the concept of the centre of gravity, or the crucial role that the Navy played in the Bay of Bengal. Despite the Navy's contribution, the only military representative present at the war termination talks in Simla, six months later, was the Director General, Military Operations.

Admittedly, all countries do not suffer the same plight as India, which has land boundaries with five nations, or China with seven. When a country has a political dispute with a continental neighbour and the armed forces contemplate the use of force, it is inevitable that, at least for the following two decades, the army will be the lead service. It is also inevitable that army action will centre on capturing territory as the method of leading to a negotiated settlement. When Fukuyama speaks of the end of history, it is obviously this very kind of politico-military action that he is talking about.[5] Nonetheless, in large parts of Asia and Africa and some parts of Europe the concept of an old-fashioned land war is alive and well. The tendency to ignore the maritime dimension of warfare is not a universal phenomenon, but for the purposes of discussing a serious maritime role in land wars, it might be useful to divide the spectrum of non-global wars into five overarching scenarios.

I label the first scenario the 'Superpower on a Divine Mission'. It is not easy being a superpower—and the prefix 'super' obviously comes from possessing global reach, which is essentially a maritime concept. All littoral powers, for instance, acknowledge that the United States of America is top dog in the Indian Ocean—a primacy that would have been disputed during the Cold War. The United States' global role comes from its ability to project more power than the local powers. In both Operation *Desert Storm* in the Gulf and Operation *Allied Force* in Kosovo, most ordnance was delivered by ground-based assets of the expeditionary air wings, but this presence abroad was ensured by United States sea control. This concept will be developed further in this chapter.

The second scenario is that of 'powers possessing predominantly coalition strategies'. Some of these states have suppressed their respective national geostrategic compulsions in favour of coalition warfare. All North Atlantic Treaty Organization (NATO) countries would fall into this group. The impermanence of this strategy would be obvious, particularly when the coalition has no natural enemies. A temporary geopolitical compulsion may hold such a coalition together with beneficial results for Europe and Eurasia. The underlying scepticism about its coherence comes from disbelief that Italy's geostrategic compulsions are the same as, say, the United Kingdom's. If the allied invasion of Italy in World War II seems to have more in common with the Punic Wars, how does allying Italian strategic objectives with those of the United Kingdom provide long-term stability? Nevertheless, coalition strategy also commits many unlikely countries into attempting power projection, or providing a component of it.

The third scenario is that experienced by island nations or remotely located nations. Such countries can prevent access to their territory through sea-denial, or can attack the enemy through sea control or sea use. Island nations with no overseas territorial ambitions would remain satisfied with sea denial, but an element of power projection is always necessary for peacekeeping and for operations other than war. Nations such as Australia, New Zealand, Iceland, Japan and Singapore fall into this category.

The fourth category reflects the experience of most postcolonial states. They have no time for Fukuyama. Imperfect colonial legacy has left many of them with disputed borders or unclear boundaries. Normally, resolving these troubles should not lead to war, but new nations often treat the give and take of a boundary settlement as a national calamity. While Pakistan and Bangladesh live in relative amity today, the suggestion that they should have been two nations in 1947—when the British left—would have led to war and a bloodbath. Many postcolonial states create large armies that develop into powerful and often dangerous constituencies. The existence of a powerful army hierarchy that only influences funding is only a small evil, but when they take over the government—as is currently the case in fourteen postcolonial states—the country's strategic outlook gets skewed into creating false apparitions that seem to need ever larger armies.

Finally, there are the problems faced by small countries. A large number of small countries have no hope of participating in any offensive coalition, but live in scenarios where the littoral warfare of the region means *their* littoral. A recent Indian Ocean maritime conference on littoral warfare came to a startling turn when it appeared that the representatives of all nations other than India were looking at littoral war as something that will be 'done to them'. Could the concerns of such states mean that there is a market for anti-littoral warfare? In theory they could, but the absence of any research literature seems to indicate that at present they merely hope that it will not happen to them.

Classical literature on maritime strategy does not address the problems of influencing the land war other than through the traditional methods of blockade, raids on the coast and a war on commerce. This is why the American maritime strategy *From the Sea* represents a turning-point in the land–sea strategic interface.[6] Its greater merit came from the fact that it was a strategy adapted to meet changing circumstances. Unlike previous strategic documents that analysed past wars and, in many cases, attempted to win the last war faster, *From the Sea* sought to change strategy midstream. In retrospect, the controversy that arose after the publication of *From the Sea* is fascinating. Some of the well-known figures in the strategic arena wrote in criticism that, although it was a strategy, it was probably no longer a maritime strategy. Early formulations of this doctrine did not go so far as to pursue the idea of 'littoral' warfare against the former Soviet Union. Consequently much of the criticism of the new doctrine avoided the question of whether it was workable or not. The Information Revolution was still in its early stages, and the concept of information dominance was some way off. Therefore, in terms of testing the new strategy in open literature, the best work still remains Tom Clancy's fictional book *Red Storm Rising*. It was just as well that it was not tested, for Clancy's scenario was heavily interlaced with the use of tactical nuclear weapons. The true significance of this doctrine lay in the fact that it proposed that a navy could forsake the sanctuary of the open ocean, and its vastness, to intrude into the messy scenario of littoral warfare. This departure was in fact a closing of the circle and a return to the earlier 19th-century idea of the superiority of the Fleet against the Shore.

Up to the end of the 19th century, fleets took it for granted that approaching the enemy coast under favourable wind conditions was a routine affair. Major portions of all coasts lay undefended. In some cases, such as the battle of Copenhagen, a fleet actually took on shore batteries, ships and artillery hulks together, defeating the lot in a single day. Perhaps the last great Fleet venture against the shore was the American landing at Vera Cruz, which eventually resulted in adding almost 30 per cent of what today constitutes United States territory.[7] Between 1850 and 1986, when *From the Sea*, was published, naval doctrine had conceded that superiority now lay with the shore in a normal correlation of forces. World War I was fought with huge fleets that were unable to interfere in any way with the slaughter in the trenches. Mines, torpedo boats and submarines had made the littoral too dangerous. Aerial reconnaissance existed only over land, and together with wireless telegraphy, it enabled shore defences to operate comfortably inside the fleet's decision cycle. World War II made the situation worse, with aerial bombing and torpedo attacks shifting the correlation further in favour of the shore. The fleet could overwhelm the shore in a few select geographical locations, such as the English Channel—where shore-based air power from England swamped German air power based in continental Europe. It is therefore not surprising that it was left to the Americans with their industrial might to build huge naval air fleets and aircraft carriers that could overwhelm shore air defences to insert amphibious forces in selected locations. Once it was demonstrated that naval air power could bring the correlation back in favour of the fleet, power projection became the ultimate objective of naval power.

In the immediate aftermath of World War II, there remained a dysfunctional relationship between naval power and state objectives.[8] During the Cold War the strategies of the previous conflict were found 'adequate' to pursue the alliance objectives demanded by NATO grand strategy. None of the Western navies were required by their governments to interfere in the land war. The pivotal war was supposed to be confined to central Europe, and naval power ensured that the United States could reinforce Europe without interference. Power projection was relevant for worldwide maritime duties such as keeping choke points open, but the force that these fleet units projected was implicit. A good instance was the infamous entry of the USS *Enterprise* group into the Bay of Bengal in 1971. Powerful though it was, the group's exact relevance in the Bangladesh War was uncertain, since the conflict was between two opposing armies of about 150 000 men each. Nevertheless, the carrier battle groups possessed aircraft superior to those flown from land bases. This discrepancy implied that punishment could be given if it came to a conflict. The promise that this capability offered was demonstrated in later cases such as the Gulf of Sidra incidents, the Malacca Straits dispute, the tanker war in the Persian Gulf, and the Taiwan incident in 2000. Why did confidence in a littoral war scenario grow as suddenly as it did in 1991? Surely the answer must include the collapse of the Soviet Union and hence the decline of a first-rate continental defence.

This doctrinal about-face leads us to consider what factors deliver superiority in the littoral to an attacking force. In the final analysis, the winning factor must be relative to the others. For instance, there are large parts of the African coast, off poorly developed parts of Angola or West Africa, where a primitive naval force could land without opposition. Such an operation would not require any level of information dominance, but would be merely a throwback to the tactical reality of the 19th century. On the other hand, any fleet approaching the northern European coast would be unlikely to obtain the requisite level of information dominance without incurring serious casualties. Ultimately, what is the factor that must be weighed in the balance? It cannot be aircraft speeds, or radar or missile ranges. It must be the relative speeds of the observation—orientation–decision–action (OODA) loop of the two opposing sides. Unclassified literature often speaks of the concept of a C-day as opposed to D-day. Presumably C-day is the day prior to D-day when our own information dominance chain is set in motion. As the days pass, the side with the superior information chain and the faster OODA loop will gradually increase the gap in information dominance over the slower side. Some estimates of those who recommend a worldwide space-based, high-resolution surveillance system argue that with such a system the gap between the faster and slower sides could be built up to eight days.[9] It is assumed that there must be an optimum number of days after which, when the faster side has discovered almost everything there is to know about the slower side, it would be advantageous to go into D-day or risk losing information dominance.

Enough has been written on network-centric warfare (NCW) for the concept not to need any more amplification, but the three grids that constitute the network of networks is hardly the most expensive part of the entire chain. For most countries, the most dramatic portion of the net—the Cooperative Engagement Capability (CEC)—is not available.[10] Consisting of a net for sensor information, the coordinates of a target detected by one unit can be transmitted to another firing unit so accurately that the second unit can engage the target without its being detected by any of the target's own sensors. Cleared by the United States for export only to the United Kingdom, the CEC will benefit both countries in that the combined number of their firing platforms can be increased, without there being the same investment in sensors on all platforms. When it works (not if), it may well replace Link 16 as the target information grid currently in use.[11] Originally an offshoot of excess capability in the SPY-1 computing system, it may currently work only in the anti-aircraft and anti-missile scene, but would surely be adapted to other kinds of warfare.

Many analysts believe that NCW will create a tactical revolution but will not have strategic implications. This view follows from the theory that the supremacy of one or another type of platform has always been transient and their relative positions on a table of merit is of no strategic consequence. For a maritime strategist who has been told any number of times that until 1850 the Fleet was invariably superior to the shore, it is difficult to accept that such a limitation is only tactical. The stalemate in the western trenches, and the battleship losses at Gallipoli did have enormous strategic consequences and were central to extending the duration of the world conflict. The plain fact is that the Grand Fleet, the greatest fleet put together before 1915, could not intervene to change the strategic centre of gravity of the World War I. Certainly, it ensured the unimpeded resupply of the army in Europe—which is what the army would call 'naval transport'. Most obviously, the prime example of the navy's role affecting the political purpose of a war was in the Pacific during the World War II. The prominence accorded the US Navy at the surrender ceremony on the USS *Missouri* reflected this central role. It takes no genius, however, to predict that any of Japan's wars will be maritime in nature, whether they be offensive or defensive. Nor is it difficult to deduce that the Pacific War would have followed a vastly different course if the United States had continued to build only battleships after Pearl Harbor.

The fundamental question for naval strategists is whether the revolution in military affairs (RMA) is going to create a parallel revolution in naval affairs (RNA). The only navy that has unilaterally accepted that there is a RNA is the US Navy, which—as early as 1986—published an acknowledged departure in its maritime strategy and subsequently went further in that journey. Russia has acknowledged no change, struck as it is by its financial collapse and the dwindling size of its naval fleet. The success of the European navies in acting together off Iraq in 1991 and their continued success off the Balkans in 1999 have shown them that acting together with the US forces to pre-empt large-scale ethnic strife is a workable grand strategy. It does not appear, though, that the European nations have made any revolutionary investments in the RMA. European navies need to pay greater attention to the lessons of Operation *Allied Force*, which was fought over Kosovo. Aircraft losses fell from 0.37 aircraft for 1000 sorties in Operation *Desert Storm* to 0.18 aircraft per 1000 sorties in Operation *Allied Force*. At the same time the percentage of smart bombs used went up from 9 per cent in Operation *Desert Storm* to 98 per cent in Operation *Allied Force*.[12] In less than a decade, the technological gap between the United States and European navies has increased, to the extent that today only Britain's Royal Navy is fully interoperable with the US Navy in all aspects of information exchange.

In the next decade, navies wishing to close the littoral will have to contend with a common range of threats that any self-respecting country might be expected to possess. Some of these threats were identified in the mid-1990s by the US Department of Defense as weapons of mass destruction; enhanced information warfare capabilities; small conventional submarines, smart torpedoes and smart mines; precision weapons such as laser-guided bombs, anti-shipping missiles and longer-range missiles; the advantages conferred by global positioning systems; unmanned aerial vehicles; an integrated air-defence network with advanced surface-to-air missiles and MIG-29 equivalent fighters; and hardened command-and-control facilities.

In both *Desert Storm* and *Allied Force*, the maritime component of this list was absent. There were no small modern submarines, no torpedoes, no sea skimmers and no maritime command-and-control system, and only a few mines. The anti-air component of this list was a factor in Operation *Desert Storm* and became even more important in Operation *Allied Force*. On both occasions the opposing anti-air capability was beaten decisively, the great part of the victory being created by the US Air Force, which had the advantage of being able to operate from friendly bases. Undoubtedly more could have been achieved, but since both international coalitions were not acting in direct defence of their vital national interests, it was politically unacceptable to absorb casualties. This would not be the case in wars of national origin where a less favourable correlation of forces might not dissuade an approach towards a hostile littoral.

The point is that Operation *Desert Storm* and Operation *Allied Force* seemed to indicate that it was possible to conduct a seamless war where the approach to the littoral and the littoral war itself could be simultaneously executed. Conducting such a war is unlikely against any serious opposition. Indeed, this author was an instructor in the Indian Staff College, where an Iraqi naval student studied during Operation *Desert Storm*. The Iraqi was an officer of exceptionally high calibre and a member of the Ba'ath Party. On being questioned why Iraq, which had eight years of war experience against the Iranians, had not learnt lessons from that war and built a navy, his answer was that Saddam Hussein was not convinced, and the naval staff were too cowed to get their point across. Perhaps dictators are notoriously unhappy with navies whose canvas is the high seas and whose leadership has an open mind that comes from traversing it. The Iraqi naval officer was quite aware that most of the decisive battles of that eight-year war were fought within 50 miles of the coast and most of them within 25 miles of the coast.

In classical terms, against any serious opposition, an approach to the enemy's littoral would have to involve a two-phase war. For the non-seagoing audience, what does this two-phase concept suggest? It posits the view that, after the first phase—the sea-war phase—large and vulnerable platforms can be moved closer to the littoral, from where they can interfere in the land war. This is a revolutionary idea and, naturally, fraught with danger—as the lessons of Okinawa suggest. Even today, a one-on-one threat analysis might produce pay-offs that favour the anti-access navy. In tactical exercises all over the world, submarines regularly sink aircraft carriers. Missile boats regularly fire missiles that destroy battle practice targets. Yet we find that in a large scenario, with fluid movements, these simple analyses are often stood upside down. Nineteen submarines were deployed by the British and German fleets on the day of Jutland. Twenty-four submarines were deployed by the Japanese and American navies on the day of Midway (with one dramatic hit).[13] As Hezlet has pointed out in his excellent work on submarine warfare, submarines have invariably failed when used in short tactical scenarios that were not structured to give a positive encounter.[14]

The revolutionary changes discussed now suggest that, although the individual correlation of forces has not changed, in any standard scenario the slower force will never get into a firing position because the faster force will constantly be a couple of jumps ahead of them. Relying on this advantage is a risky proposition, but as stated earlier, the question remains: how much faster is the faster force? This speed is largely (but not entirely) established by network-centric warfare. A combination of the three networks without space and airborne sensors is only a computer game. Since network-centric warfare has to be run on a line of sight, the US Navy's solution of using a Tracker as communications relay is not available to other navies. In any case, having got as far as the littoral, non-superpower forces are still without a land warfare picture, as they lack the Joint Surveillance and Target Attack System (JSTARS) possessed by the United States. This system provides US forces with an airborne, stand-off range; a surveillance and target acquisition radar; and a command-and-control centre. JSTARS is unmatched by any other country.

Consideration of all of the above factors leads one to conclude that approaching the littoral is only possible for some powers against a few other powers. The ordnance delivery capability of individual platforms is not in question here; what counts is the survivability of the communication nodes and sensor platforms in the information-warfare phase of the war.

Maritime powers that are not superpowers are likely to use some combination of the following platforms to create their data in the littoral: long-range maritime patrol aircraft; coastal electronic-warfare assets; a fleet at sea with helicopter-borne radars; and a maritime headquarters somewhere on the coast. It does not require the simulation of many threat scenarios to show how such a nation could be blinded. Fleet units could be destroyed in a week by a nuclear-powered attack submarine (SSN). The air picture off the coast could be monitored by an airborne warning and control system (AWACS), making maritime patrol aircraft vulnerable. Once the outer perimeter of maritime defence is breached, the destruction of the coastal radar, electronic warfare and communications nodes

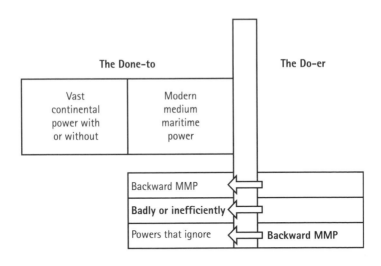

Figure 4.1 The relative positions in littoral warfare

becomes easier. However, not every nation has an AWACS or an SSN, or anti-radiation missiles. This game could therefore be played at many levels. At the next lower level, the role of the SSN may be taken by a conventional submarine utilising air-independent propulsion; the AWACS supplanted by anti-electronic warfare helicopters flying off destroyers, or by unmanned aerial vehicles. Those unable to bring anti-radiation missiles to bear may use special forces. Some medium powers have badly unbalanced armed forces, where the army-to-navy expenditure ratio is 10:1. Indeed such army-to-navy expenditure ratios are quite common in Asia, and many Asian countries could be attractive victims for those wanting to practise littoral warfare. Figure 4.1 shows a theoretical arrangement of the relative strengths of some information-warfare susceptibilities between those that seek littoral war and those that own that littoral.

A modern medium maritime power could contest the approach of a superpower's fleet carrier battle group and make that approach expensive. An example of such a power would be one of the northern European states that possesses access to satellite imagery; a great deal of satellite communications; a command, control, communications, computer and intelligence (C4I) system run off satellite communication channels; good airborne electronic signals monitoring capability; and hardened command centres. Even with these assets, however, such a power would probably not stop the battle group. Large continental powers such as China and India, which can absorb huge punishment without deflecting national resolve, also fall into the category of states that can provide this level of access resistance to their littorals. The importance of national morale in maintaining a country's resolve was demonstrated by North Vietnam during the Vietnam War. This war provided a precedent for other populous powers whose national resistance may be widely at variance with their military capability. Below this level, wars are obviously fought by the second and third elevens.

Against even middling opposition, an approach to littoral warfare would follow a sizeable victory in open-ocean war. For that reason the structure of navies may not change drastically. The first phase—the open-ocean phase—will be fought in a new way, as a result of open-ocean surveillance being integrated into a network. Such integration will result in what has been described as 'a collapse of space' in terms of time.[15] This first phase has to be sped up, so as to achieve synchronisation with the land war. Increased expenditure on surveillance and networks makes more rapid responses possible. The collapse of space will enable the 'speed of battle' to be increased, and this speed will compensate for the vulnerability of warships floating on the water, while approaching the littoral.

On the basis of defence expenditure alone, it appears possible that only the United States can indulge in a genuine RMA, using information dominance in the littoral. See item in Table 4.1 for expenditure.

The figures in Table 4.1 for the year 2001 are openly available. If the analysis is correct it would appear that the US tri-service procurement budget is about equal to the entire defence budget of Russia. This observation should not surprise anyone since Russia's gross domestic product is alleged to be less than the gross domestic product of California. The disparity between American economic power and that of other countries is even greater. Critically, the United States' expenditure on command, control, communications and intelligence (C3I) is almost equal to the defence budget of France, and represents just half the defence budget of

Table 4.1 *Some comparative defence expenditure (billion dollars)*

	Defence expenditure	Tri-service capital procurement budget	Space and naval research and development
Australia	12.2	—	—
China	45.0	—	—
France	26.0	3.0	—
India	15.0	3.5	—
Japan	54.0	8.0	—
Saudi Arabia	18.7	7.0	—
United Kingdom	27.0	4.0	—
United States	305.0	58.0	8.4

Japan and China. Does this disparity indicate a certain commitment to information warfare? Or could it simply be that when defence budgets are 'smaller', the inadequacy in the number of platforms forces most of the money into a platform-centric purchasing mode?

Table 4.2 shows the approximate ratio of expenditure on information-warfare assets to ordnance delivery assets.

In most circumstances a seamless approach to the littoral is not the scenario that prudent naval powers can hope for. Situations such as Operation *Desert Storm*—where one side possesses all the tools of information war and the other side is led by a dictator that favours continental war—are not easy to come by. Nor can the kind of support base that was provided by the European powers in Operation *Allied Force* be depended on in every case. Denying the sole superpower bases and access may have serious consequences, and hence the United States may find bases where others cannot. However, the two-phase approach to the maritime component of the continental war is the scenario that most navies could start practising. Pure maritime wars of the kind that brought Germany to its knees by blockade may not be seen again. After all, when the Germans cracked in 1918, the German army was still in France, but the will of the people was gone and the German navy had mutinied. Can navies talk of that kind of strategy anymore, when the goods in a ship belong to a multinational company, the carrier is registered in Panama, the goods are insured in London, and the ship is insured in the United States? It is difficult to ascertain who has lost money when the ship is

Table 4.2 The commitment to the revolution in military affairs (RMA)

United States	1:30	C3I budget under all heads is 20 billion. Tri-service procurement budget is 58 billion
United Kingdom, France	1:20	Approximate figures
Japan	1:40	Approximate figures
India, China	1:80	Approximate figures

sunk. With the trend towards high-value air cargo in the last 25 years, seaborne trade has declined in value from 98 per cent to 85 per cent of all international cargo.

The use of navies in a war on commerce does not sound that attractive anymore. Strategic minerals and materials are now found in many more countries than they were in 1914, when United States cotton was still being used in German ammunition manufacture and was therefore a strategic commodity. What the CIA calls 'single-commodity vulnerability' is restricted to only a few countries and a few commodities. Most countries are vulnerable to interruptions in their energy supply. Saudi Arabia, for instance, is vulnerable to a stoppage of its oil export and also to interruption in food import. The navy does, however, require time to make blockades bite. This delay may mean that the progress of the war is subordinated to the navy's strategic plans of a war on commerce—a situation unlikely to be agreed to by the army or air force in the run-up to a land war. Most large countries that have big internal markets—such as the United States and India—import and export each way about 11 to 13 per cent of their gross domestic product. Certainly 22 per cent of the gross domestic product is worth 'protecting' in principle, but in a land war the army and air force are going to be impatient for quicker results and a decisive outcome. The fact that most countries are vulnerable to interruptions in their oil traffic is, however, still an attractive option for navies. The strategic oil reserves that many countries actually keep are much lower than the figures put out on paper. While this varies from twenty days for high-consumption, highly industrialised countries to 45 days for centralised economies, these numbers often do not tell the entire tale. The amount of oil in the 'pipeline', and the availability of some critical oils, such as tank and aircraft lubricating oils, can be a critical factor. Most of all, the psychology of energy restrictions will push the land war into inappropriate and unproductive strategies, since the fear of oil stoppage increases with time.

Amphibious warfare is a good option but often not the only one. Sceptics may say that amphibious operations hardly constitute a RNA—and that is true. Substantial differences do, however, exist between a navy's new strategy in the era of a RNA and a purely amphibious war. The new strategy aims at defeating the enemy's blue and brown water capability by focusing information dominance first on the enemy fleet, and later—in phase two—onto the enemy's coast. The ultimate objective may be an amphibious landing, but other options are opened up. Some of the possibilities that come from denying to the enemy its own coast include closure of ports; support of the land campaign; fire support inland; and deep strikes. If envisaged, an amphibious operation becomes less costly owing to the wider choice of landing sites that are made available by dominance of the littoral.

Will nations be able to adjust to a new maritime strategy? Can anyone other than the United States afford an offensive war in the littoral? These questions lead us to ask both whether countries feel inclined to wage such a war and whether they feel they will need to. Countries that expect to wage war in the littorals are most likely to be those that are allied semi-permanently to a superpower such as the United States, which has the sensor and network capability to provide the alliance with the faster OODA loop. Countries not inclined to change would be those that do not see themselves in the relevant strategic scenario or those that are unconvinced about the existence of either a RMA or a RNA. Those nations that may be convinced of the reality of revolutionary change still find funding a major problem. Table 4.3 is an analytical table of military expenditures that demonstrates that some nations, such as India and China, are only at the beginning of military modernisation.

It has been estimated that, if the Chinese per-capita income even reached the level of that in South Korea, then China's gross national product (and hence military expenditure) could be 1.3 times that of the United States.[16] If that were to happen, it still does not mean that China would have a navy the size of that of the United States, given that it took

Table 4.3 An analysis of military expenditures

Country	GNP	GNP growth	Military expenditure as a percentage of GNP	Military expenditure per capita	GNP per capita
Australia	381	3.8	2.5	465	18920
China	980	7.2	2.5	53	2303
France	1427	2.4	3.1	826	26290
Germany	2079	1.2	2.0	496	26190
India	442	7.0	2.4	8	560
Israel	296	—	9.6	1646	17070
Japan	4078	1.0	1.0	401	41160
Pakistan	64	3.6	6.1	30	540
Russia	332	1.3	11.0	513	4500
Saudi Arabia	—	—	13.5	1000	6815
Turkey	186	6.0	4.0	108	2714
United Kingdom	1338	1.7	3.0	572	19020
United States	8351	4.1	3.8	1056	27550

Sources: World Development Report 2000; ACDA Summary 1998; Military Balance 2000.

the United States over 25 years to build its current stock of warships, sensors and planes. Many nations can afford the faster OODA loop only by reducing platforms. This is a difficult choice as it deeply affects the present view of war, as well as the interests of the existing service hierarchies. Countries that spend only 1 per cent of their gross national product on defence can do better. Japan is a case in point: money is obviously available for the Japanese navy to maintain 35 destroyers and frigates, and yet it is possible for Japan to invest in a RMA. Whether a country chooses to invest in information warfare capabilities may not necessarily change its place in the world order of power. Its defensive needs may still be met by anti-access strategies, but offensive maritime power will depend on littoral capabilities, which are going to cost a great deal of money.

Sharp corners: combat operations in urban areas

Roger Spiller

One of the properties of historical perspective is its capacity to sweep away the irrelevant. The hostile, the ignorant or the complacent will say that what happened in America on 11 September 2001 was more or less what had happened elsewhere, some other time. No such argument could be made, however, for the international reaction to those events, which has led to the emergence of nothing less than a global war zone.[1]

The coincidence between the events of 11 September 2001 and this conference on future warfare suffused the proceedings with an unexpected urgency. Theoretical matters were no longer so theoretical. Hypotheses were no longer so tentative. Forecasts took on a harder, more insistent edge. Set against a newly urgent necessity for effective strategic action, the claims of tradition and routine seemed less compelling than ever. Underlying this urgency was the suspicion that the dead hand of orthodoxy had once again impeded military thought and practice. There was little confidence that the prescriptions of orthodoxy would be of much use in the near future.

The effect of 11 September 2001 was definitive, rather than seminal. These attacks gave impetus to long-term trends in modern military thought—trends that share one trait if no other: the suspicion that the old ways no longer apply in the military world of the future. Interestingly, over the past decade or so, that suspicion has even taken hold inside the orthodox military world to a remarkable degree. Professional soldiers from every point on the intellectual compass now acknowledge that the art of war is on the verge of epochal change, even though they cannot agree on the nature of that change or the direction it will take ultimately.

Such professional unease was certainly detectable in the summer of 1999 when I was asked to undertake a study of contemporary urban operations for the US Army. I was given the vague impression that this request had originated at the highest levels of the Army's chain of command, and that there was some urgency for the investigation to be completed soon. The study was to be cast at the strategic and operational levels of war as the Army then defined them in its doctrines, and with the broadest possible scope, across the full spectrum of missions: from humanitarian assistance to the highest intensities of outright conflict. This guidance was not intended to limit the study in any way, however; the study was to be as unconstrained as possible.[2]

Several official concerns—some immediate, some of longer term, some bureaucratic and some operational—probably rejuvenated the US Army's interest in urban operations. At that moment, the United States and its NATO allies were conducting an air campaign against Yugoslavia in an attempt to arrest depredations of ethnic Albanians in the province of Kosovo. The official position of the United States Government, enunciated by the President himself, was that no American ground troops would be used in this campaign. While the official hope was that the precise application of air power alone might attain the objective, many within and beyond official circles speculated on what might happen if the decision on ground troops were reversed. Should ground troops have been deemed necessary after all, the speculation continued, the next question was whether their deployment would be opposed by the Yugoslavian army and its auxiliaries scattered throughout Kosovo's villages and towns.

The prospect that American troops might soon be engaged in combat operations in an urbanised environment was an unhappy one. The performance of conventional forces in recent urban operations had not been encouraging. In Grozny, in Sarajevo and throughout Bosnia-Herzegovina, and in Mogadishu, conventional forces had not proved themselves equal to the demands of the modern urban environment. The assumption seemed to be that the US Army's readiness for urban operations had not improved recently. The Army's field manual for urban operations, FM 90–10, *Military Operations in Urbanized Terrain*, dated from 1979, and the Army no longer had oversight of doctrine for urban operations at the joint level. That duty had been reassigned to the US Marine Corps, whose highly publicised 'Urban Warrior' exercises had contributed to the impression that the Marines were institutionally amenable to urban operations if the Army was not. One should not underestimate the effect of these bureaucratic and doctrinal realignments: in the fetid world of the service and joint staffs, even insignificant questions can take on a certain official gravity.

Set against this dim prospect was the generally held view that, whether the Army was ready or not, urban operations were on the rise. Indeed, although the number of unilateral operations conducted by the United States was declining, the number of multilateral operations in which American forces participated—usually under the auspices of the United Nations—was going up. Most of these operations were conducted within urbanised areas. Yet, even as these international operations demanded more and more from the US Armed Forces, among the policy and opinion elite there existed a perception that these operations cost far more than they were worth, regardless of the standard of success that one employed.[3]

These operational, institutional and bureaucratic concerns worked within a context of larger, more longstanding international problems complicated by global technological advancement. Over the past generation, the proliferation of publicly available technology that might be employed for military purposes has become a new constant in the strategic world. Most ominously, that constant includes the threat posed by weapons of mass destruction. The combination of extreme weapons with extreme political movements poses one of the most daunting strategic challenges in the 21st century.

Global demographic and urban trends appeared to conduce to the most threatening of these scenarios, in which the great agglomerations would become the new battlegrounds of the near future. Indeed, in order to employ weapons of mass destruction, one must first find the mass to destroy, and cities were ready-made targets. Soon, most of that population would be amassed in vast urban concentrations of ever-increasing size and complexity. Each of these agglomerations would test global cohesion in its own unique way, but the implication was clear: population growth was setting the stage for a succession of insoluble crises.

Under the circumstances, one might expect the US Army to have invested some professional and intellectual capital in understanding and preparing for the challenge of urban operations. Indeed, a good deal of official energy was being spent. At the level of the joint staff, a new doctrine for joint urban operations was being prepared. The Army's long-outdated field manual for *Military Operations in Urbanized Terrain* (MOUT) was being revised. Beyond the doctrinal world, at the Army's combat training centres, soldiers routinely encountered exercises in built-up areas. At Fort Knox, a new multimillion dollar training facility had been completed that was designed to exercise armoured forces in an urban setting, and even at the staff college the subject of MOUT came up from time to time. In addition to formal doctrine and training, at various meetings across the Army, discussions were under way on subjects as varied as the design and 'instrumentation' of training venues, sniper radar, miniature remotely-piloted vehicles, and a wide array of non-lethal weapons. Beyond these meetings were slightly more academic gatherings such as those sponsored occasionally by RAND in the United States.

All of these activities contribute, no doubt, to what one might consider the present state-of-the-art of urban operations. However, it is the veritable mountain of professional literature that serves as the most important source for understanding the intersection between the urban environment and military operations. These works take the form of academic and official histories, memoirs, professional military studies, staff appreciations, specific case studies, after-action reports, and research investigations of one sort or another. Taken as a whole, this body of literature conveys several impressions worth noticing.

The terms *Military Operations in Urbanized Terrain* or the British version, *Fighting in Built-up Areas* (FIBUA), and *Urban Operations* are all used as synonyms. No distinction is made between tactical and higher-level operations, the general assumption being that if one's tactics are correct all else will follow naturally. Implicitly accepting that premise, most of this literature is concerned with clearing streets, buildings and rooms, and manoeuvring cleverly between ruins and refuges. Indeed, microtactics, or the tactics of the 25-metre target, predominate. However, even perfect tactics cannot protect an orthodox army from defeat in urban warfare. Wars are not won in cities, but they can be lost there. For orthodox armies wedded to their professional traditions, cities are not important in purely military terms. Cities may indeed be politically, psychologically or otherwise symbolically important, but they never seem to offer sufficient return on the military power that is expended in taking them, and therefore it is best to do without them altogether, best to send one's armies where they will achieve decisive results.

Therefore, one might conclude that armies should never go into cities if they are permitted to avoid them. If one must go into a city, one should get out as soon as is practicable. Only bad things happen to armies in cities. The last impression one receives from this mass of literature is how little of it has been read, for most of these studies happily repeat each other; consequently, professional military knowledge is little improved upon, if at all. Ignorance is not at all necessary, however; on the contrary, for the military professional who draws an urban mission, ignorance is tantamount to failure in advance.

Once, cities were important to the art of war, and critically important in the conduct of war. Huge, often predominating amounts of military energy were spent on defending and attacking them. The ease with which Napoleon took Vienna in 1805, or Berlin in 1806, was very big news: these cities consummated his success on the fields of battle. When William T. Sherman marched into Atlanta in 1864, again big things happened: his enemies spent a great amount of their combat power defending it to no avail, weakening themselves while Sherman and his army grew more confident. Big cities were large military targets because they could produce significant military results—perhaps even war-winning results.

Then war took one of its unpredictable turns. During the Franco-Prussian War, the Germans had incontestably won on the fields of battle—Sedan, Gravellotte-St. Privat. The Emperor of France himself had been captured in battle. By the traditional terms of reference, the French should have sued for peace. The French did not. The Germans marched on Paris to force the issue. The French Government decamped, leaving the citizens of Paris to their own devices, defended only by a few national guard and hastily assembled citizen levies. They refused to surrender the city. The Germans bombarded the city. Every shell that fell on Paris injured the international standing of the new Germany. The Chief of the Great General Staff declared finally that there was only so much war could do, and that in this case his army could only posture his side for a favourable outcome at the negotiating table. Von Moltke could have ordered his half-million troops to fight their way into Paris. But what would fighting inside Paris have produced for Germany? Von Moltke knew the answer. He would ignore the city that could not give him victory. That indeed seems to have been the orthodox military view that soldiers took with them into the 20th century.[4]

This is not to say that such orthodoxy was the invariable view, merely that it served as a professional 'default' reaction. No military intellectual offered a contrary view then or later. Nor, however, did cities suddenly disappear from the landscape of modern war. The 20th century is littered with city battles, but when one calculates how many of those battles were joined intentionally and how many were purely circumstantial, the traditional aversion to using cities as essential elements in one's campaigning still held. Military orthodoxy passed through the entirety of the 20th century without serious challenge, even though evidence mounted that cities were beginning to play a more important role in warfare once again. Modern cities were more than merely 'complex terrain' to be bypassed or negotiated. Most significantly, unorthodox forces discovered cities too. If one looks at Von Moltke's siege of Paris from the inside, the city's defenders might well be described by professional soldiers as unorthodox—certainly by Von Moltke's lights. Unorthodox soldiering gained considerable ground during the 19th century, and because the city was always suspected of harbouring the most unruly elements of any society, the city seemed to live up to its own dubious reputation. As the insurrectionaries in Europe learned, cities seemed ready-made for their kind of business. Cities conduced to the sustainment of otherwise fragile conspiracies as no rural enclave ever could.

As all forces discovered, the real trouble with cities was that they did not convey an automatic advantage to any one side. In today's literature, one often reads that the urban environment always works to the advantage of the defence or that the very nature of a city redounds to the credit of the unorthodox force. Neither seems to be true, or true enough to rely on; too many other variables intervene. What was true was that, if one managed to capitalise on the nature of the city, important results were possible even for significantly weaker forces. Sometimes, what in any other circumstance would appear to be a minor tactical success could produce strategic results. A dramatic but atypical example is the nearly simultaneous, multi-city offensive (five municipalities, 36 provincial capitals, 64 district capitals and 50 hamlets) of the Vietnam War's 1968 Tet Offensive. By all accounts, the offensive was an unmitigated disaster for the North Vietnamese Army and the Viet Cong cadre in South Vietnam.[5] That, however, was true only if judged by the standards of military orthodoxy. The offensive, disastrous though it was, did excite the kind of strategic result that only a crashing battlefield victory might have had years before.

If one steps back from history for a moment, one can see that there was never any chance that orthodox armies would be able to quarantine war to the countryside where all their doctrines, organisation, equipment, training—and indeed, their professional traditions—predisposed them to operate. Yet against global trends of modernisation and consequent urbanisation, orthodox military thought has persisted in defining the urban environment as the most complicated and least promising and least productive of all the environments where one might go a'soldiering. Modern war has overtaken this definition; the old military conception of the urban environment is obsolete. Professional armies the world over must recast their old definitions of the urban world to accord with present and future realities.

In October 1999, demographers at the United Nations announced that the world's population had reached six billion. By 2056, global population will reach nine billion. If this estimate proves correct, the velocity of an unprecedented population surge will have abated somewhat. The last billion of the present population was added in only the last twelve years. The fourth of the present six billion had required only thirteen years to add. Put another way, the world's population has doubled in the past 40 years.[6] Five years from now, half of the global population will live in cities.[7] Cities, as entities, seem not to have understood the evolution of their urban fringes over the past two centuries. The vast slums of Sao Paolo or Lagos or Istanbul, for instance, do not quite fall under the neat rubrics of old. One might instead think of 'urbania'—an environment defined by its human, material and functional characteristics rather than by its identity as a particular governmental or administrative area.

Most of human history has been required to attain this degree of urbanisation. Today the world knows literally hundreds of cities or urbanias containing more than a million inhabitants. For the greater part of human history, world populations did without vast cities and got along without very many cities at all. The first city we know with some certainty to have reached a population of one million was Rome, in the year 150 AD. But Rome could not sustain this size for a catalogue of reasons, so that 750 years later, the city had declined to a mere 17 000 people, and it would not completely recover for several more centuries. In the Orient, the ancient Chinese city of Chang'an may have reached a million just as Rome did. Baghdad may have contained one million by the time the Mongols sacked it in 1258 AD, at which time by all accounts the population dropped drastically. Gains everywhere were made at a glacial pace, and depredations, once suffered, were difficult to overcome too. In the West, after Rome's relatively brief dalliance with the life of a megalopolis, some 1700 years were required for another city to reach the one million mark. In 1800, London became the world megalopolis, and four years later the global population reached its first billion.[8]

These two events were the result of escalating population growth that made its appearance around 1750, intensified beyond precedent, and has not abated. Two centuries later, the world's ten largest cities between them contain 162 million inhabitants. Table 5.1 shows how they rank at present, in millions.

Table 5.1 raises as many questions as it answers. Generalisations are difficult to frame and sustain. For example, any such accountings should be regarded as contingent on any number of other considerations. Should one include suburbs? Half of all Americans live in them, not in cities. What is the difference between city and suburb in any case? Rio de Janeiro reported a population of 5.4 million in its most recent census, but if one calculated Rio's entire metropolitan region, the total would be 10.4 million inhabitants.[9] Obviously, the equation is altered, but to what effect?

Table 5.1 Ten most populous world cities

City	Population (in millions)
Tokyo	28.8
Mexico City	17.8
Sao Paolo	17.5
Mumbai	17.4
New York	16.5
Shanghai	14.0
Los Angeles	13.0
Lagos	12.8
Calcutta	12.7
Buenos Aires	12.3

Source: United Nations, *The World at Six Billion*, p. t-31.

In any case, gross population figures in and of themselves say little about how population concentrates for certain purposes and functions: housing for the newly arrived, for instance, or communal water points, or soccer games, or a place where one goes to wait in the hope of being employed for a job of day labour. Insofar as these purposes and functions may be seen as deriving from a specific time and place, it is useful to understand how cities have changed their shape and character over the long duration. From the most ancient of times to the eve of the modern period, the physical extent of a city was fixed by how far a man might walk in half a day—say, from an outlying village to the central market. This calculation was a matter not only of distance but also of time, for one might be required to cross a river on the way into the city, and whether the season was wet or dry had a great deal to do with how far away from the metropolis one might live. Population densities were similarly influenced by physical calculations. Ancient construction techniques guaranteed horizontal cities and discouraged vertical ones. Those techniques—essentially stacking bricks one on top the other—could not support structures higher than five floors or so. Ancient Rome's apartment buildings, the *insulae*, all too often exceeded these limits, and the city's early chronicles are punctuated by grand and disastrous building collapses.[10] Even if these particular limitations had been conquered, others stood ready to exercise their tyrannies over the old cities. Water sources and waste disposal systems imposed their own important checks on growth. As late as 1858, the British Empire's business of government came to an abrupt halt when the stink emitted by the Thames was too much even for Parliament. Retching members were forced to flee Westminster altogether.[11]

We can see that the age of the 'old' city began its decline quite recently. Only in the 19th century, new building techniques, elevators and public transportation all appeared within a few decades of one another, permitting—indeed, encouraging—vertical as well as horizontal expansion. Driven by the global demographic revolution, human densities reached unprecedented levels. In 1900 social reformers in New York City were scandalised by population densities on the Lower East Side that reached 260 000 per square mile. For a few blocks here, densities as high as 1700 persons per acre were recorded.[12] By these standards, modern Calcutta's densities of 62 000 per square mile seem not so bad—until other variables are factored in.

We may be forgiven if we find ourselves mesmerised by the spectacle of the most ordinary modern city. Their image may seem strangely self-contained, like the Emerald City of the old fables, hanging suspended in the clouds. The impression is compounded by several orders of magnitude when one considers the new great cities—the vast urban agglomerations, consuming so much space, containing so many things, creating and using so much energy. These cities seem so important in and of themselves that, indeed, we have come to view them as world cities, belonging to no nation and to all nations. Indeed, one writer has imagined the greatest cities growing to a point where they would serve themselves best by seceding from the nations where they reside, creating in the process a new political entity.[13] Such a forecast distorts the nature of a city, sees the city as a kind of freestanding monolith, otherwise unattached to its suburban surroundings. Those five million other inhabitants of Rio's suburbs may think otherwise. The city is too much of this world to leave it.

Thus, to avoid being overcome by the evident complexity and variety of the global city, one should remember that, above all, cities are human creations. Long ago, 'natural cities' were thought possible; that is, that cities arose of their own accord, without direct intervention by any human agency. Now, archaeologists and urbanographers understand that no city makes itself; that cities arise when and where humans decide there is a need for them; and that, however cities may be characterised, the *sine qua non* for all of them is that they are human-built. This proposition cannot be overstated. Generals and soldiers alike have come to grief for centuries because they chose to see the city before them as an inanimate object, whereas the reality is that the city is the embodiment of animation. As one sees them in the aggregate, one is struck more and more by how they behave as complex organisms, not as merely a collection of buildings that happen to have people in them.

The interpretation of the city as the product of elaborate human and material interaction offers a different perspective on urban operations. Take, for example, the age-old myth of Carthaginian destruction: the idea that an army can erase the existence of a city. Even Carthage itself was never completely destroyed, and after the passage of a few years a 'New Carthage' sprang up close by the old city. Before one assumes that the survival of Carthage was due to the Romans' imperfect city-busting, one should recall the more modern and equally notorious example of Lidice, Czechoslovakia, when Hitler decided to revenge the assassination of Reinhard Heydrich by destroying a town. Lidice was an inconsiderable town, but within weeks of the Nazis' attempt to kill it, inhabitants were returning to the area. Nor could it be said that Lidice's smallness permitted its revival. During the worst of the blitz against London in 1940, one million people commuted to work every day. At the end of the battle for Berlin, perhaps as many as 200000 non-combatants still lived in the wreckage. Today, after more than a decade of fighting within its precincts, Grozny may be inhabited by as many as 30000 people. Being chiefly human, cities tend to adapt and persist. Although cities can be terribly damaged, they cannot be destroyed, cannot be sunk like a ship. Furthermore, it appears that the capacity for cities and their citizens to persist in the face of adversity is actually improving, that world populations are becoming more, not less, resilient. The urban citizens of Northern Ireland and Israel, to cite only two cases, have managed to pretend an ordinary life over the past generation, even while it is not.[14] This resilience permits the citizens of Tokyo who board trains two stops down from where *Aum Shinrykyo* discharged Sarin to continue about their way, even after they hear about the attack.

At least part of the reason that life can go on unhindered can be found in the complexity as well as the cohesion of the urbanscape. The functions of the city—the markets, the schools, the business zones for production, distribution and consumption, arrangements for safety and health, arrangements for the movement of the population—conduce to complexity. The needs that produce these functions seem inherently centrifugal; that is, without purposeful intervention the natural drift is toward increasing disorganisation, disintegration. City traffic is a mundane example: the mobility of an urban populace left to improvise from moment to moment would move less and less effectively. For the sake of effective—and collective—movement, urban populations must invest some portion of their freedom of action. A one-way street asks that one's movements conform to the common welfare. One need only stand at a busy intersection for a short time in order to calculate how much of what one sees is *voluntary* and how little is actually *regulatory* behaviour. Thus, the manner in which the population voluntarily responds will reflect the city's cohesion.

Of course, this scenario assumes that the city is at peace—its optimal state. How does the scenario change when a state of war is assumed? Regrettably, about this subject we know very little that might be offered as a respectable generalisation. However, it may safely be supposed that functions designed to work in a state of peace may not work at all. Thousands of common little agreements that permit their populations to live in a constricted but orderly environment would suddenly disappear. If all civil life in an urban area is disrupted by fighting, what compels non-combatants to remain in what are ever more dangerous circumstances? In April 1945, dairyman Richard Poganowska drove his milk cart through the streets of Berlin until he was stopped by Russian tanks.[15] This compulsion to remain even if an iota of normalcy remains may be related to another phenomenon—that in which cities under fire often exchange one population for another. Many urban inhabitants do indeed flee the prospect of fighting, but their places are often taken by those who began their escape elsewhere and saw the city as a relatively safe place. In the Middle East especially this phenomenon sometimes evolves into vast refugee camps, some of which are not camp-like at all. Such camps, with their strange concoctions of the temporary and the permanent, comprise a special subclass of urbanisation all by themselves (and, by extension, a special subclass of urban military problems). Indeed, one might argue that in these camps, urban life—always protean—has a new species with which it must contend.

The complex picture offered by modern global urban life, both at rest and under violent stress, poses a challenge to contemporary military thought. How is military thought to make a contribution to understanding this unique operating environment that seems at once so old and so new? What soldiers once knew about urban warfare does not translate well to modern cities of even modest size. The distance between professional military knowledge and the military's ability to overcome the challenges represented by the modern urban environment is widening at an ever-increasing velocity. The current definition of the urban environment—based on professional military knowledge and guiding modern fighting doctrines—is obsolete. The redefinition—the *military* redefinition—of the city is long overdue.

What form should this redefinition assume? The first task is to draw a precise and militarily relevant picture of the present state of affairs. An important part of this task must be to recognise that, while much of the modern urban environment is new, much of it is not, and that wantonly discarding hard-won knowledge about cities or about fighting in cities is a mistake. Second, military commanders and their staffs are not likely to be convinced that they must master the precise human and material dimensions of each and every urban area where they might operate. Professional military knowledge must therefore formulate practical generalisations about the urban operating environment that will guide military commanders and their staffs when the need arises. If military knowledge is to meet this need, it must not only be recast but in some respects created. All cities, however large or small, may now be said to possess a new attribute that may prove to be the most significant aspect of the new urban environment. Every city now occupies a cybernetic space as well as a physical space. The manner and degree in which a city's physical reality is manifested cybernetically, and the exact relation between them, are questions that should be viewed as militarily important. The answers may well suggest new means of expressing military power, and, not least, establish altogether different standards by which military power itself is measured.

Practitioners of modern war do not have the luxury of awaiting developments in military thought. In all probability, modern armed forces will find themselves campaigning in cities and urban agglomerations well before military thought can accommodate these new circumstances. Urban fighting in Baghdad was very limited. The regime forces were mainly destroyed on the fringes of the city and paramilitary forces melted away their first contact with armoured vehicles. The old vision of the military campaign, unfolding in stately, sequential fashion across the green countryside is, I suspect, now an exercise in nostalgia. As always, soldiers will be required to adapt. I do not think for a moment that the orthodox armed forces of the world will be able to 'leap ahead', or transform themselves sufficiently to anticipate when these adaptations will be necessary. Cities have their inherent characteristics, but then, so do armies.[16]

Land forces in 21st-century coalition operations: implications for the Asia-Pacific

Alan Ryan

Maintaining stability by building viable, interoperable coalitions with the forces of regional allies will remain a necessity to ensure a positive security environment in key areas of the world. Military engagement efforts produce dividends in deterrence, confidence-building, and burden sharing. They also demonstrate our commitment and resolve. However, these tasks will continue to tax our thinly stretched forces.
General Anthony C. Zinni, USMC (Retd)[1]

If the first principle of strategy is 'never invade Russia in winter', the second is 'not to get involved in a land war in Asia'. Given that apparently good advice, many strategic thinkers shy away from considering the use of multinational forces in a strategic environment that is as complex, and as unforgiving, as the Asia-Pacific. Throughout the region, policy makers come up with elaborate excuses for developing national strategic plans that pay little more than lip service to the prospect of coalition military operations. Yet, since the end of the Cold War, multinational operations—often mounted on short notice—have proliferated across the globe. Military forces are now employed in a spectrum of tasks ranging from conventional warfighting to peace enforcement, from humanitarian relief to security and stabilisation missions. In the wake of 11 September 2001 the United States assembled a global coalition against terrorism. The prosecution of operations against the Taliban and al-Qa'ida was very much a coalition effort, involving indigenous forces as well as a broad international representation. That coalition and the succeeding coalition against Saddam Hussein's regime in Iraq serve to demonstrate that in the 21st century unilateral military action by civilised states has become almost inconceivable. Nonetheless, the extra levels of complexity that are introduced by multinational participation in military operations now mean that we cannot just take coalitions for granted. Smaller powers, such as Australia, should possess a very clear vision of the nature of their objectives when they make a contribution to multinational forces and they should tailor their force packages accordingly. As Donald Rumsfeld, the United States Secretary of Defence, recently concluded, wars 'should not be fought by committee. The mission must determine the coalition, the coalition must not determine the mission, or else the mission will be dumbed down to the lowest common denominator.'[2]

When countries have to resort to the use of the armed forces—even for reasonably low-intensity operations—they are concerned to demonstrate the legitimacy of their actions. Legitimacy is most clearly proven when there is a representative array of 'flags on the ground'. Although history is replete with examples of unjust coalitions, the guarantees provided by our participation in a system of public international law now suggest that a multilateral approach is most likely to satisfy the criteria for a just war or external intervention. More to the point, the diversity of the Asia-Pacific region makes it particularly important that resort to arms has a reasonably broad level of acceptance. The security of the Asia-Pacific will therefore continue to depend on multinational cooperation.[3] Increasingly, that cooperation will require regional and extra-regional states to mount and deploy multinational forces. Many, though not all, of these operations will be carried out under the auspices of the United Nations (UN). As far as Australia is concerned, there are very few circumstances in which the Australian Defence Force (ADF) will operate by itself. When next our army fights, it will be alongside other armies. Some of our partners will be traditional allies; others are likely to be very different from us. When we set ourselves the task of imagining future land warfare, we must anticipate the complex challenges faced by heterogeneous forces. Not to do so is to invite defeat.

This chapter examines some of the lessons that have emerged from recent coalition operations and identifies the particular environmental issues that will affect multinational land forces deployed in the Asia-Pacific. The chapter does not seek to differentiate between warfighting operations and operations other than war. Although warfighting requires a far higher level of tactical integration than peacekeeping or peace enforcement, the fundamental principle of coalition operations is that the cohesion of a multinational force is generally the centre of gravity most likely to be identified by an opponent. Consequently, countries that participate in a coalition need to prepare their forces to cooperate with other national forces in advance of any operational contingency. The focus of such preparations cannot be narrow since multinational forces are required across the operational spectrum. Preparing for coalition operations in the Asia-Pacific will inevitably require land forces to conduct warfighting operations, though the nature of broad-based coalitions guarantees that these preparations will be for defensive, rather than aggressive, purposes.

In the matter of only a few years traditional assumptions about the need to rely on formal alliances have been swept away. Since the end of the Cold War, Australian forces have been employed in a range of operations with a diverse set of partners around the world. In September 1999, with little warning, Australia took command of a complex multinational peace-enforcement operation in East Timor and has maintained a substantial commitment to the UN effort in that country. Now the global response to the terrorist attack on the World Trade Center has demonstrated the need for greater compatibility between the armed forces of different countries that will have to confront the asymmetric threat.

The need for military-to-military cooperability is particularly pressing with respect to land forces. Armies from different countries face more problems in integrating with each other than do air and naval forces. In the current dynamic and unpredictable strategic environment, it is unlikely that regional countries will be able to commit to formal security guarantees. Yet regional forces need to be prepared to operate together in order to deal with a broad range of contingencies. Such cooperation requires us to develop both closer doctrinal links with likely coalition partners and second-tier cooperative relationships with regional military forces. In short, while the Asia-Pacific remains unready for the creation of a system of collective security, enhanced military—and specifically land force—cooperability will do much to bring about a positive security environment.

The thrust of this argument is targeted at an Australian audience, but when we consider multinational issues we cannot assume an Australian-centric position. As Sir Shridath Ramphal, co-Chairman of the Commission on Global Governance put it:

> For most of us values are alright if they are our values. That cannot be the prescription for a world of diversity. We have to recognise that the world is enriched by diversity not made more difficult by it; that variety is not a problem but a resource.[4]

The chance to participate in supranational military coalitions should not be seen as a problem, but an opportunity; after all, when it comes to sending our troops in harm's way, all coalition partners are in it together.

Developing a pluralist approach to security in the Asia-Pacific

Coalition operations in the 21st century will be very different from those in which we have participated in the past. Perhaps the most significant consequence of the accelerated process of globalisation that has occurred since the end of the Cold War has been the convergence of states' interests. Contrary to the fevered imaginings of the half-educated, this process is not the product of a conspiracy cooked up by the World Economic Forum, international financiers or even the illuminati. Rather, the convergence of human, social, economic and political relationships has been inevitable since the introduction of steam power, the telegraph and aircraft drama-tically shrank the globe. The unanticipated consequences of the dawning of the information age have produced a paradigm shift in human rela-tionships that is forcing states to redefine the way in which they relate to each other. Arguing that the new strategic environment does not allow us the luxury of a strategic pause, the former Commander in Chief of United States (US) Central Command, General Anthony Zinni, pointed out that states are increasingly interdependent and interconnected. Accordingly, it is no longer possible to claim that the internal affairs of states do not have implications for others. General Zinni has concluded, together with many of his colleagues, that military organisations, and particularly land forces, need to be prepared to respond to a wider range of tasks than ever before.[5] The complexity of information-age politics also means that states are no longer the only players in the global community. Faced with a threat to human security, such as the September 2001 attack on the United States, all legitimate states have little option but to cooperate to preserve their common interests. Unlike formed alliances that are built on longer-lasting perceptions of common interest, 21st-century coalitions are increasingly likely to be formed by default.

The passing of the bipolar world order that dominated the Cold War has created the conditions that have caused coalitions to thrive and flourish over the past ten years. As coalitions are formed to deal with specific circumstances, no military coalition is typical. It is important to distinguish coalition operations—which are common in a multipolar strategic environment—from alliance operations, which are characteristic of an amalgamated security environment. Coalitions may contain alliance partners, but coalitions are put together for purposes other than long-term strategic understandings. A coalition is, by definition, an 'ad hoc arrangement between two or more nations for common action'.[6] Coalition operations are the product of temporary and relatively informal combinations of states that share common interests and work together for broadly common ends—not the best foundation for the employment of military power in the information age.

The first true information-age conflict is beginning to demonstrate the problems of multinational cooperation in the delivery of security. The rather loose characterisation of the international support promised to the United States in the immediate aftermath of the terrorist attack on the World Trade Center as a 'coalition' has significant implications for security cooperation in the Asia-Pacific. Until those that have tendered their support to the United States agree to both the general objectives of the 'war on terrorism' and the measures to be adopted, it is not quite accurate to speak of a coalition. Nonetheless, the approach adopted by President Bush has left no room for doubt—those that are not with the United States are against it. Most countries of the Asia-Pacific have promised to cooperate with the United States. Although the US commitment to bringing about regime change in Iraq served to alienate many governments that supported operations against al-Qa'ida, the comprehensive nature of the war on terrorism is likely to continue to bind regional states to the global effort. Success against the rogue regime of Saddam Hussein will prove its own justification. In the long term, all countries will need to remain focused on combating the threat of trans-national fanatic terrorist ideologies.

The emergence of these commitments may well mark a significant shift in the region's security architecture. Since the end of the Cold War, many regional countries have shied away from too close an association with the United States and have placed greater emphasis on multilateral diplomatic initiatives such as the ASEAN Regional Forum (ARF). The demands made by the United States, combined with the palpable air of insecurity generated by the contemporary situation, may well see regional states become more closely associated in developing common security. It has been instructive, in the wake of the Bali bombing, to see a high level of effective international cooperation in the investigation of the outrage. At a governmental level, for instance, the sharing of intelligence and police force-to-police force cooperation has done much to restore the Australian–Indonesian relationship which had declined in the wake of Australia's role in securing East Timor's independence.

The heterogeneous nature of the region makes it difficult to forecast what combinations of national forces will be available to cooperate together in the future. Before the East Timor crisis occurred, no-one anticipated that a multinational coalition consisting of contingents from regional and extra-regional states would be required to sustain extended operations in that country. Before the end of the Cold War, no-one imagined that Australian troops would be employed in multinational operations as far dispersed as Kuwait, Somalia, Rwanda, Bougainville and the Solomon Islands. The challenge that faces force planners as they set about preparing for operations in an utterly novel strategic environment has been spelt out by Admiral Dennis Blair, Commander in Chief of United States Pacific Command:

> [A]s a combatant commander, I cannot conceive of wars in the 21st century that will not involve coalition partners. And especially in the Pacific, each contingency may require a different set of coalition partners. We cannot expect to rely on alliance protocols such as NATO [North Atlantic Treaty Organization]. We need systems that have been wrung out in the development stage with our coalition partners so that we identify what part of the operational picture needs to be seen in all coalition headquarters, what messages need to be passed back and forth, and how we can solve the daunting information assurance challenge in a coalition environment.[7]

We will return to Admiral Blair's vision for the future of security cooperation in the Asia-Pacific, but first we need to develop an understanding of why coalitions represent the future of military operations. Regardless of the level of operational intensity and despite the complexity introduced by the demands of information-age conflict in a heterogeneous global community, building and sustaining a coalition of countries with a range of interests and ideologies is the most significant way of bestowing legitimacy on a particular cause. Given the current situation in the Asia-Pacific, however, few states are capable of engaging in coalition activities at anything other than the most basic level. Learning from the international political, military and domestic levels of recent coalition efforts, it becomes obvious that the Asia-Pacific needs to evolve a security architecture that will enable rapid and effective responses to regional crises. The alternative is to accept that the region will suffer conditions of relative insecurity no longer tolerated in the West nor even in much of the Middle East.

In industrial-age conflicts it was possible to circumvent close cooperation between coalition partners. Operations could be carved up and tactical areas of responsibility could be easily apportioned to the armed forces of different states. In the European Theatre of Operations during World War II, for example, the British and American forces conducted their advances independently, coordination of their efforts being managed at the highest level. Even the two air forces divided their strategic bombing campaigns into night and day. This sort of stovepiping is not so easily accomplished in information-age operations. As opposing forces contend to get inside each other's decision cycle, the coalition that has not established internal situational awareness is starting on the back foot.

With the exception of the Russo–Japanese War, the Iran–Iraq War and perhaps the Indo–Pakistan Wars, all major conflicts of the 20th century have been waged by coalitions—at least on one side. Unlike long-term, formal alliances, their success is founded on the ability of their members to work together and preserve unity in achieving identifiable common objectives. Some members of a coalition might well have a history of cooperation, but most of the combinations of the last decade have seen disparate states forced to improvise the manner in which they work together. In contrast, combined military operations arising from alliance relationships are generally based on firmer political resolve; greater commonality of purpose; and shared training, equipment and doctrine. Preparing for coalition operations in a complex strategic environment requires much closer attention to detail than was the norm during the Cold War. As the American–British–Canadian–Australian Armies Program (ABCA) *Coalition Operations Handbook* points out:

> [P]lanners must closely study the political goals of each participant as a precursor to detailed planning. Political considerations weigh more heavily with coalitions than with alliance operations. Coalition operations are not new . . . Since human nature has not changed, conflicts over territory, religion, politics, and economics, such as those that prompted previous military operations, will continue to be widespread. The precise role of armies in these operations will vary according to each political and military situation.[8]

Lessons from Australian involvement in operations in Cambodia and East Timor

The experience that the ADF has derived from recent coalition operations has demonstrated the heightened prominence of the political dimension in contemporary military operations. Of course the employment of military force is an inherently political act. However, in an environment where coalition military forces are routinely deployed for purposes other than the defence of national sovereignty and interests, soldiers need to appreciate that the indications of a successful operation are not as clear as they are in interstate warfare. Often the need to demonstrate that a coalition achieved a viable end-state leads to the formation of a selective record of the operation. As memories are short, we too often assume that all went to plan, when what actually occurred was the result of the efforts of a few high-quality professionals combined with a great deal of good fortune. While this approach sufficed in the halcyon days of coalition operations following the end of the Cold War, it is unlikely to prove adequate for the considerably more complex operations of the information age.

In the aftermath of military operations, whether they involve combat or not, there is a pronounced tendency for participants to declare victory and go home. In contemporary conflicts this practice can result in self-deception on the part of the 'victors' about what has actually occurred. In the case of a peace operation the coalition might achieve its mandate, yet leave the state in question dependent on foreign aid, subject to internal strife, or geographically partitioned. A review of successive operations in Africa, the Balkans and the Middle East bears out the observation that few military operations are prosecuted to the point where they achieve all of their political objectives. Even wars do not end cleanly—ten years after the conclusion of the war over Kuwait, Saddam Hussein was still in power; the Marsh Arabs were totally dispossessed (those that survived); and the oppression of the Kurds and other opponents of the regime was as cruel as ever. Mounting a second war in 2003 was an untidy option, and one that with the benefit of hindsight was unnecessary. Unfortunately, when we are in the midst of a conflict, the natural tendency is to bring it to a conclusion as soon as possible.

Eleven years after the conclusion of the mission of the UN Transitional Authority in Cambodia (UNTAC) we tend to consider its operations a success. Certainly its outcome compared well with the disastrous consequences of UN operations in Somalia at the same time. Thirty-four countries contributed military forces to the former operation and eleven of those countries contributed infantry battalions. These units were provided by Bangladesh, Bulgaria, France, Ghana, India, Indonesia (two battalions), Malaysia, the Netherlands, Pakistan, Tunisia and Uruguay.[9] Far from representing an information-age force, this diverse coalition achieved its objectives and bestowed legitimacy on the peace process with a more disparate membership and range of capabilities than would have previously been considered possible.

We should not forget, however, that the military component of UNTAC was plagued with internal problems that can be ascribed to the 'wide disparities in the training, equipment and competence of the various national contingents'.[10] Some contingents showed themselves to be incompetent, while others behaved badly. Allegations against some of the contingents included drunken behaviour, overt use of brothels, running commercial enterprises for profit, and openly pursuing national agendas rather than UNTAC objectives. At the very least, such behaviour was culturally insensitive and reflected poorly on the UN; at the worst, it threatened the ability of the UN to achieve its mission. Disparities between the pay and conditions of different contingents led to tensions—even threats by some members of one contingent to kill the Force Commander, Lieutenant General John Sanderson of Australia. The ultimate success of the mission was as much due to the excellent leadership that the peacekeeping force enjoyed as it was to the cohesion of the force. It was also possible to assign national contingents to their own sectors—an option that will not always be possible to a coalition comprising units with mixed capabilities or faced with a more fluid operational situation. Most of the lessons that we can draw from the deployment of land forces in Cambodia demonstrate that information-age operations are going to require a smarter approach.

The problems that arise when forming an ad-hoc coalition in the Asia-Pacific have been amply demonstrated in the record of the international forces that have deployed to East Timor since September 1999. At the time that the Australian-led International Force East Timor (INTERFET) was completing its handover to the United Nations Transitional Administration in East Timor (UNTAET), Kofi Annan, the Secretary-General of the UN, remarked that it was 'almost a record that a UN force is able to go down within two weeks of a crisis. It is mainly to do with the leadership, the organisation, the professionalism of the

Australian Army and its leadership.'[11] In fact, the speed of the deployment in September 1999 was achievable only because INTERFET was not a UN 'blue helmet' force; instead, the leadership was 'subcontracted' under a UN mandate to Australia. Operation *Stabilise*, the multinational operation in East Timor that took place between 20 September 1999 and 23 February 2000, was deployed on a complex peace operation only five days after it was authorised. While Australia can accept much of the credit for pulling the coalition together in the field and sustaining it, we must not draw the wrong conclusions from its success.

The speed with which INTERFET was deployed and the rapidity with which it was able to establish conditions of security in East Timor make this operation an excellent model for future ad-hoc, complex, multinational deployments. In short, INTERFET was a classic short-notice coalition in that it had no time to do anything other than to make the most of the circumstances in which its members found themselves. In large part, the success of the operation was due to the troop-contributing nations' acceptance of the imperfections inherent in such a disparate force. Operational responsibility was distributed according to the capabilities of the forces assigned to the mission. The need for a robust command-and-control architecture was realised in the strong lead-nation model that INTERFET adopted. As the coalition consisted of countries that possessed a high level of interoperability at the command level, as well as countries whose operational cultures were fundamentally incompatible, the Force Commander, Major General Peter Cosgrove, had to adopt some fairly simple expedients. He later remarked of the political dimension of force cohesion that:

> I found it crucial to establish and meet the needs and concerns of each troop-contributing nation, to achieve understanding and congruence—frequently by give and take—and vitally, good will and cooperation. We were by no means faultless in INTERFET, but given the keenness of national interests involved we navigated our way through most testing times with our international relationships very much enhanced in virtually every case. Even in those first few weeks when the operational imperative was driving every waking moment, we all had to remind ourselves that every member of the coalition had to be valued and embraced.[12]

The steps that Headquarters INTERFET took to overcome the language gap, the lack of collaborative experience, and the absence of common standard operating procedures led, in some quarters, to criticism of the Australian style of command.[13] These suggestions that the Australian-dominated headquarters was overbearing in its approach and was overly belligerent were not entirely fair. Headquarters INTERFET and the Australian support-base for the operation had to satisfy the often-conflicting demands of a wide range of parties. Negotiations with contributing countries in the lead-up to the operation had made it clear that many countries, including the United States, expected that their forces would be provided with a high degree of force protection by the lead nation. The Australian, New Zealand and British forces not only shared the responsibility for establishing conditions of security in the critical early days but, as the mission developed, continued to accept responsibility for securing the porous western border. This mission remained the primary responsibility of the Australians and New Zealanders after the transition to UNTAET. Accordingly, while the primary function of the other large contingents was to meet the humanitarian element of the mandate, the primary mission of providing security required a more robust, 'no nonsense' approach on the part of the forces that were most often in contact with the anti-independence Militia units.

Given that functional interoperability was impossible to achieve at short notice with those larger contingents that had not worked with the Australians before, the headquarters adopted an uncomplicated command-and-control model. The command relationship with the Asian contingents in the eastern regencies was managed by the extensive use of liaison officers; the establishment of simple but robust communication systems and standard operating procedures; and, where seamlessly integrated operations were not possible, by the simple matching of assets and personnel to given tasks.[14]

Although many contingents remained to serve in the peacekeeping component of UNTAET, it has faced different problems from those of its predecessor force. Particular issues include the cultural complexity of a constantly changing multinational organisation; widespread unfamiliarity with the UN's procedures, and coalition operations in general; and the widespread lack of technical interoperability. None of these factors is critical in what has been stabilised as a low-intensity military operation. For those countries that expect to continue to participate in multinational operations, the need to address training and force preparation issues has become a priority. This imperative requires military organisations and their supporting institutions to focus on the practical aspects of overcoming the linguistic, cultural, doctrinal and educational gaps that bedevil international missions.

INTERFET was a heterogeneous coalition, as is its successor force UNTAET. Both forces consisted of partners that possessed vastly different operational cultures, and many of them had no experience of working together. Consequently, the prosecution of the mission relied on the force commanders, their staffs and the senior national contingent commanders devising workable expedients for the distribution of operational responsibility. Both INTERFET and UNTAET have succeeded because the officers that commanded and staffed them have excelled in working in the less-than-perfect conditions of a multinational headquarters. More significantly, neither operation faced sustained or particularly professional opposition. Had the Militia targeted the cohesion of the coalition by causing unacceptably high casualties in those contingents that were not structured for combat operations, the outcome might have been different. We have no guarantee that similar circumstances will arise in the future. In fact, any determined opponent could learn from the lessons of Somalia, Cambodia and East Timor, and take advantage of the internal contradictions that exist in any multinational force. For this reason multinational military coalitions need to assure their internal cohesion before they are tested in the field.

Warfighting and peacekeeping: keeping our options open

The Asia-Pacific region has not the same tradition of coalition operations as has Europe, or for that matter, the West as a whole. In the past, the disparate nature of the region has militated against the formation of broad-based coalitions. However, global pressures now mean that there is a greater co-identity of interests between states than was the case during the Cold War and before. While the likelihood of major global war between the great powers appears to have receded, the possibility of aggression by marginalised states and failing states remains. In addition, we now face the threat of asymmetric attacks by non-state actors such as terrorist and criminal groups. The proliferation of novel threats to human security in the Asia-Pacific has resulted in more willingness on the part of regional countries to employ their forces in coalitions for purposes other than war.

During the past ten years, within our immediate region alone, Australia has been involved in multinational peace operations in Cambodia, Bougainville, East Timor and the Solomon Islands. While these operations have not involved warfighting, the ability of the Australian Army to prosecute military operations offshore, and to bring with it the promise of potent warfighting skills, has made it a valuable asset to these multinational forces. The same can be said of Australian contributions to extra-regional coalitions such as those in Somalia and Rwanda. Australia's willingness and ability to take command of INTERFET demonstrated its commitment to regional stability and enhanced its credit within the region. Like those of our neighbours in the Asia-Pacific, the direction of Australian national policy and our current pattern of deployments indicate the likelihood of involvement in future cooperative partnerships. As the current Defence White Paper points out:

> Over the next ten years the ADF will continue to undertake a range of operations other than conventional war. Preparing the ADF for such operations will therefore take a more prominent place in our defence planning than it has in the past.[15]

We must therefore consider those factors that might influence the use of land forces once they are committed to a multinational force. It is also important that we identify the roles that Army units will have to undertake in regional coalitions.

In many military forces there is considerable resistance to the notion that they will be called upon to execute operations short of 'warfighting'. The conservative argument is that armies are designed to fight wars and that other functions, such as peacekeeping and humanitarian relief efforts, more properly belong to other bodies, for example, police forces or non-government organisations. As well as being short-sighted, this argument does not follow history. Land forces have traditionally fulfilled a range of roles. During the 19th century, European forces performed constabulary tasks around the world. During the postwar period of decolonisation, troops across the globe took on the thankless task of preventing the independence process from descending into total chaos. Not for nothing do we speak of the Pax Britannia—and in retrospect that period of vile imperial repression is beginning to take on a roseate hue. Commencing with the Roman legions, soldiers have generally spent more of their active careers serving as engineers, administrators, lawgivers and police than in combat roles. Their authority is, however, only as good as their capacity to enforce their will.

In the aftermath of the Cold War we are experiencing a variety of challenges to international security. Some of the most immediate threats requiring the potential employment of military force include the disintegration of states; ethnic and religious conflict; small wars and large displaced populations. Consequently, there is a greater demand than ever before for legitimate and militarily capable armed forces that can enforce order and lay the foundation for reconstruction. As the former Chairman of the US Joint Chiefs of Staff, General John Shalikashvili, used to joke, the US Armed Forces did not have the option of hanging a large sign outside the Pentagon saying 'I'm sorry, we only do the big ones'.[16] Soldiers have to be able to fight wars, but that is not a sufficient condition. In the fluid strategic environment that is the Asia-Pacific today, we require forces that can win on the battlefield and provide the conditions that will guarantee the peace—in either a pre-conflict stage or the aftermath of violence.

Given the need for such forces, as well as the fact that they will almost inevitably be employed in a coalition context, we need to question why in the information age we should adopt the comparatively messy option of deploying land forces, rather than avoiding personnel-intensive operations. The answer is simple: whether conducting peace operations or fighting a war, the task of pursuing political objectives through the use of force in a land-based environment requires the physical presence of troops. Conrad Crane of the US Army's Strategic Studies Institute recently made the point that:

> Army units are the preferred forces to form the core of the joint force
> required for the type of enhanced conventional deterrence that can

compel an aggressor to back down and defuse a crisis. Not only do Army forces possess significant capability, the deployment of heavy units also is the strongest possible signal of American intent. The effort that goes into their movement and relative permanence of their placement shows the maximum national commitment to defend US interests. Lighter Army units also clearly signal commitment intent and usually serve as the spearhead for American ground involvement in any crisis.[17]

What applies to the actions of a superpower also applies to the efforts of a multinational effort seeking to demonstrate its legitimacy in a situation where order has either broken down or is in the process of breaking down. However, the very potency of wielding land power in a multinational context brings its own challenges. It is important that we identify what these potential pitfalls are.

The distinctive role of land forces in a coalition environment

The Australian Government's recent Defence White Paper identified the need to develop a 'professional, well-trained, well-equipped' land force that:

> is available for operations at short notice, and one that can be sustained over extended periods. This type of force will have the flexibility to deal with operations other than conventional war, and contribute to coalitions.[18]

The requirement that Australia's Army be capable of contributing to coalitions recognised the particular challenges faced by armies when they are required to integrate their efforts with those of dissimilar coalition partners. Unlike the other services—which are traditionally 'platform-based'—land forces are human-based organisations. When we think of deploying air and naval assets, aircraft and ships immediately spring to mind. By contrast, the range of capabilities that land forces bring to a coalition are diverse and complex. Consequently, the way in which land forces are structured, commanded and employed on coalition operations must be distinguished from the way in which air and naval forces might be used. While we are accustomed to thinking of coalition operations as joint efforts involving the synergy of air, land and maritime forces, we must recognise the particular characteristics of land forces that affect ground-based operations. These characteristics are cultural, organisational, tactical and political. It is important to appreciate how the complex interplay of relationships between different forces will affect land operations.

The way in which armies operate reflects the culture from which they are drawn, as well as their particular history, their longstanding alliances and the doctrinal influences that have shaped their thinking. Although soldiers from many countries have the opportunity to train and conduct operations overseas, armies are inherently parochial and self-centred organisations—and this is not meant as a criticism. The history of land forces deployed as part of a larger effort bears out this observation, regardless of whether they are engaged in warfighting or military operations other than war. Any contingent assigned to an operation is a cultural microcosm, a unit or formation sealed in time and defined by its constituent elements. In contemporary operations, national forces can find themselves deployed at short notice into an unfamiliar environment and as part of an ad-hoc multinational force. In those circumstances the national characteristics of the forces deployed become particularly evident.

The considerable differences that exist between national forces are nowhere more obvious than in the Asia-Pacific. The lack of cultural and organisational compatibility between forces is obvious to most observers, but in recognising these 'soft' factors we must not forget the significant differences that exist in the capabilities of many forces. As the revolutionary potential of information-age warfare opens up to us, the gap between cutting-edge military forces and industrial-age organisations is likely to widen. Nowhere is that gap more obvious than when assigning tasks to the disparate land forces that countries contribute to coalitions. As the former Commander in Chief of the United Nations and US–Korean Combined Forces Command, General Robert RisCassi, observed in 1993:

> Air and naval forces, because they must operate in international mediums, are equipped with communications gear and common

protocols and procedures to provide for organized space management. All of the 'vessels' that operate in the air or the sea can be readily classified for their strengths and weaknesses to perform the various missions of air and naval warfare. Ground forces come in all shapes and sizes, and their equipment may be entirely dissimilar and incompatible. Technological differentials, particularly in this era of revolutionary change, can be vast. Therefore, fundamental commonalities become even more important.[19]

As we have already seen, for most crises requiring a military response, there is no dispensing with land forces. The temptation in recent coalition operations has been to employ platform-based weapons rather than the much messier option of troops on the ground. In asymmetric conflicts the Western democracies see distinct domestic advantages since ships and aircraft are less likely to incur casualties and are easier to deploy, being mobile by their nature. By comparison, soldiers are more vulnerable to both conventional and unconventional weapons. Nonetheless, land forces are required in both peace operations and warfighting—since only they can enforce compliance on the ground.

The employment of land power does present operational planners with a particularly complex set of problems. As Colonel Anthony Rice pointed out in an article published in *Parameters*, the journal of the US Army War College, the 'ground component has invariably been the most difficult to integrate, because doctrinal and equipment differences affect the lowest echelons of command in all armies'.[20] The tempo of operations can, however, make a significant difference in the level at which forces need to be integrated. Where a major conflict such as the Gulf War raises problems of sustaining resource-hungry, high-intensity operations that require a common logistic system capable of rapidly supplying the needs of the whole force, low-intensity operations such as peacekeeping may allow forces to be resupplied at a much lower level. On low-intensity operations, countries can take direct responsibility for maintaining their own forces and thus relieve the strain on the coalition's logistical arrangements.

Air and naval units can more easily establish a symbiotic relationship with dissimilar forces. Navies can do this by matching capabilities to needs, and air forces achieve it by matching the characteristics of their aircraft to specific missions. As these functions are highly automated, or at least essentially platform-based, they do not involve the political dimension of human interaction in the same way that integrating ground forces does. Ostensibly, platform-based units appear to be better suited to coalition operations, but it is a mistake to think that all coalition operations will lend themselves to stand-off weaponry. Low-level operations will always require a human presence, and any operation that requires troops to take and hold ground to achieve the mission's political objectives involves the need for ground forces.

Ground forces devoted to coalitions raise particular problems for commanders. The prominent US scholar of coalition operations, Thomas Durrell-Young, has demonstrated that land commanders require a greater level of command authority when conducting coalition operations than that required by their naval and air counterparts.[21] In addition, land forces are extremely vulnerable and their presence on an operation raises specific issues of force protection, interoperability and operational autonomy.

To develop the same level of symbiosis between ground forces as is possible with platform-based services, armies need to train together. Also, as part of their preparation for command, commanders need to develop specific skills and aptitudes in order to meet the demands of ad-hoc combined operations at every level of conflict. As US Navy Captain Terry Pudas pointed out, senior officers need to appreciate the effect that different coalition combinations will have on key planning factors, and accordingly officers at all levels need to conduct exercises in order to familiarise themselves with the variables that are inherent in multinational operations.[22]

Security pluralism and principles for cooperation by land forces in the Asia-Pacific

If land forces are to be successfully employed on coalition operations, a high degree of cohesion has to be present from the beginning of their mission. This requirement implies that multinational forces will have established a pre-existing level of understanding and functional interoperability before they arrive in-theatre. Looking for ways of improving the conduct of coalition operations, General RisCassi focused on the factors of doctrine and leadership. He argued that doctrine and leadership are the keys to achieving order in the chaos of battle and that this truism rings doubly true for multinational operations. Nonetheless, he noted that, despite long experience of coalition membership, the United States (and by extension all other states) remained remarkably ill-prepared for combined action. Although his comments focused on warfighting, they apply to any coalition force facing armed opposition. The fog and friction of operations, he wrote, were best overcome by:

> accentuating the commonalities that exist: first, between our national interests; second, between how we intend to deal with threats to mutual interests; and then in how we actually apply our combined forces in battle. Where commonalities are required but lacking, we move quickly to create them ... The key to achieving this unity is by promulgating a doctrine for warfighting that is commonly understood and applied. Planning systems must be collective and participatory, yet responsive and unerringly timely.

General RisCassi concluded that the friction inherent in coalition operations was best overcome by rapidly analysing and testing combined tactical integration; command-and-control systems; training; and logistic arrangements. Provision could then be made to 'sew' these coalition systems even tighter.[23]

The task of developing coalition doctrinal principles that are both capable of being applied by the states of the Asia-Pacific and politically acceptable to them is a daunting one. However, that task is perhaps not as difficult as we might think. Attitudes to multinational operations are often shaped by experiences of UN-run missions. The past record of such operations does not provide an ideal starting point for a consideration of the most efficient way to deploy coalitions—a fact that the UN is honestly, if belatedly, accepting. The *Report of the Panel on United Nations Peace Operations*, which was released in August 2000, frankly exposed the problems that many coalitions faced. Such problems included the overly bureaucratic distribution of responsibility in coalitions; shortfalls in officers qualified to serve in command and staff positions on coalition headquarters; the lack of training and equipment; and the inability of many states to honour the commitments that they had made to the UN.[24] These findings emphasised the gross disparities that generally exist between forces hurriedly cobbled together for multinational operations.

Despite these criticisms of the manner in which the international community currently mounts multinational operations, there is another dimension to the military profession. Whatever their cultural origins, almost every military force recognises a list of principles that guide its actions. Most of these principles are derived from a common body of professional literature and enable officers, despite their own unique backgrounds and disparate force capabilities, to communicate complex concepts to each other. Working from a foundation of commonly accepted principles, professionally trained officers can establish understandings that will form the basis of a coalition and enable command relationships to be formed. Although we often concentrate on the 'bad news' about multinational forces, we should be surprised that they ever work at all. How many other professionals, sent far from home at short notice, could achieve anything in a polyglot team drawn from twenty or more countries?

With coalition operations becoming more common, soldiers can now expect to serve on a number of such missions during their career. The requirement to sustain operations in East Timor has resulted in the rotation of most active-service Australian Army units through that theatre. In addition, many Australian officers have gained valuable operational experience in multinational headquarters or as liaison officers with other forces. Officers from other armies participating in the operation often have even more experience of multinational operations than their Australian counterparts. From a regional perspective, a middle-level officer in the New Zealand Army is likely to have served on three or four overseas peace operations, and a Fijian soldier may well spend half of his career overseas on operations.[25] If the operational tempo currently maintained by the Australian Army persists, frequent overseas service may well become the norm, not the exception, in a soldier's career.

In these circumstances it makes little sense to reinvent the wheel for each operation. Longstanding, well-trained alliances such as NATO forces, or for that matter the forces of the Warsaw Pact, have demonstrated the value of possessing formed doctrine. The existence of such doctrine does not presuppose a commitment to particular operations, but does demonstrate a capacity to collaborate effectively if required. Different levels of cooperation are achieved within every interstate relationship: military, political and economic connections operate in different dimensions and at distinct levels. For example, the formal treaty-based special relationship with the United States is supported and supplemented by the specific operational synergies with other armies that the Australian Army gains through its participation in the American–British–Canadian–Australian Armies Program. In fact a comparative reading of Australian, US and British doctrinal publications will demonstrate extraordinary conceptual similarities—similarities that often extend to the order of the words themselves. (In the academic world we might call it plagiarism. In the drafting of military doctrine it is considered a full, frank and open exchange of ideas.) The high level of intellectual understanding that English-speaking and other NATO forces can establish only emphasises the problems faced by ad-hoc coalitions, which are often required to coordinate military operations in a matter of days.

Due to their complexity, land forces are particularly reliant on doctrine. Historically, the development of doctrine has reflected the particular national and cultural characteristics of individual forces. Their cultural similarity explains the ease with which English-speaking armies can share operational philosophies. In the Asia-Pacific, where even the simplest level of understanding between disparate forces is difficult to achieve, it is not possible to share common doctrine. In the absence of linguistic and cultural ties, it becomes even more important to seek alternative means of building common understanding. A recent joint US–UK–German–French working group on improving cooperability on coalition operations found that:

> Coalition partners working with very different doctrines will obviously have problems harmonizing their efforts. Indeed, regardless of the degree of technical interoperability they might achieve, genuine cooperability will be all but impossible to achieve. In simplest terms, forces that operate on different fundamental principles become vulnerable to misunderstandings, poorly coordinated actions, and even working at cross-purposes. Doctrine can, if harmonized, be the glue of coalition operations. Finding ways to harmonize doctrine is, therefore, a priority effort to ensure improved coalition operations.[26]

It is a mistake to believe that the task of improving the level at which land forces can cooperate is fettered to the state of relationships between states in the Asia-Pacific. Nor is it in the long-term interest of regional states that the level of security dialogue should be pinned to formal diplomatic instruments. As Lord Palmerston famously commented: 'There are no permanent friends, only permanent interests.' It is in the interests of states that they be prepared to cooperate at short notice, even if it is impossible to foresee the circumstances that might give rise to joint action. In a proposal with particular relevance for the Asia-Pacific, Colonel Michael Smith, Director of the Joint Doctrine Directorate in the US Army's Training and Doctrine Command, suggested that:

> To overcome the problems associated with the lack of common doctrine, regional organizations should develop regional doctrinal publications which identify doctrinal 'considerations' for commanders and planners. The term 'considerations' is used because it is unlikely that anything more detailed or prescriptive would be adopted and endorsed by all potential coalition members from a region.[27]

Unfortunately, the nature of the strategic environment in the Asia-Pacific militates against the creation of a 'strong' security community. The region is simply not ready for developed multilateral cooperation in the way that Europe is.[28] Not only does the region not share a monolithic security architecture, but historically it has not shared many of the presumptions on which international law and the notion of collective security are based. The security implications of the heterogeneous nature of the region are particularly clear in the case of the member states of the Association of South-East Asian Nations (ASEAN). In a paper published in 1996, Nicola Baker and Leonard Sebastian highlighted the extreme reluctance of ASEAN states to commit themselves to formal alliances:

> Formal multilateral security agreements and structures were not considered feasible or desirable by the founding member states of ASEAN for three ... reasons: they lacked the defence capacity for any form of collective security, their relations were complicated by unresolved territorial disputes, and they had quite different threat perceptions. Regional

defence capabilities have since improved significantly but few have reached the point where adequate forces could be committed to, and sustained in, any form of collective action beyond the occasional military exercise.[29]

To a certain extent, operations in East Timor have disproved this last assertion. Regional forces have established a precedent for cooperation on active service. Importantly, both INTERFET and its successor, the peacekeeping force element of UNTAET, have enjoyed regional leadership—in turn generals drawn one each from Australia and the Philippines, and two from Thailand.

Despite initial worldwide and regional support for the US-led 'coalition' against terrorism, we are unlikely to see overtly formal cooperative security structures established in the region in the near future. At the intergovernmental level, such an initiative—particularly if it originated in a Western state—is likely to be unwelcome.[30] Although initially most East Asian governments pledged support for the planned US retaliation against the al'Qa'ida organisation, these governments have often had to face hostile domestic constituencies. The promises made to the United States have placed many regional countries in a difficult position—particularly those countries where the United States does not enjoy domestic popularity. As Bruce Gilley of the *Far Eastern Economic Review* wrote:

> Domestic pressures in every country will force most governments to keep their cooperation with the U.S. low profile. Anti-American sentiment, and more commonly a lack of support for a U.S. response, runs deep within the region. Some countries—particularly Singapore and Malaysia—are wary of making themselves targets of terrorists. Yet a failure to support U.S. efforts would put a country in danger of being labelled an undependable ally, or a rogue regime. So far, that is providing a formidable incentive to stand up and be counted.[31]

While current circumstances provide indications that regional resistance to security cooperation may not be permanent, we must not be naive about the political constraints on the task of creating the preconditions for military coalitions. Over and above questions of language, culture and technical interoperability, many regional military forces play political and economic roles in their own countries. In some instances they have been implicated in human-rights abuses. The usual Western response to this concern was summarised by the Canadian scholar Brian Job, who made the quite valid point that:

> expansion of the extent and scope of military to military activities is viewed positively by Asia-Pacific security analysts who see substantial longer term benefits from opening dialogues among national militaries, as preliminary steps toward creating understanding, advancing transparency, and promoting important functional [links].[32]

Nonetheless, liberal democracies cannot afford to be seen to be providing implicit support to the armed forces that might not fully represent the legitimately expressed aspirations of the populations that they are meant to protect. It would be naive to believe that we would never act in concert with such forces; instead, we can expect to belong to coalitions with a diverse composition when our national interests are involved and the particular operation or cause is demonstrably legitimate. Issue-based coalitions—rather than formal, standing defence relationships—will continue to be the norm so long as regional military forces remain active participants in their countries' political and economic affairs. The question that confronts us in the immature strategic environment that is the Asia-Pacific is how to create cooperative synergies with essentially dissimilar militaries.

Although multilateral diplomatic engagement has its place, post-Cold War regional diplomatic initiatives have singly failed to improve conditions of security. As Frederick the Great is credited with saying, 'diplomacy without arms is like an orchestra without instruments'. Security needs to be backed up by potent military force, and in the information age the talisman of military power needs to be transnational. At the level of military-to-military cooperation, US strategic engagement in the Asia-Pacific provides a model that regional forces need to embrace wholeheartedly. The challenge to US Pacific Command and its regional partners that Admiral Blair enunciated requires an information-age response that can only be achieved when armed forces have developed a high level of familiarity with each other. In the Asia-Pacific the US policy has been to support the growing pattern of security pluralism in the region.[33] Admiral Blair has been particularly active in promoting the notion of 'security communities' that will enable specific-issue cooperation between military forces, even if more comprehensive political links do not exist between countries.

The notion of security communities—which was the brainchild of Karl Deutsch, the noted Harvard-based political scientist—is used to describe a group of nations that share dependable expectations of peaceful progress. Recognising that many regions were not yet ready for amalgamated security arrangements, much less shared political and economic systems, Deutsch identified three factors that could substantially enhance the prospects of a pluralistic security community. The first of these was the widespread unattractiveness of war as a means of resolving conflict among the potential members of the community. The second factor was the spread of intellectual movements favouring security interdependence. Thirdly, Deutsch promoted:

> the development and practice of skills of mutual attention, communication, and responsiveness, so as to make possible the preservation of the autonomy and substantial sovereignty of the participating units, and the preservation of stable expectations of peace and peaceful change among them.[34]

The first factor is almost a foregone conclusion in a region that seeks stability for economic growth and where most countries would regard war as a calamity. The second process is certainly in train, through measures such as the second-track diplomacy of the ARF and the Council for Security Cooperation in the Asia-Pacific (CSCAP). The third process is one that could be substantially enhanced by the practical security collaboration that will arise from preparation for coalition efforts.

The concept of the security community is particularly useful for those states that are likely to come together to form coalitions and that need to prepare their forces to do so. As already demonstrated, land forces require the most preparation for multinational operations, and they have the most to benefit from the sort of cooperation envisaged by regional security cooperation. Admiral Blair has pointed out that:

> An attractive feature of security communities for Asian states is the absence of any requirement for security institutions or regimes specified

by treaty. Communities may be based on a non-military organization such as the ASEAN Regional Forum; or their membership may be based upon geography or common concerns rather than any multilateral security forum. The key is that the members are committed to policy coordination, including combined military cooperation on a particular regional security issue, or a series of related security issues, to advance peaceful development of their region over time without major conflict.[35]

As far as land forces in the Asia-Pacific are concerned, cooperation can be engendered by practical measures to prepare regional land forces for the most common operations that they will have to carry out. In the current strategic environment, this requirement entails preparing for peace operations and countering transnational threats such as terrorism, smuggling, piracy and other crimes that threaten regional order. In the absence of more formal cooperative instruments, a useful expedient would be the formation of a multilateral army-to-army program, modelled on the highly successful ABCA system and building on the excellent relationships formed in recent regional peace operations.

The ABCA program provides the region with a useful model for inter-army cooperation since it is not an alliance, nor has an ABCA force ever been employed under the program. The program began after World War II to take advantage of the unprecedented levels of standardisation achieved by the American, British and Canadian armies. Australia joined the program in 1963 and New Zealand joined as an associate member two years later. The member armies conduct formation-level exercises on a biennial basis in order to identify technical interoperability issues and to test the abilities of the armies to operate in coalitions should the need arise. These exercises do not, however, imply a commitment to alliance operations; rather, they are a recognition of the common interests of the member states and signify an awareness of the fact that the member armies are likely to continue to serve together in the pursuit of common objectives. The program produces standardisation agreements, advisory handbooks and planning guides that help the armies to operate together when they are called on to do so. Although achieving total technical and doctrinal interoperability between armies from such varied operational environments is not likely, or even desirable, the experience of the synergies that they have been able to achieve demonstrates the value of this arrangement. The adoption of an ABCA-style model in the Asia-Pacific would not commit regional land forces to common doctrine, but it would enable them to harmonise their operational styles.

Nascent infrastructure for army-to-army cooperation already exists. The Pacific Armies Management Seminar (PAMS), which is annually co-hosted by the US Army and the army of one other Pacific Rim country, has been in existence since 1978. Representatives from 33 countries attended the seminar in 2001. Similarly the biennial Pacific Armies Chiefs Conference (PACC) involved fifteen army chiefs at its second meeting in Kuala Lumpur in September 2001. Although significant adjustments to the circumstances of the Asia-Pacific would be necessary, the adoption of a standardisation program would build on the goodwill and shared experience established by the Australian Army's participation in recent operations in Cambodia and East Timor.

Conclusion—forging the coalition warrior

Anyone that attempts to make recommendations about the manner in which their country should contribute to international coalitions does so at their own peril. Coalition operations are based on accommodation and compromise, neither of which is popular domestically or within the armed forces. Multinational forces take us out of our comfort zone. It is possible to score cheap points out of the differences that exist within a multinational force—and indeed, some of the differences can be very entertaining. The melange of cultures that make up the Asia-Pacific countries makes this observation doubly true. In our contemporary strategic environment, however, we would be mistaken if we thought that Australia's ability to contribute one, or even two, brigades to a coalition is enough to advance the long-term security of our region. Australia is not going to be able to field large land forces in the future—and it may well be that in information-age warfare such forces are not required. What is required is the capacity to make potent contributions to regional coalitions, and those contributions—whether they be of personnel, equipment or other support—need to be geared to the complex demands of disparate forces. Accordingly, Australia's strategic preparations need to concentrate on developing combined- and joint-force synergies with its likely partners in future operations.

In a region as large as the Asia-Pacific, air and sea power is critical. The obvious need for air and naval assets does, however, often lead to the overlooking of the necessity for a sustainable land-force contribution in coalition efforts. Quite understandably, many countries are tempted to tailor their contributions to contemporary coalition efforts so as to reduce the possibility of casualties. Providing an air, naval or non-combatant capability is one way of minimising risk. Nonetheless, most operations will need a substantial ground presence, and for this reason only land forces will do. Writing recently about the role of the US Army in the Asia-Pacific, Dr Andrew Scobell of the US Army's Strategic Studies Institute pointed out that:

> [T]he Army is the ultimate symbol of a rock-solid U.S. commitment to the enduring peace and prosperity of the region. The Army is the core service in the labor-intensive process of peacetime engagement. Moreover, when hostilities break out and the commitment of U.S. forces is required, the Army forms the nucleus of any mission force. Finally, only the Army, the sole service that can occupy land, can guarantee a decisive strategic (i.e. political) outcome and an effective transition to a desired end state.[36]

Dr Scobell held up operations in East Timor as an example of an effective regional coalition and proposed a number of initiatives that would enhance the ability of regional forces to manage operations in the region. These proposals included deterring potential aggressors by demonstrating an ability to undertake large-scale sustained land combat and improving the level of engagement between the US Army and the armies of the Asia-Pacific. He pointed out that a different approach was needed when engaging with the US 'linchpin' partners—South Korea, Japan and Australia—and other countries that he characterised as 'powder keg' states. Most importantly, he advocated the improvement of regional force capabilities to execute smaller-scale operations, such as peacekeeping and humanitarian relief operations. To achieve this end, he proposed the establishment of a regional training centre to rehearse Asia-Pacific forces in the conduct of these operations. He concluded that 'the most logical place for such a facility would be Australia . . . [s]uch an initiative would be particularly timely and appropriate because it would follow on the heels of the successful Australian-led multinational operation in East Timor'.[37]

The circumstances of the contemporary strategic situation favour Australia's taking the initiative in helping advance security cooperation among regional forces. The formation of the East Timor coalition provided a significant watershed for the land forces of the Asia-Pacific. A multinational force with a heavy regional representation has operated successfully since September 1999. If the will is present, regional armies can capitalise on that experience. The incentive to develop combined-force synergies has been provided by the need for enhanced security cooperation arising from the war on terrorism. Without ignoring the problems that are inherent in regional coalition operations, we need to start preparing for the complex challenges that the information age will bring.

Although Australia cannot bring about change by itself, it is in an excellent position to initiate and facilitate military cooperative measures. As a result of operations in East Timor, the standing of the ADF, and the Army in particular, is high within the region. At the relatively non-controversial level of defence cooperation, Australia can play the role of honest broker, without any of the complications that hinder higher-level political and diplomatic arrangements. Yet, as we have seen, the development of a pluralist security community can greatly enhance the prospects for regional cooperation and goodwill. Colonel Michael Smith of the US Army Training and Doctrine Command has listed some of the initiatives that will enable regional forces to improve the efficiency and effectiveness of regional coalition operations:

> Publication of regional coalition doctrine considerations, common terminology, and institutionalized training and exchange for coalition operations would be significant steps to improve such operations. Implementation of these steps would enhance the chance for successful missions, and would most assuredly save lives.[38]

To that list might be added the need to rethink the industrial-age model of national autonomy in defence matters. Whether we are willing to acknowledge it or not, the era of globalisation has ushered in a range of comprehensive threats to human security that ignore national borders. The future of land forces in the Asia-Pacific lies in cooperation and building common purpose. It will be interesting to see what form the future coalition warrior takes.

Part II

Future challenges

7

Creating a culture of velocity: the Western military mindset and the challenge of digitisation

Lieutenant Colonel Robert Leonhard

In February 1921, the *Journal of the Royal United Service Institution* published a lecture by Captain B. H. Liddell Hart, titled 'The Man-in-the-Dark Theory of Infantry Tactics and the Expanding Torrent System of Attack'. Since that time, the man-in-the-dark analogy has been a vivid and useful way of thinking about battlefield tactics. With the US Army's recent advances in developing and acquiring information technologies, however, perhaps the time has come to shed some light on the man-in-the-dark.

In his lecture, Liddell Hart began by offering a simple analogy with which to examine modern tactics. Due to his experience as an infantry platoon leader and company commander in World War I, Liddell Hart had a solid foundation for both understanding and teaching small-unit infantry tactics. He likened battle between two opposing units to hand-to-hand fighting between two men in a dark room. Since neither opponent could see the other in this fictional contest, each had to adapt his stance and fighting techniques to the fundamental uncertainty of darkness. Liddell Hart showed that the problems faced by the men in the dark were conceptually the same as those faced by military units on the battlefield.

Imagine standing in a pitch-dark room, and all you know is that your opponent is somewhere in the room with you. Instinctively, you crouch. Why? Because you want to lower your centre of gravity and assume a defensive posture in the event that the enemy surprises you. Liddell Hart noted that, just as the man-in-the-dark would crouch, so also armies on the battlefield assume a constantly defensive stance—even when they are moving or attacking. Good armies are constantly thinking about the possibility of ambush.

The man-in-the-dark will tend to move slowly—much more slowly than he is actually able to move. He does this because he cannot see the floor or the opponent, and he does not want to stumble or wander into the enemy unprepared. Likewise, on the battlefield, armies move much more slowly than their components could move. An MI tank can reach speeds of 50 miles per hour. In battle, however, a tank battalion will move at perhaps a tenth of that velocity. The unit moves slowly and cautiously, taking time to use overwatch tactics and to post air guards and flank guards, and so forth.

Among the techniques used in the blind fight is the outstretched arm. We can easily visualise ourselves standing in the dark, knowing that our opponent is nearby but being unable to see him. Instinctively, we raise the arm and extend the hand. In essence, the hand must assume the duties of the eyes. The first purpose of the extended hand is to find the enemy. In military parlance, this function is called 'reconnaissance'. Reconnaissance is an enemy-oriented function because, in order to perform it, the unit must go where the enemy is and collect detailed, precise information on enemy dispositions and capabilities.

The second purpose of the extended hand is to avoid a surprise attack. Again, this concept has a military term that defines it: 'security'. Security is oriented on the friendly force and seeks to prevent observation by the enemy and attack on friendly formations. There is a third purpose for the extended hand: grasping the enemy. In military terminology, this is called 'fixing' the enemy. Just as a man in the dark would grasp the throat of his foe to immobilise him and set him up for the decisive punch, so military units on the battlefield must immobilise enemy units. The fixing function serves to hold an enemy in place and divert his attention so that another attack—such as a decisive envelopment—can be more effective.

With this germane comparison, Liddell Hart went on to explain the principles of infantry tactics in detail and provided a useful perspective for thinking about war. Yet recent developments in information technologies and related advances in weaponry suggest that a new analogy may be appropriate. It is time to consider the 'man-in-the-light'. As the US Army continues experimentation with digitisation and related information technologies, it will probably face a spectrum of threats in the future. Future adversaries may employ information technologies equal to, or perhaps better than, those of the US Army, while others will have advanced little in this regard. It is instructive, then, to think first about what might happen to tactics when facing the latter. What would occur if US forces were enhanced with information technologies, while those of the opponent were not?

With apologies to Liddell Hart, we must begin by modifying his analogy. In this case, one of the contestants can see, and the other cannot. Again, we must admit that the situation on a real battlefield will rarely be so clear-cut. Advantages in perceiving the battlespace would be relative, not absolute. For the sake of our exploration, however, let us proceed at first with the absolute: we can see, and the enemy is blind.

It is obvious from the start that such a fight is asymmetrical in the extreme. This is a key point, and one that has its good and bad sides. It is almost inconceivable that the friendly force would not prevail in such an encounter. The blind opponent is at an overwhelming disadvantage. If, however, future US military units obtain a clear edge in information operations, what would be the effect on battlefield tactics?

To begin with, the stance of the man-in-the-light would change. If we were to picture ourselves in a well-lit room in which we could clearly see our blind opponent, it is unlikely that we would crouch, tense and extend the arm as we did in the dark. With our eyes functioning properly now, we would not use our hand for reconnaissance. Although reconnaissance would still be a critically important function in the fight, we would use our eyes rather than our hands to do the work. On the battlefield, then, we should expect that a clear-cut advantage in information dominance would lead to less reliance on manoeuvre forces for reconnaissance in favour of other battlefield sensors. The information dominance resources of future commanders may include 'eyes' processing data fused together from an array of sources: optics, radar, imagery, electronic intelligence, local populace, and so on. If realised, this notion would offer welcome respite since reconnaissance by ground forces can cost time and lives.

Anyone with experience in combat or at a combat training centre understands the arguments against a reduced emphasis on ground reconnaissance. In the past, there was no viable substitute for having stealthy groups of soldiers or combat vehicle patrols probing enemy positions. In the past, existing technology was neither responsive nor precise enough to supplant ground reconnaissance. Hence, while commanders would exploit whatever intelligence they could garner from other assets, they would rely on their own soldiers to gather the detailed intelligence necessary to prevail in combat. We simply do not yet know whether emerging technology will overcome this challenge; if it does, then the reconnaissance function must move from the hand to the eye.

A clear example of this dynamic can be drawn from the Battle of Britain in 1940. One of the problems the Royal Air Force (RAF) faced was how to detect incoming German aircraft. Although Ultra and ground observation teams helped considerably, the RAF would have had to rely on fighter pilots conducting surveillance from the air. The pilots and the aircraft would have quickly been worn out using this method. Fortunately, the British had developed radar. The Chain Home radar system allowed the RAF to keep pilots on the ground until they were needed for the interception. Hence, by using information technology, they were able to reserve pilots and aircraft for the decisive fight.

The outstretched hand would remain an effective security measure even in the now well-lit room, but again, the eyes would take over some of the security function. The man-in-the-light who can observe his blind opponent will not feel compelled to raise the hand for security until he has closed the distance to striking range. Hence, by using his eyes, the man-in-the-light employs the hand more precisely to protect himself. This analogy, if sustained in experimentation, may have a fundamental effect on tactics. In short, by employing the eyes to detect a threat, the man-in-the-light does not need to remain in a crouching, battle-ready stance continuously. Instead he can relax (thus using less energy), plan and stalk his blind opponent—tensing himself only moments before he strikes.

In battlefield terms, this phenomenon may mean that units can avoid the inefficiencies that attend current security measures and instead move, strike, protect and refit more economically. For example, let us consider a mechanised infantry brigade combat team operating in a theatre of war. In the context of current technology, the brigade is in a similar position to the man-in-the-dark and it must compensate for the uncertainty of the situation with active security measures. Units must patrol aggressively; establish manned observation posts; and develop, supervise and execute sentry procedures. All these activities take time, consume resources, tire soldiers, and sometimes result in death or injury.

If future technology can instead provide the brigade with battlefield visualisation that is good enough to detect threats reliably in a timely manner, we could perhaps dispense with many such security measures, thereby saving time, supplies and lives. Security is an economy-of-force activity, and the principle of economy of force directs that we garner our energies, time and resources for the decisive action. Future technology may move us closer to the goal.

Again, we must be circumspect. The unit that relies solely on technology for security, allowing the organisation to ignore other measures, will be annihilated by an attacker that defeats or avoids the technological defences. Therefore, as we move from theoretical extreme to practical reality, we must recognise that information technologies may lead to a relative reduction of security measures. Even so, relative changes will result in tangible economies.

In the asymmetrical fight of the man-in-the-light against the blind man, the concept of fixing must also change. Because enemies in war will always have their own intentions, capabilities and strengths, US Army doctrine calls for tactics in which the army 'fixes' enemies as it seeks to defeat them. The fixing function accounts for enemy strength and attempts to immobilise or divert it, so that it cannot be brought to bear against the friendly plan.

With its recent emphasis on information operations, the US Army must now consider whether it is feasible to fix the enemy in a way that is different from before. Whereas the US Army used to have to fix the enemy with ground forces, it may now be possible to fix the enemy with his own ignorance. Consider our analogy. The man-in-the-light looks across the room and sees his blind opponent groping about, trying to sense and understand the battlespace while avoiding destruction. Armed with his perfect intelligence, the man-in-the-light stalks his opponent, perhaps sneaking behind him, while the blind man is completely unaware. When it comes time for the decisive blow, the man-in-the-light does not need to spend the energy to fix his opponent, because the blind man is fixed by his own ignorance of the situation. The attempt to grasp the blind man would more likely serve only to alert him of the danger.

In a similar manner, it may be possible for the US Army to employ information operations on the future battlefield to fix the enemy with less reliance on ground combat for this critical function. In the asymmetric fight, the friendly force is planning, mounting and executing operations more quickly than the blind force. Through active and passive command-and-control warfare, the friendly force could conceivably manoeuvre and shape the battlespace to the point at which a decisive operation could be launched without first having to engage enemy forces to fix them. Instead, for example, the commander launches a high-tempo enveloping attack, exploiting the enemy's lack of awareness. The enemy is fixed by his own ignorance.

Once again, we must consider the counter arguments. In real warfare, the enemy is rarely fixed in the absolute sense even when engaged in ground combat. Fixing in practice is relative and produces relative advantages. The same would be true with information operations. The enemy will not cooperate and is likely to be not totally ignorant of the battlespace, but merely partially so. If we employ this concept, what we must avoid is using the 'fixing by ignorance' idea simply to wish the problem away. Fixing by ignorance will not work unless we combine aggressive information operations with high-tempo manoeuvre and fires. In common practice, it is likely that future fixing operations in an asymmetric scenario will combine information operations and ground operations to achieve the desired outcome.

The asymmetry of the 'one man-in-the-light' scenario should result in an unprecedented display of the principle of economy of force. The friendly force in such a contest should adapt itself to exploit the advantages that it has, resulting in real savings in time, logistics and lives. Precision warfare—particularly when pitted against its converse, mass warfare—should lead to economies in every dimension. It should also lead to overwhelming victory. Therein lies the danger of the asymmetric scenario. It is human nature to adapt when confronted with a challenge. The enemy will do the same. As we investigate future warfighting concepts, we must put ourselves in the enemy's shoes and ask the question: If we were faced with an enemy who had overwhelming advantages in battle, would we simply give up? Usually, the answer is a resounding 'no'. Instead, humans figure out a way to adapt themselves to the new situation.

It is this innate capacity to adapt that underlies the theory of combined arms and, incidentally, confounds theorists who envision a future battlefield dominated by a single arm or weapon system. No single system will ever prevail in real war because, no matter how effective it is, the enemy will eventually adapt to it. It is also true that the greater the effectiveness of the friendly force, the more quickly and urgently the enemy will react to diminish the advantage. Since the asymmetric fight we envisioned here confers such an overwhelming advantage to the friendly force, we can anticipate that future adversaries will race to defeat or avoid that scenario.

How would an enemy react to the asymmetry of the one man-in-the-light scenario? Obviously, the US Army can count on opposing nations and groups to continue their own technological innovation programs. When we demonstrate a technological advance in battle, we can be certain that future adversaries will attempt to develop their own technologies in order to defeat that capability, or at least to imitate it. Technological adaptation takes time and money, however. The enemy will also adapt itself through battlefield tactics. If the fight is too asymmetrical, the enemy will urgently avoid battle altogether and prosecute unconventional warfare instead. In extreme cases, the US Army will see its battlefield advantages become nullified through political realignments or even cultural revolution. By various means, potential enemies will adapt themselves to the US Army's successes, with the result that the asymmetric scenario will be short-lived.

Two men-in-the-light

It should not be a surprise that fighting in a symmetrical conflict will cause the US Army to modify its tactics again. The analogy offered earlier can help to point to some possible future warfighting concepts. Instead of reverting to the darkness of Liddell Hart's model, we must instead consider a fight between two men in a well-lit room, both of whom can see. How would such a fight differ?

First, there are some continuities. Reconnaissance remains a vitally important function. When both sides are in the light, reconnaissance is still accomplished primarily with the eyes. Likewise, on the battlefield, between two forces, each of whom can perform information operations, most reconnaissance will tend to be from sensors, rather than from ground action. It is clear that future contestants in war will emphasise information operations in general, and command-and-control warfare in particular, in order to defeat enemy 'eyes'. With both forces able to 'see', and with thorough reconnaissance being the prelude to victory, forces in war will develop an array of passive and active measures to reduce the enemy's perception of the battlespace and increase the perspicacity of the friendly force. If such a disparity can be produced, then the nature of the fight becomes, at least temporarily, asymmetrical again.

In the symmetrical fight, there will be little difference in the pattern of security operations discussed earlier. Both contestants will continue to employ the eyes in order to economise security. Both sides will tend to avoid the wastefulness of extreme security measures until the eyes detect an actual threat. It is obvious that, when the opposing forces each have greater reconnaissance capability, long-range strike operations will become a fundamental part of battle. Therefore, the two men-in-the-light will have to guard against hand-thrown weapons. When both sides were in the dark, long-range strike operations were of limited effectiveness. The advent of robust information operations will, however, lead to precision-strike capabilities that will extend the length, width and depth of the battlespace.

Of the three possible roles for the man-in-the-dark's outstretched hand, the fixing function will re-emerge when both contestants are in the light. It was posited earlier that in the asymmetrical fight, the friendly force could fix the enemy with ignorance, rather than with ground manoeuvre and fires. In the symmetrical contest, however, fixing by ignorance will not be possible. Commanders will again have to portion their available combat power between the fixing function and the decisive action. Combat between forces of similar capability tends to resolve itself in continuous attempts by both sides to fix the other. The delivery of the decisive action is often unfeasible and postponed while both commanders struggle to set the conditions for victory. It is even conceivable that a campaign will end in a tactical stalemate, with neither side being able to fix the other well enough to launch a dislocating blow.

For this reason, future warfare between forces that are similarly equipped and trained will feature fewer instances of positional dislocations such as envelopments and turning movements. Rather, such symmetrical contests will be characterised by functional dislocation—the attempt to render the enemy's strength irrelevant through the defeat of some key capability. There is a strong theoretical foundation for this assertion. In biology, the more advanced and complex an organism is, the more vulnerable it becomes to an ever-increasing array of threats. The diseases, injuries and other maladies that can kill a single-cell creature are infinitely fewer than the myriad that can harm a human.

The same is true in military theory. There was only a handful of ways to defeat enemy forces in the ancient world. An enemy had to defeat the phalanx's momentum, disrupt its lines or take it in the flank. Ultimately, the phalanx was defeated only when its men were routed. A modern division has many more vulnerabilities than a phalanx. It is a complex organism with physical, cybernetic and psychological weak-spots that are far greater in number and scope than those in primitive warfare. For this reason, symmetrical combat in the future will centre around each side's attempt to discern the critical vulnerabilities of the other and attack them, shattering and dislocating enemy functions as a prelude to defeating enemy units.

In general, future technology should bring about a reduction in the use of ground forces for reconnaissance, but only when that technology and the procedures that attend it are mature enough to provide the immediate, precise detail that ground reconnaissance now offers. Technological enhancement of the US Army's ability to perform information operations should move it into precision warfare, the theoretical converse to mass warfare. As a result, security operations—still a vital battlefield function—should become more economical.

Last, we should expect to see a form of 'cybernetic fixing' in future fighting, particularly in the asymmetrical scenarios. If the US Army can adapt its tactics to the advantages that come with information dominance, it can fix the enemy with his own ignorance rather than spend the time, resources and lives that it takes to do the job with ground forces. In more balanced contests, however, fixing is likely to re-emerge as a manoeuvre problem and become more difficult than before. To break the tactical stalemate that may occur, future commanders will seek to dislocate the enemy, primarily through attacking its critical and vulnerable functions, rather than its units.

With the entire US Army looking in earnest at future warfighting concepts, it can be sure of a lively and productive debate as the process advances. The US Army must continuously try new and innovative ideas—fully understanding that some may be wrong—until it emerges with a fielded digital force that is equipped with dynamic, effective and adaptive tactical doctrine. Switching on the light to illuminate Liddell Hart's blind men may be a useful way to fuel the debate.

8

Asymmetric warfare: myth or reality?

Group Captain Ian MacFarling

> *One is weak because he makes preparations against others;*
> *The other has strength because he makes others prepare against him.*
> Sun Tzu[1]

A symmetric warfare is a reality. There is no doubt that, since the beginning of the recorded history of war, people have fought wars in the way that suits their best interests—politically, socially, culturally and technologically. As a consequence, warfare has, by definition, always been unbalanced.

It is worth considering the events of 11 September 2001 and placing them in their historical context, but only as a side issue because the attacks on the United States should not be considered as an act of war. Terrorism is a security matter, not a defence issue. While defence organisations will become involved in responding to terrorist incidents, there are a number of ethical, social and legal problems that come to the fore when such crimes are seen as acts of war.

This chapter includes a consideration of what we mean by 'war' and what we mean by 'asymmetry', so that it is made clear how such asymmetry is an inherent part of warfare. What intellectuals have said about war is also considered. Most of these people have been non-military. In fact, we might go so far as to say that war and intellectuals are dichotomous. Intellectuals are often hopelessly impractical, and war—as Freud reminded Einstein—is essentially a practical activity.[2] The chapter concludes with a discussion of how we see warfare in the 21st century so that future potential asymmetries can be identified.

An issue for all scholars in the study of war is that few people define it clearly. The reason for this lack of clear definition is that war is essentially an archetype in the correct, dictionary meaning of the word. Accordingly, we can only understand it by its outcomes or consequences. It has no real definition of itself. The person who comes closest to a definition is Quincy Wright, who notes that 'war is a legal condition which equally permits two or more groups to carry on a conflict by armed force'.[3]

This definition raises the important point that war is an affair of states. How one defines a state is outside the terms of reference for this chapter but, if one accepts Quincy Wright's view that war is a legal condition, it is difficult to see how anything other than states can make war. His term 'groups' must mean nation-states. What is important to understand is that states have always been with us in one form or another.[4] Sun Tzu was quite clear in his statement about 'laying plans' that the art of war is of vital importance to the state.[5]

In his treatise *De Re Militari*, written around 390 AD for the Emperor Valentinian II, Vegetius refers to war as being an affair of the Empire. He argues that all warlike preparations should be towards its defence, while noting that 'no state can either be happy or secure that is remiss and negligent in the discipline of its troops'.[6] Given that Vegetius's small manuscript was the standard textbook for royal leaders—including Charlemagne; Foulques the Black, Count of Anjou; Richard I of England; Henry II of England; and the Prince de Ligne of Austria, who severally commanded armies in the service of their states over a millennium—the relationship between war and states throughout recorded history should now be clear.[7]

Any doubt that war is the province of the state is most memorably dismissed by Shakespeare's soldier, John Bates, speaking before the Battle of Agincourt in *Henry V*, '[W]e know enough, if we know we are the

| PEACE | OPERATIONS OTHER THAN WAR | WAR |

Emergency aid

Alliance warfare

Aid to the civil power

Localised war

Regional war

Maintenance of law and order

Peace enforcement

General war

Limited intervention

Hijacking

Protection of allied interests

War of regime survival

Terrorism

Wider peacekeeping

Sanctions

Humanitarian assistance

War of national survival

Coercive diplomacy

Peacekeeping

Figure 8.1 The spectrum of conflict

King's subjects. If his cause be wrong, our obedience to the King wipes the crime of it out of us.'[8] That is drawing a long bow, but as Michael Walzer notes, 'war as it is conceived, both in international law and in ordinary moral judgment, is the king's business—a matter of state policy, not of individual volition, except when the individual is the king'.[9]

We should also mention in passing Clausewitz, who was an intellectual and could never have met the demands he set out for a military commander in his own writings. He argued that 'war could not be divorced from the political life of the nation—it is not an abnormal situation, but merely the forceful realisation of a political aim'.[10]

Asymmetry

The spectrum of conflict set out in Figure 8.1 clearly shows the asymmetry in war. The range is between peace and all-out war, with a wide variety of activities in between.

It is possible that one side—such as the North Atlantic Treaty Organization (NATO) Allies in Kosovo in 1999—will regard the conflict as one where they apply coercive diplomacy at the left-hand end of the spectrum shown in Figure 8.1. Conversely the opponent, in that particular case Slobodan Milosevic, will see it as a war of regime survival, or might try to portray it as a war of national survival to ensure as much popular support as possible. Consequently, the way in which the contending parties fight will be determined by their perception of the nature of the conflict and the risks involved. Few of us would want to buckle in the face of great threat and—it is hoped—we would respond as the Melians did to the Athenian generals Cleomedes and Tisias when those two thugs threatened 'they that have odds of power exact as much as they can, and the weak yield to such conditions as they can get'.[11]

It seems therefore that asymmetry is natural. There will never be a situation where both sides in a conflict are so similar that they have the capacity to meet each other's manoeuvre in kind, and the opponents will severally view the conflict through the spectrum of their own interests. It also appears likely that we have misidentified asymmetric warfare as the tool of the weak. We see the weaker side resorting to stratagems that have the aim of negating the superior side's power. In fact it is a two-way street. The small street fighter will go for the groin but, when his big opponent gets up, the small combatant is in for a hard time. In short, size—as they say—matters. When we consider the US Air Force, we realise that that organisation has the same power as all other air forces in the world combined. In literary terms, it is analogous to being an English playwright in the reign of Elizabeth I. Unless your name was William Shakespeare, you would have spent your time in cynical emulation, rueful resignation, or jealous irritation. *Schadenfreude* would have also been a factor: there would have been the unspoken hope that the next production would be a flop.

In accepting the inevitability of asymmetry, there is another, less obvious, problem. The danger is that such imbalance will generate its own threat within the body corporate of the larger and more powerful player. Power brings with it the seeds of hubris, and one reason we need to consider the writings of the Roman scholar Vegetius is his longing to bring back the values that made Imperial Rome so formidable. Vegetius thought that, if only the Romans had kept to the standards of earlier times, they would not have lost so badly in the 4th century.[12] History, as Mark Twain loved to say, does not repeat itself, but it rhymes. There are plenty of examples in history where, as the belief in one's own omnipotence grew, weak opponents had an opportunity to get under the guard of the once great. There is a danger of great powers becoming so mentally and physically flaccid that they believe their own myths and no longer realise that their power is ebbing away.

Only when there exists a constant threat to provide context for a nation's military preparedness is it possible to develop skills that provide superior power, even when one is relatively small. The Israelis combined professional skill and sophisticated technology to defeat numerically superior enemies during the latter half of the 20th century. The main thought that arises in this instance is 'why on Earth would you want to live in a situation where threats are ever-present?'. Nonetheless, the conundrums posed by a long period of relative security also cause problems. We would all like an easy life, but the easy life makes us weak. To enlist Shakespeare once again, we face 'the cankers of a calm world and a long peace'.[13]

Military thinkers

Sun Tzu and his disciples were quite clear that all warfare is based on deception.[14] The aim is to achieve surprise in how you attack, with what, and when. These elements are all contextual. For example, if your enemy is very strong and difficult to attack, you must be prepared in case he uses the advantage of his strength to attack you. If, however, your enemy is recuperating, perhaps from an earlier campaign, then you should continue to harass him so that he cannot recover and present a threat to you. Also, though Sun Tzu did not mention it explicitly, this method of warfare gives you the advantage, because you are the one who keeps the initiative and thereby controls the combat.

The interesting issue with Sun Tzu's concept of asymmetry is that he places morality and ethics above all else. This approach conflicts with many—particularly Western—attitudes where 'win at all costs' drives the thinking. Sun Tzu then moves on to command and leadership as it is exemplified by a general's ability. The focus of asymmetry is therefore in many ways at the top of the organisation and it is all centred on the leaders. Thereafter it moves down to contextual issues. We move to the benefits of having the tactical advantage—or perhaps working to gain it. Then we come down to aspects of the force we command— which side is more disciplined—though to a Western mind this seems to be a repetition. The commander should define the level of discipline within his force.

All the way through his discourse Sun Tzu keeps giving us paradoxes. He mentions strength on the one hand as if it is a vital aspect, while later telling us that smaller sides with better skills and disciplines are the likely winners in any conflict. This observation leads us to consider the importance of training, which will produce an asymmetry because a trained unit will always beat a rabble, and the side that has the fairest system of punishments and rewards will be the best trained with the highest morale and best capabilities. We could say that the army that comes quickest to mind from Sun Tzu's description is that used by the greatest emperors of ancient Rome.

The writings of Vegetius do, however, reflect the fact that Rome was past its prime when he wrote the small book that would later become so influential.[15] He was a product of his time, and he provided the model text for all commanders in Christendom for at least the next millennium precisely because of his anguish at the decline of the Empire. It is interesting to note that, while he addresses most of the issues that Sun Tzu had considered long before in a different culture, Vegetius tends to look inward for the solution to the question of how military organisations should counter the inherent asymmetries between their own forces and those of the enemy. Four of the six elements that he stresses in his writing are related to one's own organisation. Only when the balance between discipline and the other essentials of training, strength and courage, has been achieved does Vegetius suggest that the generals need to consider the context of battle as defined by the tactical situation and the enemy to be faced. It is worth stressing that his view of war is that it is an affair of the Empire and the asymmetry within warfare is natural.

Intellectuals and warfare

The reason for delving—regrettably rather thinly because of constraints of space—into the works of the intellectuals is that they have much to tell us, which military officers frequently miss. Their seemingly innocent questions cause us to reflect more deeply on what it is that we do. In this short section we will look at three of the great minds of the last hundred years and one from the 19th century.

In 1932 the International Institute of Intellectual Cooperation, a subordinate body of the League of Nations, asked Albert Einstein to participate in its activities. The institute suggested that Einstein should open a frank exchange—with a person whom he was free to select—on any problem that seemed to be the most insistent of all that civilisation had to face. Einstein consequently wrote to Sigmund Freud in July that year on the issue of war.

Einstein had watched the increasing lethality of weapons with horror. He was also concerned that politicians could not provide the leadership necessary to prevent war or to stem research into new and even more lethal arms. It was obvious that some of those jockeying for power in several Western European nations during the early 1930s were intent on using military force to buttress their own position.

Einstein came swiftly to the point. He knew he lived in a cloistered environment, working on problems of theoretical physics, which did not help him offer solutions to the problems of humanity. He therefore turned to Freud for advice. He then asked the question that goes to the heart of this discussion. The proposition is that, if we accept that war is an affair of states, then it is a logical step to accept that those with power and influence within a state will be the ones that make the decisions for the rest of the citizens of that state. Einstein wanted to know how the majority could be persuaded—or coerced—into doing the bidding of a small and implicitly illegitimate group, especially when the majority stood to lose so much because of the actions of that minority. That is a question that remains with us today. There is a certain innocence about Einstein that is both endearing and astonishing. He had lived in such a closed world that he did not understand how unpleasant the real one was. One has the feeling that Einstein wanted something that was concrete—and completely unattainable. He wanted Freud to supply him with a neat template that provided a sequential list to guide his actions in dealing with these dangerous people and the problems they caused. It is perhaps pleasant for mere mortals to realise that even geniuses can be astonishingly naive, particularly in an epistemic sense.

Freud was not susceptible to Einstein's blandishments. He had met the scientist once before, in 1927, and had reported to a friend that 'Einstein understands as much about psychology as I do about physics, so we had a very pleasant talk'. He thought that he was about to embark on a sterile and tedious discussion, and the tone of his reply suggests some condescension. He started off with the relationship between might and right. Freud was insistent that war is a *practical* problem. He also felt that he could only offer observations on issues of war as they appeared to a psychological observer. He pointed out to Einstein that the use of violence was a normal way for people to resolve their differences. He noted that human instinct plays the major part in all relations—and both love and hate are essential: 'They are phenomena [that] arise from the concurrent or mutually opposing action of both',[16] or—as Doris Day used to sing in the plastic morality days of the 1950s—'you can't have one without the other'. Freud felt that the outcome was all-important. He came to two conclusions concerning the resolution of interstate conflict. First, he noted that one side had to abandon its claim. Second, the only way to achieve that outcome was to increase the pain by raising the level of violence being directed at that side so that they would eventually realise that the damage was too high a price to pay.

There is a good balance here in the practical issues outlined by Freud in that force meant violence, and when brought to bear, force would ensure that the victor achieved his end state. It is important to realise the essential nature of an end state in war, and we shall come back to this discussion later. The final issue, which bears so heavily on this discussion, is the issue of killing one's opponent. The world has changed significantly since Freud wrote about this matter in his letter to Einstein, though we still have 'darkness and the death hour rounding'.[17] The issue for us in the West is that we now have a situation where one side will achieve its final purpose by either dying as a martyr for a cause or by forcing the West to abandon its plans because it is not prepared to accept casualties at all.

This is true asymmetry brought on by a limitation in the collective psyche of one side rather than by the application of force on a vast scale.

As an aside, it is interesting that the correspondence between the two great men never reached its potential, and both saw the start of World War II fought with an asymmetry that they would never have considered possible when they began their discussion in 1932.

Freud's view of conflict in many ways paraphrased Clausewitz, who had few illusions about war and the behaviour associated with it. The issue for asymmetric warfare is that nowadays, with political concerns driving a desire to ensure minimal casualties, war, as waged by the Western powers, tends to be self-protective in nature, rather than balanced between attack and defence. Added to this newly discovered caution in the conduct of war, the laws of armed conflict should prevent excesses by prescribing proportionality and legality while proscribing revenge.

How different is the concept of restraint from Clausewitz's opinion. When we descend to his concept of absolute war there are no limits, and there is no imaginable act of violence—however treacherous or cruel— that falls outside the province of war, or in the realm of what he calls 'not-war', for the logic of war is a steady thrust toward a complete moral vacuum. That is why war is so terrible and why it is so awful to set the wheels of conflict in motion. In fact Clausewitz is telling us that each side in a conflict must seek an asymmetric advantage to ensure that they gain the initiative and win without losing everything to the other side.

The fourth and final intellectual considered in this chapter is the American scholar, Michael Walzer. His continuing civilised discourse should be a matter for our complete attention when we discuss all forms of warfare. He notes that philosophy and deep thought *should* help us in such difficult times—but they only do so indirectly. People are not usually philosophical in moments of crisis: there is often not enough time for this luxury. Walzer makes the apt comment that 'war especially imposes an urgency that is probably incompatible with philosophy as a serious enterprise'.[18] We can extend this assertion and say that those that have thought about the chances of war and its consequences will have developed a favourable asymmetry, because they will have canvassed the important issues in advance and are therefore less susceptible to surprise.

Several paradoxes continue to appear in all the writings that intellectuals produce on war. On the one hand—like Clausewitz—they tell us that 'anything goes', while on the other they maintain that there is 'a code'. Walzer tells us that going to war is a crime unless it is for the protection of the nation. When war commences there is—or should be—a set of rules for the behaviour of combatants. The protection of prisoners, the wounded and other innocents is paramount. There must be discipline to ensure that combatants behave as they should in moral terms. Yet, in demanding discipline and unfailing obedience, the state is actually requiring that its troops kill the enemy. It is odd that military discipline should be seen as antithetical to the morality of the state; yet in the last analysis, it is. It must be stressed that, without the authority of the state, combatants are just brigands, or 'wilful wrongdoers', as Walzer calls them—rather than loyal and obedient subjects defending, at great personal risk, what they believe to be right.[19] Without the state we have no legitimacy and all of our acts are criminal.

A historical example of asymmetric warfare

The campaign chosen as an example here is the Allied Combined Bomber Offensive against Nazi Germany during the period 1943–45. It is one of the best examples of asymmetry in warfare from the 20th century, because neither side could be called weak at the outset and ways had to be found on both sides to win what was—particularly after Casablanca in 1943—a contest to the death.[20]

This chapter will not revisit the bureaucratic wrangling and bitter inter-service battles, particularly in England, Australia and the United States, that characterised the debate over military policy in the years immediately following World War I. By the early 1930s the politicians—particularly in Western Europe—had come to believe the theories of Douhet, Trenchard and Mitchell, as well as the apocalyptic fiction of H. G. Wells. In late 1932 the British Prime Minister, Stanley Baldwin, summed up the current thinking about the terror of aerial attack on civilian targets:

> There is no power on earth that can protect the man in the street. *Whatever people may tell him the bomber will always get through* [emphasis added].

> The only defence is offence, which means that you have to kill more
> women and children more quickly than the enemy.[21]

People tend to remember the line in italics while forgetting the rather
nasty sentence that follows. In his remarks Baldwin argues for asymmetric warfare. This certainly happened, with the solution found, not only in
the Combined Bomber Offensive, but also in its counter—the integrated
air defence system that had its first test in the Battle of Britain—when the
Royal Air Force (RAF) managed to defend England against the German
attacks and stave off the Nazi plan for an invasion.[22] The lessons learnt
there were not lost on the Germans, who developed a particularly effective air defence system. The point of this example, though, is that this air
defence system denuded other elements of Germany's war machine to the
extent that it left holes through which Soviet and Allied ground forces
could move, albeit with great difficulty.

The Allied air offensive was conceived in the aftermath of the Allied
debacle at Dunkirk in May 1940 and Churchill's subsequent accession
to the prime ministership of England. Churchill wrote to Lord
Beaverbrook, the Minister for Aircraft Production, that he could only see
one way to defeat the Nazis. The British Army's losses in manpower and
equipment in north-western France had been so great that it could not
defeat the Wehrmacht on land and, with the German acquisition of the
Western European ports from Norway to the South of France, there was
no way the British Royal Navy could maintain the blockade it had
enforced with great success until May 1940.

Churchill was, however, convinced that, after Hitler had directed his
forces towards the Soviet Union, the one factor that would succeed in
bringing the Nazis down was a sustained aerial attack on the German
nation.[23] This was a fight for national survival, and Churchill validated
Clausewitz's theory that in the last analysis there are no limits to war. The
attack was sustained for the entire duration of the war, though there were
times when it looked shaky. The consequences for both sides were bad,
but the Germans were pounded to the point where they were on the verge
of defeat while the British Government only used a minor part of its total
war effort in prosecuting the Combined Bomber Offensive.

The British and Commonwealth rate of effort and consequent losses are staggering. They reflect the toll of around-the-clock operations.[24] Raids of varying sizes were launched on occupied Europe for almost 72 per cent of the nights between 1940 and 1945. There were over 307 000 individual sorties launched, and almost 8000 aircraft were lost. These losses represent an average attrition rate of just under 2.6 per cent of aircraft per mission. Raids of varying sizes were launched on German targets in occupied Europe on over 52 per cent of the days between 1940 and 1945. With respect to daylight operations, just over 80 000 daylight sorties were launched, and 1000 aircraft were lost, representing an attrition of 1.25 per cent per mission. Over this period, the weight of bombs dropped totalled almost one million tons. Overall the British and their Commonwealth and Dominion partners sent 125 000 aircrew on these raids. Tragically, the total casualties numbered almost 74 000, which represents 60 per cent of all aircrew.[25]

It is important to note at this juncture that the RAF bombing campaign of Germany constituted only 7 per cent of the total British war effort during World War II.[26] Attrition was horrendous among the bomber crews, but they created far more damage than they sustained. The US Army Air Forces—particularly the 8th and 15th Air Forces—suffered similarly high casualty rates. In the six months leading up to the Allied landing on the Normandy beaches, the attrition was astonishing. The details of American losses were recorded in Samuel Stouffer's groundbreaking study and are set out in the Table 8.1.[27] If it was not a defeat, it was—to quote the Duke of Wellington—a near-run thing. The consequences for the German population and for its war production were dire. Absenteeism rose to a 19 per cent average in 1944. Thus, when the German economy was finally getting on a war footing, it was functioning at about 80 per cent of what was planned through this factor alone. In addition, 9000 additional workers were used simply to repair bomb damage on a daily basis—further reducing planned production. The targeting of population centres caused massive displacement, with consequent disruption to the war effort. For instance, Berlin's population dropped by 1.3 million in eighteen months. This drop created a housing and food distribution problem in many other places that were also being bombed. These shortages must have been a further drain on the war effort. Moreover, the bombing had a significant psychological impact on

Table 8.1 United States Army Air Force losses in Europe January–June 1944

	KIA/MIA (%)	Wounded (%)	Total (%)
Fighter pilots	48.4	3.9	52.3
Light Bomber	23.8	11.2	35.0
Heavy	71.2	17.5	88.7

the population. Over 90 per cent of people surveyed immediately after the war stated that the constant bombing was the most difficult experience to bear.[28]

There were many reasons for the Germans to hate the bombing. Just under 600 000 were killed by the Allied bombing campaign. Another million or more were injured. Almost 3.5 million homes were destroyed, of which 600 000 were in Berlin. It is amazing to find that the statistics for German war production still managed to increase significantly. The effect of the bombing was to stop the Germans from expanding their arms production rapidly and supplying their forces in the field. A German analysis completed at the behest of Albert Speer noted that, while production had gone up, it nevertheless fell far short of what had been planned the year earlier. In all aspects of the production of military equipment, the Germans suffered a shortfall of at least 30 per cent. In essence, the Combined Bomber Offensive had stopped Germany from becoming an economic superpower.[29]

Furthermore, the Combined Bomber Offensive had caused a significant diversion of German resources from the various fronts to defence of the Nazi homeland. The Germans diverted at least 900 000 troops to the task of manning the anti-aircraft defences. They deployed almost 15 000 heavy anti-aircraft guns. When the effectiveness of the 8 mm gun against armour is considered in both the Western Desert and Normandy, the loss of these weapons represented a significant drop in defensive anti-armour firepower. About 42 000 light anti-aircraft guns were deployed in the German homeland; therefore the combination of the weapons and the ammunition they needed meant that there was a dearth elsewhere.[30] To perform the tasks associated with the Combined Bomber Offensive, the Allies had 12 000 frontline combat aircraft in the form of heavy bombers, light-attack bombers and fighter escorts. These aircraft had taken the war to the Luftwaffe so effectively that, on 6 June 1944, the Germans had 309 fighters and bombers to defend the Reich and make attacks on the invading Allied forces in Normandy. It had been not only a remarkably effective use of asymmetric warfare, but a devastating war of attrition that the Allies won handsomely.

The irony of the situation was that the German population did not collapse, and this is a subject for discussion in the aspects of future war. The average German's only aim in life was to survive the war. It seems that the Germans gave no thought to developing any form of resistance to the Nazi regime because that regime, with its SS and Gestapo, was more of a threat to its citizens and its armed forces than the bomber offensive was. It seems that there was a feeling that bombs were a matter of luck. Chancing your arm against Hitler was a matter of stupidity because, as von Stauffenberg and his co-conspirators found out in the latter half of 1944, there was no recourse to mercy.[31] The main point, however, was that the need to counter the Allied bombers distorted the later German war effort—and that is what asymmetric warfare is all about.

The Combined Bomber Offensive has been criticised from a number of perspectives: moral, political, strategic and economic. Also at issue is the question of leadership arising from Portal's failure to rein in his subordinate Air Marshal Harris, the Air Officer Commanding-in-Chief of Bomber Command. In his memoirs written in Spandau Prison, Albert Speer's reflected on the impact of the Bomber Offensive, but he was often suspected of trying to curry favour. The Nazi propaganda chief, Josef Goebbels, described the situation clearly when he wrote in his diary: 'The air war has turned into a crazy orgy. We are totally defenceless against it. The Reich will gradually be turned into a complete desert.'[32] The bomber offensive against the Reich had destroyed the German air defences and certainly made the final ground attack all the easier.

This example shows that asymmetry works both ways. To be sure, the Allies won and the Germans surrendered unconditionally in the end. Clausewitz had been vindicated. It is, however, clear that the strategy and tactics had been based on the victors' own views and outlook rather than those of their enemy. It seems that we make it far more difficult for ourselves if we do not understand the basis for our opponent going to war. The Allies saw the Germans as evil and demanded that that evil be cauterised by unconditional surrender. They did, however, still fight them as if the Germans were civilised. The Allies did not link the effects they wanted to achieve with the methods needed to persuade the enemy to surrender much earlier. They saw the war in terms of what we would now call national survival, while the Nazi leadership did not care tuppence for their people and were fighting a war of regime survival. When we misidentify the reasoning of our enemies we add to the complexity of war and add a few extra dimensions of asymmetry to our calculations.

The 1991 Gulf War

The most appropriate example of asymmetric warfare in the recent past is the 1991 Gulf War. The Allies' objective was to drive Iraqi forces from Kuwait. Later commentators have added another task, which was—if possible—to remove Saddam Hussein from office. It is unlikely that this latter plan was ever the case. If this were one of the coalition's objectives—which is by no means clear—then we can say that the first aim was achieved while the second failed miserably. Saddam remained in power for over a decade and three US Presidential elections later. It took another war, led by the son of the man who left him in power in 1991, to remove him.

The man that has probably had the most influence on airmen's thinking in the last 50 years is Colonel John A. Warden III. He was the US Air Force intellectual that developed the concept for Operation *Instant Thunder*, which was devised to target Saddam Hussein's leadership infrastructure. Warden was dismissed for his pains, but it was his plan that formed the basis for the air campaign against Iraq in early 1991.[33] As time went by, he modified his ideas and introduced the concept of the concentric rings that form the target grid of any enemy infrastructure. This plan is shown in Figure 8.2 where the rings have been superimposed over Germany in a comparison with the objectives of the combined Bomber Offensive of World War II.[34]

In strategic level targeting, the first target is the command structure and the communications system that connects it to its troops and the outside world. The second target is the key production sites, which in this

1. Command structure
2. Key production
3. Transportation system
4. Population and food sources
5. Fielded military forces

Figure 8.2 Warden's Rings: strategic level targeting

case would have been Saddam's nuclear–biological and chemical facilities. The third target set is the transportation system, which would have provided the logistic support to Iraqi forces in Kuwait. The fourth target is the people and their food—though the aim in the 1991 Gulf War was dislocation rather than physical harm. The final target is the fielded military forces—in this case the Iraqi military forces deployed in the Kuwait Theatre of Operations.

Warden's thesis has long been that, with the accuracy provided by the new weapons systems and the protection of the delivery system by stealth technology, it should be possible to attack all elements almost simultaneously or—as he put it—to conduct parallel warfare. This means that the sequence set out as one to five in Figure 8.2 does not have to be in that order. It can be tailored to match the enemy's structure but—and this is the big but of asymmetric warfare—it means that you have to have exceptional intelligence. Of course the Americans were deficient in intelligence, and they were not as culturally skilled as they could have been.

Following his work in the late 1980s Colonel Warden focused his plan for *Instant Thunder* with the use of air power's inherent advantages; speed, range, flexibility, precision and lethality. His target was Saddam Hussein and his Command, Control, Communications and Intelligence (C3I) system; and the fielded military forces that supported the maintenance of his Ba'athist regime. The general idea was to inflict strategic and operational paralysis on the adversary by striking key nodes in the adversary's war-making potential. The particular military target that took the greatest concentration of bombing was the Republican Guard, because its role was partly misidentified by American intelligence agencies.[35]

Saddam's power network was built on a set of organisations, which he controlled by fear.[36] The whole structure was designed solely to keep him in control. He achieved control by putting people from his tribe and family into the other elements of the structure. He then maintained his grip through his intelligence and security network, which up to and including the Gulf War hid its importance and the size of its structure. The infrastructure of totalitarian control devised by Saddam Hussein permeated every aspect of Iraqi life. Yet, while John Warden and his colleagues were targeting the Republican Guard as the most important element for regime maintenance in the Iraqi Armed Forces, they appeared to know nothing about the security and intelligence Network, which included 26 000 troops of the *Special* Republican Guard. Even then, this organisation was not the most important element in the 55 000-strong praetorian guard that Saddam had created for his own protection and survival.

As a result, Saddam survived despite being subject to one of the most asymmetric military campaigns in recent history. The air campaign developed by Colonel Warden and his colleagues certainly ensured that Saddam could not control his forces on the battlefield, made the ground campaign swift and introduced a fog of war that the Iraqi leader found difficult to penetrate, but it did not bring about his downfall. One of Warden's most respected colleagues is Colonel Philip Meilinger, USAF (Retd). He notes that air power—which brings about the greatest asymmetry in warfare—is all about targeting, and targeting is all about intelligence.[37] Destruction on the Basra road may be devastating, but if the leader does not care—and probably does not even know of the damage—then it might be a negatory effort.[38]

Sun Tzu was absolutely right in claiming that if you know yourself and your enemy you cannot lose, but while we often quote from him we seem to avoid actually implementing any of his ideas. Meilinger has used the tenets in his air-power theories. We must have another look to see if we can use any others.

From 11 September 2001 onwards

The terrorist attack on the World Trade Center on 11 September 2001 deserves some mention. We saw the normally peaceful skyline of Manhattan destroyed in a matter of hours by evil men. The destruction and surrounding damage is difficult to comprehend, but it was not an act of war. In simple terms, it was a criminal act that succeeded because of a failure of domestic security within the continental United States.

The attackers did not represent any nation-state. Michael Walzer was right when he pointed out that people such as these are merely a robber-band.[39] They did not use weapons, but employed normally peaceful equipment in an unprecedented and devilishly cunning way. Their leader is not acknowledged as a leader or member of any nation—even a rogue nation—and none have claimed him or accepted responsibility. This was a crime against humanity. It was not war. It is important to note, however, that, had a rogue nation carried out this sort of attack, it would definitely have been one of the cleverest acts of asymmetric war the world has seen. The choice of the method of attack would have been a hallmark of weakness in the rogue state, as well as of the inability of the international community to prevent such attacks completely.

Given that we still do have rogue states in the world, it is appropriate to direct some effort to considering what lessons they might have learnt from the events of 11 September 2001 and whether they might believe it necessary to act this way.

Asymmetric warfare is the only way of war. It is a reality and has been so since wars began. It will generally be the act of the smaller against the larger—though the stronger, the more professional, and the better-equipped can still defeat the weaker. The most worrying problem in the nature of asymmetric warfare is that, when the weak are pushed to the limit and there seems no way out except to bow to the inevitable (as was the Melian case reported by Thucydides), they will usually seek an apocalyptic outcome because they have little or nothing to lose. One nuclear weapon or other forms of nuclear, biological or chemical weapons will wreak havoc on the strong. We must avoid the Athenian thuggery and disavow the concept that Thomas Hobbes so ably translated: 'They that have odds of power exact as much as they can, and the weak yield to such conditions as they can get.' Not only is it totally amoral, but it is a call to disaster.

So what does this mean for armies in the future? As far as a liberal Western democracy such as Australia is concerned, we will never be guilty of prosecuting an unjustified war. Armies such as our own will either be protecting those that Michael Ignatieff calls 'the people who make the misery of strangers their business', or we are going to be defending ourselves against unjust aggression.[40] Countries such as Australia still occupy the high moral ground; such an attitude should therefore enable us to be a force for good and also the trusted broker, if that is a role we are allowed to play.

From an Australian perspective, we need to realise that the Australian Defence Force (ADF) is one of the small street fighters of the world. We must therefore develop superlative warfighting skills that accentuate the positives in our inevitable asymmetric situation while reducing as far as possible the negatives. Consequently, the ADF needs exceptional intelligence—in both meanings of the word. All of the good intelligence in the world is worthless if we are not intelligent enough to use it properly. We need to ensure that everyone understands what air power really means so that we fight where our side has control of the air—for without it we will surely die. The need to ensure control of the air means that we must be able to prosecute joint operations—and joint must not fall prey to single-service rivalries. The ADF must evolve beyond the mere appearance of cooperation and the Services must understand each other's cultures to maximise mutual trust and remove those stupid prejudices that—even now—abound within the military. If we can do those things we might just win.

Whither the close battle—British Army operations: 2015 and beyond

Colonel Richard Cousens

There is a general assumption in Western armies that the close battle is the pivotal and most significant aspect of warfare. This has certainly been the case in past history, but there are some indications that the revolution in military affairs (RMA) might be signalling the eclipse of the close battle, if not its demise. This chapter explores our love affair with the close battle and its continued relevance for the future. It describes the British Army's vision of the 2015 battlefield together with the significance of the close battle within it, in order to identify some difficult decisions on the horizon that may strike a chord in the Australian and other armies. I will discuss UK thinking on the framework of the future battlefield and identify some bitter pills that may have to be swallowed.

We are having difficulty in identifying the true potential of digitisation and we are hampered by a cultural malaise that is emotionally wedded to the equipment program rather than to the concepts to which the equipment should be subordinate. This is a problem with which many modern armies are familiar. Conceptual thinking in the United Kingdom for the battlefield of 2015 and beyond is mature and effervescent. Following a fixation with peacekeeping, we are now focusing back on warfighting—the gold standard of military capability. We need to explore a particularly sensitive idea: the notion that the primacy of the manoeuvre elements in the prosecution of decisive operations is fading and that consequently the significance of the close battle is changing. These considerations provide a signpost to possible changes in our structures over the next fifteen years.

In a recent paper titled *Close Combat—Lessons from the Cases of Albert Jacka and Audie Murphy*, Dr Michael Evans makes the categorical statement that 'close combat has been the defining feature of war in the past and is likely to remain so in the future'.[1] Evans concludes that 'success in war usually requires first-class infantry to close with, and to finish off, an enemy. There is no other way of winning.'[2] He also refers to the 'mystical appeal of close-quarter combat', alluding to a 'long history of eager participants'.[3] Finally he offers the thought, 'men-at-arms, not military machines, give Western society the mythology to nourish its martial pride and traditions'.[4] Most soldiers can readily identify with all these sentiments. They stem from our history, our culture, our tradition and heritage. The walls of infantry messes all over the world are adorned with tributes to those that fought and died in bloody close combat. I select but one example of the pivotal significance of the close battle in war:

> When dawn came, it was found that friend had bayoneted friend, foe foe, and that the .303 bullets poured so furiously inwards, had gone equally furiously outwards to the other side of the perimeter and there settled in many an Australian limb. [*sic*] From that time onwards the order was that the enemy was to be engaged at night only with bayonets—and we gunners, who had previously used bayonets solely for the purpose of opening condensed milk and bully beef tins, now had to view these beastly weapons in a new and more serious light which filled us with dismay.[5]

There is no better description of the bloody nature of the close battle at its closest than that of Russell Braddon in *The Naked Island* describing the battle for Malaya in December 1941. It reinforces all of Evans' remarks and most soldiers would identify strongly with them. There is certainly no denying that some close combat will indeed be an enduring feature of war. However, as someone who was recently Director of Force Development for the British Infantry, I have to ask whether this is becoming an institutional comfort-blanket that is masking a genuine RMA. Is it an excuse for clinging to branch-specific structures that have less and less relevance in a battlefield involving the orchestration of capability rather than branches and cap-badges? Perhaps it gives credence to Field Marshal Slim's remarks that:

> Generals have often been reproached with preparing for the last war instead of for the next—an easy gibe when their fellow-countrymen and their political leaders, too frequently, have prepared for no war at all.[6]

I will not deviate from my aim by exploring the nuances of the RMA debate. They are familiar to most soldiers, and there is a similarity between the United Kingdom and Australian approaches. Michael Evans has addressed the issues in depth in his recent paper on Australia and the RMA, which he concludes with the remark:

> The designation of information capabilities as a separate capability grouping—with more funding than that assigned to improving current strategic strike—is perhaps the most fundamental indication of how Australia has come to view the knowledge edge as the foundation stone of its military capability in the 21st century.[7]

The foundation of the British approach to the RMA is similar and has been best described by Dr Tim Benbow of Oxford University. Dr Benbow identifies the various RMA schools of thought as being the 'radicals, visionaries, moderates and pessimists'. To declare my own position on this question, I am in the camp of the radicals.

It is no secret that, as we prepare to refocus the British Army for high-tempo expeditionary operations, we are equipped with major weapons systems that weigh over 30 tons and are a legacy of a previous era, configured for continental warfighting. The problem is that, if one takes today's ideas—or worse yesterday's—as the point of departure, there is a danger of compounding the error of taking an evolutionary approach. Only by making a clean conceptual break from the present can we design an army for 2015 and beyond. Like the Australian Army, the British are making some progress in achieving the necessary break with old ways of thinking. Making such a conceptual break is a big challenge for us. We still have some officers who have a romantic fixation with the I(BR) Corps structures in

Germany, and there is often an assumption that all the capabilities deployed in Germany must be replicated in the future. Such an idea would result in all of the intellectual, financial and equipment problems inherent in the evolutionary approach to developing future military concepts. There is no more precise description of the need to break with the present than that offered by General Gordon Sullivan (former US Army Chief of Staff) and Michael Harper in their book titled *Hope is not a Method*. In it they explore the need to look back from the future rather than evolve from the present. Strategically, this idea is perhaps the key point of this chapter from which all else stems. Sullivan and Harper believe that:

> Looking back from the future begins by going back to the most basic questions: what is your purpose as an organisation; what business are you in? What will your purpose tomorrow be? What will the characteristics of your strategic environment be? What will it take to win in tomorrow's markets? Don't ask yourself what the 'next' organisation will look like. The 'next' organisation is constrained by today; it must evolve from today's organisation. By imagining the 'after next' organisation, you can take off today's blinkers and imagine your organisation in a world unconstrained by its present reality. This technique does not deny the reality of the present but rather helps you think beyond it.[8]

In short, if we focus on tomorrow, we are almost guaranteed to get it wrong. The key therefore is to focus on the day *after* tomorrow. Taking General Sullivan's advice to heart, it is appropriate to describe briefly the British Army's view of the 2015 battlefield and, in so doing, identify some of the more controversial issues for resolution over the next few years. Most of these issues indicate the direction of ongoing Australian analysis, and this is certainly the case for the fundamentals that reflect three constants and five changes.

First, warfighting will remain the benchmark against which to train and prepare. Operations in Bosnia, Kosovo, Macedonia and Sierra Leone notwithstanding, we remain an army configured for high-intensity warfighting in the belief, to put it crudely, that you can 'dumb down' to peacekeeping but you cannot 'dumb up' to warfighting. Second, asymmetric attack will become a more prominent feature of warfighting and we must be configured to conduct asymmetric attack ourselves as well as defence. In the light of the horrific attacks in Washington and New York in September 2001, this is the understatement of the century. Nevertheless, we must not pretend that, because the term is currently in vogue, it is new; it is not. Third, the need to preserve fighting spirit and a unique ethos remains important. We accept that a regimental system is inextricably enmeshed with the ethos and fighting spirit of the British Army and that it provides the enduring foundations of the moral component of its fighting power. These then are the constants. What about the changes? The multinational dimension of warfighting will increase; future adversaries will be more diverse and unpredictable, and are unlikely to accept the moral and legal constraints that impinge on us. Operations in 2015 and beyond will be set within a joint campaign, with the army commander drawing on joint capabilities to a far greater degree than today—facilitated by digitisation. Indeed, the availability and use of information will profoundly change the way in which the army operates. This last point is the most important one of all and it merits expansion.

Brigadier Jim Wallace, who recently retired from the Australian Army, has written extensively on the effects of digitisation. In a recent paper he stated that 'one of the main motivations for digitisation in advanced western military establishments is the belief that the process will impose a new order on the inherent chaos of the battlefield'.[9] Wallace rightly identifies the enhancement that digitisation brings to decision making and emphasises the need for it to be balanced by firm battlefield leadership. However, in the context of 2015, digitisation is much more than command and decision making, and the British Army has been slow to appreciate the more holistic benefits to warfighting as a whole. As for the Americans, the debate has been fogged by the Gulf War, which was perceived to be revolutionary but actually was not. In his book, *The Next World War*, James Adams suggested that:

> The 1991 Gulf War was the last hurrah of the armed forces and generals who had trained on the legacy of the Second World War. War had changed its form with the arrival of stand-off weapons and precision guided munitions.[10]

He noted that, though the equipment had changed, the tactics had not and observed:

Mile after mile of tanks, armoured personnel carriers and fuel trucks; serried ranks of tents marching in perfect order over the horizon and runways shimmering in the desert heat.[11]

What, then, are those changes in tactics and structures that digitisation will facilitate? It is my belief that they will have their greatest impact on doctrine.

The constants are the manoeuvrist approach and the notion that tempo is the key to success. Manoeuvre warfare theory will continue to be the doctrinal bedrock for the British approach. As for the changes we expect, they include terminology, more emphasis on capabilities that enhance tempo and greater interoperability through common doctrine. Herein, incidentally, lies considerable scope for a revitalised and more dynamic American–British–Canadian–Australian (ABCA) armies program. As the recent chairman of the ABCA Quadripartite Working Group (QWG) on Manoeuvre, I remain an ABCA enthusiast but feel that perhaps the bureaucracy and fixation with process tend to inhibit dynamic output. The question of how the whole ABCA program functions has been addressed by Lieutenant Colonel Grant Johannsen, who has published an important paper on the topic.[12]

In 2015 and beyond, what will be the relevance of the traditional framework of the battlefield (deep, close and rear) in a battlespace that is acknowledged to be dispersed, non-contiguous and non-linear? Does it continue to have relevance when operations are progressively enemy-focused rather than terrain-focused and where holding information is arguably more significant than holding ground? How can one describe close and rear operations in such an environment? These questions reflect a deep debate within the United Kingdom and, at the 2001 Future Army Study Period, hosted by the Chief of the General Staff, a number of one-star officers who participated actually voted to dispense with the old framework. Whither the close battle indeed?

Once again, there is merit in identifying constants and changes. In deep operations the constants might be summarised as follows. The first constant is that the corps, division, brigade and battlegroup hierarchy remains valid. Whereas today the lowest level at which deep operations are prosecuted is the division, we believe that around 2015 it will become the brigade. Attacking the enemy's centre of gravity is the second constant. The third constant is the need to commit ground forces in deep manoeuvre. Overcoming the considerable difficulties involved in the indirect engagement of moving targets is the final constant.

The changes, however, are far more significant and far-reaching than the constants, and perhaps point to the eclipse of close operations as we know them. Deep attack will be increasingly joint and integrated, and deep operations will be increasingly *decisive*. There will be much greater reach: long-range precision artillery, air manoeuvre, electronic warfare and the contribution of both maritime and air fixed-wing and long-range missiles will deliver synchronised fire at ranges out to 300 kilometres or more. Digitisation is the enabler, not just the enhancement to C2 but also the sensor-to-shooter links. Air manoeuvre will deliver greater operational impact than ground manoeuvre and planning will be much more complex.

As for close operations, some form of close combat continues to be inevitable, but the changes are profound. There are several alternatives to striking including, perhaps, isolation and neutralisation. The range and volume of the close-combat zone will increase, rendering existing capabilities inadequate—a legacy of the analogue era. The RMA comes into its own in this case. Sensor and shooter will be much more difficult to conceal. There will be enormous changes in the way that combat arms fight. These changes include more capable infantry that is smaller, digitally empowered, light, lean and lethal; highly significant and much more integrated artillery, with increasingly joint effects and the demise of dedicated forward observation officers; and a much greater contribution by aviation and hence, if there is a close battle, it is likely to be a product of air manoeuvre—not ground manoeuvre—with a significantly reduced logistic drag. Another change is that the armoured effect will be less likely in decisive operations; they are unlikely to be there, but if they are, their effect will be from much more dispersed locations.

We need to examine the implications of having a smaller but more capable infantry. At a recent infantry trial of battle group thermal imagery installed in the Warrior armoured fighting vehicle (AFV), a corporal remarked, 'Who needs close recce now?' He had a good point. He was sitting in an AFV with better firepower, mobility, protection and surveillance equipment than his colleagues in a reconnaissance platoon equipped with Combat Vehicle Reconnaissance (Tracked) (CVR(T)). In addition, the Warrior would not offer the unique signature of a reconnaissance unit. We are arguably wedded to the concept of manned reconnaissance but, with the technology now available, do we need dedicated reconnaissance platoons anymore? The scope is huge: equip the mortar platoons with 120 mm mortars and top-attack precision-guided munitions and dispense with anti-tank platoons but, above all, equip the soldier to cue and initiate effect from fire units that may not be integral to his unit. The days of the decisive close battle at less than 2000 metres must surely be numbered. The see–tell–act cycle can now include the manoeuvre elements and suddenly the potential exists for an infantry company commander to see, to tell and to act at ranges far deeper than today. The answer for us lies in the Future Infantry Soldier Technology (FIST) program. It is the UK equivalent of the US Land Warrior program.

FIST has particular potential in urban operations, an area in which concepts, tactics, techniques and procedures have changed little since 1945. The British approach is to acknowledge that close combat remains one of the most demanding tasks of all but that the trend should be to make close combat less close. Thus, while developments will never completely negate the need to close with the enemy, the aim will be increasingly to locate the enemy, neutralise their capabilities and break their morale and will to fight while at a distance. We owe it to our soldiers to use technology in order to remove them from danger, where this is feasible. Some current US Marine Corps modelling of urban warfare projects a casualty rate of 33 per cent. No small army such as ours can afford to sustain a high-casualty rate from an old-fashioned, close and attritional activity. There has to be another way.

Of course rear operations continue, but those that cling to the linear divide between rear and other operations may be mistaken. The battlespace will be more seamless and the United States concept of 'an expanding area of close combat' is becoming very attractive in the Directorate of General Development and Doctrine. The need for any commander to maintain his freedom to manoeuvre, and to support and sustain operations while preserving his force, will be increasingly important. It represents a role for medium forces. There will be a definite impact on future structures as a result of some of the conceptual thinking outlined in this brief account.

A prophetic article in *The Economist* of 4 January 2001 sums up the strategic drivers nicely:

> As late as 1938, Britain's Neville Chamberlain could get away with calling Czechoslovakia a far-off country of whose people we know nothing. That is a vanished past. Now, except for a few sealed-off corners of Africa and Asia, what a ruler does to his people is swiftly revealed by camera, satellite and Internet to a large, interested and reasonably well-informed audience; and, if what he does is outrageous enough, the audience is likely to want something done about it.[13]

The UK defence *Future Strategic Concept* paper indicates that Britain is likely to have to deploy forces more rapidly in order to deliver strategic effect. The emphasis is not just on rapid deployment but on operational impact once deployed—what we call 'rapid effect', which requires sufficiently capable forces to be effective in theatre in order to deter, pre-empt, or contain a crisis, that is, a 'medium capability'. We foresee that a medium capability will be based on the enhancement of existing forces, in particular by the merging of light and mechanised infantry into light mechanised infantry. We also intend to improve the characteristics of armoured reconnaissance, taking advantage of enhancements in firepower, digitisation and ISTAR (Inteligence, Surveillance, Target Acquisition and Reconnaissance). Significantly, there is an opportunity to do this within the current equipment program through the Future Rapid Effect System (FRES). The FRES concept aims to develop a group of armoured platforms that have broad utility, greater tactical and strategic deployability, and greater commonality. The FRES might blend the armoured battle group support vehicle (ABSV), multi-roled armoured vehicle (MRAV), TRACER and the future command and liaison vehicle (FCLV). The FRES concept is an important issue, but the key point is that the transition towards medium forces is well under way.

Structures are bound to change. The British Army will continue to benefit from the retention of a regimental system that reflects the fighting traditions and ethos of its soldiers. This being said, we require *a* regimental system and not *the* regimental system. As it has always done, our regimental system will continue to evolve. The emphasis for ground manoeuvre on balanced forces, versatility, high tempo and a growing 'medium' capability may begin to prove that the traditional distinctions between armour, armoured infantry, and mechanised and light forces become less helpful. Similarly, the traditional boundary between firepower and manoeuvre could become blurred in close combat, leading to a much closer integration between the two. Indeed, we are likely to acknowledge the subordination of manoeuvre to firepower and an effects-based approach. Hence not only whither the close battle, but also whither the Directorates of Infantry and Armour as separate entities?

In the 2000 edition of *The Australian Army in Profile*, Captain Glenn Jones wrote an excellent piece on 12/16th Hunter River Rifles. His conclusion is a classic:

> The history of the regiment is proud and honourable. Its continuing success is grounded in its traditions, values and its ability to incorporate change as needs have changed over a century of continuous capability.[14]

He has identified the central theme. Status quo is not an option and the current generation of staff college graduates in the United Kingdom are not as wedded to the past as some of their predecessors, particularly because they have been educated at a joint staff college. Ownership of assets is no longer an issue; the key is the ability to cue those assets in order to produce effect as deep as possible. The close battle will indeed, as Michael Evans suggests, remain an enduring feature of war but it will not be *the* defining feature of war. Our love affair with close combat leads perhaps to backward-looking evolution when what is required is a lust for the deep battle and forward-looking revolution.

A debate on the challenge posed by terrorism

In this chapter a symposium of senior officers and security experts consider the implications of the terrorist threat for future conflict. The symposium is an edited version of a remarkable panel discussion that took place at the Chief of Army's Land Warfare Conference in Canberra on 10 October 2001. The panel discussion was a free-flowing dialogue between a group of authoritative military and civilian thinkers, and was interpolated with questions from an audience of military officers and security experts. The panel included authors of other chapters in this book: General Sir Michael Rose, Major General Duncan Lewis, Lieutenant Colonel Ralph Peters and Rear Admiral Raja Menon. Also participating was Mr Clive Williams, Director of Terrorism Studies in the Strategic and Defence Studies Centre at the Australian National University.

Lieutenant Colonel Ralph Peters has previously expressed the view that, to face the threat of terrorism, Western armies may be faced with a new requirement to act with degrees of brutality that they are not used to. What implications does this have for the rule of law?

Ralph Peters: I have to say that I have never subscribed to Michael Walzer's view of just and unjust wars with that rigid peacetime, academic, on-the-safe-campus view you get. Sometimes you fight not the just wars but the necessary wars, and it is necessary to win them. In the aftermath of 11 September in the United States, a number of instant myths sprang up, or returned, from the dead. One of the myths—really pernicious, and always from leftist-campus intellectuals—is that, if we behave with the brutality of our enemies, we become as bad as them. As an aside, I do hope that, as a result of 11 September, we will witness a rebirth of the intellectual Left. One consequence of the brutal attacks on New York and Washington has been to expose the more utopian cultural relativist fantasies of many ivory tower-based scholars. They are still in confusion now because all these supposed folk-dance groups are bombing the World Trade Center.

As Ian MacFarling suggests in his chapter on the combined bombing campaign during World War II, we answered Japanese and German aggression and savagery with literally immeasurable brutality of our own. We fire-bombed German and Japanese cities, and ended up by dropping two atomic bombs. By the end of the war in the Pacific, US marines and soldiers were enjoying burning Japanese soldiers alive with flame throwers—and they did not read them their rights first. Those soldiers did not come home to the United Kingdom or Australia or the United States to stage a military coup or to transform it into a police state; they came home gladly, to liberal democracy and at peace. I often hear intellectual arguments, or insistence—they are not even arguments, but insistence—that if we behave badly, if we fight hard, we will become evil. Such arguments are an insult to our people. The people of our countries can do a dirty job well and come home without turning into monsters.

Sir Michael Rose: I would disagree totally with everything that Ralph proposes. I also disagree with those that suggest that terrorism is an inextricable part of all warfare. You can have isolated acts of terror—a person planting a bomb in a supermarket trying to extort the owner of the supermarket to pay money—but that is not at all what we are up against.

Terror is a part of warfare; it is a part of revolutionary warfare. Anyone who has read anything about revolutionary warfare will know that the onset of revolutionary warfare is the creation of acts of terror among the civilian community in order to get the government to respond in certain ways—it is to be hoped in oppressive, violent and brutal ways. If we are going to fight a war, and we are going to win that war, we have to understand that it is a war. Secondly, we have to understand that we have to obey the rules of war; that is, if we carry out counter-acts of terror even more efficiently than the terrorists carried out their acts, then we are playing into the terrorists' hands, and we are making the problem worse. The way you win terrorist or counter-revolutionary wars is to stay within the law. It is about people's attitudes; it is not about body counts. It is about the acquisition of extremely good intelligence, and you do not get intelligence from people if you are bombing them. If you take the current global war against terrorism, the centre of gravity is clearly the attitudes of the majority of the nearly one billion Moslem people around the world. If we overreact to what happened on 11 September, we are merely going to play into the hands of the people who perpetrated these crimes. We have to keep the majority of the Moslem people on this planet on side, and we have to gain the intelligence that we need to target our attacks specifically and precisely in the way that we can do with all the modern technology that we have.

If we obey the rules of counter-revolutionary warfare—which is that it is going to be protracted; it is about the gaining of intelligence; it is about the winning of the sympathy of the people that are the oppressed people from among whom terrorism has been spawned—then we will win. You can be mighty violent while you are doing it, but you will have to be violent in a specific way.

Duncan Lewis: I also disagree with the comment that Ralph made, if I understand correctly the thrust of his comments in answering that question. I think there are limits with regard to the way one manages terrorism. Inevitably, there is going to be—as there always is in conflict—brutality on both sides. I do not resile from the brutality, but I think the point of your question was related to the legality. I can tell you now that, in my personal view, you must never step over those lines that your government defines as being legal, and I for one would certainly not do that.

Ralph Peters: I will just clarify that point. I am not arguing for bombing Afghanistan flat, by any means. I am not arguing for wantonness. I am saying: 'Do what is necessary'. That is all.

Sir Michael Rose: I would just add that any violence has to be very well directed because if it is not, you provide further ammunition to the adversary, who can then use the media to portray the violence on our part as unacceptable. I think we have to maintain the moral high-ground at least.

There is of course another legal aspect, which separates what happened in Hamburg, Würzburg and Dresden in the last war from what we can do today; and that is the postwar Geneva Protocols, which quite specifically state that attacks on civilian persons or property are prohibited.[1] Since we all have ancestors—fathers, grandfathers, uncles—who fought so that we would live in a better world, it would seem retrograde to go back to the pre-protocol days.

Raja Menon: This question has got into some very interesting areas. Terrorism grows not straight out of peace. It grows through acts of insurgency first. By the time you get to the levels of terrorism being conducted in certain areas, you can be quite certain that the courts will not be functioning. The reason why the courts will not function is because no witness will be prepared to give evidence. Look at the Sikh terrorist movement. The result of their activities was that no court was functioning. If a court functioned at all, it had to function *in camera*, because even if there was a suggestion that a witness was going to give evidence, he would be murdered. There are practically no courts functioning in Kashmir today, not because the judges do not sit, not because the Public Prosecutor is not there, but because no witnesses come forward. I will give you an example of one of the biggest counter-terrorist operations we ran against the Liberation Tigers of Tamil Eelam (LTTE). On 16 January 1993, we captured a ship, the MV *Ahat*, with 28 people in it. They were carrying 55 tons of arms and ammunition on the high seas, 220 miles south-east of Madras. We shepherded the ship into territorial waters and then asked for its surrender. Then everything went wrong. People on board started biting on cyanide capsules, jumping overboard, setting the ship on fire. The commanding officer lost his nerve and opened fire, and there was no way they were going to surrender. What we did not realise at the time was that Sathasivam Krishnakumar, alias Kittu, the number two man in the LTTE was on board, and no way were they going to surrender. Everyone who jumped overboard was picked up.

Given that in the entire State of Tamil Nadu there would not have been a single man willing to give evidence against the LTTE, a special court was set up in a different State. They were taken there. The LTTE's organisation in London provided the best Admiralty lawyers, and so after a trial of one-and-a-half years every one of them walked. Thereafter, when we did catch people like these on the high seas, we let them approach the Sri Lankan Coast and merely told the Sri Lankan Air Force where they were and looked the other way.

Sir Michael Rose: Can I just make a point about the use of law in any terrorist war, any kind of terrorist action. Of course the British have had 25 years' experience of this in Northern Ireland, where it is still going on in a lesser form. When faced with terrorism, all countries have to adopt new measures and emergency provisions in order to combat terrorism because the laws that are designed to combat crime are totally inadequate for combating terrorism. Therefore you do have to give people the right to stop and search; you do have to have non-jury trials. Incidentally, the southern Irish Government brought non-jury trials in long before the British Government in the North did so. There are several such measures. France, Spain, Italy and Germany have all done the same when confronted with terrorism within their own countries. However, when you introduce this kind of terrorist legislation, you have to be careful that you do not allow it to act against you in the long term. For example, if it is seen as an oppressive measure and is perpetuated after the terrorist campaign comes to an end, then of course you will be playing once more into the hands of the people who carried out the original terrorist act, but of course you have to have different laws to fight it.

Ralph Peters: One of the problems that is emerging from this exchange is that 'terrorism' is not an adequate word to describe all the varieties of violence we are seeing. There are differences between the Basques and Osama bin Laden in motivation, scope, skill and practice. It is necessary to be explicit. We will never be loved by certain parts of the world, and where we cannot be loved, we must be feared.

Now, that sounds harsh but think about something please. Consider who is participating in this debate. It is an historical anomaly that we now hear the cutting edge of military thought from representatives of the world's greatest, oldest and largest democracies. Has there been a time in history when democracies were the cutting edge of military thought? The reason we are is not that we are such a grand bunch of guys, but it is because we have to be. We are hated.

Duncan Lewis: What I prefer to address is al-Qa'ida, which is obviously going to be an area of interest to you. In recent years we have generally regarded 1968 as being a watershed in terms of terrorism because at that time there was a considerable amount of change taking place. There were the after-effects of the Six-day War; there was the social ferment in Europe; there was the antiwar campaign in the United States and so on. From that point, there was a great increase in the amount of terrorism, particularly involving Palestinians internationally, but the event on 11 September represented a sharp turning point in terms of the numbers of people that were killed. Until that point, the most that had been killed were 329 people on an Air India flight in 1985, and now suddenly we are looking at over 3000 people killed. That is a substantial difference.

Al-Qa'ida has been mounting attacks since 1992, and if you look back over the number of attacks that they have carried out and the nature of those attacks, one thing that comes through is that they are becoming increasingly sophisticated. Some of the points that came out of 11 September were the sophistication of the operation itself; the fact that they achieved surprise; the fact that very careful preparation and planning went into it; that, in terms of target selection, they have gone for both military and civilian targets over the years; and more recently they are going for symbolic targets as well. The fact that we are seeing 'propaganda of the deed' is another issue that we need to consider. Most of us are aware of what al-Qa'ida says it is about and why it is doing these things. Its priority has been its objection to the US presence in Saudi Arabia. It has, however, also invoked the situation with the Palestinians and the Israelis. Its third major cause, which is perhaps less well known, is the fact of the people that have been already convicted for terrorist offences in the United States, such as Sheikh Abdul Rahman, who was imprisoned subsequent to the 1993 attack on the World Trade Center.

We have known quite a lot about al-Qa'ida for a long time. What we lack, though, is some knowledge about their capability and a great deal of knowledge about their intent. That is where we certainly need to do considerable catching up in the future. It is very difficult to deal with al-Qa'ida because the way it operates is out of sanctuaries in Afghanistan. It is very difficult to get at the leadership. They have operational and support cells in a number of countries. They use human couriers to go backwards and forwards carrying messages. The agent handlers never leave Afghanistan. The couriers have a limited amount of information. Consequently, if you roll up one cell, you are not going to get another cell because it is a different agent handler dealing with that. What they tend to do is that they set up an operation with a number of simultaneous events often unknown to other cells. The attacks against the US embassies in East Africa demonstrated the security provided by the existence of these cut-outs.

At the end of 1999, when al-Qa'ida was planning to conduct attacks on Los Angeles Airport, in Jordan and against a US ship in Yemen, each operation proceeded in isolation from the others. The Yemen attack was subsequently the attack against the USS *Cole* because the original attack had to be aborted when the suicide boat carrying the explosives sank. Obviously, despite having fewer explosives, the attack on the USS *Cole* was successful and it demonstrated that al-Qa'ida had learnt from its mistakes. This is an enemy that is difficult to penetrate from an intelligence point of view and difficult to deal with militarily as well. The evasive nature of this opponent is an issue for us in terms of our future operational strategy. The initial US response, which was to mobilise Reserves and call up the National Guard, did not address the real problem. It did, however, make people feel better that something was being seen to be done.

The problems that have arisen in the course of successive conflicts in Afghanistan reflect many of the challenges that we may face in the future. In terms of dealing with terrorism generally, longer-term issues involve finding—as has been the case in Northern Ireland—a common ground where we can deal with them after working out exactly what their political aims are. When the pain has diminished in the United States, it might be prudent to think about reducing the US military presence in Saudi

Arabia, and putting pressure on Israel to come up with some sort of accommodation with the Palestinians. I do not expect that people will be released from gaol in the United States: that would not, perhaps, be appropriate. These are some of the issues that need to be considered for the future in dealing with the sort of threat that al-Qa'ida presents to us. Ultimately, even if we kill or apprehend Osama bin Laden and his senior associates, we will still be faced with the problem of these Wahabi cultists who will continue to be a difficulty for us.

One of the questions that is on all of our minds is the implications of 11 September for national and international security. We have been watching the kinetic attack going on against targets in Afghanistan—targets that are quite difficult to identify. Even at the time that these attacks took place, Secretary Rumsfeld stated that they were not the complete solution by any means. In fact, I would argue that it is doing more to make us feel better than to resolve the problem. There are, however, two consequences of the events of 11 September that have changed things profoundly. The first one is the effect in a global sense: that those events have now touched everybody in this global village. If you take the global village analogy one step further, we have had an attack on the High Street in the global village in New York, and the marketplace—the World Trade Center—is lying in smouldering rubble. There are very few folk on this globe that will not be affected one way or the other, either directly or indirectly, as a result of those events. Then you cannot help but draw down: how does that affect us locally, coming from the global level to the local level?

I can recall, as a cadet, going up to Sydney—I was eighteen years of age—and for the first time seeing a policeman with a weapon. I had never seen police armed in the streets before in my life. I went to Heathrow as a lieutenant and for the first time had my bags frisked as I went through the airport security guards. We just had not experienced that sort of thing in Australia in the past. I recall parking my Avis hire car outside a pub in the Cotswolds. I had parked illegally while I went in for a couple of glasses of orange juice, to find that it had been towed away by the local authorities for fear that it was a bomb. The point I am making is that Australia has had, with one exception in 1942 for a short period of time, a situation of absolute community security and safety. I am not sure that is the case anymore, and I fear that for all of us there is going to be a massive intrusion in our domestic arrangements and our domestic lives. This intrusion will be both an irritation and, as importantly, maintaining high levels of security will impose significant costs on the government. The last and probably the most telling aspect is that this conflict is going to leave a legacy for our children. They will be living with this sort of arrangement for the rest of their lives.

Raja Menon: I am not very familiar with the network of terrorism that arises from West Asia or the Hezbollah Syrian–Iraqi–Iranian connections. I am only familiar with what happens in the subcontinental nexus. That is quite big, with 360 000 Muslims. There are 70–80 000 Madrassas in Pakistan alone—and I am not trying to make a point just about Pakistan. The reason why those Madrassas have grown is that the education system in Pakistan has collapsed, and the reason why that has happened is that government spending has collapsed, and there are two reasons for such a collapse in public spending. One is that Pakistan's Government has no money because people do not pay any taxes, because there is no law and order. The other is that Pakistan spends four times what India spends per capita on its Army.

The reason why this situation has come to pass is that, after Partition, India adopted democracy and eventually got a parliament consisting of people whom the elite in India looked down upon because they eat with their mouths open and do not know what clothes to wear. These people, however, represent the very population that votes for them. There is therefore a political process. When I was ten, I was traumatised by the fact that when the communists came to power they took away all our land and we were left with just seven acres. It has left a very deep impression in all our minds.

In contrast, land reform has not come into Pakistan even today. The Bhutto family owns 14 000 acres. Within the estate of that there are private armies, private transportation corps and all kinds of things. It is true that 22 families rule Pakistan. Unless social reform comes in, economic progress is not going to take place. Nawaz Sharif said that the reason he wanted the Army's help in running Pakistan was that, as he put it, 'I have 2500 schools on the rolls of the Education Ministry that actually do not exist'. You cannot get 2500 fictitious schools unless the legal process, the police, the CID, the income tax have all been brought into the net. He said, 'The only way I can get rid of this fictitious number is to tell the Army to go in and find out whether these schools exist or not'.

Without significant social reform Pakistan will not get the money to run schools so that the Madrassas lose their appeal. The existence of the Madrassas is in a way like the Roman Catholic Church, which is transnational, but in a benign way; however, there is also a transnational Islamic movement. The biggest of these movements is the Tabligi Jamaat, which is again a benign organisation, it is to be hoped. The Tabligi Jamaat is an organisation that asserts a missionary and charitable function among Muslims, not only in Pakistan, but in other countries. Its last meeting was in Singapore, when around 50000 people met. Their funding is international and the organisation conforms to what the Koran says, that Islam recognises no national boundaries.

The reason I raise this issue is that these international organisations administer significant financial transactions. It is much easier for the people who run finances to run centralised non-government organisations. You do not fund one terrorist organisation. Terrorist organisations are grouped together under umbrella organisations. For instance, there is the Harkat-ul Mujaheddin, which was previously called the Harkat-ul Ansa. Members of this organisation kidnapped the five foreigners in Kashmir and the organisation was then banned by the Americans in 1997. The organisation merely changed its name so that it could open accounts in Pakistan under a new name: Harkat-ul Mujaheddin. There is the Jaishe Mohammed, which has carried out a series of car bomb attacks. There is the Lashka-e Toiba and then there is the al-Qa'ida. They all have big funding organisations, the source of which is very interesting. You can say that it was originally the Afghan poppy trade, but the Afghan poppy trade was being converted into heroin. The heroin is then transported from the north to the south through the help of the Interservices Intelligence (ISI) Organisation of Pakistan. The largest industrial organisation in Pakistan is the Pakistan Army, which runs the Fauji Foundation, which has over 250000 employees. It also runs the National Logistics Corporation, in whose trucks the heroin is transported. The eventual umbrella organisation for all this is in fact the ISI Organisation. The structure for these arrangements was set up by General Hameed Gul, who is a loose cannon and who was eventually sacked by the Pakistani Army.

The reason I mentioned this is that all these terrorists are not as other-worldly as you might imagine. A terrorist operating in Kashmir gets 25 000 rupees a month, which is the same pay as that for a three-star general in India, but he serves for a much shorter period. When he dies, his family gets 500 000 rupees. All this money is made available through somebody, and this money, which used to run through the heroin trade, does not run anymore. General Musharraf has done much to bring the poppy trade under control—which has been a positive development. However, stocks still exist: close to 700 to 800 tons. Money for terrorism is still coming from private Saudi financiers. There is an Islamic tradition that every year you give a certain amount of money for charity. There is a Saudi gentleman who comes every year to Muridke, which is the training centre for terrorist activity in Kashmir run by the Lashka-e Toiba. He comes to see how his money is being spent, and he is very happy when he is shown people running to shoot and kill. He goes back to Saudi Arabia very happy every year.

We have had discussions with French Intelligence and with American Intelligence about Saudi money. This money is coming through banks. The *Time* magazine says that the money is coming in through Hawallah (or *hawala* in Arabic), which is an unofficial method of moving money through intermediaries, thus getting around financial regulation systems. However, Hawallah is not what is being used for funding terrorism. The money is actually coming through banks. Most of these banks are reputable, international banks in which you and I bank. Through personal contacts, I also know that there are keywords that have been put into the banking system so that when you make a money transfer, if words such as Hizbul, Mujaheddin and Osama appear in that system, they can be removed. The international banking system is already sensitive to this matter. It is therefore not clear to me why this money flow cannot be stopped. We also know in India that, for instance, most of this money comes through the Gulf states, whose rulers are taking a cut.

It is axiomatic that terrorism does not procreate if terrorists do not have access to media coverage. In what way can governments get the media to assist in somehow mitigating the effect of terrorism on a community, especially international terrorism? The sight of those aircraft hitting the twin towers of the World Trade Center was horrifying. It was like a movie created by Spielberg rather than reality. That shock went through the whole of the Western world and delighted many people in other places. Is there a way that the press can support us in somehow limiting the propaganda effect of this terror?

Sir Michael Rose: It is a problem that the British tried to confront a number of years ago in Northern Ireland. When she was Prime Minister, Margaret Thatcher decided to starve the terrorists of their oxygen—the media coverage they were getting—and we had the absurd sight of actors on television acting the words of Gerry Adams as he was giving some speech somewhere. The message that came through after a year or two was that you cannot control the media even within your own country, let alone around the world. It is a problem that you have to confront. You can confront it because the majority of people in this world do not like terrorism. There has been no example in history of terrorism ever over-throwing a state.

Tony Blair went on television the day after Osama bin Laden had been on television specifically to counter his points. You have to engage constructively with the media. If you try to suppress what the terrorists are saying, you are playing into the terrorists' hands. They will get their message across some other way. It is far better to allow them to spout the nonsense that they do, for the horrors of their acts to be seen around the world, and let them condemn themselves.

Ralph Peters: We have heard a great deal since 11 September about address-ing the root causes of terrorism. I do not underestimate the importance of the mistakes that the United States and other countries have made in the Middle East, but the root cause is that we are succeeding and others are failing. We cannot force others to succeed, so sometimes we must force them to behave. We can do that if we have the strength of will. Although there has been great international reaction to this incident and people can visualise aircraft going into the Houses of Parliament or the Champs Elysées, I still do not think that it has come home that you are not dealing with rational actors with serious political goals. These are fanatics in the true sense of the word. These are people that, if they could push a button and kill every one of us, would push that button and call it a good day's work well done. Make no mistake, despite the crocodile tears and the protestations throughout much of the Islamic world disowning these acts of terrorism. The hijackers of 11 September will go down in Islamic history as true and revered martyrs. Osama bin Laden is on the road to being remembered in future centuries as a successor to Saladin. We are dealing with a serious threat and at some point you just thrust the sociology aside and without wanton killings, without the slaughter of the innocents in Bethlehem, you do what must be done.

This is ultimately a contest of strength of will. I think we can muster that strength of will. There is a point past which discussion in the theology of theory has to be set aside. We must not be wanton in the exercise of our power; it is too easy to sound like a warmonger, and we do not want to kill everybody from Suez to the Hindu Kush. We must have the strength of will to do what must be done, and if we do not, then we will be the victims for a long time to come. One last point: we hear nonsense about how killing terrorists makes them into martyrs. The quickest way to make a terrorist into a martyr is to apprehend them, charge them, try them and put them in gaol. Then you have no end of kidnappings and hijackings and other terrorist incidents trying to set them free. Osama bin Laden has made the point that the imprisonment of terrorists in America is one of the reasons for his attacks. There are no good terrorists, but the best possible terrorist is a dead one.

In his chapter, Group Captain MacFarling invoked the Roman author, Vegetius. Now Vegetius did long for the lost virtues of republican Rome. These lost virtues included, when necessary, levelling Carthage and sowing the ground with salt. I do not really think that we are in screaming disagreement here. Although I am wearing the black hat in this discussion, I will simply observe that success will always be forgiven.

Clive Williams: In my view, people such as bin Laden are rational actors. They have a game plan; they know what they want to achieve. He probably miscalculated the reaction that would occur from the United States. Anyone that sits down with a council of four and works through an operation, decides how they are going to do it, what the likely reaction will be, and how they will exploit that, has to be someone that is a rational actor and knows what they are trying to achieve. It is not the kind of thing that you would expect if somebody does things on the spur of the moment. That to me is an irrational actor, who has not really thought through the consequences. I certainly think that, in the case of al-Qa'ida, they are very careful about what they are trying to achieve and they know what they want.

Is it possible to forecast Osama bin Laden's next move? Does he have any options, or does he have to remain in the region and tough it out? Do you believe that it is viable for him to stage other attacks to try and draw attention to his dilemma in Afghanistan?

Clive Williams: I think what is going to happen is that Kabul will fall fairly quickly and the Taliban will pull back into the Kandahar area. If they are forced out of Kandahar, they will go into the mountains between there and Pakistan. They will be supported there by the ISI, which has supported them up till now. Therefore I think that it will be difficult to get at Osama bin Laden. They probably have a couple of operations in the planning stage, given that in some cases they have gone several years in advance. Obviously there would be a greater degree of difficulty in undertaking those operations now. It might be possible, for example, to contain their cross-border infiltration of that area and their movement through Pakistan. It will, however, be very difficult to contain them. One of the concerns is the use of weapons of mass destruction. I would rate the risk of chemical and biological attack as low, and radiological attack as a possibility. One concern, though, is nuclear attack. People tend to discount that, but I do recall back in 1998 that General Lebed was talking about the nuclear charges that were to be carried by Spetnatz to detonate behind enemy lines. These charges were to be used against NATO. They were 1 kiloton. The Russians apparently had 132 of those weapons. They have accounted for 48, but they have not accounted for 84. Bin Laden has been interested in those nuclear charges, and so have the Chechens. There were media reports only a few of weeks ago saying that the Chechens had managed to obtain a couple of those weapons.

The threat of such an attack is a dimension that we need to think about as well because it sounds extraordinary, but so does flying aircraft into the World Trade Center. Putting a suitcase-sized nuclear device in

Trafalgar Square gives you a lot of leverage. Such an attack would reduce to ground level everything within 500 metres. Therefore it is quite a catastrophic weapon. I am not necessarily saying that Osama bin Laden will always go for catastrophic events, but obviously those have more impact than anything else. Taking out the Golden Gate Bridge during rush hour, for example, would focus people's attention. Perhaps he will go for lesser attacks, as he did with the USS *Cole*. He is very difficult to predict; that is why we need much better human intelligence than we have now.

Duncan Lewis: It has been interesting to watch the various Western Alliance leaders dancing around the issue of the relationship between mainstream Islam, radical Islam and terrorism and how they are trying to break the nexus between fundementalism and a major world religion. Like probably many other people here, I have had the privilege of living in several Islamic countries for protracted periods of time. When you have had that experience you come to understand very well where those dividing lines are between what you regard as the noble form of another religion that is fine in its pure sense, and at the other extreme this issue of terrorism.

There are, in my personal view and my personal experience, a great many people in the Islamic communities in the less-developed world that do, as Ralph pointed out earlier, dislike us. That dislike ranges from a little bit of dislike through to an intense hatred. It goes right through the spectrum of less-than-positive emotions. One of the issues to which we are going to have to pay a great deal of attention, as a global community, is how we address that question and bring what are largely disaffected slabs of our community into the whole. This task of reconciliation is not going to happen overnight; this is something that our children will still be addressing.

Raja Menon: I am sure that most of you have read Mohammed Attah's last will and statement. He was one of the hijackers—the pilot of one of the aircraft that flew into the World Trade Center. If you read his statement, you find him exhorting his people to die and to approach God in a clean state and fix their resolve to go through with the act. What struck me most was: why pick on the United States? If something in his own psyche, his teaching, his desire and his religious beliefs required him to die, and exhort all his fellow conspirators to commit suicide, what has that to do with the United States? It is bizarre. His intense desire to die has nothing to do with this country on the other side of the globe. Somebody has put that into their heads. The formation of such attitudes is taking place in their religious indoctrination. Who is turning out the preachers that are imparting these messages? It is the Madrassas. Of course not all theological schools deal much in fundamentalism. However, the source of the theological exhortations—teaching, preaching—is starting from these schools. It is not impossible to interfere with the prevailing philosophy of these schools because they are by and large pretty broke. It is possible to influence financially the way in which these religious schools function. It is an option that we ought to consider.

The military profession in Australia: crossroads and cross-purposes?

Hugh Smith

The military profession in Australia faces critical challenges—not from an external enemy but from pervasive technological, social and political change.[1] The so-called revolution in military affairs is permeating the business of fighting, increasing its complexity, pushing up budgets and demanding greater skills from personnel. Changing attitudes and expectations in the community are causing young people to be more reluctant to enlist in the military and are making it increasingly difficult to retain serving members, while in the eyes of society the status of the military profession seems less secure than in the past. World politics is giving rise to conflicts that are entangling the armed forces of many nations and proving resistant to easy resolution. At the same time globalising trends are leading to more complex and subtle threats to the security of states—from people-smuggling to pollution, from transnational crime to international terrorism.

These developments combine to present the military profession with fundamental challenges. Modern military forces are being asked to take on a wide range of non-military tasks that are of a continuing nature and perhaps set to increase in number. The question arises whether armed forces should continue to focus primarily on their inherited warfighting role at a time when traditional war seems less and less likely. Furthermore, these developments have brought the human factor to the fore. People have always been essential to military effectiveness, but today the requirement to understand and lead people has become absolutely critical. To handle the ongoing process of transformation, armed forces need people who are capable of dealing with three major challenges.

First, they should be able to understand emerging threats to security. No longer do militaries direct their attention mainly to dealing with organised, armed forces that, while dangerous, are more or less rational and predictable. There is a need to understand communities where groups and factions deploy violence in unfamiliar ways, and individuals act with apparent irrationality. Second, they must know how to develop strategies for dealing with the complex range of tasks now assigned to the military on a more or less continuous basis. Taking on new roles raises fundamental questions about the *raison d'être* of the military profession as well as problems of force structure, equipment, doctrine, training, education and the ethos of military service. Third, they must manage and sustain the profession itself. Recruitment and retention of military personnel has become problematic in many Western countries—in part because of changes in society, in part because of uncertainty as to the present and future role of armed forces. The challenge here is not only that of numbers and quality of personnel but also that of ensuring the military profession is able to contribute to the debate about its own future.

Against this background the military profession is at a crossroads and perhaps at cross-purposes. Failure to meet this array of challenges is liable to be just as fatal to national interests as poor equipment or faulty strategy. It goes without saying that meeting them will be all the more difficult if budgetary constraints apply and perhaps increase. This chapter sets out the nature and implications of the growth in military roles. It examines some of the problems as they have been manifested in Australia; and concludes by offering suggestions for dealing with them by reforming reserve forces, making the best use of education, and sustaining military professionalism.

Table 11. 1 Expanding roles of the military

	Australia	International
Warfighting	World War II	World War I, World War II, Korean War, Vietnam War, Gulf War, Afghanistan
Force, short of war	Aid to the civil power, counter-terrorism	Counter-insurgency (Malaya, Vietnam) Peace enforcement (Somalia, East Timor)
Constabulary roles	Offshore law enforcement	Peacekeeping (Cambodia)
Humanitarian tasks	Assistance to the civil community	Natural disasters, mine clearance

Changing roles of armed forces

Underlying these challenges to the military profession is a fundamental shift from traditional roles and structures to what has been called the 'postmodern military'.[2] In place of large, heavily equipped and often conscript armies designed to fight one another—as we saw in the 20th century from World War I through to the Gulf War—many countries are adopting smaller, all-volunteer, specialised forces that are preparing not only to fight wars but to conduct peace operations, engage in law enforcement, and undertake humanitarian missions. Where once soldiers were recruited to prepare for and fight wars, they now train for, and engage in, a wide array of tasks.

Governments have always turned to military forces to perform tasks other than war which they consider useful. What is different now, compared with the last two centuries, is the scale, scope and political salience of the wide range of roles now assigned to the military. Four main types of activity can be identified—each of which can have a national or international focus (see Table 11.1).

Warfighting

The traditional task of Australia's armed forces is warfighting whether in defence of the nation or to protect Australia's wider interests, either in isolation or as part of an alliance or international force. Traditional war is directed primarily against the organised forces of other states or political entities, although irregular operations may also take place. In such a war lethal force is used, and used extensively. Since Vietnam, Australia's involvement in warfighting has been relatively small and infrequent.

Force, short of war

This is the application of force where the opponent is not a regular military formation and/or where violence is unstructured. At home, aid to the civil power and armed counter-terrorism fall into this category. Abroad, Australia has taken part in counter-insurgency operations and in Chapter VII peace enforcement. (The Vietnam War, it may be noted, embraced both warfighting in the form of combat against regular North Vietnamese forces and counter-insurgency.) In these situations lethal force is always likely and may often be necessary, sometimes on a large scale. But hostilities generally take place among civilians and against opponents difficult to identify.[3] Force, therefore, is liable to be highly constrained by political, legal and moral factors.

Constabulary roles

This includes ADF assistance to law enforcement agencies at home and offshore policing of fishing, smuggling, people movements and other, similar roles. In the international context it refers to Chapter VI peace-keeping, peace monitoring and similar tasks. Force is unlikely to be employed but is always possible, particularly in self-defence. When force is employed it is generally on a small scale, and with a preference for non-lethal action. Having armed force in reserve during constabulary operations, however, may help gain acquiescence from recalcitrant parties.

Humanitarian tasks

At home and abroad, humanitarian tasks include search and rescue, assisting communities during and after natural disasters, the delivery of emergency supplies or medical support. Force is not normally part of such activity though it might prove necessary on a small scale, for example, to deal with looters or to protect the delivery of humanitarian supplies.

Like many other Western armed forces, the Australian Defence Force (ADF) has shifted rapidly and perhaps irreversibly from a mission-based institution solidly focused on the traditional role of warfighting to a task-oriented organisation expected to perform any or all of a wide range of activities. This expansion of tasks has demonstrated that armed forces are particularly versatile and valuable organisations in times of uncertainty and change. Far from losing their utility as conventional war seemingly becomes less probable and less valuable to states, armed forces are proving extraordinarily useful to governments. They have three types of advantage over other entities—organisational qualities, physical assets and human resources (see Table 11.2).

Of the three sorts of advantage, human resources are the most important. Good people can perform well with poor equipment and inadequate organisation, but good equipment and good organisation rarely make up for inadequate people. An organisation with good human resources, however, is not easily created and is not cheap to run. Investment in people is a long-term and inexact science. Nor can money always solve people problems in the way that it can solve equipment and even organisational problems. Critically, too, human resources are mobile. Physical assets can be locked up or screwed down; organisational qualities can be preserved and protected. But human beings can simply get up and walk away.

Problems facing the Australian military profession

The problems facing the military profession are troubling armed forces in many Western and non-Western countries. In Australia, personnel

Table 11.2 Advantages of armed forces

Organisational qualities
- direct government control
- hierarchical structure and disciplined action
- readiness to act
- flexibility
- coordination of information and communications
- persistence against opposition and endurance

Physical assets
- destructive power
- protective capacity
- transport
- logistic capability
- surveillance, collection and analysis of information
- communications

Human resources
- skills and capabilities (training)
- knowledge and learning (education)
- judgment (intuition, empathy)
- initiative, flexibility
- teamwork and cohesion
- discipline (external) and commitment (internal)

matters have received increasing attention in recent years both inside and outside the Department of Defence. The Defence Efficiency Review of 1997 led to the creation of a Defence Personnel Executive to bring together all human resource matters, including education and training. Other Defence-initiated reviews include *Serving Australia*, which reviewed the full range of issues and put forward of a set of principles for managing personnel; the Grey Report, a review of harassment at the Defence Academy with implications for the ADF as a whole; an inquiry by Justice Burchett into military procedures following allegations of 'rough justice'; and a comprehensive study of military remuneration.[4]

Outside Defence, the Australian National Audit Office has taken a particular interest not only in financial matters and project management but also in personnel questions.[5] Another important barometer of public concern is the number of inquiries by federal parliamentary committees into matters relating to personnel—a total of five major reports between 1994 and 2001 (see Table 11.3) as well as many other inquiries that have

Table 11.3 Parliamentary inquiries into personnel matters

Sexual Harassment in the ADF	1994
Senate Standing Committee on Foreign Affairs, Defence and Trade	
Officer Education: The Military After Next	1995
Joint Standing Committee on Foreign Affairs, Defence and Trade	
Military Justice Procedures in the ADF	1999
Joint Standing Committee on Foreign Affairs, Defence and Trade	
Rough Justice? An investigation into Allegations of Brutality	
in the Army's Parachute Battalion	2001
Joint Standing Committee on Foreign Affairs, Defence and Trade	
Recruitment and Retention of Defence Personnel ·	2001

Source: Senate Foreign Affairs, Defence and Trade References Committee.

touched on these issues. Such interest is important not only because it engages politicians and is often bipartisan, but also because it offers opportunities for serving and former members of the ADF to air their concerns while protected by the privileges of parliament. Thanks to modern technology their words are placed on the Internet for the entire world to see. This alone suggests a radical change in the nature of military service.

It is clear that the military profession will face its challenges under the close scrunity of other agencies of government, parliament and the media. Three key issues for the military profession in Australia can now be identified.

Can the profession recruit and retain personnel?

The first issue is the challenge of recruitment and retention.[6] The ADF has faced declining recruitment across the board in recent years. Shortfalls have occurred despite a nearly 30 per cent reduction in the size of the Defence Force—from about 69 000 personnel in 1991 to about 49 500 in 2001—and despite an absolute increase in the number of the population in the 15–24 age group. (Numbers in this group will continue to increase in absolute terms until about 2013 after which steady decline will set in.)[7] Though inquiries from potential recruits have risen recently, the proportion of those inquiries that resulted in actual enlistments has fallen.[8] Advertising may be running up against the law of diminishing marginal utility.

As long ago as 1974, Professor T. B. Millar's report on the Citizen Military Forces noted less respectful attitudes towards constituted authority and the changing priorities of younger people.[9] For whatever reason, we live in what has been called a post-deferential society in which ready acceptance of military service is rare. But there is another fundamental factor that underlies recruitment difficulties. Only fifteen years ago the appeal to potential recruits was relatively straightforward: prepare to fight in defence of Australia and its interests. Today, the appeal may be anything from combat to humanitarian assistance.

The dilemma is that if the Defence Force presents itself as a multitasked organisation (as much current advertising does), it loses the traditional focus on warfighting—the unique reason for its existence. This image may discourage potential recruits (and dismay some serving personnel) who are keen to prepare for war. If, by contrast, it presents itself simply as a warfighting organisation, the Defence Force may lose the interest of those who want to do other things apart from preparing to fight wars that may never happen. At the same time such an approach misleads those who join with the expectation that they will be engaged primarily in warfighting.[10]

Retention, too, remains problematic as serving personnel place the desire for more satisfying employment, family concerns and the option for second careers ahead of undivided loyalty to the Defence Force.[11] These considerations have long been known, but seem more influential than before in decisions to leave. It is also apparent that retention is being affected in various ways by the range of new tasks the military must now perform.

What is the military profession for?

The challenges posed by the increasing diversity of military tasks lead to a second set of questions concerning the role of the military profession. What does a military professional do? Traditionally, soldiers trained for and fought wars—defending national borders against military attack or promoting national interests abroad by force of arms. During most of the 20th century this was the unquestioned *raison d'être* of Australia's armed forces among both military professionals and the general public. Today, however, the prospect of conventional war between states has waned (and the prospect of major conventional attack on Australia almost disappeared). Instead, armed forces find themselves gainfully and continually employed in a wide range of activities other than war. This inevitably impacts on structure, doctrine, training and ethos as personnel prepare for what they actually need to do. Yet they cannot simply abandon the traditional focus on warfighting without undermining essential organisational qualities. The ethos of the warrior is the glue that holds armed forces together.[12] In these circumstances debate within the profession is essential and desirable, albeit sometimes wearying and seemingly endless.

The nature of the new tasks also means that personnel have to function under pressure at a high tempo. They are likely to be deployed overseas or in the field more frequently. These commitments often 'overstretch' individuals and are liable to cause discontent and family stresses. Personnel are expected to prepare for war and to exercise aggression, but also to show patience and compassion in dealing with civilians in difficult and possibly dangerous circumstances—from starving populations to rioting mobs to fractious 'boat people'. Dealing with such problems may be traumatic for the individual soldier and lead to long-term psychological effects. Society, moreover, expects higher standards of personal behaviour from the military than the rest of society in relation not just to military performance but to harassment, sexual relationships, political activities and so on. Those in uniform may wonder whether too much is being asked of them.

As well as internal difficulties, there are organisational challenges from without. Any institution that performs a diverse and expanding range of tasks that extend beyond its traditional boundaries can expect existing or proposed organisations to seek to take on some of those tasks. Other agencies may develop to take on some of the law enforcement and peacekeeping functions performed by the ADF. The proposal for a separate coastguard such as exists in many other countries is a clear case of the trend to disperse security functions more widely. The growth and use of private security and protective services (including by the military itself) is another example. Even the deployment of violence is increasingly seen in many parts of the world as suitable for operations by other government agencies (the CIA now controls a number of missiles) and by civilian contractors as the provision of security takes to the marketplace.[13]

Can the military profession sustain its own identity?

The broadening range of institutions engaged in the provision of security bears on a third kind of problem for the military profession: can it maintain a positive self-image and retain (or restore) its status in society? The military is not alone in facing this challenge. In Western societies there has been a widespread loss of trust in professionals, perhaps as the public becomes more educated and more ready to criticise, perhaps as some professionals have been found wanting in ethics and competence. Most professions have come under greater scrutiny from the media, clients and consumer organisations, often with unhappy results.

The military in Australia have a fine record—that extends from Gallipoli to East Timor—consequently they enjoy general public esteem and respect. There is high regard for the individual in uniform and broad public support for the ADF.[14] But this could be dissipated. In recent years the media have made much of spectacular embarrassments. These have included: harassment on Royal Australian Navy ships and at the Australian Defence Force Academy (ADFA); allegations of mismanagement over the *Collins* submarines and other high-cost projects; the public sacking of the Secretary of Defence; and criticism of senior leadership evident in the consultation processes in 2000.[15] Dealing with these sorts of problems is important out of consideration for equity, efficiency and effectiveness, not simply out of a desire to improve public relations.

Another fundamental challenge to the military profession is to be found in the sustained efforts to consolidate the Australian Defence Force and the civilian Department of Defence into what is termed a single Defence Team. While some administrative and policy-making benefits exist, there are drawbacks. A distinct military contribution to policy-making is not always evident, and complaints have been heard that a distinct military voice has been lost or diminished.[16] Forums conducted in the Defence Force as part of the 'Action for People Plan' revealed a concern that the distinct character of the military profession was being eroded and its contribution undervalued. Similar complaints have been heard in Britain.[17] The key point is that the military and the public service are really different professions with different perspectives and ethical priorities. Rather than trying to harness a horse and an ox to a single cart, it is preferable to recognise a distinct profession of arms and a distinct profession of Public Service.

A third challenge is presented by the Commercial Support Program which has seen more and more tasks contracted-out to civilian contractors. There are benefits in terms of cost-effectiveness and of minimising the use of expensive military personnel. But the downside must also be understood. Contracting-out reduces internal reserves of personnel, leaving the Defence force 'lean, mean and vulnerable' as one study noted.[18] It also undermines the distinctiveness of the military profession. Civilian contractors, for example, may now be expected to serve in an area of operations. Such developments may be inevitable, given personnel shortages, and on balance desirable, but they do blur the boundaries between the military profession and the civilian world.

The need is for the military profession to be able to debate its problems and its functions both internally and in the public arena. There are fundamental questions of concern not only to the military but to society. Why, for example, do we maintain armed forces? What are the implications of taking on wider roles such as law enforcement?[19] The military profession needs to be provided with the means and the opportunities for debate and analysis of such questions. This will enable it to better deal with the challenges facing it, and to play a fuller role in society and government decision making. A profession that is more visible and vital will in turn assist recruitment and retention.

Strategies

In the following pages I suggest three broad strategies to respond to these challenges. The focus is not on tactical questions such as forms of advertising for recruits, posting and family issues, or terms and conditions of service. All these issues—and more—must be effectively dealt with, although they have been studied and studied again without producing easy answers. The three strategies that aim to equip the military profession to better confront and deal with the problems facing it require: first, the reform of the reserves; second, more effective approaches to military education; and third, the promotion of military professionalism.

The strategies are broadly based on the growth of the information age, the importance of education, and changing patterns of individual employment, education and training—in short, information, intellect and the individual (I3). Each looks for a wide range of effects, whether directly or indirectly. They do not require radical revision of military structures or ethos but they do call for some new approaches and some difficult decisions. The problems facing the military profession in Australia, however, warrant what Sir Humphrey Appleby would call 'courageous' measures.

Reforming reserves

Reserves have grown in importance in many Western states for several reasons. First, the shift to all-volunteer forces means that recruiting and retaining sufficient numbers of full-time personnel now depend on individual choice not central direction. Reserves offer a way of attracting people into uniform who would not otherwise consider military service. This may be all the more important as those inquiring about enlistment in recent times seem to be more ambivalent than before as to whether they want full-time or part-time service.[20]

Second, reserves come into their own as the range and intensity of tasks undertaken by the ADF increase. Small full-time forces have to respond to surges in activity that exceed normal capacities, that are often unpredictable, and that are sometimes prolonged. Useable reserve forces not only relieve the problems of inadequate numbers but also address the demands of heightened operational tempo on the regular forces.

Third, reserves are valuable in importing expertise from civilian society which would be prohibitively expensive to maintain in uniform on a permanent basis. This expertise includes: medical, legal, language, civil affairs and information technology skills. Many of these skills are particularly in demand in operations other than war. In some cases commercial providers might suffice but from a military perspective, reserves offer better prospects for control, training and cohesion.

In Australia the problem is not that the Defence Force lacks reserves. About 20 000 reservists are maintained at an indicative cost of $1 billion per year ($0.9 billion for the Army Reserve) in 1999–2000.[21]

The problem is that Australia does not and perhaps cannot use them, other than as individual volunteers. In marked contrast to the United States, not a single Australian reservist has been called up since World War II. Many individuals have volunteered for full-time service, notably in East Timor, performing well and adding to capability. Many Australian Navy ships would be unable to sail without reservists volunteering for particular voyages. But the bottom line is that the government has been unable or unwilling to call out reserves, individually or collectively, for full-time duty. Three reasons can be identified.

One reason is that legislation prior to 2001 permitted call-out of reserves only for the direct defence of Australia. Many other contingencies, including combat outside Australia, were therefore not covered. Amendments to the *Defence Act* remedied this deficiency in formal terms so that reserves can now be called out for almost any purpose, including defence emergency and defence preparation, peacekeeping and peace enforcement, defence assistance to Australian or overseas governments, humanitarian and disaster relief, and support to community activities. In place of successive call-outs each limited to three months, call-out can now be for continuous service. Parts of the reserve and individual members can also be required to serve. In legal terms, at least, reserves have become fully employable.

A second reason continues to restrain call-out of reserves, namely the likely disruption to the lives, families and employment of individuals. About 45 per cent of reserves are married (plus 6 per cent divorced or separated) and their families are less accustomed than those of regulars to enforced and extended periods of absence.[22] More critically, perhaps, the great majority of reservists are employed or self-employed and would face difficulties of one kind or another in taking lengthy or unexpected leave. The *Defence Reserve Service (Protection) Act 2001* provides statutory protection for the jobs of those called out. Employers are simultaneously threatened with fines for failing to preserve the jobs of reservists and offered financial support in the form of an Employer Support Payment equal to adult average weekly earnings for employees absent on duty longer than two weeks.

But these sticks and carrots will not necessarily prove effective. Businesses with small numbers of workers, for example, may find difficulty in securing replacement staff or in making positions for those returning from compulsory service. It is hard to imagine small businesses being pursued in the courts in such circumstances. Compromise will be the better approach and the Office of Reserve Service Protection established in 2002 is intended to facilitate this. Some self-employed still face intractable problems in leaving their livelihood for lengthy periods. Without the entrenched social attitudes such as those in the United States that favour the use of reserve forces, it will still take considerable political courage for any Australian government to call out personnel from their families and their workplace.

The most important reason preventing the call-out of reserves, however, is the lack of trained personnel in large enough numbers. The posted strength of Army brigades, for example, ranges from 35 per cent to 50 per cent of authorised establishment with some units as low as 19 per cent of establishment.[23] This situation is called 'hollowness'. If units or formations are to be called out at short notice, they cannot be effective if a high proportion of positions are still to be filled. Nor will they be deployable if their personnel need extended training before they can be used. Making up these deficiencies not only takes time but ties down both trained reservists and full-time personnel involved in the training process. This sort of approach may have sufficed in World War II but is not appropriate for likely future operations. What is needed are elements of trained reservists ready to go at short notice and made up of personnel who can be deployed without causing major social, employment or personal disruption.

It seems that we must go back to a form of reserve service that approximates the Ready Reserve scheme that existed from 1991 to 1996 before its abolition by the incoming Liberal–National Party Government. It is worth recalling the key features of the scheme.[24] Ready Reservists received one year full-time training and on-the-job experience essentially identical to that received by regulars. After twelve months the reservist was as well trained as the regular recruit. Thereafter Ready Reservists undertook a minimum training obligation of 50 days per year for a period of four years—less than the regular but sufficient to maintain skills at a reasonably high level. A new scheme could have some flexibility around the figure of 50 days.

The majority of Ready Reservists were planning to enter tertiary education or already undertaking it. By 1995 about 80 per cent of the Army's recruits into the Scheme were planning to become tertiary students. In the case of the Air Force, which had smaller numbers, the proportion was lower but still over 50 per cent. During their period of part-time service, student reservists were not only available for training during long vacations but also likely to be able to undertake full-time duties for periods of six or twelve months. Most tertiary courses can be interrupted without serious difficulties. (The new *Reserve Service (Protection) Act* also extends to educational enrolments.) Indeed, Ready Reservist students would likely have been strongly attracted to, say, a six-month deployment in Timor—in part out of enthusiasm to use their skills, in part because of the financial incentives, in part for a worthwhile experience. Since they would not be in the workplace, moreover, there is no need for employer compensation.

A related benefit was that the presence of several thousand Ready Reserves in tertiary education institutions provided information about the military to other students in an informal fashion. Contact with fellow students actually in the military also has the effect of exposing a wider pool of educated people to the prospect of service and can exert a positive influence on recruitment, whether part-time or full-time.

The Ready Reserve scheme sought to influence key social attitudes by attracting individuals into the services who were likely to become influential in the community later in their civilian careers, including future business and community leaders. They would carry an understanding of the Defence Force into the wider community and perhaps be in positions where they could encourage or help others to enlist in the military. The Young Australian of the Year in 2000, for example, spoke positively of his Ready Reserve experience. The scheme also promised to counter a long-standing handicap of the ADF, namely that children of the élite in Australia rarely enlist in the military (this is also the case in the United States since the end of conscription).

The Ready Reserve scheme attracted a new pool of recruits who would not otherwise be reached. This is a critical advantage. Young people regard one year full-time plus four years part-time in a totally different way from joining up full-time (even if it is easy enough to leave the regular force after one year). Many also saw the benefits of a year off between school and university—to think about whether they really wanted to study, to have a break from education and not least to earn some money with a guarantee of support while at university. Whatever the psychology, it is a phenomenon of which the ADF needs to take full advantage.

In the early 1990s regular recruiting was suspended because—it is hard to believe—the Defence Force had sufficient recruits. Some who were turned away joined the Ready Reserve so that they could undertake the necessary training and later transfer to the regulars—the reservoir effect. Other recruits to the Ready Reserve found—sometimes to their surprise—that they took to military life, and sought to transfer to the full-time force. Consequently, the scheme produced both 'reservoir' and 'siphon' effects. This siphon effect was counted as a loss to the Ready Reserve but was a major bonus from an ADF perspective.

The stated reason for the abandonment of the Ready Reserve scheme in 1996 was its cost—not far enough below that of regular forces, too far above the cost of General Reserves. The figure for the individual Ready Reservist was estimated as 45 per cent of a regular over a five year period; for a unit (taking into account the employment of a proportion of regulars in that unit) the cost was 65 per cent.[25] The cost of a General Reservist, by contrast, has been estimated as low as 10 per cent of that of a regular soldier.[26]

There is little benefit, however, in partly training large numbers of low-cost reservists who cannot be used, certainly not in formed units. The existing cost of reserves is already some $1 billion per annum and is set to increase. The Employer Support Payment will in effect fine the government for employing reserves at a rate of over 800 dollars per week after the first two weeks. Efforts to improve retention among the general reserves are also likely to increase costs. A survey in 2001 indicated factors that reservists said would exercise 'considerable' or 'very considerable' influence on any decision to stay in. The six highest-ranking factors were full medical and dental services (79.9 per cent of those surveyed), increased pay (74 per cent), retention bonus (72.4 per cent), improved allowances such as travel (70.1 per cent) and Defence-sponsored superannuation (62.9 per cent).[27] All of these would add to the cost of existing forces without necessarily adding to individual readiness.

Against this background, a relatively small number of reserves with extended training looks to be value for money. Nor is the option of increased full-time personnel likely to be available. Recruitment is falling short of the targets set, a situation which seems unlikely to change for some time, if at all. While some might prefer a larger regular force (and there is a case for this) the likelihood is that the desired numbers simply could not be recruited—assuming standards are maintained and massive pay increases are not possible. The essence of a Ready Reserve scheme, by contrast, is that it attracts many who are not otherwise going to put on uniform.

In terms of the range of tasks performed by the ADF, a new reserve system also makes a great deal of sense. The original scheme focused on the Army, providing mostly infantry who would have been highly useable in those deployments, such as occurred in East Timor, that have severely stretched Army's regular numbers. It seems quite possible that the Ready Reserve scheme could have raised a battalion for service in East Timor on a voluntary basis. At the same time, call out would also have been a viable option for the Government since it would be more politically acceptable than call out of general reserves with all its drawbacks. Army, facing the likelihood of ongoing peacekeeping commitments, could gain particular benefit from an effective reserve scheme.

As far as the Royal Australian Air Force is concerned, the original scheme included a small component for airfield defence. This was and remains a classic function for reserve forces (and might need to extend to civilian airports given the current threat). Protecting twelve or more major airfields in a large-scale conflict or in a low-level contingency would require large numbers of Airfield Defence Guards. It is not viable to maintain that number on a full-time basis. Nor could the Army be expected to have enough spare personnel for this purpose in an emergency. In the event, the Air Force quietly re-introduced a reserve service scheme for airfield defence that looks like the Ready Reserve but is not called by that name. It entails eleven months full-time training and four years part-time service.[28]

The Royal Australian Navy used the original Ready Reserve scheme in idiosyncratic fashion, for the most part recruiting former regulars on generous conditions of service rather than using it to attract new blood.

What I suggest is that a naval reserve be raised in order to carry out primarily patrol boat operations. These operations are mainly—but not exclusively—law enforcement tasks. Reservists could live anywhere in Australia and be able to plan deployments ahead of time, travelling to a patrol boat base as required (as reservists already do for major surface ships). Reservists could operate the boats as formed crews, or mixed with regular personnel. Reservists of acceptable quality could transfer to full-time service (and vice versa). Navy might well find this a better option than a separate coastguard.

Other voices have been raised in support of thoroughgoing reform of reserve service. The bipartisan report of the Joint Standing Committee on Foreign Affairs, Defence and Trade supported a reserve scheme of this kind in a report tabled in August 2000.[29] The Defence submission in May 2000 to the Senate Committee on Foreign Affairs, Defence and Trade inquiry into recruitment and retention noted that '[t]he cessation of the very successful Ready Reserve (RRES) Scheme in 1996 resulted in a significant downturn in Reserve retention and recruitment'.[30] The Ready Reserve was a hybrid scheme, disliked by some full-timers and part-timers alike. It may be, however, that this mongrel quality is precisely what is needed at a time when future roles of the military remain uncertain.

Exploiting education

Education is clearly critical for the ADF—in the broadest sense of equipping people with analytical skills and encouraging them to think. It is important in an age when information is increasingly recognised as a source of power, when information is more readily available both to Australia and its opponents, and when uncertainty about the character and course of future conflict is greater than ever. Failure to understand the nature of war and conflict and to incorporate that understanding in doctrine, education and training is liable to prove disastrous—as the French found in the years leading up to 1939. United States forces in the same period, by contrast, encouraged critical professional analysis and laid the foundations for victory in World War II.[31]

The need to understand the full context in which armed force is deployed is greater today than before 1939. The proliferation of new roles requires the military to understand and deal with individuals and groups who are often civilian rather than military, who are from different cultures and speak different languages, and who are not accustomed to Western customs and traditions of warfare. Many areas of academic learning have become relevant, directly or indirectly, to the military profession.[32] If it was once considered sufficient to learn the history of famous campaigns and battles, this no longer suffices (and may be counterproductive if it creates a mindset about the character of warfare). The politics of Afghanistan, the social structure of East Timor, the economy and topography of Bougainville, the languages, history, religions, culture and politics of Australia's Asian neighbours are likely to be of value to the military professional—not to mention familiarity with computers, communications, engineering, project management and human resources.

There are two main ways in which education can assist Australia's military. The first relates to the quality of the academic and professional education that it provides to its members through its own institutions, notably staff colleges and the Defence Academy. The ADF has shown considerable commitment to this purpose over many years.[33] There are, however, traps into which the military might fall if they take a too instrumental approach towards education. The second main way in which the Defence Force can exploit education is to get educators and students in the mainstream tertiary institutions more interested in defence issues. This requires considerable change in those institutions but circumstances are such that change is feasible at minimal cost.

Quality university education for ADF members

The ADF can no longer be characterised as anti-intellectual though the occasional dinosaur might still be found. Jurassic Park has given way to Campbell Park.[34] The problems are rather more subtle. Given the wide range of subjects about which military professionals need some knowledge, and given the limited time available, there is a natural tendency to narrow down areas of study on the basis of perceived 'relevance'—this is the trap of vocationalism. Organisations are also increasingly anxious to seek formal recognition of some kind for the training and education of their members. While this has benefits, credentialism can be taken too far. The Defence Force, finally, must ensure that quality is maintained in the institutions on which it relies for the education of officer cadets (University College, Australian Defence Force Academy) and for the professional development of middle-ranking to senior officers (The Australian Command and Staff College).

The trap that is vocationalism reflects a desire to make academic learning of direct and immediate practical value. Some professions naturally take this path. Doctors must know certain basic things if they are to cure illness; lawyers must immerse themselves in the detail of the law and its procedures. There is therefore a more or less agreed body of knowledge that must be taught at medical or law schools, although there are occasional fierce debates about inclusions or exclusions at the margin. In these circumstances the term 'learned profession' is appropriate.

The military profession is different. There is a body of essential knowledge and expertise relating to the deployment of violence which is unique to the profession of arms though much differs as between land, air and maritime warfare. But military professionals, not universities or other outside institutions, teach this knowledge. Academic learning is necessary—not as part of core professional knowledge—but because it provides understanding of the context in which armed force is used or threatened. This context has grown enormously in importance since World War II. War itself has become more complex through technological developments, because armed forces have become far more intricate and specialised organisations, and because the political and social situations in which armed forces are likely to be deployed have become more difficult and more varied.

The military must therefore never be content with an established body of academic knowledge (nor with its own professional knowledge of the means of violence). It must learn how to learn, and professionals must continue to learn throughout their career. The rationale for this was well put by the Department of Defence when it stated in a submission to the Senate inquiry into higher education that 'creative people who can readily adapt and innovate to confront new threats and challenges are a valuable commodity'.[35] The military profession must be not a 'learned profession' but a 'learning profession'.

Faced with seemingly endless learning, however, there is a natural tendency for a military organisation to adopt a 'requirements' approach, seeking to identify priorities in learning and then directing students to follow those priorities. But this is to misunderstand the role of education for the military profession. It should serve two principal purposes: to develop skills of analysis and argument (which can in principle be gained in any academic discipline); and to enhance understanding of the context in which armed force is used. Education, unlike training or professional studies, is an indirect rather than direct means to the end of increasing capability.

Attempts to use it directly in vocational fashion are liable to give rise to problems. This can be illustrated with regard to the introduction of compulsory courses for all officer trainees at the Defence Force Academy. The ADF has proposed that every officer cadet and midshipman at University College, ADFA take two academic courses, one in 'Strategic Studies' and one in 'Leadership and Management'. Known as 'directed studies' these courses are intended to be introductions to the topic. Two sets of problems arise, at least with regard to strategic studies. The first relates to implementation, the second to substance.

As far as implementation is concerned, the course in 'Strategic Studies' is intended to be identical for Arts, Science and Engineering students.[36] This is pedagogically unsound. Tertiary courses work best when tailored to the academic background and experience of students. Compulsory subjects also tend to de-motivate students. It is better to allow them to choose from a range of subjects, thereby also demonstrating some trust in them as future professionals. Most problematically, compulsory courses must be passed. Given students from diverse academic degrees, at different stages in their degree and under compulsion, setting an appropriate level of achievement for all students seems impossible.

The second set of objections concerns substance. Though insistent on 'Strategic Studies' the ADF has not defined what it actually wants taught. At least six areas of knowledge could be intended from campaign history to nuclear strategy. In the event the content will be left to academic judgment—again inconsistent with the idea of a common body of knowledge. Moreover, if strategic studies is taken to cover the use of force in relations between states, this is not an independent discipline but rather a combination of other disciplines. Ideally, it should come after students have some grasp of the basic disciplines that strategy must call on, notably history and politics, but extending to economics and geography, science and technology, and so on. A purist, indeed, would argue that strategic studies—perhaps any field with 'studies' in the title—should be left to postgraduate level—after a student has three years grounding in relevant disciplines. But undergraduates should, at least, not begin with strategic studies.

Another objection of substance is that directing future professionals into a particular field assumes that it will be of continuing importance and that other fields of study are less relevant. Innovative thinking, however, tends to come from a wide mixture of disciplines. The development of nuclear strategy in the 1950s, for example, was greatly enriched by mathematicians, game theorists, biologists, anthropologists and others. The case for diversity was put well in a Department of Defence submission to a recent Senate Inquiry:

> Rather than limiting the nature and type of graduate recruits and postgraduate courses undertaken by ADF personnel, Defence sees it in its best interests to encourage diversity in both as an insurance against an unpredictable future. This helps ensure a depth of knowledge across a range of academic disciplines.[37]

This expectation does not apply, apparently, to ADFA. University College with only twelve Schools covering Arts, Science and Engineering can offer only a limited range of courses compared with other university campuses. A School of Behavioural Science, proposed by the Academic Planning Council for ADFA, was never established.

We come back to the principal idea that education provides the context, not the subject, for the military professional. Once the ADF decides that some subjects are necessary for the military professional, the problem is that education becomes more instrumental than enlightening. And another slippery slope beckons. If strategic studies is essential, so too perhaps is the study of ethics—plus law, political-military relations, psychology (to understand people), sociology (to understand Australian society), anthropology (to understand other societies), and so on. Who can say these are not necessary to the military professional?

When the military meets education, the temptations of vocationalism are strong. The Zimmer-McKern Report on education at ADFA, for example, acknowledged 'the clear tension between the growing "vocational" requirements of Defence and the academic integrity of the [University College] programs'.[38] But it did not challenge the basis of such requirements, simply coming down on the side of vocationalism, and accepting that Defence knows best what academic knowledge and skills are relevant to its future officers. Reflecting current departmental thinking, the Report also proposed that the agreement between Defence and the University of New South Wales be re-negotiated and operate for a period of no more than ten years (rather than for an indefinite period as with the original agreement). This will further strengthen the hand of those who now or in the future seek to manage academic programs in greater detail.

Associated with the problems of vocationalism are the perils of credentialism. The quest for credentials—public statements of achievement to show that certain competencies have been reached—is a longstanding part of the academic system. 'Credentialism' takes this practice too far. Degrees, diplomas, certificates and so on are awarded for ever greater numbers of courses and for on-the-job learning. Consequently, individuals come to expect recognition for more and more of what they do in the normal course of their employment; and organisations come to expect employees to have more and more paper qualifications. In short, there are more boxes to be ticked, and ticking them becomes important.

The ADF has gone down the path of securing formal public recognition for many of its courses.[39] There is much benefit in this. It reassures individuals that their military education is of a high standard and assists some to secure advanced standing in civilian educational institutions; it increases public recognition of the skills and competence of military personnel; and it informs future employers that ex-Defence Force personnel have particular skills and achievements. However, there are dangers in taking this practice too far, particularly in relation to tertiary education.

It is tempting for the ADF to assume that some military courses are comparable to university qualifications, and that study at university is therefore unnecessary. This is true even if a university agrees to award one of its own qualifications for what is primarily a military rather than academic course. It is all the more true if the accreditation process has simply deemed a course to be comparable to a postgraduate degree or diploma. The ADF should not confuse a badge for the real thing—a genuine university education.

In addition, where military courses earn some exemptions (advanced standing) for individuals enrolling in university courses at postgraduate or undergraduate level, this should be limited and carefully related to what has actually been learned in military courses. The process is in the hands of university authorities but in a competitive environment the temptation may be to offer more advanced standing than is strictly justified. The whole process needs to be monitored and restrained, lest the ADF end up with less than it bargained for.

The ADF has a natural interest in maintaining quality in its premier educational institutions, notably the joint Command and Staff College and University College at ADFA. In place of three single-service colleges and a joint service college there is now a tri-service Australian Command and Staff College (ACSC) offering a year long course for officers around the rank of major or equivalent. Also located at Weston Creek in the ACT is the Centre for Defence and Strategic Studies (CDSS) which offers a year-long course principally for colonels and equivalent. Both organisations are part of the wider Australian Defence College (which also includes the Australian Defence Force Academy) and have their own arrangement with a university whereby a substantial part of the syllabus is the responsibility of the university which grants an award to successful students.

The benefit of this system is to inject significant academic content and methods into courses which would otherwise be run by military personnel together with 'guest lecturers' on selected topics. The traditional approach often brought in leading experts but lacked overall coherence in the syllabus and failed to provide depth in given subjects. The new approach makes staff colleges a little more like universities while retaining their practical military focus. But the fact that universities are involved and that the CDSS in particular aims to 'approximate postgraduate study' does not mean that a staff college education is the same as a university education.

There is scope for further reform. In a study of officer training and education, the leading Israeli strategic expert, Martin van Creveld made some trenchant criticisms of staff colleges.[40] Highly sceptical of the value of courses which every student must pass, he put forward ways in which intellectual standards might be raised, some of which are worthy of consideration in Australia. They included competitive entry, for example, by selecting for promotion *before* attendance at staff college as is the case in some countries. Second, a longer course for better students, providing an incentive to perform well. Third, high-quality military instructional staff who should have both academic experience and military prospects. For example, some instructor positions in the Canadian Forces College at lieutenant colonel level and higher require a Master's degree.[41] Such changes, it may be noted, are characteristic of university education. However, they could be implemented without losing the necessary professional military focus and without the need for major change in existing structures.

Expanding university interest in defence-related studies

The foregoing discussion of reserve service emphasised the importance of the tertiary education sector in Australia. But the ADF can do more than have a few thousand reservists on university campuses around the country. The tertiary sector is the most significant source of the best educated people in the country. At present there are about 600 000 Australian tertiary students of whom three-quarters (74 per cent) are aged under 30—which is to say that they are of recruitable age.[42] Overall, about 50–60 per cent of the total population will undertake tertiary education of some kind at some stage.

Historically, tertiary institutions in Australia have taken little interest in what is broadly defined as 'defence studies'—in part due to antipathy towards the military dating back at least to the Vietnam War, in part due to simple lack of contact with the military. The great majority of Australian universities do not offer courses in strategic studies, military history, political-military relations, defence policy, peacekeeping, armed forces and society, military sociology, and so on, either at undergraduate or postgraduate level. There is considerable research in scientific and engineering fields of interest to the military—indeed, much is commissioned by Defence—but the impact of this is likely to be limited as far as disseminating information and encouraging interest in military matters is concerned.

In short, few tertiary students even have the opportunity to learn about the military and its roles. Nor do staff (who are mostly graduates of Australian universities) have the academic background to present courses that might stimulate interest in military matters. This situation contrasts with the United States and to a lesser extent the United Kingdom, where research and teaching on military matters is common, including on personnel matters. The level of publications, conferences and public debates on military issues is also much greater in these countries so that the wider public also gets some idea of contemporary military matters. The ADF misses out on the direct and indirect benefits of wider academic and public discussion of its activities.

For a relatively small investment the Department of Defence could promote a wide range of defence studies in tertiary education institutions around Australia. The aim would be to disseminate knowledge about, and increase general understanding of, the military—all the more possible given the expanded roles of the ADF. At the cost of approximately $2 million to $3.5 million per annum, Defence could rectify the neglect of military studies that has become entrenched over the last two generations. Between $300 000 and $500 000 per annum for a period of five years would need to be allocated to each State and the Northern Territory. Universities in Canberra could be excluded from the scheme, since the Australian National University and University College, ADFA already conduct courses and research in the defence field, while the University of Canberra has recently become involved in teaching at the Australian Defence College. Canberra also has the newly-established Austra-lian Strategic Policy Institute. In addition, tertiary institutions (or groups of institutions) in each State and the Northern Territory would bid for funds, setting out proposed expenditure such as: new courses to be offered; new staff to be appointed; research areas to be developed; special projects linked with Defence needs; and undergraduate and postgraduate scholarships. Bids would also indicate the funding and infrastructure to be provided by the institution itself to supplement the grant. Defence would monitor the activities of institutions receiving funds but not control the agreed program in detail. A review of progress could be undertaken after three years.

By way of example, an institution might develop a specialisation in personnel issues by appointing staff, presenting courses and offering PhD scholarships in military sociology. The ADF produces an enormous quantity of data on personnel and family matters which would provide topics for analysis by academics and postgraduate students. One current example is a postgraduate study of the impact of the East Timor deployment on ADF families under way in the Department of Social Work at Monash University.

Tertiary institutions are likely to respond positively in the present financial climate. The immediate benefit would be to raise interest in defence within the tertiary sector among both staff and students. This should lead to greater knowledge of, and debate about, defence issues of all kinds across the community. It also promises to make more young people think about the ADF as a career, whether full-time or part-time. There are also long-term benefits. In a submission to the Senate Employment, Workplace Relations, Small Business and Education References Committee, the Minister for Defence stated that '[t]o Defence the public universities are strategic assets' which act as 'sources of new ideas, knowledge and techniques'.[43] The gains from making a relatively small investment in this 'strategic asset' could be of major significance for the future of the profession.

Promoting professionalism

The difficulties facing all professions in modern society and the military profession in particular were noted earlier. There are, however, some steps that can be taken to revive and sustain military professionalism. Three are suggested, each of which seeks to restore self-confidence to the military profession and to demonstrate to the community that the profession is tackling questions of importance to society. The aim is not to prejudge debate but to ensure that the military professional voice is well argued and clearly heard.

Publication of a high-quality professional journal

Every self-respecting profession has a journal (or several) in which new ideas can be put forward, critical issues debated and future challenges anticipated. It is a public indicator of intellectual vitality among those bearing important social responsibilities. Australia lacks such a forum in which genuine debate and discussion about defence can take place. The ADF's existing publication, the in-house *Australian Defence Force Journal*, attracts few leading thinkers or original analyses, and is hardly read outside the Defence establishment. What is required is a publication of standing that will allow rigorous discussion of ideas, arguments and policies, both new and old. The aim would be to promote serious debate within the military, to gain interested readership outside Defence, and to regularly raise issues that are taken up in the popular media.

A quality professional journal would serve as an intellectual free-fire zone where ideas stand on their merits and where rank carries no intrinsic authority. It would therefore need to be independent from direct control by the ADF, the Department of Defence and the Minister. A strong and independent editor would also be essential in order to ensure high quality contributions and seek out stimulating contributors. The *Joint Force Quarterly* in the United States is in some respects the kind of publication envisaged; in a good test of the quality of contributions it recently re-published a selection of leading articles from its first five years.[44] Canada finally secured a professional journal, the *Canadian Military Journal*, after pressure from the Minister for Defence whose advisers saw it as a 'litmus test' of the Canadian Forces' 'stated intent to embrace education and intellectual debate'.[45] Australia is perhaps the only first-rank military force among Western countries without such a journal.

Establishment of a centre for professional military ethics

All professions need a lively sense of ethics. Professionals are not governed by rules and regulations alone but also by an inherent sense of values and duty to society, often in the form of a code of ethical conduct. The military profession above all faces severe ethical dilemmas precisely because its members are given power of life and death over other soldiers (both the enemy's and its own) as well as over civilians of all kinds. Where discrepancies in power are great and where action often takes place away from the public gaze and beyond legal remedy, the need for strong ethical values is paramount. The burgeoning of peacekeeping operations and law enforcement tasks has already placed many soldiers of all ranks in situations where they must take decisions about life and death in volatile and ambiguous circumstances.

In Australia interest in military ethics has focused on two extremes: financial fraud and unacceptable behaviour by individuals at one end of the scale, and the international humanitarian laws of armed conflict at the other. There is rightly much emphasis on the moral integrity of individuals and the importance of group solidarity. Chaplains also play an important, if limited, role. But more can be done to encourage ethical thinking in the ADF and to promote wider discussion in areas where little ethical analysis has taken place—such as peacekeeping, law enforcement and training. It is also desirable to inform society that such thinking is taking place in a serious and sustained fashion.

The ADF should establish a Centre for Professional Military Ethics at the Australian Defence Force Academy under the auspices of the University of New South Wales. University tutelage would ensure that the Centre is academically sound and substantively independent. There is no value in a Centre that is simply an apologist for the ADF, the Department or the Minister. As with a professional journal, such a Centre might create some discomfort from time to time but in the long run both military people and the general public will have more respect for a military profession that is actively, honestly and intelligently debating its dilemmas.

Both the US Military Academy and Naval Academy have set up centres of this kind in the last three years with a remit to promote ethical thinking not only at their academies but across the profession.[46] There is also an active professional organisation in the United States, the Joint Services Conference on Professional Ethics, that conducts and promotes debates on ethical issues of concern to the military.[47] The military profession in Australia surely cannot take ethics for granted.

Greater public prominence for the military profession

While some military leaders achieve public prominence—the Chief of the Defence Force, by virtue of his high office, and leaders of major peacekeeping operations by media exposure—they are not usually noted for their contribution to public debate about the military profession as such. Much of this is due to the traditional abstention of the military from activities that might be construed as in any way political, and to the sensitivity of recent Australian governments to anything that looks like criticism from those in uniform. A non-political military is essential in a democracy but this should not require military personnel to refrain from ever expressing contentious views on issues central to the military profession. The current leadership may be accustomed to 'silent service'; future generations may not be so reticent.

To be fully recognised as a profession in the community, the ADF needs people who represent it in public, who explain what it is about, and who lead discussion about military matters. If members of the profession do not speak for it, who will? Both serving and, perhaps especially, retired officers could make a greater contribution to public debate. In this country only a handful of senior retired personnel have contributed on occasion to the discussion of professional issues, and only former Air Marshal David Evans has been a continuing and noted contributor to the defence debate. There are three single-service 'think-tanks' (the Sea Power Centre, the Land Warfare Studies Centre and the Aerospace Centre) but these are relatively small and heavily constrained by protocol. Compare this with the broad and active debate in the United States that engages many serving and former officers and benefits from numerous non-military think-tanks that focus on defence issues from right, left and centre perspectives. Such Australian debate on military matters as takes place is notable mainly for the absence of military voices.

None of this was helped by Defence Instruction (General) ADMIN 08–1 issued on 8 August 2001. It begins by reminding civilian and military Defence members that 'to achieve a credible image and a well-informed public, co-ordination over information dissemination is essential' and that the government must have the final say over what information is released. The types of public comment and dissemination of information falling under this rubric are very widely defined, from interviews or providing background to the media to 'discussion or correspondence with members of the public'. The Instruction also requires Defence members to report 'all approaches and contact by the media' and to submit all speeches and writings on topical issues for clearance by the Public Affairs and Corporate Communications directorate. In an Orwellian touch Defence members are nonetheless permitted 'to increase public understanding of matters that complement Government policy making'.

The effect, of course, is to stifle public discussion and debate about defence and to undermine the sense of professionalism. As one commentator put it, the Instruction 'betrays a total want of confidence in [Defence members'] discretion, judgment and intelligence' and serves to 'deny even the possibility of Defence building a credible professional image'.[48] The pulping of an edition of the *Army* newspaper in 2000 on the grounds that it contained material possibly critical of government policy similarly reflected a certain paranoia on the part of politicians uninterested in hearing a range of opinions.[49] Of course, military professionals must observe some constraints in public forums; but to issue heavy-handed instructions not only inhibits debate but also undermines any sense of professional responsibility. There is a danger, too, that professional debate within the military will be constrained for fear of leaks to the public, and that what internal debate does take place will be uncontaminated by ideas from outside.

As of April 2002 it appears that common sense has prevailed and the Instruction will be relaxed. Australia certainly needs to permit its military personnel to use the education with which they are expensively and (mostly) liberally provided. At a time of great change for the military profession, the views and ideas of military professionals who are widely educated (the 'soldier-scholar') or who have extensive political experience (the 'soldier-statesman') are needed more than ever. The responsibility to facilitate and encourage professional debate lies primarily with the government of the day. But it also depends on an opposition that does not exploit debate and discussion by ADF personnel for party purposes. Australia has generally enjoyed a high degree of bipartisanship on defence matters (despite efforts to the contrary by a recent minister). This needs to be extended—not necessarily in the sense of unity of policy but in terms of permitting genuine and responsible debate regardless of party line. The media also need to cover military professional issues in the same spirit. For such reasons this may be the most optimistic of the proposals outlined here.

Conclusion

The military profession is facing a difficult future. Fundamental problems will continue for an indefinite period since no easy or early solutions exist.

The challenges facing the profession of arms most notably include the three issues discussed in this chapter. First, recruiting and retaining high calibre personnel. Second, determining the role and character of the armed forces. This requires that the ADF prepare people to carry out a diverse range of traditional and non-traditional tasks that require both changed norms and ethos on the part of the organisation and different attitudes and patterns of behaviour on the part of individuals. Third, the ADF must take steps to revitalise and sustain military professionalism as it is sorely needed to deal with problems of crucial importance to the profession and to society at large. At the same time, the ADF will be in the midst of organisational and budgetary pressures that question the roles it should engage in, and even its very existence.

The strategies proposed here will go some way to dealing with these challenges. They are intended to be more than tactical responses (which are necessary) or strategy maps (which lack content) or motherhood statements (which need to be abandoned). They seek to give the military profession a place in society which remains subordinate to civilian control but which is more active and identifiable. They need cooperation on the part of the military profession itself and the government of the day (and to some extent the opposition and the media). The strategies are designed to promote substantive change without being unduly expensive or radical, though some will find them hard to accept. The cost of failing to act—and to act early—is liable to be great.

Defending the 'other': military force(s) and the cosmopolitan project

Graeme Cheeseman

The military forces we know today have not always existed. They are the product of a particular time in history, the so-called Westphalian age, which grew out of the violence and chaos of the Medieval era and was marked by the emergence of the modern state. During this time, the private armies that had characterised medieval times were gradually replaced, initially by mercenaries contracted by the state's sovereign, then by citizen-based militia forces, and finally by professional defence forces. The primary role of these various military forces was determined by the realist notion of systemic anarchy. This saw the world in terms of a series of independent states whose individual sovereignty and security was to be ensured through the acquisition of strong military forces and strong alliances, and disputes between states were ultimately to be settled by recourse to war. As Mary Kaldor describes, this basic approach to international relations 'implied a clear distinction between war and peace, between internal and external, between military and civil. Periods of peace alternated with periods of war. The internal territory of a state was peaceful or civil compared with what went on beyond the state's borders.'[1]

The military forces we know today are therefore inextricably linked with the states and societies they serve. Military forces are often the agent of the state's birth. They provide the means of defending national sovereignty, of projecting the interests of the state (or state elites) beyond national borders, and of underpinning, and sometimes enforcing, governmental authority within the state. Military experiences and traditions play a central role in the construction of national identity.[2] Military service, and particularly service in combat in the defence of the state or its interests, is often posited as the most important, and noble, responsibility of the state's (until recently male) citizens.[3] The wartime experiences of the state's armed forces and its citizen-soldiers are used by politicians and historians to define what it means (and does not mean) to be a member of the state. During peacetime and especially in the face of adversity or change, national military forces and their associated cultures are also often seen as an appropriate model for the state's *Gemeinschaft* function, its continuing internal cohesion and legitimacy.[4] Indeed, in a globalising world, state-based militaries are one of the last repositories of national independence, pride and assertiveness.

As we enter the 21st century, all of these traditions and practices, and the assumptions that underpin and inform them, are being questioned or are under challenge. The Westphalian world order that gave birth to the modern state and its armed forces is said to be ending and we are entering a fundamentally new era in international politics. The role of the state in these 'new times' is being circumscribed by a combination of forces beyond its control and the emergence of other key political and social actors. The twin dynamics of globalisation and fragmentation are blurring the previously clear distinctions between peace and war, between the state's domestic and external environments, and between society and the military. Traditional notions of citizenship and identity are changing. The first half of this chapter surveys these various pressures and changes, some of the key questions and debates they have engendered about the future of military force and military forces, and how they are being perceived and responded to by state-based defence planners and their advisers. The second half of this chapter explores the place of military force and military forces in a future globalised world, one that is informed by cosmopolitan rather than communitarian views and values.

Military force(s) in a post-Cold War and post-industrial world

From defence to security: the changing roles of military forces

Contrary to realist expectations, military forces today are being employed less and less in the defence of the state and more and more on broader regional and international security tasks. The post-Cold War era has witnessed a significant number of UN-sponsored or sanctioned military interventions including the establishment of the 'safe havens' and 'no-fly zones' in northern and southern Iraq, the United States and UN operations in Somalia, successive NATO operations in the Balkans, and the use of Australian-led forces in East Timor. These various interventions were triggered by human rights violations and suffering of such magnitude that they were seen by the UN to constitute potential threats to international peace and security and, as such, warranted collective action under Article VII of its charter. Together they may represent a new, if qualified, norm in international relations: a right to intervene in the internal affairs of states or, more specifically, a 'right to secure the delivery of humanitarian assistance by force'.[5] Even if this is not the case, calls for the United Nations to intervene in various civil emergencies and intra-state disputes will continue, and the meaning of peacekeeping will continue to expand beyond earlier, Cold War understandings to embrace so-called 'second-generation' or 'wider peacekeeping' activities that include the option of peace enforcement.[6] Following the demise of the Soviet Union, the answer to the perennial question 'security from what?' is also being expanded beyond other states and their military forces, to include such new sources of insecurity and conflict as: disputes over the control of, and access to, resources; various non-military threats to societal harmony and wellbeing posed by such things as traditional and cyber terrorism, drugs, trans-boundary crime, epidemics and disease; and population migration caused by poverty and overcrowding, political oppression or instability, and growing environmental degradation.[7] Armed forces are now expected to help deal with these so-called 'threats without enemies',[8] and to contribute to the pursuit not only of military security but 'economic security', 'energy security', 'food security', 'societal security' and 'environmental security' as well.[9]

The growing employment of national military forces on peace operations and other non-traditional security tasks is requiring them to expand their existing repertoire of functions, capabilities and skills. Post-Cold War peace operations, for example, have required the intervening forces to, among other things, provide humanitarian assistance of various kinds, manage the movement of refugees and displaced persons, help conduct elections, provide safe havens and protection for humanitarian workers, establish cantonment areas or demilitarised zones between warring parties, disarm military or paramilitary forces, clear mines and other leftovers from war, negotiate local ceasefires or the safe passage of aid, provide civil administration, help restore civil society, and contribute to the reconstruction and development of local economies.[10] Military establishments in industrialised countries in particular are, to varying degrees, beginning to recast their policies and doctrines to reflect these broader roles and responsibilities. The armed forces of both Great Britain and Australia, for example, are now described as 'forces for good'. Both are being required to defend security interests that extend well beyond their territorial boundaries. And both are expected to help deal with such non-traditional military threats as illegal immigration, terrorism and cyber attack.[11] While acknowledging that their military forces will be involved more and more in so-called 'operations other than war', defence planners in most countries remain reluctant to (re)structure their military forces for such operations. As Ian Malcolm described in the case of Canada, they tend to see peacekeeping as an 'accepted activity rather than a core concern',[12] and argue that national forces should continue to be structured and prepared primarily for defending the state against armed attack or threat of attack by another state. They further argue that forces structured for the defence of the state are sufficient for carrying out likely non-traditional security roles although some changes at the margins may need to be included.

The changing nature of military forces

The growth in the number and importance of peace operations and other non-traditional security roles is said to be part of a broader shift in the general nature of military organisations generally whereby the existing modern military organisation is evolving into a new, postmodern form. According to Charles Moskos and his colleagues, modern and postmodern militaries differ in quite significant ways.[13] The modern military organisation is a product of the Westphalian and Weberian eras. It consists of volunteer and conscripted lower ranks operating under the command of an increasingly professionalised officer corps. It is 'war-oriented in mission, masculine in makeup and ethos, and sharply differentiated in structure and culture from civilian society'. The postmodern military, by contrast, is 'more multipurpose in mission, increasingly androgynous in makeup and ethos, and [has] greater permeability with civilian society'.[14] A related trend has been the recent expansion of the types of military forces beyond state-based ones. Military forces are becoming, on the one hand, increasingly trans-nationalised with national forces being deployed under the control of such regional and international organisations as the United Nations, NATO and the Commonwealth of Independent States. We are also seeing a growing array of private military services and mercenary organisations that are often 'organised around a charismatic leader' or 'attached to political movements or organized criminal networks or both'.[15] While they may not have cruise missiles and the other high-technology weapons that are owned by national and transnational forces, these 'post-Fordist' militaries can easily access the range of small arms that have flooded the world in the wake of the end of the Cold War.[16] They are likely, too, to benefit from what Kaldor and her colleagues describe as the increasing 'informalization' of the international arms trade, a process whereby surplus weapons from the arsenals of the rich countries are sold 'downstream' to Third World governments or newly independent states in the Balkans or the former Soviet Union. Redundant soldiers sell their weapons or services for hard currency. Weapons scientists sell their knowledge to outlawed governments. Obsolete bases or stores are raided by black marketeers. Often, illegal small-scale craftsmen copy light weapons to arm informal groups.[17]

These trends are part of a much wider process in which the sovereignty of the state and its longstanding relationships with the military and society are being challenged from both above and below. In a rapidly globalising world, the economic, physical, cultural and psychological underpinnings of state sovereignty are being eroded or circumscribed by the unimpeded flow of goods and capital, ideas and information, lifestyle cultures, criminal activities, drugs and pollution. Governments are having to contend with increasingly powerful transnational economic actors as well as global social movements of various kinds. They are also being confronted by a growing array of what Anthony Giddens calls 'manufactured risks'—nuclear oblivion, global environmental pressures of various kinds, AIDS and other pandemics, and so on—which are a product of human activity and against which individual states are relatively powerless.[18] As a result, the image of the state as posited by classical realist and neorealist thinking is becoming increasingly problematic.[19] In some places, the 'sovereign' or 'territorial' state is being reduced to what some describe as the 'residual state' and others the 'enabling state', one that is more and more the agent of global capitalism and less and less the representative of civil society.[20] In other areas we are witnessing the emergence of so-called 'phantom states', or 'failed or failing states'—states that exist on paper, that may have a government and be represented at the UN, but have ceased to provide the services that are paid for and expected by people within their borders.[21]

These pressures are producing in turn, a 'crisis of governance' in which people everywhere are beginning to question traditional sources of authority and to look to other institutions and ideals for meaning and leadership. Citizens in the postmodern era are assuming multiple identities or have multiple loyalties which are often locally and globally as well as nationally based.[22] Military organisations are not immune from these processes. As James Rosenau describes, today's service men and women are likely to identify themselves, not only with a particular service or country, but with specific religious, ethnic or secular groupings that exist within the state—and which also often have global connections—as well as broader social movements concerned with such global issues as gender, human rights and environmentalism. This 'disaggregation of interests' within the military itself is likely to have important operational and other policy consequences ranging from the need to adhere to a range of global norms and expectations through balancing the interests of the state with those of self or family, to dealing with soldiers who refuse to fire on fellow or like-minded citizens.[23]

The changing nature of war

The stated primary purpose of modern militaries is to be able to fight and win wars against other states. Yet there is a growing view that major interstate wars may be becoming a thing of the past. This view, which admittedly is not shared by everyone, is seen to be heightened by the end of the Cold War, the continuing spread of democracy and the phenomenon of globalisation itself which is facilitating growing levels of interaction within and between states, and the gradual spread of globalised cultures and associated norms.[24] The decline in the prospect of war between industrialised nations does not mean, however, that armed conflict will disappear completely—for the foreseeable future at least. As evidenced in the upsurge of violence in Africa and the Balkans, the post-Cold War political landscape is witnessing a range of armed disputes and conflicts that are variously called 'new wars', 'uncivil wars' or 'wars of the third kind'.[25] These conflicts differ from their predecessors in a number of important ways. They are taking place largely within society rather than between bordered states, and in relatively remote regions on the periphery of the developed world. Unless taken up by the international media, they usually have little relevance much beyond the immediate vicinity of the site of the conflict. They often arise in the wake of the disintegration of existing states or the destruction or marginalisation of local economies. They are more often directed at civilians than opposing military forces. They are marked by a decline in earlier patron–client state relations and the emergence of a range of new external connections and actors including various diaspora communities, transnational commercial networks (both legally and illegally based), foreign mercenaries, and non-government organisations. And they are more about the politics of identity than traditional concerns with *Realpolitik*.[26]

These and the other changes described earlier are raising questions about existing military mindsets, doctrines and structures. Donald Snow questions, for example, whether the high-technology weapons and forces flowing from the 'revolution in military affairs' are entirely relevant or appropriate for most of the conflicts likely to be faced by the United States and its allies in the future.[27] Carl Builder of the RAND Corporation suggests that the size of active forces required for warfighting roles will almost certainly decrease, whereas missions and associated forces 'involving the rapid projection of infrastructure (transport, communications, surveillance, rescue, medical, humanitarian assistance, civil emergency and security) are likely to increase disproportionately'.[28] Mary Kaldor argues that security planners are failing to recognise the importance and character of the 'new wars' taking place around the globe, seeing them as secondary to traditional interstate conflicts, and when they are engaged, responding to them in largely Clausewitzian terms.[29] Others, including those from the environmental, feminist and critical security movements, suggest that it is time to broaden our traditional and largely militarised understanding of security to include the various non-military sources of insecurity described above, or to have individuals or the globe as a whole replace the state as the key referent in future security calculations.[30]

As evidenced by the proliferation of workshops, journal articles and conferences on such topics as the 'revolution in military affairs', the 'future of warfare', the 'military after next', 'new era security', 'information warfare' and 'asymmetric warfare',[31] defence and security establishments around the world are aware of many of these changes and, as noted earlier, are beginning to adjust their thinking and policies accordingly. Yet Western military planners still tend to ignore the social and political roots of continuing ethnic conflict. They often overstate the incidence and potential impact of intrastate conflict in order to argue that the world is becoming a much more dangerous and unstable place.[32] They continue to posit non-military sources of insecurity as dangers to be defended against rather than problems to be solved. And, in many countries, they continue resolutely to resist suggestions that the concept of security be extended beyond traditional politico-military concerns usually on the grounds that this would divert attention from more serious threats to national security and overly complicate defence planning.[33] Yet as we have seen, the world is becoming more complex, not less, requiring policy makers to develop more sophisticated and nuanced ways of examining and responding to the global security *problematique*.

The future of international politics and its implications for the role of military force(s)

States and their military forces are the products of the Westphalian age. Yet in the view of many commentators, the Westphalian age has ended and we are entering a new era in international politics. Just what the post Westphalian world will end up looking like remains a matter of considerable contention.[34] Some see the world returning to the kind of situation that existed before the Treaty of Westphalia—a world of chaos and anarchy as portrayed on the screen by the Mad Max movies, and we find in reality in countries like Rwanda, and other places in West Africa.[35] Some see a continuation of existing state-centric structures based around realist, rationalist or liberal internationalist systems of world order in which states remain the key actors.[36] Some suggest that future fault lines will occur between civilisations or so-called 'zones of peace' and 'zones of turmoil'.[37] Others argue that existing state-based systems are being complemented or replaced by a complex, increasingly interconnected and globalised international political economy and associated global society, a world that has porous or no borders, and is increasingly dominated by a range of non-state entities, transactions, structures and norms. These contending world visions have different implications for the meaning of security—in particular who or what is being secured and against what—as well as the future roles of military force and armed forces.[38]

It is difficult to tell at this stage which one or combination of these visions of the future is the most appropriate or will prevail. Depending on when and where we look, some models seem to be more valid than others. Certain parts of Africa, for example, seem closely to fit the 'new medievalism' thesis, while western Europe is a clear exemplar of the economic security community postulated in both the liberal internationalist and zones of peace–turmoil models. Given that the process of globalisation cannot be reversed, it would seem reasonable to suggest that we are slowly moving towards some form of system of global order or geogovernance. How quickly and how uniformly we complete this transition and what kind of system of geogovernance we end up with, however, remains uncertain and will depend, in large measure, on the actions and decisions we take now.[39] Depending on these decisions, we could move towards a system of world order that is inequitable, unjust, unrepresentative, and, for many, profoundly insecure; a system of 'predatory globalisation' marked by structural inequalities, global economic apartheid, and continuing conflict 'between the forces of globalisation and the territorially-based forces of local survival seeking to preserve and to redefine community'.[40] Or we could oversee the transition to a world that is both enlightened and humane, in Richard Falk's words:

> an imagined community for the whole of humanity which overcomes the most problematic aspects of the present world scene ... [and where] difference and uniformities across space and through time are subsumed beneath an overall commitment to world order values in the provisional shape of peace, economic well-being, social and political justice, and environmental sustainability.[41]

How such a system of humane geogovernance might be organised, and the role of military force and forces in such a system are the subjects of the second half of this chapter which examines the cosmopolitan project and cosmopolitan militaries.

A 'force for good': military force(s) and cosmopolitan world orders

The cosmopolitan project responds to the imperatives of limiting transnational harm, controlling and overcoming violence, and reconstructing democratic legitimacy in a globalising world characterised by both intensified spatial and temporal interconnectedness and increasing exclusion and marginalisation. A cosmopolitan approach to security takes into account the security of individuals and communities and is concerned as much with the conditions for peace as the causes of war. It anticipates an emerging post-Westphalian order in which 'sovereign statehood and territoriality are loosening their grip on modern political life'.[42] A cosmopolitan approach identifies statist approaches which are associated with particularist and exclusivist values as inadequate or even counter-productive in the search for just and equitable responses to many contemporary challenges. The cosmopolitan project is not simply an intellectual or theoretical account of the good political community, rather, as McGrew points out, it 'identifies the political possibilities inherent in the present',[43] and seeks to put in place the means to translate these into future actualities.

In developing alternative and transformative models for the practice of world politics, contemporary cosmopolitan thought rests on a number of key propositions. The first is that humankind is bound together as a single moral community with shared rights and obligations which 'transcend the morally parochial world of the sovereign state'.[44] The consequences of such a world, cosmopolitan scholars argue, is that a right violated anywhere is felt everywhere and so we have a moral commitment to those who are not our co-nationals.[45] Thus, as Andrew Linklater argues, many exponents of cosmopolitan citizenship 'support the project of enlarging the moral rather than the political boundaries of community'. In line with Kant's original conception, they believe that if citizens (and leaders) of bounded states imagine themselves as 'co-legislators in a universal communication community', this would be enough to 'place powerful moral and psychological constraints on the wrongful exercise of state power'.[46]

But others believe that cosmopolitan citizenship needs to go beyond a moral commitment not to exploit others. In their view, political action is also required to form a global democratic political community in which centres of power are diverse and overlapping and in which structures and practices of governance are representative, accountable and equitable. A second feature of contemporary cosmopolitan thought therefore is that compassion to outsiders must extend beyond Kant's cosmopolitan right of hospitality to include a powerful normative commitment to the creation of democratic or humane forms of global governance. This notion of cosmopolitan democracy recognises that our world is becoming increasingly complex and interconnected. It is a world where states are not the only and, in some cases, not the most important actors in the management of international affairs, where citizens have multiple and often conflicting identities and responsibilities, and where problems affecting the wellbeing and security of citizens everywhere have to be dealt with locally and globally as well as nationally. This expanding notion of citizenship, responsibility and accountability requires the creation of new institutional arrangements and universal frameworks of communication that are based on the principles of dialogue and consent rather than power and force.[47]

Exactly what these new arrangements should be and how they might be implemented is the subject of some difference and contention. Daniele Archibugi argues, for example, that cosmopolitan democracy should be concerned with utilising the positive features of both the confederal and federal models of state systems while avoiding their pitfalls. In his view the actions of states can be constrained by strengthening existing world judicial powers, including the International Court of Justice, changing the membership of the security council, and establishing a UN Peoples' Assembly.[48] While not ruling out such measures, others, like Andrew Linklater, call for the development of new forms of political community in which 'citizens and aliens come together as co-legislators within a wider public sphere'. Citing the European experience as a possible model, Linklater sees these new structures complementing and extending existing state-based arrangements by providing representation to people with both sub-state and transnational allegiances. Such structures are said to be necessary in part because the vast number of existing international organisations are neither democratic nor publicly accountable and, in part, because without them the considerable achievements of national citizenship will be increasingly at risk.[49]

The third feature of cosmopolitan thought suggests that these expanding political arrangements need to be embedded in a growing body of cosmopolitan law which embodies both democratic and humanitarian principles including international humanitarian law and the laws of just warfare. Among other things, cosmopolitan law permits and facilitates military intervention in the internal affairs of states in order to protect the rights of individuals or groups of individuals against the actions of others or their own state.[50] As a consequence, military forces of some kind are likely to be needed to underpin and, if necessary, enforce the emerging *pax cosmopolitica* and its body of cosmopolitan law. This is the fourth (and possibly most contentious) proposition of cosmopolitanism and the one that informs the remainder of this essay.

Cosmopolitan militaries

While much has been written in recent years on cosmopolitan citizenship and cosmopolitan democracy, no significant work has been done on the place and role of military force(s) in a cosmopolitan world order. What are the theoretical arguments for, and the operational expectations of, military force and military forces in a cosmopolitan world order? Should they be defined primarily by the purposes for which they are deployed or by their normative structures and value systems? Can state-based militaries, traditionally hierarchical, closed and non-democratic, be deployed as agents of what is an essentially and inherently democratic, open and non-hierarchical normative purpose? Can they serve both cosmopolitan and statist objectives at the same time? What follows are some preliminary thoughts about some of these questions grouped under three key headings: the perceived roles of militaries in cosmopolitan world orders; how cosmopolitan militaries might be constituted; and their preferred organisational and ideational structures.

The role of militaries in cosmopolitan world orders

Just as the roles of national military forces stem from a statist approach to international politics, so the roles of cosmopolitan militaries are shaped by the key principles that underlie the notions of cosmopolitanism. As described above, these include, at its most basic level, the idea of the world as a single moral community in which people everywhere share certain basic rights. These rights are enshrined in a growing body of international cosmopolitan or humanitarian law which is upheld and, where necessary, enforced by the key actors in this Kantian world. In the case of the military, this involves a capacity to be ready and able to protect the citizens of the planet, wherever they may be located, against gross violations of human rights whether by states or by other actors. The conduct (or not) of such humanitarian interventions will be determined, in part, by the circumstances surrounding the violation. The recent experiences of UN or UN-sanctioned humanitarian interventions provide us with an indication of the kinds of operations and basic roles that may be required to be mounted by cosmopolitan forces in the future. As described above, these include such things as the protection of ethnic or other communities, the delivery of humanitarian aid, and the establishment and policing of 'safe havens', 'humanitarian corridors' or 'no-fly zones'.

Those who see cosmopolitanism as a political as well as a normative project[51] would see the role of militaries extending beyond protecting individuals against gross violations of their human rights to helping facilitate the transition to a humane system of global governance and its subsequent protection. Just as, within a realist world, military force is used to advance the political interests of the state, so in this case they would be used to advance and defend key cosmopolitan values and objectives. Therefore cosmopolitan militaries might be expected, first, to be used to help defend and, where necessary, restore civil society especially in areas where it is under threat from criminal activities or various destructive forms of particularist politics. This is certainly the view of Mary Kaldor. In her analysis of the 'new' or 'uncivil' wars that have become a feature of the post-Cold War political landscape, she argues that the international community and their militaries should be less concerned with the negotiation and oversight of agreements with the warring parties as with enforcing cosmopolitan norms largely through the 'provision of secure areas in which alternative forms of inclusive politics can emerge'. In her view, such a role lies:

> somewhere between soldiering and policing. Some of the tasks that international troops may be asked to perform fall within traditional ambits, for example separating belligerents and maintaining ceasefires, controlling airspace. Others are essentially new tasks, e.g. the protection of safety zones or relief corridors. And yet others are close to traditional policing tasks—ensuring freedom of movement, guaranteeing the safety of individuals, especially returned refugees or displaced persons, and the capture of war criminals.[52]

The position taken by Kaldor is not entirely removed from that advocated by certain mainstream military thinkers. In his 1995 essay on 'The Guardian Soldier', for example, Gustav Daniker, a former Major General in the Swiss Army, suggests that the military's primary missions are now to promote peace and to facilitate the current transition from an era of confrontation to one of cooperation. Military forces are 'no longer solely an instrument of countering enemy power, but increasingly an instrument for building and cementing a new era of inter-state relations'.[53] This is said to require a 'paradigmatic shift' in strategic and defence thinking involving, first, the view that military victory will become a tactical goal, sublimated to the broader strategic purpose of creating 'favourable conditions for new, more comprehensible and durable peace settlements' between the combatants.[54] As such, the ultimate goal of military doctrine is reconciliation, and combat plans must endeavour to minimise not only friendly force casualties but those of the adversary as well.[55] This requires that existing military roles and structures must also be expanded and provide for much greater flexibility and multifunctionality than previously. This cannot, in Daniker's opinion, be improvised but must be included in the military's force structure calculations and its training and equipment schedules.

> In a contingency, combat troops can carry out aid missions, but technical or logistics units would be better qualified. It would be even better to train in advance for such missions. Armed forces which will be equally well prepared for combat, protection, aid and rescue missions—apart from a certain degree of specialization which is indispensable—will be best suited to measure up to the variety of challenges which may arise. Even in the past, armed forces had to comply, for different non-military reasons, with various and costly regulations which were sometimes contrary to their combat missions. Therefore it should be possible in the future, in the light of clear requirements, to develop organisational patterns, operational principles and equipment for a multiple employment of modern armed forces.[56]

While there is considerable overlap in the positions of Kaldor and Daniker, there are nonetheless some important differences or potential differences. Cosmopolitan militaries would be seen to be acting in the interests of the victims of the conflict—usually the local population—rather than its interested parties (externally as well as internally located). They would be guided by the precepts of cosmopolitan rather than international law which they would seek to carry out both impartially—no distinction made on the basis of nationality, race, religious beliefs, class or political opinions—and effectively (ordinary people would be persuaded of the advantages of abiding by the rules whereas those who seek to break them are both isolated and marginalised). While the peace enforcers must be prepared to use force against those who threaten the local population or seek to undermine the operation's mandate, the use of such force would be demonstrably reasonable, proportionate and appropriate. Thus 'unlike warfighting, in which the aim is to maximize casualties on the other side and to minimize casualties on your own side, and peacekeeping, which does not use force, cosmopolitan law-enforcement has to minimize casualties on all sides'.[57]

A second purpose of militaries in a cosmopolitan world order might be to help protect and defend the global environment or global commons. As described earlier, traditional, militarised approaches to environmental security tend to see environmental degradation and resource depletion as further sources of insecurity and potential conflict between states. They therefore focus on identifying and dealing with the consequences of environmental decline rather than its causes. Scarcities in water resources, arable land and other environmental services are posited as potential threats to be prepared for or overcome rather than environmental problems to be solved. Thus military planners focus on maintaining access to certain 'strategic resources' only. Their involvement in the mapping and monitoring of the environment is driven by operational rather than normative considerations (information that provides an operational edge or advantage is not shared). And, in the event of conflict, environmental obligations under both national and international law are ignored. Cosmopolitan militaries, by contrast, would give priority to securing the environment over securing states. Their roles could include the physical clearance of landmines and other 'leftovers from war'; the decontamination and clean-up of land and other toxic sites used for military purposes; the clean-up of pollution and restoration of environmental damage in areas that are outside the jurisdiction of states or that are beyond the capacity of individual states to deal with; the monitoring and policing of global environmental agreements and laws; and the protection of specific world heritage areas, resource zones or even endangered species.

Constituting cosmopolitan militaries

There is some debate over how such forces should be constituted. In his 1995 book, *Democracy and the Global Order*, David Held thought it reasonable that 'a proportion of a nation-state's military (perhaps a growing proportion over time) ... be "seconded" to the new international authorities and, once moulded into coherent units, placed at their disposal on a routine basis'. He preferred, however, that the global authorities 'increase enforcement capabilities by creating a permanent independent force, recruited directly from among individuals who volunteer from all countries'.[58] In an article published in Peace Review two years later, Held argued that the main problem with existing means of enforcing international law is that they depend too much on powerful states, such as the United States, which are likely to operate on the basis of their own interests rather than those of the community as a whole. A true system of cosmopolitan democracy, he continued, required

> new enforcement mechanisms that are genuinely transnational, and thus transcend the boundaries of nation-states and existing geo-political interests. International law enforcement should not depend on particular nation-states lending part of their military apparatus to regional or global democratic institutions. To the contrary, a global military force should be internationally recruited, based on individuals not countries.[59]

Mel Gurtov similarly argues that a key agent in a 'truly new world order' in which the world community does not 'walk away from mass violence on the basis of narrow calculations of national interest', may be a permanent international peace force (IPF) that acts under UN command and is deployed in the 'event that non-violent measures fail to produce compliance with UN resolutions'. This force, which would comprise national military contingents that are brought together for training in advance of actual need, would:

> Act on behalf of the international community, not an individual government or regional organization. Its primary purpose would be rapid deployment to prevent or minimize large-scale threats to human life, such as by creating safe havens for civilians. A specific threshold of violence would automatically trigger the deployment. Secondly, and not automatically, the IPF might be used in select instances of 'peace enforcement', meaning the use of deadly force to assert the world community's will.[60]

Like many others who have proposed or examined the establishment of some kind of permanent UN-based force, Gurtov acknowledges the concept of an international peace force is a contentious and problematic one which 'must answer to a large number of political and ethical questions'.[61]

The ideational and organisational structures of cosmopolitan militaries

Should and how will the organisational and ideational structures of cosmopolitan militaries differ from those of existing state-based forces? Mary Kaldor believes that her cosmopolitan law enforcement role, described above, will 'require considerable rethinking about [existing military] tactics, equipment and, above all, command and training'.

> The kind of equipment required is generally cheaper than that which national armed forces order for imagined Clausewitzian wars in the future. Transportation, especially air and sealift, is very important, as are efficient communications. Much of this equipment can be bought or rented from civilian sources although military equipment tends to be more easily available and flexible ... While tactical air support and, indeed, air superiority may prove to be the decisive advantage of multinational peacekeeping forces in controlling violence, the utility of large-scale, sophisticated air strikes is limited in relation to its disadvantages—collateral civilian damage, difficulty of hitting hidden targets, lack of control on the ground.[62]

She further suggests that a member of a cosmopolitan military force will need to be a 'new kind of soldier-cum-policeman', a professional who understands and can apply the laws of war but who is motivated by cosmopolitan rather than traditional, national ideals. 'Above all', she argues, 'the motivations of these new forces have to be incorporated into a wider concept of cosmopolitan right. Whereas the soldier, as the legimate bearer of arms, had to be prepared to die for his country, the international soldier/policemen risks his or her life for humanity'.[63]

Conclusion: towards a cosmopolitan world?

What are the prospects of us seeing a future system of geogovernance that is informed by the ideals of cosmopolitanism? Rather than try to deal with this question in any rigorous way, I will make some preliminary observations. The proponents of the cosmopolitan project can take heart from a number of factors. First, as described above, many of the basic building blocks of a cosmopolitan world are already either in place or in prospect. Second, global civil society seems to be expanding and we are seeing the emergence of a range of important non-state actors—global social movements, international non-government organisations, epistemic communities, regional governments, and so on—which are concerned with advancing key elements of the cosmopolitan agenda. Third, there is a growing consciousness among the different sectors of society that the key issues of human survival, security and prosperity are systemic in nature and can only be dealt with holistically and cooperatively.[64]

The proponents need to recognise, though, that there are also forces present in the contemporary world that, for various reasons, would see us move towards altogether different and less democratic or humane forms of global politics. These include, of course, terrorists and other fundamentalists who have little or no respect for human rights and freedoms. But they also include authoritarian regimes, new-Right governments and opposition political parties, unprincipled and opportunist politicians who manipulate public fears and uncertainties, certain economic and business interests, ardent communitarians, and academics and others (including radio and other media commentators) espousing exclusionist ideologies and doctrines. The move towards a cosmopolitan or humane system of geogovernance will depend in the end on the outcome of the political struggle between these two sets of forces, between, if you like, the forces of globalisation from above and globalisation from below.[65] Unfortunately at this point of time, it looks as though the former may be gaining the ascendancy and we are moving towards a global orientation in which there is little or no normative agency and any past sense of community is being replaced by 'cold, practical calculations of interest'.[66]

What of cosmopolitan militaries? At one level, the emergence of cosmopolitan militaries will depend on the success of the overall cosmopolitan project. But this doesn't have to be so. There is no reason why cosmopolitan or cosmopolitan-like militaries should not prefigure the transition from the Westphalian to a cosmopolitan world. Indeed there is considerable evidence that we are seeing the emergence of cosmopolitan militaries at least in an operational or material form. As we saw earlier, the international community is sanctioning military intervention on humanitarian (that is cosmopolitan) grounds, and militaries in Western liberal democracies in particular seem, in the wake of the end of the Cold War, to be recasting their roles and purposes in ways which resonate, at least implicitly, with cosmopolitan values. Military forces everywhere are performing a range of non-traditional security tasks and their activities are being constrained, in peacetime certainly, by the expectations of global social movements and the growing body of global norms and conventions. And, in the debates about whether a UN standing army should now be commissioned, about establishing a European army or reaction force, and about the role of NATO forces in Kosovo, we seem to be witnessing a gradual move towards the transnationalisation of military capacity in support of cosmopolitan goals.

On the other hand, as we have also seen, there remains strong resistance within many military establishments to any suggestion that their 'core business' be directed away from warfighting and the defence of the state. There is also as yet little evidence of any shift in the ideational structures of current military forces away from their statist roots. And militaries and their traditions are being called on by New Right governments to assert particular brands of nationalism, to protect the inroads of globalisation into their internal societies and, even, to advance their own domestic political interests. These trends are being variously reinforced by the lure of technology and the RMA, the search for stability in a time of change and uncertainty, a degree of 'peacekeeping fatigue' among governments, and 'compassion fatigue' on the part of their populations. Again these forces appear to be gaining the ascendancy. But the emergence of cosmopolitan militaries depends not just on the interplay of external political pressures. Internal factors will play a role as well. Particularly important here is the phenomenon of identity and interest disaggregation described earlier. Like others in society, those in the military are having to decide whether they are first and foremost a member of their national armed forces or a member of a broader community of interests, a national or a global citizen.

As evidenced by the increasing numbers of personnel leaving the military (often in disgust) to work as civilian mine clearers or with international organisations or non-government organisations, for example, many are choosing the latter identity. We might expect this refocusing of loyalties within the military to increase as we move from a Clausewitzian to a post-Clausewitzian world as existing militaries are employed more and more on broader cosmopolitan security tasks and as younger officers (both male and female) with peacekeeping experience move up through the ranks and gradually replace the present generation of leaders. This raises the interesting possibility that military forces may move, over time, to be at the forefront of the movement concerned with seeing in a more just, equitable and humane world, to become a kind of global social movement for peace and security, or a true 'force for good'.

13

Preparing the Australian Army for 21st-century conflict: problems and perspectives

Major General Peter Abigail

Introduction

The challenge confronting all defence organisations is to prepare the right force to do the right things in the right timeframes. The right force is one tailored to the strategic circumstances and strategic culture of the nation. 'The right things' refers to the array of military options a government may call for in particular circumstances, and the ways in which military force is applied. Additionally, all modern armies must adhere to international norms of behaviour, and the provisions of international law. The right timeframes reflect notions of preparedness and responsiveness, and particularly the capacity for timely changes when confronting volatile shifts in strategic circumstances. The task of preparing military forces for operations is a complex and demanding one. It is made difficult by the requirement for expensive military forces to retain their relevance over time and avoid being structured and trained to fight the last war or the wrong war, and not the next war.

To that end, those of us addressing the challenge pitch our minds forward many years to examine the possibilities and then craft a view of what is likely to transpire. We then design a force to meet those needs, convince our political masters of the rightness of our course, and set in train a development program to deliver the new force. In the fullness of time, if we have been wise and lucky, the force-in-being and the strategic environment will match. If not, then our successors may need to make changes, and if they are lucky, they will have sufficient time to do so. This chapter outlines the Australian Army's approach to the challenges that it faces in preparing for 21st-century conflict.

21st-century conflict—a generic outlook

Already, it is reasonable to suggest that we know something about the likely nature of conflict in the next ten to twenty years. The conflicts of the last decade of the 20th century and some trends that have emerged recently set the pattern that will probably endure for most of this period. We live in an era of limited wars, both interstate and intrastate conflicts, which have been accompanied by large-scale population movements. Over recent years the world has seen a flood of refugees and displaced people ejected from or fleeing their homelands. In Africa, the Balkans, Central Asia, the Gulf and the Middle East the story has been the same: violent conflicts, indiscriminate and deliberate targeting of civilians, ethnic cleansing, and barbarity on a scale more resonant of the Middle Ages than that which we would expect of modern civilisation.

We also live in an era of interventions in such conflicts, usually led by the major powers and often at the behest of the United Nations. These actions have broadened the spectrum of conflict and the type of operations for which forces must be prepared. Although Western armies rightly hold to the view that we should give priority to the most demanding warfighting requirements when designing and training our forces, we must also be able to undertake a wide range of peace, humanitarian and security operations. Over time we may see shifts in emphasis between these different types of conflict, but the days when military forces could focus just on warfighting against peer competitors are behind us. Forces, particularly those of nations that respond to, rather than initiate, aggression, have to be versatile and adaptable. Across this spectrum of conflict we can discern features that will likely characterise warfare in the years ahead. Some of these features are enduring; some are emerging. Some relate to increases in capability; others will serve to constrain the employment of that capability.

First and fundamentally, warfare will continue to be chaotic, unpredictable and bloody because it will also continue to be determined by human interaction. The notion of clinical, antiseptic conflicts driven by all-powerful technologies is a fantasy. Conflict will continue to exhibit operatic qualities to the extent that 'it won't be over till someone kicks in the door'. Invariably, that someone will be a soldier, although he will need a lot of help. Whereas the 19th and 20th centuries saw conflicts caused by thrusts for imperial expansion and aggregation, we are now in an era of nationalism and fragmentation. Issues of ideology or religion, the rich–poor divide and the availability of resources fuel these trends. Harvard professor Samuel Huntington, who in 1996 proposed that the next major conflict would arise on the 'fault lines' between cultures, might not be completely correct in forecasting the clashes of civilisations, but the possibility is apparent. Changes in the causes of conflict are also being reflected in its nature and participants. No longer the exclusive pursuit of nation-states, modern conflict encompasses a wide range of players from supra- to sub-national military forces, non-state belligerents, civilian populations, and a plethora of non-government organisations and other aid agencies.

The methods employed in conflict vary with the nature of the belligerent. Large industrialised and information-age nations continue to seek to exploit the clear advantages that advanced technologies can provide to find, fix and neutralise an adversary. At the other end of the spectrum, less conventional belligerents seek to avoid the strengths and exploit the weaknesses of their stronger adversaries through the adoption of asymmetric methods including guerrilla warfare and terrorism. The latter, of course, brings the conflict directly into people's homes and lives. Most conflicts will occur where people live, and the battlefield of the future is likely to be centred on urban concentrations within 50 kilometres of a coastline. Thus, we will be fighting in a complex and littoral environment, where operations will be multidimensional in nature. A former commandant of the United States Marines, General Charles C. Krulak, captured this notion with his concept of 'three-block war', which postulated that a force had to conduct fighting, peacekeeping and humanitarian-aid distribution within a single theatre.

Warfare, and particularly interventions, are increasingly joint and coalition in nature. A key feature of recent major campaigns has been the need to construct and maintain multinational 'coalitions of the willing' in order to achieve the necessary legitimisation of the action. Within these broad international groupings, there is also usually a core 'coalition of the capable' that includes the more advanced military forces with higher levels of interoperability. These forces conduct joint operations orchestrating the employment of land, air and maritime forces under unified command-and-control arrangements. Thus, the complexity of operations is increasing with a corresponding need for coordination and synchronisation across multinational forces and civilian agencies. The history of warfare is the history of technology, and we have ample evidence of the ways in which the application of advanced technologies is changing the way armies, navies and air forces fight. Advances in information technology, weaponry and mobility allow operations to be conducted at an increased tempo. This increased tempo enhances manoeuvre on the battlefield, particularly when disparities between belligerents lead to a technological overmatch.

In this context, information is the key to successful operations, and those with the advantage should prevail. Information is now more accessible, however, and the Internet makes a great deal of it available to a much wider audience. In some ways this situation can support our endeavours; in others it can be positively dangerous. Hence the growth in interest in information warfare. For example, the important role that the media plays in the dissemination of information has made it a key factor in operational planning. If the media is free and open it can be a powerful force for accountability and exposure, but it may also be subject to manipulation by adversaries. As a tool of the state, it can be used to disseminate misinformation and propaganda. A number of trends that are likely to persist impose constraints on the application of conventional military power. The emphasis on international and humanitarian law and the law of armed conflict is an important expression of our values and should underpin our use of force, even when our adversary opts for a different course of action. However, political pressure in democracies for low-risk military options sets limits on offensive action that match the limited objectives sought in most humanitarian aid operations. The desire for the avoidance of casualties, and the increasingly litigious nature of Western society may act on military commanders' attitudes towards political or military risk, forcing changes to concepts of manoeuvre.

The Australian Army context

All of these trends will impact on the Australian Army and the Australian Defence Force (ADF), just as they will influence other forces around the world. However, in looking at the challenges that we face in coming to terms with warfare in the 21st century, there are a number of domestic factors that also come into play.

One factor is Australia's strategic culture of minimising the size of its standing army in peace and mobilising in times of crisis. For many years we adhered to the concept of a 'core force'—one that provided a capability to meet small commitments from within the force-in-being while most of the Army was a mobilisation base for a much larger force. The modern variant of this approach is expressed in the Defence maxim 'structured for war and adapted for peace'. This is the security equivalent of 'just in time' manufacturing, and demands an assured capacity for timely mobilisation and expansion. In benign strategic circumstances the risks in this approach are low; in more volatile times the hazards rise and the need for surety increases—a point that will be discussed later in the chapter.

The product of this approach is that the Australian Army is small, comprising only about 25 000 full-time and 16 000 part-time personnel out of a population of just over 19 million; that is, two in a thousand. It is perhaps noteworthy that on 1 March 1901, shortly after Federation, 28 923 colonial soldiers, mostly militia and unpaid volunteers, were transferred to the Australian Army. We have come a long way since then, but today's Army is very much a last-quarter-of-the-20th-century army—modern, but not postmodern. We have some state-of-the-art systems but much of our equipment is aging, having been introduced into service in the 1970s and 1980s. Significant updating and upgrading of most of our major weapon systems and vehicles is required. Thankfully, a program to start the process is now under way.

Ours is a pre-information age army. We employ compartmentalised management information systems and we are only now at the threshold of moving into the digital era, with the introduction of nascent operational command-and-control, communications and computers (C4) systems. We share a problem with other America–Britain–Canada–Australia (ABCA) armies, of keeping up with the United States in the application of digital technology, although we gain great benefits through our access to their development processes. Despite these deficiencies, our army fields some world-class capabilities, such as our Special Forces, and we still match anyone in terms of our professionalism and the quality of our soldiers. This is apparent wherever we commit soldiers to operations. At any one time, we have soldiers deployed on peace missions in a dozen countries around the globe. The experience base of the Army is now as healthy as it has been since the Vietnam War era, although it must be conceded that this experience has been limited to low-intensity conflict and peace operations. Nonetheless, we are an army that has put theory into practice recently and learnt or relearnt many lessons.

The professionalism and quality of our soldiers has always been one of our strengths, although it should never be taken for granted. As our society has changed, we have seen changes in the attitudes and expectations of soldiers. The 'diggers' of today are different from their predecessors. Today's diggers are better educated and do not contemplate a long military career. They have, and are looking for, alternatives. They expect their personal needs to be met. If we do not meet these expectations, then we may not be able to generate the middle- and senior-ranking leaders required in the years ahead. These social changes have presented an increasingly difficult challenge for a variety of reasons. Reductions in authorised personnel numbers, perceptions of a decline in conditions of service, and an onerous operational tempo have led to a surge in separations that has nearly matched the high levels of 1988, which were the worst in recent memory. Retention is therefore a problem, and recruiting is not much better. All three services are having problems with low recruiting rates resulting from declining interest in defence service in our target population. Outdated personnel policies are also an issue. In the Australian Army's case, these problems extend into the reserve, where we have been going backwards in strength for a number of years. These dual problems in recruiting and retention have led to undermanning in many units, and this in turn has exacerbated the difficulties of meeting the increased operational tempo. In essence, the organisation is stretched and many of our people are simply overworked.

Many of these issues are legacies of the 20th century—legacies that we cannot afford to carry too far into this century. Fortunately, the passage of the Millennium sees the Army poised at the threshold of major transition. We are introducing changes in our strategic and operational concepts, and designing a force structure that is relevant to Australia's needs. We will field new combat systems that change the way in which we fight, and we will considerably modify the employment of reserves. We will also modernise our management processes and, significantly, our management of information. These important transitions are possible because our world changed on 6 December 2000.

Our world changed on 6 December 2000

The release of the Defence White Paper, *Defence 2000—Our Future Defence Force*, set the Australian Army on a new path. In contrast with earlier strategic policy documents, this paper identifies a central role for land forces to assist air and naval forces to control the approaches to Australia, defeat incursions and secure operational bases as part of a maritime strategy. Such a strategy implies that we must maintain land forces that are balanced to meet the demands of both operations on Australian territory and deployments offshore, especially in our immediate neighbourhood. For these reasons 'Defence 2000' is a watershed in the future development of the army.

The White Paper provides a prudent assessment of our international security environment, a clear definition of our strategic objectives and tasks, and a comprehensive outline of capability enhancements required to develop our forces in the next decade. It identifies clearly what the Government wants, and where it expects us to be employed. Thus, it gives senior military planners a solid strategic foundation on which to build our forces and design our training.

Several strategic themes are developed throughout 'Defence 2000' that are important to the Army. First, there is a clear emphasis on warfighting and providing a capable ADF that is trained and equipped to meet the demands of conventional war. Linked to this is the fact that self-reliance is identified as a key requirement for defending Australia, though the nurturing of external alliances to provide security in our region is addressed. Second, the paper also highlights the critical role of personnel in the ADF and foreshadows significant initiatives to improve support arrangements. Finally, the focus on capability enhancements reflects a sensible thrust towards evolution, and not revolution, in capability.

The Army's focal plane is Australia and our immediate neighbourhood. The most likely locus for ADF operations is offshore and the central concept for the employment of the ADF should be joint operations in a littoral environment. Within this setting, it is the Army's view that we must be capable of prevailing in up to mid-intensity conflict in this setting. Such a capability means serious warfighting that includes the employment by an adversary of joint forces in conventional operations. Such forces could include air and sea power, light to medium armoured forces, sophisticated modern weapons technologies and Special Forces. Mid-intensity conflict in this context connotes force projection by all parties, but does not include, inherently, the tactical employment of weapons of mass destruction.

The White Paper outlines a capability goal for the Army, with the overall emphasis on providing a professional, well-trained, well-equipped force that is available for operations at short notice, and one that can be sustained on deployment over extended periods. The Army is to be structured and resourced to ensure that we will be able to sustain a brigade on operations for extended periods, and at the same time maintain at least a battalion group available for deployment elsewhere—the capability to handle a 'bushfire' and a 'brushfire' concurrently, as it were. Such demands have significant implications for our preparedness and, particularly, our capacity for timely mobilisation of lower-readiness units.

The Army has been analysing these requirements to determine the optimum force structure and preparedness levels that we can achieve in the context of the force we have, and that which can be delivered in the White Paper timeframe. The force requirement set out in the White Paper can be briefly summarised. First, the Army is required to furnish a rotatable brigade group to be deployed offshore for low to medium intensity warfighting tasks. We need one such group at high readiness for a deployment of up to twelve months and two others available following mobilisation. Second, the Army must be able to provide a battalion group, also at high readiness to be deployed offshore for limited duration evacuation and other contingency tasks. Third, the Army must maintain a forcible-entry capability, comprising airborne and commando elements at high readiness that can facilitate the projection offshore of either the brigade group or the evacuation force if necessary. Fourth, Special Forces are required to contribute to the first three requirements and provide a counter-terrorist capability. Fifth, the Army needs the capacity to expand to meet defence of Australia tasks within capability warning time for a force of nine deployable brigades and an expanded special operations group. Finally, and by no means least, the Army must retain a logistic support force to sustain all of the above concurrently.

The fulfilment of these requirements will not be possible unless we adopt a true total force approach—one built on the complementarity of the full- and part-time components of the Army.

Our world changed again on 11 September 2001

As with so many other nations, Australia's vision of its place in the world changed again on 11 September 2001. The events in the United States demonstrated with searing intensity the potential for terrorist attacks in our national heartlands and the horrific effects such attacks can produce. President Bush's declaration of the 'first war of the 21st century'—one of nation-states versus transnational terrorism—has galvanised reactions and prompted quick reassessments of homeland security arrangements around the world. The invoking of ANZUS has occurred under circumstances that few would have contemplated, but there can be no doubt of its relevance and the appropriateness of the action. Yet the Australian

Government's response has, understandably, provoked questions and apprehension in the community. Is Australia 'a "soft" target with our head above the parapet', as some commentators have suggested? Does such a threat exist here? What do we need to do to protect ourselves?

It seems reasonable to assume that a heightened terrorist threat has emerged and that it will demand some changes to our security posture and capabilities in Australia. Some are in hand; more will follow. Other questions have focused on the types of contributions that Australia could make to the war on terrorism. There should be no doubt that we can contribute quality forces for the types of military operations that are likely to feature in the earlier engagements against terrorist elements. The Prime Minister has announced some already. Beyond that, it very much depends on the nature of the war, but it is possible that, in time, we could and might have to participate 'to the limit of our capability'. Australia will be expected to contribute how and where we can within a coalition campaign. What is emerging steadily is the acceptance that this will be a long campaign. This will not be a repetition of the Gulf War, or Kosovo. The campaign will be complex, measured and embrace multiple phases with many potential branches and sequels. Military force will be but one of many tools applied by governments in pursuit of the desired outcome. As nations embark on this campaign we do not yet know where the task will take us, but it seems certain that it will not be confined to Afghanistan.

Noting the comments I made earlier about 21st-century conflict, one might ask: Are we reinventing 'war' or redefining 'peace'? For me it is probably the latter: the security profile for 'peace' has been raised, perhaps enduringly. In Australia I expect that the security focus will be on anti-terrorism, homeland security, border control and expeditionary interventions for some time, perhaps many years, with possible growth paths to more significant conflict. These will not be separate requirements; they will be interconnected and will require close coordination. For the purpose of homeland security, military forces may be needed for protective security, crisis response and consequence management in support of civil authorities. The ADF will also have to sustain current operations as well as meet demands for warfighting, peace operations and humanitarian assistance.

The ADF's policy as well as its conceptual, capability and organisational solutions are still emerging; our role and tasks in the 'war on terrorism' are therefore not yet clear. Some prudent adjustments to national counter-terrorist capabilities have been announced and others may follow in the longer term if the need is confirmed. These thoughts beg the question: Will the White Paper policy settings be adjusted? 'Defence 2000' was predicated on a concept that differentiates between conflicts of choice and conflicts of necessity, and the assumption of a relatively benign homeland security environment. The threat assessment has changed slightly, but the concept remains valid. Australian governments will retain their prerogatives in deciding whether to engage in conflicts of choice, and even in conflicts of necessity such as the war on terrorism, they will preserve the right to set the parameters for Australia's involvement. Therefore I expect that, if there are to be changes, they might be at the margins only, addressing improved homeland security; otherwise, the fundamentals have not changed and probably will not need to. We still need to cover the wide range of military options sought by the Government, and our focus should remain those key areas defined in the White Paper. Of course, should the Government determine the need for force expansion, additional capabilities or some form of mobilisation, then this would come at a cost. As it stands, the implementation of the White Paper presents a real challenge for the Army. The 'devil', as always, is in the detail.

The Australian Army approach to the challenges of the 21st century

The story of the Army's implementation of the White Paper is the story of our approach to the challenges of the 21st century. In essence, we have been through the process of determining the 'right force', the 'right things', and the 'right timeframes'. The Army's task is to deliver the force that the Government wants and support other aspects of Defence policy in the next decade while also framing our answers with some consideration of what might follow in the longer term. Analysis of this task suggests a number of key tasks that need to be undertaken by the Army.

First, the Army should maintain a balanced force structure and operational concepts to conduct joint manoeuvre operations in a littoral environment and homeland defence. The Army is committed to concept-led capability development, and our force structure will therefore be guided by the needs identified in our central concepts for the employment of the ADF. The entire ADF should be optimised for the conduct of joint manoeuvre operations in a littoral environment as the logical complement to our strategic guidance; this idea is consistent with our expectations of future conflict. Joint capabilities should be at the core of a future Australian way of warfighting. Homeland defence is an essential and enduring ingredient in our national security framework—something that has been made even more pertinent by recent events.

A balanced force structure might seem a statement of the obvious; who would aspire to an unbalanced force? The language is, however, important to us because the force we have today is out of balance. We need to make adjustments in order to provide the coverage of military options sought by the Government and to ensure that we can deploy balanced force groupings when required. We must posture the force so that we have sufficient depth in the full range of capabilities in order to be able to sustain a commitment. An important element in our solution to this problem will be the level of complementarity that we can establish between our full-time and part-time components. We are finalising plans that will dramatically change our employment of reserves, but we must be careful that what we ask is feasible.

Striking a balance between the combat force and the enabling or supporting component is also important. A decade of rationalisation has left us with a Training Command that is barely capable of meeting the training throughput required for the current force and incapable of surge should we need to mobilise. We plan to increase the number of staff in the Command, with the offsets coming from the Combat Force. The Army has already had to make similar adjustments in other functional areas to ensure that service provision levels can be maintained.

This quest for balance presents many challenges, and the Army envisaged in the White Paper will still be small, with many limitations. The land capability requirements have been examined by means of a Combat Force Sustainment Model, which clearly exposes problems in our force structure. We suffer from major deficiencies in personnel and equipment, particularly in our lower-readiness reserve units. Many of our capabilities are shallow; some reside in single units. We need more specialists in intelligence and counter-intelligence, engineers, linguists and civil affairs. Our deployable logistics capability requires urgent remediation, following a steady decline over the last decade. Some of our logistics specialists have now done four or five operational tours in East Timor and Bougainville. Our Special Forces are stretched at a time when their commitments have just increased. We face a particular problem in this area because the rest of the infantry base of the Regular Army is insufficient to sustain much growth in our Special Forces community—something that might be needed if the Army is allocated a larger role in homeland security.

None of these problems is a showstopper, and we have plans to redistribute personnel across the Army to provide a more balanced force. We aim to use all components of the Army to meet the government's requirements, but our plans are reliant on timely mobilisation.

The Army, and the ADF as a whole, must attract, train and retain the necessary people. Hugh Smith has addressed this subject comprehensively in his chapter, so there is no need to reiterate the importance of the human factor in gaining and maintaining a qualitative edge in the standard of our military personnel. Without labouring the point, there is compelling evidence to suggest that this will be the greatest challenge confronting Defence and the Army during the next few decades.

Our prospects of manning the force adequately, in the absence of a national 'call to arms', appear bleak. Our marketing and engagement policies, and the conditions of service that we offer are going to have to change. In addition, the costs of training are increasing because of trade rationalisations, the introduction of new technologies and the necessity for the adoption of common competencies across the full-time and part-time components. These factors will require that more of Defence's dollars be devoted to personnel, but it will also require that we amortise our investment in people over a longer period. To that end, the notion of mandatory reserve service, including in the Standby Reserve, for say five years after a full-time engagement has many attractions. The biggest part of the challenge may be maintaining the position set out in the White Paper on manning levels. Our people may well ask: What is going to stop Defence leaders from defaulting in the face of funding pressure? After all, it has happened before.

We need to benchmark our land combat forces to be the region's best in complex or restricted terrain, 24-hour operations, information warfare and decisive close combat. We must certainly seek the advantages offered by the information age but in the context of our likely operating environment, which limits the application of some advanced technologies. We must secure the optimisation of both people and technologies to prevail; ours is not an environment where technology has significantly reduced the need for people on the ground.

The Army's leadership will face some big choices as we seek to balance our future force. We will have to be very conscious of criteria such as relevance, cost-effectiveness, practicality and sustainability in making our choices. Our options will be tested through experimentation under the umbrella of the Headline series and we will also aim to use the experiences of other armies. Some of the themes we might examine include: the necessity for military specification as opposed to commercial-off-the-shelf equipment; the minimisation of the number of different platforms we employ; the right mix of conventional and special forces in a small army; the optimum range of infantry variants (airborne, mechanised and amphibious); and in terms of the application of information technologies, whether we should aspire to create the 'networked digitised battlefield' or just work towards very smart process improvement.

We must maintain force preparedness levels that provide for directed short notice contingencies, the immediate reinforcement and round-out of deploying units, the timely preparation of rotation forces, and mobilisation for the defence of Australia within capability warning time. These contingencies demand a major reassessment of Defence's approach to preparedness. Until recently, preparedness tasking has been confined to those units required at high-readiness notice. We are now developing a comprehensive preparedness framework to embrace all elements of our combat forces. Such a framework, in turn, requires considerable refinement of our understanding of mobilisation processes and practicalities.

We should permanently base forces in specific locations in order to optimise readiness for short-notice deployments, recruiting and retention, and the utilisation of available defence estate and community resources for mobilisation. To the extent that our disposition does not satisfy these criteria, we attract additional costs, complicate our management processes and degrade our mobilisation potential. However, relocating forces is very expensive.

The Army needs to maintain interoperability with allies and selected regional armies in order to enable coalition operations. The Australian experience on recent humanitarian and peace support operations is that the Army needs to prepare and anticipate a requirement to be more politically and culturally sophisticated in the conduct of operations in the future.

We must increase our investment in civil-affairs capabilities as well as language and cultural training. This training should not be left to the last minute as part of pre-deployment preparations.

Similarly, commanders, their staffs and the leadership of the ADF should not be meeting diplomats, aid agency representatives, police and regional neighbours for the first time when an operation is in the last stages of planning. The Army should engage other government departments, regional neighbours and the numerous national, regional and international organisations that work for the common good of peace as a prudent way of doing business, not as a necessity in crisis.

At the same time, the ADF must continue to take every opportunity to conduct combined military exercises with Australia's neighbours and traditional allies. Command post and field exercises lay the foundations for a better understanding of our relative strengths and weaknesses for coalition operations. As a contribution to understanding different national styles of operation, these exercises assist in developing a level of understanding akin to the interoperability of equipment. In fact, they may be more significant in determining the success of future regional coalitions. The Army will continue to conduct military shaping activities in order to minimise the potential for the development of threats to Australian interests. This entails a wide range of engagement activities within the region and further afield, conducted under the auspices of the Defence International Engagement Plan.

We must maintain the security of information, forces, Defence facilities and members' dependants. This is a matter of heightened concern in the current circumstances. We must monitor events in order to ensure timely responses to demands for the commitment of land forces. Monitoring involves participation in Defence strategic and operational level reviews conducted on a regular basis.

The Army must be able to adjust the preparedness of forces through mobilisation and demobilisation in order to meet strategic needs. Maintaining adequate levels of preparedness is the linchpin of the Army's strategic posture. We will not be able to fulfil the land capability requirements set by the Government unless we can mobilise in a timely manner.

The ADF's comprehension of mobilisation is not what it needs to be, particularly in terms of the processes and timeframes required to mobilise low-readiness reserve units. Our understanding has improved in recent years, primarily through the limited defence mobilisation that we conducted in 1999 and the subsequent preparation of force elements for duty in East Timor. However, these have been relatively simple activities. The 1999 effort was a redistribution exercise, with some additional procurement; in short, it was not that demanding.

A large-scale mobilisation would severely test the entire Defence organisation, and highlight the complex and disjointed nature of our management and support arrangements. I am not suggesting that it could not be done; but perhaps Defence would need to adapt its peacetime structure to meet a wartime requirement. Such a mobilisation would also expose the 'Achilles heel' that is represented by our current equipment holdings in the Army. Our reserve units differ from their American counterparts in one important way: whereas US units have most of their equipment, ours do not. We provide minimal holdings to our units, sufficient only to sustain training, and would need substantial procurement programs to deliver large quantities of equipment in a relatively short time. Unfortunately, we cannot have a high level of confidence that such requirements could be met. The lead times applying in the global rationalised armaments industry suggest that we might have to wait years, not months. It is apparent that the Army needs more equipment than we have in order to provide the necessary foundation for timely mobilisation. We are working on it. The other big challenge in a large-scale mobilisation scenario would be the provision of trained people. Raising the necessary manpower would be a matter for government policy—and I leave you to draw your own conclusions about that—but the training of those people would be our problem. One of the early measures would see the expansion of training capability, but we would also need to find ways to fast-track the development of competencies. This is one area with great potential for exploitation of the products of the information age, and Training Command has already made important advances in leading-edge training applications of information technology.

Conclusion

The Army is evolving a clear and shared view about the right force, the right things, and the right timeframes. We are reshaping our force around new operational concepts. We are continuing a process of modernisation that will reap the benefits available to us from the advanced technologies of the information age and change the way we fight. Land Command is rebuilding capability in important areas of the Army, such as our deployable logistics units, and redressing some of the imbalances that resulted from a decade of expediency and reductions. We are at the threshold of an era when we should realise a true total force with the complementary employment of full- and part-time personnel. As an institution, the Army is addressing many of the concerns of our people, aiming to attract more recruits and stemming the excessive outflow of trained soldiers. We are busy—in some areas a little too busy. The future presents many challenges and I have attempted to address those that are apparent and of significance to the Australian Army. Of course, others will probably emerge and surprise us. If we are lucky, we—or perhaps our successors—will have time to respond.

Part III

Operational lessons

14

Lessons from Bosnia: a British perspective

General Sir Michael Rose

The terrorist attacks on the United States on 11 September 2001 have clearly changed many of the strategic imperatives of the post Cold War—among which is our current view of what constitutes a state of war. Peace has traditionally been defined as the absence of war, but some confusion must now exist as to where the dividing line stands between war and peace. What is certain is that war has never been defined by the degree of violence inflicted on human beings—for in the last century 130 million people died violent deaths in so-called peacetime, compared to a 30 million in war. Thus, I believe that although we may have just embarked upon a war against global terrorism, peacekeeping will still have a central role to play in the search for peace and order on this planet.

It has sometimes been argued that wealthy nations who are at peace should not concern themselves with what is happening elsewhere in the world—in the same way as the founding fathers of the United States regarded their country as a land of liberty to be preserved for itself—rather than one which would use its might to re-shape the world in its own image. Such an isolationist position has long been untenable. Leaving aside the moral position so eloquently expressed by the 17th-century poet, John Donne, when he said that no man is an island, political reality dictates that we all are engaged in a struggle to make the world a better place.[1] We have an interest in reshaping the world so that peace and security, and consequently prosperity and freedom can flourish. It makes absolutely no sense to talk of globalisation in one breath and isolationism in the next. Human security involves us all.

Immediately following the terrorist attacks on the United States, there were understandable calls for immediate action to be taken. But as Lord Melbourne, Prime Minister of Britain from 1834 to 1841 once said, 'When I hear people saying something must be done, I know that something foolish is about to happen.' The missiles fired in 1998 at Sudan and Afghanistan were examples of such a foolish response—for while the missile attacks did little damage to the terrorists, they succeeded in greatly swelling the ranks of militant extremists in the Middle East opposed to US foreign policy. At the same time they created political difficulties for America's allies abroad—especially the moderate Arab rulers.

When NATO in 1999 launched air strikes against Yugoslavia, once again it was shown that it is not possible to solve complex political, social problems by military action alone. The primary purpose of the war should have been the preservation of human life—not the destruction of an enemy war machine. The failure to make a distinction between the two resulted in a terrible tragedy for the people of Kosovo in spite of two months of one of the most intensive bombing campaigns in the history of war. During that period, while the combat troops of the most powerful military alliance in the world stood helplessly by, thousands of Kosovo Albanians were brutally slaughtered, and a million people were driven from their homes. Notwithstanding recent claims made by NATO, that somehow the Alliance 'won' because the people of Yugoslavia—more than a year after the war—decided to vote Milosevic out of power, it is a fact that the alliance failed to achieve its three declared objectives when it went to war. In the words of Javier Solana, the Secretary General of NATO, the main objective of the war was 'to prevent more human suffering and more repression and violence against the civilian population of Kosovo'.[2] It did no such thing. On the political level, NATO's air war achieved no more than what Milosevic had already agreed to during the talks held before the war at Rambouillet.[3] Even on a military level, NATO failed—for the Serb military machine, far from being progressively disrupted, degraded and destroyed (as forecast by the NATO commander General Wesley Clark) left the province an undefeated army.[4]

When I was in command of the UN forces in Bosnia in 1994, I was under continual pressure to launch an intensive bombing campaign against the Bosnian Serbs in what was called a 'Lift and Strike' policy. The siren voices calling for war were fortunately ignored, for a war at that time would have resulted in the end of the state of Bosnia and creation of more than 4 million refugees. If the free world is to prevent the sort of dreadful events that happened in Kosovo, New York and Washington from becoming commonplace this century, then it needs fundamentally to redefine its collective approach to human security. Dealing with such emergencies, giving hope to the oppressed and dispossessed who now make up a quarter of the world's population, will in the future demand an understanding of what it takes to sustain the condition of humankind on this planet rather than seeking solutions that emerge from the belly of an aircraft or the barrel of a gun.

Although the military are likely to play a central role in attempts to bring peace and security to the world, it is clear that military force can only be effective within a credible political and social framework. But in reviewing future strategies, it must be remembered that the principal priority of any armed force must remain the defence of the nation. It is particularly important that armies should continue to be able to fight at the intense, hi-tech end of the spectrum of conflict, for while they will always be able to move down this spectrum, they can never move in the opposite direction. In any case wider peacekeeping and even counter-terrorism demand all the disciplines, structures and technologies of warfighting.

As we examine the changed operational circumstances that face peace-keepers today, and as we define new doctrines and concepts, it is of course important that we understand the legal and moral basis on which nations intervene in another nation's internal affairs. The principle of non-intervention under Article 2 of the UN Charter which establishes the equal sovereignty of all nations, remains central to international law. Yet today the international community is increasingly opting for a policy of military intervention—usually under Article 39—on the grounds that the UN has a duty to intervene where civil wars are in danger of spreading, or where there is a dire need for humanitarian aid, or where there are gross violations of human rights.

There are also many moral questions posed by military intervention. To which crises should the international community respond, and which ones should be ignored? We cannot act as a world policeforce everywhere—nor is it appropriate to intervene in all crises. The peacekeeping mission in the Balkans was the largest that the world has ever seen. Thirty-six thousand peacekeepers were deployed in an operation which cost billions of dollars. Yet when General Dallaire asked for 3000 soldiers to go to Rwanda, to stop what was a genuine genocide where at least a million people died, the world failed to respond. There is obviously no defensible moral basis for such inequality.

Mandates for United Nations operations

Liddell Hart once said that strategy was the 'art of distributing and applying military means to fulfil the ends of policy'.[5] But in the confused and brutal circumstances prevailing in much of the world today, it is often impossible to know what are the 'ends of policy'. While it may be obvious that there is a need for clarity in any UN mandate, it is less obvious that the mandate must also define the limitations of the mission—and not merely express the aspirations of the international community. This will prevent a confusion of aims, as happened in Bosnia, where the peacekeeping mission was asked to deliver warfighting goals. To step up to combat operations was something that it clearly could not do, nor was it possible for NATO to respond to the demand that it achieve humanitarian objectives in Kosovo without being given the military means to deliver them.

I went to Bosnia in 1994 because of the early resignation of my predecessor who believed that he could not continue in his post given the confused aims of the mission caused by the many United Nations Security Council Resolutions that had been passed over the preceding months of constant crises. In his words, 'Just do something' is not a sufficient mission statement for a military commander.[6]

I believed that the UN mission in Bosnia had three fundamental elements. The first was to sustain human life and alleviate suffering. The second was to create the conditions in which peace could be obtained, and the third, which was implied rather than specific, was to prevent the war from spreading. I took this re-defined mission statement to Kofi Annan, who at that time was head of the peacekeeping department of the United Nations in New York. This mandate was generally agreed by the ambassadors of the troop-contributing nations as well as with the United States and Russian ambassadors.

If this mandate is today measured against what was achieved by the peacekeepers, the United Nations mission in Bosnia can be judged to have been a surprising success—though this was not the image created at the time. First, the aid program managed to keep 2.7 million people—who were wholly dependent on aid—alive, even though the aid had to be delivered in the midst of a bloody three sided civil war. Second, vital progress was made in creating the necessary conditions for peace by halting the fighting between the Muslims and the Croats—thus paving the way for the Dayton Peace Accord. Finally, the war in Bosnia only spread to neighbouring countries five years later through NATO's action against Yugoslavia.

The use of force

Peacekeeping is about the resolution of conflict through peaceful means. Nonetheless, in the new conditions of world disorder, to achieve the successful outcome of even humanitarian-based missions, a peacekeeping force will have to be extremely robust in its use of force. In the circumstances in which peacekeepers are likely to find themselves, they cannot afford to be pacifists, and the United Nations Protection Force in Bosnia (UNPROFOR) was no exception. Millions of rounds of small arms, tank main armament, artillery and mortars were used—as were air strikes by NATO aircraft. However, in any peacekeeping mission there will always be limits on the use of force—indeed this is what distinguishes it from warfighting.

Despite the limitations that exist on the use of combat power, the line between peacekeeping and all-out war is determined less by the level of force used than by the purpose for which it is used. Furthermore, the level of military force used must be appropriate to the sort of conflict in which it is engaged. The level of force may be far removed from the level and type of force that is applied in warfighting. This distinction is not widely understood. In Bosnia when I called for NATO close air support, I was often accused of using pinpricks against the Serbs. This would have been true had I been at war—but I was not. In a peacekeeping operation, only a minimum level of force should be used to achieve a specific aim. The use of force should also be evenhanded, impartial and only applied after due warning. Force cannot be used to punish an aggressor, deliver military solutions or solve the underlying political problems of a country in the midst of civil war. It can merely help create the necessary conditions for a peaceful resolution to the conflict. It is vital that warfighting goals are never pursued by peacekeeping forces as happened in Somalia, for a peacekeeping force can never become a combatant itself. You do not go to war in white painted vehicles.

Command-and-control

There are three elements present in any peacekeeping or humanitarian action: political, security and humanitarian aid. All three need close co-ordination as the warring parties will be quick to set one element against the other if they perceive any division or uncertainty among the three elements. It is especially important that the civil power remains in overall control and that the military respond both to the political dictates as well as the humanitarian requirements of the situation. In Bosnia the coordination between security and humanitarian requirements was achieved by co-locating all military operation cells with those of the principal aid agency, which was the United Nations High Commission for Refugees (UNHCR). Once this was done, the tonnages of aid delivered immediately started to increase. However, unity of political action was never successfully achieved between the UN, NATO and the rest of the international community, and this was one of the main failures of the political aspects of the UN mission in Bosnia.

The media in Bosnia

The effect of global communications is to compress the strategic, operational and tactical levels of command. This is especially significant where the handling of the media is concerned. The war in Bosnia has been described as a war of information and misinformation—a war for the sympathy of the world in which the media itself all too often became manipulated by the protagonists. One of the greatest failures of the United Nations in Bosnia was its inability to win the information battle. Indeed, the negative international image of the United Nations operation was so great that on many occasions troop-contributing nations began preparing for the withdrawal of their troops—in spite of the fact that the UN were largely succeeding in their mission. In order to change international perceptions about the effectiveness of the mission, I took personal control of the handling of the media at the local level. It had become clear that the professional United Nations public relations staff were unable to provide the necessary level of argument with a generally hostile media.

The ability to handle media will be an increasingly essential personal quality for leaders at all levels in the future. I was nevertheless surprised in Bosnia how often eminent journalists and commentators would fall for the oldest propaganda trick in the book, in which the innocent are accused of crimes while the war criminals are described as the victims. As President Truman said, 'the road to peace is long and difficult and costly. But those who do not wish to pay the cost, must be prepared to pay the price of war.'[7]

Lessons from East Timor

Major General Duncan Lewis

Introduction

The course of any military operation sees the deployed force move through a cycle of transitional stages, ending—if the operation is a success—with the intended political outcome. Consequently, this chapter does not examine the experience of other commanders in East Timor, when the situation was markedly different from that which prevailed when I served there with the peacekeeping force. My own experience covers the closing days of the International Force East Timor (INTERFET) and the transition to the United Nations Transitional Administration in East Timor (UNTAET). The significant changes that occurred during the handover from a UN-mandated, but Australian-run operation to a more traditional UN-led multinational operation makes it worth paying particular attention to the formative months of the UN Peacekeeping Force in East Timor. The period in which the UN consolidated its position witnessed considerable military and community-building activity, and extended through most of 2000. This chapter focuses on the particular period that witnessed the transition from the INTERFET experience into the UNTAET peace-keeping force.

My own perspective of operations in East Timor was shaped by my command of the western border sector. It proved to be an active area of operations. During the period from January to September 2000 in Sector West, there occurred 82 shooting incidents and eighteen exchanges of fire. There were, sadly, losses in the case of the militia groups, the local community, UN workers and among our own forces. It was a period of quite active military operations and also of nation-building operations, which started to gather full momentum at that time. The early period of the UN-led operation was critical. Only five months after the post-election bloodbath, INTERFET had achieved its mission, stabilised the situation and provided adequate conditions of security to enable the UN administration to take control of the territory. That transition of power was an interesting period. It was done sequentially from the eastern end of the island back towards the border. The passage of authority was completed in good order, although the nature of the handover sometimes made it unclear as to who was responsible for what. Given that some forces were remaining with the UN peacekeeping force while others were leaving the territory, some minor confusion was probably inevitable. More important, however, was the fact that any handover is potentially a vulnerable point in the progress of an operation.

The UN Security Council passed Resolution 1272 on 25 October 1999. That resolution gave rise to UNTAET and the peacekeeping force. The Secretary-General appointed the experienced Brazilian administrator Sergio Vieira de Melo as his special representative (SRSG) at that time. It is important to note that the SRSG had ultimate authority as the transitional administrator in East Timor. Beneath him were three branches of adminstration, known in the UN as 'pillars'. The first was the Governance and Administration pillar (GPA) of UNTAET; the second was the Peacekeeping Force (PKF); and the third, the Humanitarian and Emergency Relief pillar. Those three pillars were the legs on which UNTAET was framed. Militarily, responsibility for the territory was distributed across a number of sectors: Sector West, Central, East and the Oecussi Enclave, as well as the Headquarters of the United Nations Military Observer Group. The last was originally a freestanding organisation but it was later held to have a line of responsibility—if not reporting—through the commander of the PKF. The PKF also had a

Force Logistics Squadron, and functional areas of responsibility that included Air Operations, Maritime Operations, Engineers and Medical. This structure consisted of some 8500 soldiers, of which Australia contributed approximately 1600 at any one time.

Sector West comprised a diverse collection of forces. It consisted of a headquarters of about 45 people; a Pakistani Engineer Regiment in support; a Pakistani Force Communications Unit of about 80; and two infantry battalions, supported by a New Zealand Aviation element and an Australian Aviation detachment. A Brazilian Military Police Platoon was attached to the Australian Battalion. The New Zealand Battalion was a composite battalion involving Fijians, Nepalese and originally Canadians—there was a Canadian company when we first arrived; they were replaced by the Nepalese—and an Irish Platoon. In total there were about 4300 troops. The Australian Battalion was located in the north at Balibo. In the south there was a whole range of units: the New Zealand composite Battalion, the Pakistani engineers and the Pakistani communicators located near the provincial town of Suai, which is where my headquarters was established. Both the New Zealand and the Australian Light Observation Helicopter Detachment were down in Suai. During my period of command, the Australian Blackhawk helicopters that had operated with INTERFET returned and were located in the Australian Area of Operations (AO) in the north.

Running through the centre of this island is a cordillera, or spine, of mountains. There are therefore very different weather patterns in the north and in the south. They get more than twice as much rain in the south as in the north, which is comparatively dry. The weather in the south could significantly inhibit our freedom to conduct operations. That spine of mountains divided the AO into two—very much like the division between the north and south coast in Papua New Guinea.

My task was to establish and train a formation-level headquarters to take over responsibility for border operations from the Australian Brigade that had established itself at Suai during the INTERFET period. We had to assume responsibility for border security as well as manage the security of the two border districts of Bobonaro and Cova Lima.

Our experience in East Timor leads me to make a number of general prefatory points. First, these operations taught me to be positive about the potential of the international community to conduct multinational peace operations—particularly robust peace operations under the provisions of Chapter VII of the UN Charter. During my period of command, the level of operational intensity ranged from relative periods of calm to periods of violent conflict. Whenever we contemplated moving to a Chapter VI peacekeeping mandate, the resurgence of violence confirmed the wisdom of remaining with a Chapter VII mandate until the prospects of violence were demonstrably reduced and greater security prevailed. Second, the application of military force or the threat of application of military force under a UN mandate will continue as an important vehicle for change—a vehicle for arriving at stable but internationally acceptable solutions to conflict within or between communities. Third, military operations in East Timor meant breaking a lot of new ground for Australia: our government, our strategic level processes, our operational level plans and support mechanisms, and our tactical units all found themselves facing new challenges. It has been argued that there was no bigger challenge than our national leadership of the INTERFET coalition. The exercise of this responsibility impacted directly on my period in command because while the UN had clearly and officially taken control following the transition of authority from INTERFET to UNTAET, Australia still had an enduring legacy of responsibility within the mission well beyond that which we as a middle-power would ordinarily expect to hold.

Coalition operations

There are many lessons to be learnt from the multinational dimension of operations in East Timor. The fact that particularly affected me as a commander within a coalition operation was that we had a number of external political forces that influenced the way we behaved and the way we operated. It is worth examining the effect of those forces in some detail. There was a three-way political relationship between Australia, Indonesia and the fledgling East Timor state. The United Nations organisation and its interests represented another dimension of this relationship. On the issue of interests, it was Lord Palmerston that reminded us that there are no such things as enduring friendships, only enduring interests. I can only say that, so far as a multinational coalition is concerned, he was completely accurate. During the whole time I was in East Timor, although we did not necessarily experience tension, there was not always a confluence of interest between all the contributing governments. I learnt at a very early point that each government is a sovereign entity and will exercise its sovereign right to do what it wishes with its people. Even though governments hand over troops to United Nations command, there is still a string that is attached from the national government. It is quite right and proper, but it is enormously frustrating at times when you are trying to execute a military plan and you are fighting almost with one hand behind your back. That is all part of the challenge.

Another external factor that had an impact on us was something as far away as the Fijian coup. Right in the middle of my time in Timor the coup took place in Fiji, the emergency there commencing on 19 May 2000. We had 185 Fijians in the New Zealand Battalion. Those soldiers were absolutely distracted for a period of some weeks while that political hiatus in their own country took its course. They were particularly worried about their families; they were also worried about where their next pay packet was going to come from. I must say that, to the very great credit of the soldiers and their commanders, they did get back on the job after a week or two. It did, however, knock them around for a period and they were less than effective while the coup was at its height.

Training and international staff

We were particularly indebted to my predecessor, Brigadier Mark Evans, and the staff of his 3 Brigade headquarters for the assistance that they gave us in establishing our headquarters in Sector West. We were lucky because the headquarters was largely monocultural and because it shared a common language. Being an Australian–New Zealand headquarters, it had the advantage of being an ANZAC headquarters. We also had several Fijian officers and an Irish officer on our staff. I thought therefore that we would be able to swing into action in a very short period of time. However, we were not a formed headquarters prior to deployment. We came in as a group that was largely unfamiliar with each other and sat in over the top of 3 Brigade, watching the 3 Brigade officers perform their functions. During the transfer, we took over the task and were watched by them for a period of time. Then 3 Brigade withdrew. It took about two weeks for that process to see its course, and I think that it was very effective. It is also worth noting that, while we had a largely monocultural headquarters in Sector West, the headquarters of the PKF in Dili did not enjoy that situation. That headquarters consisted of officers from more than twenty countries—it was multicultural and multilingual. Consequently, it took them some time—and it was a mighty feat on behalf of all those officers that were involved—to get Headquarters PKF up to an efficient and effective state.

National limitations and restrictions

This is a big issue. It goes back to the string of authority that links a contingent to its government. A simple example of the limitations on a non-national commander arose with the New Zealand Battalion—a unit that was not only integral to operations in Sector West, but with which I had developed excellent relations. I had issued an order that Claymore anti-personnel mines were to be withdrawn and held in company headquarters locations. Some months before, I had issued an order that Claymores were appropriate weapons to be employed and that they could be used in accordance with the operational need. After a period of some quiet, my appreciation of that need changed and I decided that their use at platoon level was no longer necessary. For several months we lived comfortably with that arrangement, until one day I was flying along in a New Zealand helicopter monitoring the New Zealand Battalion net when I heard the commanding officer give an order to issue Claymores. I flew directly to his headquarters and shredded him over the matter. However, when he told me that he had been ordered to deploy Claymores by his national government, I realised that we had a problem. The only way I could bring the issue to a head was to order him not to issue or deploy Claymores, to which he said that he would get back to me. This he did, through my very good friend, Brigadier Lou Gardner, a classmate of mine from our time at the Royal Military College who was then the

New Zealand Senior National Officer (SNO). The New Zealand Government, exercising its sovereign right, confirmed that they would persist with the issue of Claymores—and they did. It was necessary for me to bring the problem to a head because it had to be at the feet of the New Zealand Government that this decision was taken, and not at mine. As the Commander, my professional call at the time was that that weapon system was not required.

This situation is just one of many low-level examples of the type of tensions that can occur when the national card—the red card—is played. Of course the New Zealanders were not alone in invoking their right to national autonomy. At one stage the New Zealand Battalion Commander and I tried to move the Irish Platoon from one hill to another. They had been comfortably ensconced on one hill for about four months and I wanted to shift them across to where a New Zealand company was operating, and had been operating in comparative safety for months. We were half way through this move when Dublin became involved. They were intensely interested in the movement of a platoon of Irish soldiers. Again, they were exercising their sovereign right.

Sometimes the limitations on a contingent's ability to undertake an operation are driven by factors other than military capability. The resolution of the Atambua incident demonstrated both the strengths and weaknesses of a multinational force undertaking a very sensitive mission. This tragic incident arose on 6 September 2000, when members of the Laksaur militia, who had been responsible for the massacre at Suai Cathedral, attacked the officers of the UN High Commissioner for Refugees (UNHCR) in Atambua—some five kilometres across the border in West Timor. Three international staff members of the UNHCR were brutally murdered. The Indonesian military gathered the UNHCR survivors together at Atambua and informed the UN that they could not safely arrange their evacuation. It was agreed that UNTAET would send helicopters to arrange the evacuation. The problem that arose was that, because the mission involved crossing into Indonesian territory, the UN needed to get permission from the national command authority of the country whose forces would undertake the operation. Both Australian Blackhawks and New Zealand Iroquois helicopters were available on the border. In fact the Blackhawks were closer to Atambua and had greater lift capacity. Nonetheless, it was a sensitive situation, and given the urgent need to proceed with the evacuation it was clear that the New Zealanders would be able to secure the authorisation of their national command authorities with greater despatch. Accordingly, I approached Brigadier Lou Gardiner in his capacity as SNO of the New Zealand contingent and asked him whether it was possible for the 3 Squadron detachment and a team of soldiers from the New Zealand battalion to do the job. The request then went up very quickly, through the New Zealand national command chain, and approval was almost immediate—and I greatly appreciate this speed of reaction to this day. Within three hours, we had a number of helicopters and some ground forces in Atambua. The helicopters took off, crammed with as many people as possible and in two trips flew the 43 UNHCR staff out of Atambua into Balibo.

The reason I would not have chosen the Australian Battalion in Balibo gets back to the question of: What is Australia's position in East Timor? We have a very special position in that country. We are what could be described as a front line state; we are engaged. The threshold for Australian soldiers to go over that border into Indonesia would obviously be much higher than that for other troop-contributing countries. That essentially was the basis of my decision, but it was an important one. To its credit the Australian Government gave approval the following day that, if there was to be any follow-on evacuations required—and there were other UN workers in Atambua—we could use Australian assets to go backwards and forwards. Again, the lesson here is that you must, as a UN Commander, always consider the interests of the governments of the troop-contributing nations.

International command relationships

Establishing and maintaining personal relationships with other levels of command proved to be a highly important factor in ensuring that operations proceeded smoothly. It was also vital to establish good communications between the various national commanders. The Force Commander, General Boonsrang Niumpradit, and I would talk every day on the telephone. He was always the first one to call when matters were not proceeding smoothly at the border or if we were in any strife at all.

He was extremely supportive and I found that, as an experience of working with a superior officer from a very different culture, it was a success. I have already mentioned that Brigadier Lou Gardner had been a classmate of mine at Duntroon. Lou was not only the senior national officer of the New Zealand contingent, but also the Chief Military Observer with the UN Military Observer Group (UNMOG). Clearly our background of common military experiences and cultural compatibility helped us work together. I do not, however, think that we need to lie awake at night worrying about the problems of transcending military cultural gaps. With goodwill among commanders you can make it work. I know that there can be problems, but in this particular instance it went well.

Relationship with the local community

We had obviously identified at the start that maintaining good relations with the local population was going to be a critical issue. The local community was fragmented. It was fragile and in a state of shock. INTERFET had been there for five months, but the scars of what had happened during the election were still evident. It was necessary that we nurtured this community and made sure that they were not afraid of our continuing presence, but were in fact positively disposed towards our being there. To assist us in our task I used the sort of information—the quality and the volume of information—that we were getting from the local community as a yardstick of how well we were doing there. It was a pretty good barometer. You could see if we were doing well in certain areas because the information would start to flow about the location and activities of the militia; whereas, if you were not cutting it so well in any particular village, the information flow would just dry up.

Relationship with the Indonesians

General Kiki Syahnakri, who was the commander of the military district that owned West Timor, was an officer whom I had known personally for many years. Mercifully I spoke what I called Indonesian—though he might not have recognised it as such. Kiki Syahnakri and I had a one-on-

one linkage, which we would exercise from time to time. You may recall that there was an incident in August 2000 in which it was alleged that an Australian soldier had set up an East Timorese to go over into West Timor to spy. This news started to hit the media and it was beginning to escalate as a potential source of further conflict. I was able to ring Kiki and invoke his trust. I told him that this did not happen as it was being reported and it was not a sanctioned activity in any way, shape or form, nor would it be. We were able, therefore, on that personal basis, to take the heat out of that issue. The relationship with the Indonesians was thus an absolutely critical one.

Originally this relationship was maintained through the workings of the Tactical Coordination Working Group (TCWG). The meetings of the group took place every two weeks. They were a legacy from INTERFET. It became critical to the whole UNTAET operation because it was the only linkage between the UN and the Indonesians on the island of Timor, and it was that for about three or four months. Eventually other linkages came into place as political and economic co-ordination efforts started to develop. It was a tactical-level meeting, designed to coordinate the forces deployed along the tactical coordination line, because we did not call it the border. These meetings were important because we did not agree on where the border was. In fact the border was in disagreement by up to 1700 metres at one point. So we did agree on a tactical coordination line, on one side of which were Indonesian soldiers, and on the other were UN soldiers. The TCWG meetings were designed to make sure that we managed a critical aspect of the relationship.

Relationship with the UN military observers

This relationship was another complex issue. Again I emphasise the point that each nation that contributes troops has its own interests. In most cases those soldiers come with their own cultural experiences, which are not necessarily the same as ours. They may view a situation from a very different perspective from our own. It was therefore always difficult for the United Nations Military Observers (UNMOs) who were not deployed in national units but served in an oversight capacity in small, multinational groups. Their reports often differed substantially from the perceptions that I had developed as a commander. Therefore we had to make sure that this relationship was well managed to prevent cultural misunderstandings from causing confusion higher in our respective reporting chains. It was a point of tension occasionally, but by August 2000 we had started to settle down. After six or seven months we had got it right, but it did take a long time to get right.

Relationships with the FALINTIL

The FALINTIL Liaison Team of three was sent to Suai, joining my Headquarters in March 2000 and stayed with us for the remainder of the operation.[1] These three men had interesting backgrounds. They represented a significant asset from the point of view of developing our relationship with the local communities. They were a great source of information, but they always had to be watched because they also had their own interests, and they would be attempting to pursue those interests with the local community. This would sometimes be at variance to what the UN was trying to achieve. Remember that these people were a politically interested party, but they were highly useful from a military point of view. There was a great deal of sensitivity throughout Sector West about these men when they first came to join us. There was a lot of suspicion, particularly from the Australian Battalion, about whether they should be allowed to operate in and around the battalion, and what their relationship would be with the battalion. We always ensured that we had them on a fairly short string, but they were a necessary part of the whole operation, and at the end of the day we had no choice. It was a political decision that they would be part of the solution, not part of the problem.

The militia

Obviously, the relationship with the militia was adversarial. We had to reintroduce a number of militiamen into the East Timor society when they came back from West Timor. Some of these men were merely miscreant youths, but others were quite dangerous and had been involved in some very nasty business. It was quite difficult to work out who was who and to make sure that those that were most at risk coming back—at risk from their local community of being badly beaten—were properly and safely reintegrated into the community. It was comparatively easy during my time because we tended to get the less vicious of the militiamen back. As time went by, though, we were getting down to the bottom of the barrel, and there were some fairly hard cases coming back into East Timor. There were efforts of reconciliation in progress. Xanana Gusmao was talking almost daily about the business of reconciliation and how necessary it was. Politically, that is the right answer, but we were confronted with the practical problem of taking these hoods back into their communities and having to reintegrate them.

Humanitarian organisations

Every UN commander for probably the past 50 years has spoken about the awkwardness of reconciling the objectives and procedures of military peacekeeping with the humanitarian efforts being undertaken by a range of non-government relief organisations. It is probably no surprise to any of us that these folk come from a very different background to those of us trained in a military environment. They do not have the same approach to problem solving and they often work to a different rulebook. Consequently, when we meet to discuss how we might solve a problem, they have quite different views as to how it should be done. One example occurred when there was a group of about 150 refugees brought to the border by the Indonesians for handing over to us. We were all lined up, ready to take them over, when a UNHCR official said, 'Oh, no. We're not going to take these folk because we think that they are here under duress'. It may well have been a fact, but I could not see it from where we were. Clearly, there was a conflict of interest. I had an interest to repatriate these refugees back to East Timor and to help them settle back into their communities. However, the UNHCR and the International Organization for Migration (IOM) were hung up on their charter, which specifies that they may not process anybody or have anything to do with people that have been moved in a coercive sense. The refugees were a considerable logistic strain on our limited resources. We had to provide water, sanitation, sometimes shelter, and sometimes support with transport. We were constantly having military resources—I will not say diverted because it was quite justifiable—allocated to the business of repatriating refugees. There was no choice in that; it was part of the job.

Another humanitarian function that required our involvement was the provision of security for family reunions. For about six months we ran these family reunions, which were points of great stress for us each weekend since every Saturday morning we would get a huge crowd. On one Saturday over 13 000 people attended a family reunion. The idea was that families that had already been repatriated and were in East Timor could meet with their relatives that were still in West Timor and convince them that it was safe to return. It was hoped that such meetings would act as a catalyst to get these folk back. With a very large crowd gathering every Saturday at a predictable place and a predictable time, these reunions set up a perfect target for anybody wishing to create mischief. On a number of occasions we had outbreaks of violence. At one particular outbreak that took place, Indonesian troops fired over 500 warning shots, which caused a panic in the crowd and several people were injured in the rout that ensued. Events such as that, where there are large numbers of people, represent a significant management and security problem.

Logistics

In his brief but classic book, *Generals and Generalship*, General Wavell made an argument that gave rise to the observation that 'amateurs talk tactics and professionals talk logistics'.[2] Nothing could be more true. Dealing with the militia and sorting out the refugees was comparatively easy for us. The difficult part was where our next feed was going to come from. We were dependent on one main supply route across the island from Dili that was episodically open and a Logistics Over the Shore (LOTS) Operation. Logistics Over the Shore refers to the procedures that are followed to unload cargo from ships where no port facilities exist. During May and June 2000 we experienced the wettest season for 53 years. In the town of Betun about 150 people were drowned. In the town of Suai, where our headquarters was, we had about 30 or 40 deaths. The main supply route from Dili was completely washed away. We were therefore cut-off. As for seaborne supply across the beach at Suai, at one point we had four ships washed up on the beach at Suai. We had to attack one of them, the MV *Bosavi*, with an oxyacetylene torch, cut a hole in the side and then use a front-end loader to unload the supplies so that we could get fed. The ship owner did not appreciate the damage done to his vessel, of course, but it worked a treat! That is the sort of situation that confronted us because during the wet season the conditions at sea deteriorated to the point that we were unable to maintain our logistic supply line. We always had sufficient combat rations and could find potable water locally, but the fresh-ration train just dried up completely.

The problems of supplying a force deployed in such a remote area were compounded by another factor. In the transition from INTERFET to UNTAET, much of the logistic support, and in particular the fresh rationing, was handed over to civilian sources. The company that was chosen to do the fresh rationing did not have anywhere near the capacity to produce the goods. It was able to supply fresh food to Dili but not to Suai. We were getting rotten food. In fact the New Zealand Battalion was delivered 300 kilos of beef liver to feed New Zealand soldiers. I had it put on a helicopter and flown back to Dili, and presented to the chief logistician because I was so disgusted with this disregard for the troops in the field. The system of commercialised rationing just did not work. The lesson is that, if you are in the business of contracting out logistic support for operations in the field, you had better make sure that you get it right because it can come back and bite you, and bite you badly.

Medical and surgical support

In Sector West we had surgical capability both north and south of the ranges. We worked on the Australian Army standard of one hour to resuscitation and three hours to surgery. Throughout the period the New Zealand Battalion maintained a surgical facility in their battalion area. On the north coast we had a joint medical facility in Dili that was manned by Australia, Egypt and Singapore.

We had a number of operational casualties. The most important part of responding to these events was the provision of aeromedical evacuation (AME). With the drawdown of INTERFET, many of the assets that had been supporting INTERFET were brought home to Australia.

The Blackhawk helicopters were one of the key capabilities that were withdrawn. We were therefore left with a hole in our AME. The United Nations promised to fix this problem, again with civil hire. That particular effort was an extraordinary failure, and for months we were left in the situation where we had suboptimal AME. Night AME was a particular issue for the Australian Battalion. As this battalion was fully equipped with night vision equipment, it was capable of fighting completely by night, except for the fact that we were incapable of evacuating the wounded. When we conducted the risk analysis for night-time operations, we found that, without the ability to evacuate our men, the troops were having to concentrate around the places where they could be evacuated by road. This limitation restricted the areas in which operations could occur. Once the Blackhawks came back, all of those problems disappeared. In fact, on the night of 10 August 2000, there was a rather nasty contact between a band of militiamen and a Nepalese company, in which Private Derim Jaisey was killed and three other Nepalese soldiers were quite badly wounded. The Australian helicopters were brought over to do a night AME. Mercifully we had already practised such an evacuation. However, they were doing a night AME with a group of soldiers that did not speak English and there were no Nepalese speakers on the helicopters. It was a very challenging operation for our men to be engaged in, but it demonstrated that it was necessary to have good night AME cover.

The law and rules of engagement

In May 2000 an armed militiaman was shot and wounded near the border by soldiers from the Australian Battalion. He managed to make it back into West Timor, where he presented himself at an Indonesian Army post. What ensued was a nasty investigation. I must confess that I was caught a little flat-footed on this one. An international team of officers, which did not include an Australian, was put together to conduct an investigation into the shooting. We already had our national investigative system working. All of a sudden this UN investigation came in and conducted its own process. The results of that duplicate inquiry were very uncomfortable from my point of view and absolutely incorrect. I was even asked by the force commander at one stage whether the Australian

Government would contemplate giving compensation to this fellow, who had come into East Timor armed. I said, 'You must be smoking something, General. We are clearly not going to do that'. The incident did, however, demonstrate that the investigative process for any contact that you have in an operation needs to be clearly understood in advance of events.

As the year progressed, we became more adept in both representing our soldiers' interests and in facilitating the investigation of incidents. Private Manning of New Zealand was brutally killed on 24 July. The issue here was the way in which the New Zealand Government and the United Nations went after the perpetrator of this crime, a fellow by the name of Jacobus Bere, who has since faced trial in Indonesia. We had to pursue the Indonesian Government very hard to make sure that this fellow was brought to justice. It is interesting that a national government had to step in to pursue the issue of what happened to its soldier. On 2 August two militiamen were killed in a contact with Australian troops. By this time our investigative procedures had greatly improved, and both the UN and our national investigative team handled this situation far more slickly.

The important factor for all commanders is to make sure that their soldiers understand their rights. Mercifully a few of us in Headquarters Sector West had been involved in counter-terrorism for many years and understood very well what it meant for soldiers to be shooting people in circumstances where they would be called to account. We were aware that soldiers needed training in what they could and could not say, and how they should behave. Our legal officers were working overtime to ensure that soldiers were trained.

Force protection

After an attack that took place in March, we had gone to extraordinary measures to ensure that all our positions were in fact defended properly: we sand-bagged and put up anti-grenade screens and so forth. In one particular instance, where there was a doorway, we had hung up a screen with a weight on the bottom. The idea was that, if a grenade was thrown at it, the grenade would bounce back. That is precisely what happened.

The grenade made a hole where it landed. Inside the door there was a mosquito net covering a bed—one of nine. That first bed space was shredded by the grenade, and it is the only one that was not occupied. The soldier was outside on gun picket duty. The rest of the bed spaces were occupied and the occupants were unscathed. There were five grenades thrown into that area and about 400 rounds of ammunitions fired at the wall. The lesson here is that you must ensure that your soldiers understand force protection and know how to construct and carry out the necessary defensive precautions. We had another incident in May where a further grenade was thrown. There were five Australian soldiers in a weapon pit. The grenade went off five metres from the pit. One of the soldiers had slight lacerations under the arm. Mercifully they were below ground, and damage was minimal.

Force protection is not only an issue of enemy action, but has to do with accidents as well—industrial-type accidents, accidents with ammunition and incidents that arise from the inherently dangerous nature of military activity. These events demonstrate the need for personnel at all levels to take precautions in order to prevent wasteful and needless death and injury. In August, Corporal Stuart Jones was killed when a weapon accidentally went off inside an armoured vehicle. Other accidents included an explosion in which four soldiers were badly wounded. This incident occurred because a soldier had stashed an unidentified plastic rubbish bag of grenades under his bed when he went on leave, and another soldier who had come in to do a clean-up threw the bag into the rubbish tip, causing the explosion. Even more tragic was an explosion that occurred at the rubbish dump in the New Zealand area of operations. An allegedly empty 44-gallon drum of petrol—which obviously still contained some fumes—was thrown on the rubbish tip and caused the deaths of two locals, including a child, who had been scavenging in the vicinity of the tip. Nine other people were injured in the incident, which caused a number of nasty burns cases. It was a terrible scene. Inevitably, it was difficult to maintain a good relationship with the local community when preventable accidents of this nature took place.

I was absolutely confident that all the soldiers under my command in Sector West had been well trained. This observation is particularly true of the Australian Battalion. It speaks volumes for our Army training system that we were able to produce soldiers who, in my view, were absolutely prepared for the task at hand. There had been a lot of work done in Land Command and throughout the Army to prepare these diggers for the job that they had to do, and it was done in an exemplary way. I was never in any doubt that the soldiers deployed to East Timor were up to the task. I also had every confidence that my subordinate commanders were fully and adequately prepared for the task at hand.

The experience of conducting operations in East Timor has done a great deal for the professionalism of the Australian Army. The Army has made significant advances from where we were in September 1999. Carrying out this type of complex peace mission has been a highly valuable experience for commanders, for soldiers and for government. During the period of INTERFET, the issue of coalition management was the greatest single challenge for the Australian Government and for the Australian military—a challenge that we were able to meet successfully. It was a maturing process, in terms of our relations with other countries. By the time that UNTAET took charge of operations, we were well prepared to contribute to the multinational effort and to play an effective part in supporting the nation-building mandate of the UN mission.

Lessons learnt from multinational operations

Brigadier Dominique Trinquand

Introduction

Multinationality will be a necessary element of military operations conducted in the 21st century. This chapter focuses on building a picture of the lessons learnt by the French Army in the operations it has led outside France during the past ten years. In particular, it concentrates on the issue of the operational implications of multinational representation. However, before addressing the problems and benefits arising from the conduct of combined operations, it is worth considering the perspective that the French Army brings to any coalition. For one thing, France's armed forces are currently deployed all around the world. In addition, the French military has received strategic guidance that has focused its efforts on force projection. An inevitable consequence of that development has been a greater emphasis on multinational operations. The French Army's operational contract means that unilateral operations are now the exception rather than the norm. The lessons learnt from multinational operations are consequently the result of both long experience and recent deployments. In addition, France understands the necessity for cooperation from both a political and an operational viewpoint.

Whether we like it or not, multinational operations exist. During this century they will become increasingly common. Although everyone agrees on the fact that a national operation—with a chain of command and troops coming from the same nation—would be more efficient, it no longer corresponds to the reality facing the prosecution of contemporary missions.

There are three major reasons for a number of countries to be involved in an operation. First, as members of the United Nations (UN), our countries have committed themselves to use force only in self-defence, or upon an order given by the Security Council of the UN. Legally speaking, an operation requires international support in order to be recognised as legitimate. Second, to enable an external intervention to take place, and to be able to exercise an influence on the outcome of a crisis, we need to achieve agreement among a number of nations. Political agreement among a number of countries is therefore necessary for a mission to have a chance of succeeding. In most cases, it is not possible to mount an intervention without international support—even when the influence and standing of the country initiating the operation is undisputed. Building a firm basis of international support is a major asset when any state sets out to obtain international acceptance of an operation. Lastly, since the end of the Cold War, the defence budgets of many countries have diminished. At present there is only one country—the United States—that can have at its disposal all the capabilities required for an intervention, with a few countries able to have some of those capabilities at their disposal at any one time. Accordingly, the need to adopt a multinational model is heavily influenced by economic factors.

The range of situations in which military intervention might occur has undergone great changes over the past ten years. Both the nature and types of operations that are likely to take place are far broader than in the past. In addition, we have witnessed the redistribution of responsibility for the conduct of operations and the apportionment of different roles to distinct civil and military organisations.

In the aftermath of the Cold War, conflict is more likely to break out within states rather than between countries. The cause of contention can be cultural, ethnic, religious or even criminal, and many of these characteristics can coexist. Consequently multinational forces are confronted with a broader range of missions. These missions include prevention and deterrence, and peace enforcement or peacekeeping—all of which take place in a joint and, most of the time, inter-allied environment. The political restrictions imposed regarding the strength and the nature of the multinational force give rise to constraints that increase the complexity of each operation. It is particularly difficult for contributors to these operations to react to changed circumstances and modify the mission bestowed on their forces. This difficulty is often the result of the fact that responsibility for the operation is placed in the hands of an international institution (or institutions) and is no longer under the direct control of a national authority. The transfer of responsibility to international bodies produces a novel level of complexity, with which national militaries have to contend. In Europe we experienced these problems both in Bosnia (when the distribution of authority was between the UN and North Atlantic Treaty Organization (NATO)), and in Kosovo (involving the European Union and NATO).

The environment in which contemporary conflict is likely to take place is more complex than in the past. The trend towards intrastate conflict has meant that forces are more likely to be deployed in urban or heavily settled areas. Consequently, the forces engaged in a conflict have increased contact with the civilian population and generally have a stake in gaining their support. Other participants also influence the conduct of operations in this environment. The part played by the international media in reporting and even influencing the course of a crisis is well documented. Numerous other entities are also to be found in operational theatres and include formal international organisations such as the Red Cross and the United Nations High Commission for Refugees (UNHCR) as well as non-governmental humanitarian relief organisations with a wide variety of individual agendas.

In considering the advantages and disadvantages that multinationality represents in the conduct of operations, it is worth applying the three main principles of the conduct of war developed by Marshal Foch before he became allied commander in Europe at the end of World War I. These principles were freedom of action, concentration of effort and economy of effort.[1] They provide very useful criteria in evaluating the problems that coalitions face. The famous dictum about coalition command that is also usually ascribed to Foch is probably the best starting point for this analysis: 'Since I have been commanding a coalition, I have far less admiration for Napoleon's victories.'

The disadvantages of multinational operations

Limitations on freedom of action

The restrictions on the freedom of action available to commanders are almost inherent in coalition operations. The disadvantages of coalition command-and-control are obvious to all soldiers. All of us seek to obtain certainty and predictability from our command structures. In a multi-national environment, however, we inevitably encounter something more complicated. In working with forces from outside our national command systems, we naturally find that the political factor is closely linked with all the disadvantages of multinationality. The political constraints on the freedom of action of commanders at all levels are far more severe in an operation carried out within a multinational framework. These constraints generate delays, misunderstandings or even tensions between national contingents because of conflicts of interest or of diverse cultures. The problems that NATO encountered in agreeing on the use of air strikes in Kosovo serves to remind us of this fact.

Similarly, the mandates bestowed on a mission are often of a limited duration. This restriction does not take into account the fact that the engagement of a force can hardly be decided for a given period of time, since its aim is the resolution of the crisis. The time factor represents another form of political constraint, owing to the limited nature of the engagement, and it represents a restriction on the efficiency of the multi-national force and is potentially an impediment to its final success. Again, it is worth recalling the problems caused by the initial time limitations set on the deployment of NATO forces in Bosnia.

Finally, national interests remain of paramount importance. They are expressed through the options available when delegating command authority; through the parallel national intelligence chains that coexist on operations; and through the drafting of independent evacuation plans for national contingents. Indeed, the protection and security of the troops has been given an unprecedented significance because of terrorist actions, organised criminal groups, clans, or even technological and industrial risks. Here again, there are heavy political constraints. The acceptable risks would not be the same for the defence of major interests. Once more, the examples of limitations set to the employment of troops are numerous in the former Yugoslavia.

In most circumstances, the centre of gravity of a multinational operation will probably be located more in the preservation of the coalition's cohesion than in the accomplishment of the mission. Thus, the factor determining the extent of the commander's freedom of action is often the search for the lowest common denominator.

Obstacles to the concentration of effort on coalition operations

It is difficult to apply the principle of concentration of effort in a multinational environment. The task of constructing a mixed force is difficult to master: the force must be adapted to the political and budgetary constraints that vary considerably from one country to the next. The principle of force packaging provides the necessary adaptability, but the contribution that each country makes is dependent on the benefits that they each intend to gain from the operation. Besides, one must be careful not to scatter the smaller units too much, and to preserve the *esprit de corps* of national forces. The setting-up of the force is therefore a genuine tightrope-walking exercise between the interests of the mission and those of the contributing states. The time that it takes to set up a multinational force is often longer than it would take to establish a unilateral operation.

The concentration of effort is of paramount importance in the area of command, but the assimilation of multinational specificity within a headquarters requires a lot of energy. This problem inevitably arises where cultural differences exist, and where multiple liaison officers are posted at all levels. The ability to integrate other contingents must be the product of building an atmosphere where all parties feel that they are welcome and also play a role in welcoming others. A command system naturally requires the compatibility of the various systems, but the human and cultural dimensions of interoperability should not be forgotten. Despite the widespread use of the English language and the international standard represented by NATO structures and procedures, an effective contributor to a multinational headquarters should have additional language skills and have training in coalition adaptability.

In the intelligence field, the existence of complementary national assets for the gathering and processing of operational intelligence, as well as the multiplicity of national or allied intelligence organisations, can induce misunderstandings. Each nation wants to preserve a certain freedom when it comes to making decisions. Also, countries are inclined to use intelligence resources as a kind of currency. However, the protection of sources and intelligence-gathering methods can be an impediment to the necessary coordination of actions. Besides, the commander on the ground can be deprived of information which, though gathered nearby, is too often transmitted only to the national contingents.

Civil–military cooperation is now an essential component of operations, since, in addition to the activities undertaken in support of the force, they can help lower tensions and partly settle the consequences of the crisis. Nonetheless, if this cooperation cannot address the root causes of conflict within a failed state, it can prove to be a bone of contention among those states contributing forces. The competing agendas of the different contingents comprising the United Nations Operations in Somalia between 1993 and 1995 (UNOSOM II) demonstrates how varied points of view on the part of the engaged nations can induce differences in the goals of the operation.

Obstacles to economy of effort in a coalition

It is difficult to impose economy of effort on a multinational force. When a country assumes the responsibility for providing the infrastructure for a multinational operation, it becomes liable for the cost of providing the various contingents with the mission-essential assets. The lead nation has to accept responsibility for ensuring that its own officers possess the appropriate staff competencies and training. Indeed, the size of headquarters tends to increase, and is no longer proportionate to the volume of forces that the headquarters command. The organisation of the headquarters is also modified in a coalition. There is a distinct increase in the number of liaison detachments, as well as an increase in establishment positions designed purely to ensure that all contingents are represented in proportion to their contribution.

In the area of logistics, NATO standardisation is an obvious advantage. Even within such a longstanding alliance, however, the search for procedural and technical interoperability is an ongoing process. When conducting multinational operations, logistics is a national responsibility and, because of the weakness of some contingents, of the know-how of others, and of the scattering of units, there is a risk of redundancy.

In recent years, the working conditions of personnel deployed on operations have been constantly upgraded so that they more closely reflect the comfortable, if austere, standards of urban life. Troops employed on multinational operations, particularly peace and humanitarian relief missions, enjoy access to clean clothing, accommodation, food and entertainment that would have been unavailable in the past. We do, however, have to be aware of the fact that this equipment also represents a serious logistical burden in terms of both weight and size. Access to these basic comforts is widely appreciated and makes a significant contribution to morale. Nonetheless, despite the cultural differences that exist between national forces, obvious discrepancies between contingents may cause tensions.

The process of setting up a force often complies with a need to preserve the representativeness and not the overall cohesion of the force. This need often results in the duplication of capabilities and the consequent redundancy of some force assets. The tendency to arrive at unbalanced force contributions is either the result of attempts to ensure the coherence of a national contribution, or arises from a policy of ensuring that a country is represented with sufficient 'boots on the ground' to enable it to exercise a real influence over the course of the operation. Although both aims are understandable from a national perspective, they do not, strictly speaking, do much to promote economy of effort.

The advantages of multinational operations

After examining the disadvantages experienced by multinational forces, we should now consider the advantages of multinationality. The point is not to convince ourselves 'to make the best of a bad lot' but to see that 'diversity is enriching'. This idea is one that should be easily shared by countries created through immigration—such as Australia and the United States—but it is not necessarily an opinion that all share.

Relative freedom of action on operations

On contemporary operations, the media generally have a major presence and influence on the public representation of military actions. Consequently, each contingent shares responsibility for communicating information to both national and international media organisations. An operational media strategy has several key elements. It enables the force to help shape international public opinion, which in turn helps demonstrate the legitimacy of an operation. It is a means of communicating key messages to local populations and authorities. Full media coverage can also help consolidate the cohesion of the deployed force and to 'sell' the operation to domestic constituencies and the troops' own families. Here again, the national level is closely interwoven with the multinational level but, this time, the multinational dimension is an advantage. Indeed, the larger the media presence, the more target audiences can be made aware of the importance of the mission. The various national media assets can be enlisted to communicate a range of messages to different groups. In order to do so, the deployed force must coordinate the messages that it wishes to provide. In this sense, the commander, his staff and the various national command elements have a degree of operational autonomy that might not be available to a more homogenous force.

Alternatively, the presence of competing national interests can represent a constraint on the commander's freedom of action, the limits of which need to be defined so as to integrate them into the planning process. By identifying these limits on the employment of the force, the command element can avoid last-minute surprises. The formal delegation of authority to a force commander clearly identifies what level of command he can expect to wield in respect of the different contingents. Because this is factored into the Status of Forces Agreement (SOFA) that is made prior to the deployment of a national contingent, the commander should be fully aware of what capabilities are available in what circumstances. The existence of a reserve in the force must, in that respect, be specified in the granted delegations of power.

The coexistence of several countries in an operation is not always an impediment for the accomplishment of the mission, and it can sometimes even create a competitive spirit. Indeed, the existence of a degree of legitimate national pride usually induces each contingent to do its best, and this can contribute to the success of an operation. The commander who has the honour to be entrusted by the participating countries with the command of their troops will know how to use this competitive spirit for the benefit of the mission.

Consolidating the efforts of a multinational force

National armed forces, with very few exceptions, are increasingly less likely to have the full range of military capabilities at their disposal. The complementarity of national capabilities thus makes it possible to make up for gaps that occur at the time the force is established or as operations progress. For example, engineers from different countries can put their efforts together in order to provide the necessary assets; and specific units specialised in crowd control can be held in reserve and used to intervene at a critical point where reinforcements are necessary.

A broad range of participating contingents provides a commander with a spectrum of response capabilities that are often useful in controlling outbreaks of violence. The origin, the language and even the specific training of some contingents make them more able than others to commit themselves in certain phases of the operation. This diversity in competencies enhances the force's ability to concentrate its efforts.

The cosmopolitan composition of many coalitions often enables a force to devise various approaches to a single problem. The resulting flexibility makes the entire force more able to adopt an asymmetrical point of view, which is becoming increasingly necessary in peace support operations. This is especially the case in the area of human intelligence.

Economy of effort using multinational resources

In the area of logistics, paradoxically, multinationality can be a source of economy. Indeed, the search for operational economies induces participants in a coalition to try to combine functions such as transport, or to designate a steering nation for one function, such as the provision of petrol, oil and lubricants. Even in very sensitive areas such as medical support, agreements signed beforehand can make it possible to reduce the costs for each country by providing the force with the necessary assets. In the intelligence area, the process could be the same and thus, despite the existence of separate national intelligence chains, the merging of these various assets could reduce costs, especially with the provision of strategic intelligence or rare assets, such as those of electronic warfare. The complementarity of assets in this specific area is often very important, and it requires the sharing of the intelligence production and analysis capabilities.

Generally speaking, multinationality can only save money if procedures and training make it possible to make the most of the complementarity of assets. Optimising multinational assets is currently being done for NATO procedures, and reflects what Europe is trying to do in the procurement area.

Conclusion

Multinationality will be an unavoidable condition for the operations that take place in the 21st century. It is no longer appropriate to think about national operations or to attempt to make the other contingents on an operation act according to whatever our criteria are for a national operation. For example, the efforts that Western states make to ensure the wellbeing and the security of our men and women generate a logistical burden. These conditions are obtained at the detriment of simplicity and the acceptance of risks, which can be essential factors for success—particularly when we are faced with belligerents who do not have the same value systems as we do.

Multinational cooperation will enhance our chances for success if we limit its disadvantages by pre-preparing common procedures and specific agreements that will permit us to start an operation with a set of good conditions. The constraints imposed on us by multinationality, especially during the planning phase, must be taken into account in order to assess the limits on the commander's freedom of action. Finally, a high level of mutual awareness—particularly in cultural, linguistic and technical areas—must be developed, in order to reap the benefits of multinationality. This last factor is essential since diversity is enriching, as emphasised earlier. We have to learn how to maximise the benefits of national differences in order to empower multinational forces and to contribute to the success of their missions.

Conclusion

Early 21st-century armies and the challenge of unrestricted warfare

Alan Ryan

The challenge of conducting combat operations in the information age presents affluent, democratic and technologically advanced societies with a number of conundrums that are peculiar to our current historical period. As the ability of information-age forces to apply stand-off, surgical, kinetic effects to particular targets increases, so too might we expect that close combat and the role played by ground forces would diminish. This has not proved to be the case. High explosive, however smartly delivered, is a poor tool for resolving those causes of conflict that reside in the human heart. Current indications are that future conflict will require the active participation of land forces with access to high technology. These forces will also need to apply the soldierly functions that have long been entrenched in Western modes of warfare. A recurring theme throughout this book has been that, although technology has changed the way that land warfare is waged, the core functions of modern armies are little changed from the days when Roman legions defended the borders of the empire and enforced a cosmopolitan peace within it. Soldiers have always been more than just warfighters, though a century of struggle between the great powers made it a priority that they be able to fight and prevail in total war. In the inherently more complex conditions of protean global insecurity that confront us today, armed forces do not only exist to win wars, but are also an integral part of the liberal democracies' struggle to win the peace.

The challenges that are being played out in the current battles of the war on terrorism presage much of what is yet to come. We are witnessing a global struggle between wealthy, politically secular, post-industrial societies on the one hand, and fanatical ideologues, opportunistic warlords and sub-national ethic groups that inhabit the marginalised fringe of a bifurcated global economy on the other. The disparity between the methods and character of such fundamentally different combatants requires a re-adjustment of our concept of military service from that which prevailed in the 20th century. Warfare is reverting to its more usual condition—not internecine conflict among states striving for economic and political dominance, but struggles between the haves and the have-nots, fuelled by religious, racial and cultural antipathies. This is not to say that warfare between states is a thing of the past. Nonetheless, armed conflict is more likely to take place between parties that have little in common. Pluralist, information-age states have experienced a convergence of interests brought about by globalising pressures. Modern states have too much to lose by fighting each other. The greatest effect of the information age has been to build a community of interests between states whose economies, digital networks and populations are trans-national. Unfortunately, the downside of the information revolution has been to drive a wedge between the information-rich haves and the economically backward, information-poor have-nots. It is in this rift that most of the modern causes of conflict reside.

The affluent world is finding that, in this sort of conflict, its technological edge does not automatically guarantee its security. In many cases our reliance on technology makes us even more vulnerable to attack—a fact that was graphically demonstrated on 11 September 2001. As Edward Luttwak pointed out in his classic, and recently re-released book, *On Strategy*, paradoxically there is no necessary correlation between military might and military effectiveness.[1] All military capabilities are made redundant at the time that they are fielded because a resourceful enemy is already dreaming up counter-measures to overcome them.

Defeating future enemies

The contributors to this book examine a range of potential adversaries across a broad spectrum of conflict. They range from the challenges of peace enforcement in failed states where First World forces confront feudal clans, to combat operations against terrorist forces and their state-based supporters, to full-scale open warfare against state-based armies. For the most part, the authors consider the advantages and disadvantages that arise from Western dominance in the fields of military technology and military information. In most contemporary conflicts, potential adversaries are unlikely to possess these advantages and are therefore more likely to act unpredictably in order to gain a comparative advantage. This observation is as true for a terrorist organisation as it is for a warlord who controls a country. Unfortunately for us, in the current environment of protean insecurity, it is quite possible that a rogue actor might have access to weapons of mass destruction and might consider that their use is quite legitimate. The existence of this threat has pre-occupied the Bush Administration since 11 September 2001, and it is the strategic concern that has the greatest influence on our immediate future.

Although the operational methods employed by information-age forces will vary considerably according to the nature of the conflict in which they find themselves engaged, the most likely enemies that we will meet share one thing in common. No force—whether from the industrial or the pre-industrial era—will think of challenging information-age forces in their area of strength. During the 20th century, even the most bitter battlefield confrontation was fought according to certain rules and within a broadly shared perception of reciprocity. Even the horror of the trenches during World War I was justified according to principles of attritional warfare—however misguided. In World War II the use of terror-bombing techniques was explained by reference to the effect that it had on the ability of the opposing side to support their war machine. Even the use of nuclear weapons was justified by a cost–benefit analysis of the value of immediately terminating the war. Those (Western) calculations of advantage are not necessarily shared by fundamentalist ideologues who know that they have God on their side and do not feel constrained about the ways in which they might further His ends (in their theology there is no question that 'He' might be a 'Her').

Religious fanatics are not alone in rejecting conventional notions of proportionality and restraint, much less state-based notions of what constitutes victory. The work that is likely to have the greatest long-term effect on war in the 21st century is *Unrestricted Warfare*. Senior Colonels Qiao Liang and Wang Xiangsui of the People's Liberation Army (PLA) published this vision of the future of conflict in 1999. The authors argue that, given the overwhelming military power wielded by the United States, those that wish to challenge America or its Western allies will have to adopt other means than conventional military attack. They consider terrorism, cyber warfare, economic attack and weapons of mass destruction. They conclude that:

> Non-professional warriors and non-state organisations are posing a greater and greater threat to sovereign nations, making these warriors and organisations more and more serious adversaries for every professional army. Compared to these adversaries, professional armies are like gigantic dinosaurs which lack strength commensurate to their size in this new age. Their adversaries, then, are rodents with great powers of survival, which can use their sharp teeth to torment the better part of the world.[2]

Perhaps most frightening is that the two colonels suggest that information-age warfare may be beyond the capabilities of traditional armies and traditionally trained 'managers of violence'. It is no use preparing to fight a conventional state-on-state war that will be a contest of strength fought out on an identifiable battlefield and governed by mutually accepted conventions if the enemy attacks in other ways. The recent spate of mass-casualty terrorist attacks has served to demonstrate that plural democracies are vulnerable to attack anywhere. We confront 'Mad Max'-style warriors who have the option to use our own advanced technology against us, but who are often more effective fighting the war of the rodent, gnawing away at our social structure and avoiding open conflict with our security and defence forces. In the West, this is a theme that has been expounded by authors such as Ralph Peters and Martin van Creveld, and it is a concern that lies at the heart of this book.[3]

The development of the essays that form the content of this book took place in the eighteen months following the events of 11 September 2001. During that time we saw the United States use military forces in innovative and novel ways in order to deal with a very different enemy. In Afghanistan, the internationally recruited forces of al-Qa'ida and their Taliban allies sought to use the country's traditional obstructions of terrain, weather and remoteness to stave off invasion. They were brought to battle by the forces of the Northern Alliance—armed, equipped and constituted very much like themselves. However, what proved decisive in this conflict was the presence of modern and highly unconventional special forces as well as coalition light forces that were able to deploy into the theatre and establish a presence with a facility not dreamt of by earlier armies. Despite the Cassandra-like lamentations of those pessimists who prophesied that the operation would come to grief in the mountains of Afghanistan, the international coalition, under the no-nonsense leadership of the US military, designed a smart campaign. It was a campaign that was appropriate given the nature of the enemy and the particular circumstances of the conflict. It was unlike any war we had seen before—perhaps because, in order to defeat this enemy, the United States selectively used its military strengths. The US military did not, however, resile from the fact that, in order to contend with this enemy, its forces had to become partly like those of the enemy. It was innovative, information-age warfare against an opponent whose lack of information resources caused it to fight blind. The theory developed by Robert Leonhard over the past few years and which is spelt out in Chapter 7 was given dramatic vindication.

The images that emerged from Afghanistan were markedly different from those that we imagine when we consider conventional state-on-state conflict. Instead of armoured formations battling it out in rolling open country or desert, the United States committed small teams that prepared the political conditions for victory well in advance of the deployment of ground forces. These groups included teams from the Central Intelligence Agency's Special Operations Group (SOG) whose mission was to win the support of the Northern Alliance and coordinate their efforts with those of the coalition forces coming into the theatre of operations. As combat operations developed, special forces troops fought alongside their Afghan allies travelling with them on horseback, but using hand-held laser designators to bring overwhelming aerial firepower to bear on their enemies.

This strategy maximised the technological superiority of the United States, but enabled it to exercise political influence on events on the ground. The same forces were able to employ lethal force with a degree of discrimination that is not possible when a weapons platform and its pilot are moving at high speed at an altitude of 30000 feet. Where appropriate, the use of light forces capable of bringing accurate but overwhelming firepower to bear will be the 21st-century equivalent of the guerrilla tactic of 'grabbing a superior foe by the belt'. In Afghanistan, instead of the technologically superior force being rendered helpless by an inability to use close fire support, the Taliban and al-Qa'ida were brought to battle and destroyed. The aim of contemporary operational commanders should be to possess the advantages of Lieutenant Colonel Leonhard's 'man-in-the-light', while leaving the opponent in the dark.

A similar principle will apply to future conflicts, though the methodology will differ according to circumstances. This theme is developed in Chapter 9 by Colonel Richard Cousens, who points out that the point of battle is not the combat itself, but the effects that it achieves. In any major conflict—whether it be against a fundamentalist non-state movement, a Third World warrior state, a Second World totalitarian dictatorship, or a combination of all three—First World forces will employ capabilities that are more joint, integrated, precise, lethal and decisive than previously considered possible. What is more, as Colonel Cousens points out, planning such operations will involve a greater level of complexity than ever before. When engaging enemies that wage war using civilisation rather than terrain as the battleground, strategies need to be developed that use all elements of national and supra-national power to achieve victory. As Colonels Qiao and Wang concluded:

> Faced with warfare in the broad sense that will unfold on a borderless battlefield, it is no longer possible to rely on military forces alone to achieve national security in the larger strategic sense, nor is it possible to protect these stratified national interests. Obviously warfare is in the process of transcending the domains of soldiers, military units, and military affairs, and is increasingly becoming a matter for politicians, scientists, and even bankers. How to conduct warfare is obviously no longer a question for the consideration of military people alone.[4]

In the era of asymmetric and unrestricted conflict, armies, the other services and their professional-officer classes only possess partial responsibility for the human, cultural and social security of the societies that they represent. Traditional, state-based military forces do, however, have a special responsibility in this changing, protean security environment. The military has traditionally been entrusted by states with a monopoly on the legitimate use of force. Consequently, the military possesses the greatest expertise in the development of strategies to use force in the defence of the state. In the information age, the military must share that knowledge and learn to rely on other aspects of national and transnational power. Perhaps the greatest challenge to military men, politicians, policy-makers and theorists will be to accept that violent and destructive conflict has moved beyond the bonds of state-based entities and that all parties now share the responsibility for understanding and, if necessary, prosecuting war. In his chapter, Professor Hugh Smith demonstrates the challenge that the transformation of conflict poses to military professionalism. His prescription is utterly correct. The military is no longer merely responsible for the mechanics of war against identifiable enemies. Defence forces are an integral part of the national security establishment; they must therefore assist in preparing and coordinating national and transnational responses to attack. Although the future of warfare remains uncharted, military professionals retain the special responsibility that their training and position in society bestows upon them. In this complex new world they have more, rather than fewer, roles to play.

Asymmetric war

At the heart of the new insecurity lies confusion about the implications of the varieties of asymmetric warfare being waged against Western societies. It is easy to become bogged down in the confusion of definitions and competing explanations of the phenomenon. As the discussion of terrorism in Chapter 10 demonstrates, even among experts from a broadly similar background, there exists a wide range of opinions concerning the best way to respond to attacks that target our communities' vulnerabilities rather than contend with our military power. There does, however, appear to be little disagreement that asymmetric warfare—in the sense of an attack on areas of weakness by an intrinsically incompatible opponent—is here to stay.

The essence of asymmetric strategy is that an antagonist must step beyond accepted norms of armed conflict in order to achieve its desired outcome. For a variety of reasons, states cannot usually do this. There is nothing particularly unusual about asymmetric warfare. In fact the internecine slugging matches indulged in by great states during the 20th century are more the exception than the rule. Throughout history, most armed conflict has not been between states. Military power has most often been employed for the purposes of what we now call 'operations other than war'. During the 19th century, the great European imperial states most commonly employed their troops in what we now call constabulary tasks. Many of the non-state actors that they fought have since evolved into states themselves, but that does not negate the fact that the military forces of states were engaged in warlike activities against other types of human organisation. In our own age, peace operations and interventions in failed states require armed forces to conduct military operations that are often difficult to distinguish from combat operations. The challenge of the present and the future is to deal with the realisation that Pandora's box has been opened once again. The ability to wage war is no longer the monopoly of states, and armed forces must now contend with an infinite variety of potential opponents and allies. The assertion that all war between dissimilar states is asymmetric is a meaningless proposition that fails to deal with the true threat posed by those parties that choose to target our civilisation's soft spots.

Asymmetric modes of violence as well as attacks on the civil infrastructure of a state have already been adopted by non-state actors such as religious and political groups, criminals, warlords in failed states, and even single-issue groups such as radical environmentalists and economic luddites. These acts of propaganda by the deed have even won partial acceptance in some circles—a worrying postmodern trend that will make it more difficult to combat future terrorists. Some pundits have made great cause of blaming the United States for the attacks of 11 September 2001, and voices have been raised in Australia and elsewhere warning against participating in the international war on terrorism for fear of inviting another attack like the bombing in Bali. In the meantime, Australians and other Westerners travelling and working abroad must accept that they are the targets of indiscriminate violence simply because of who they are. War is being waged, not just on conventional military establishments, but on all of us. Inexorably and largely unnoticed, a novel and extremely unpleasant environment of global insecurity is being thrust on us. Western liberal pluralism is under attack and its own characteristics of the open society, freedom of speech and tolerance are being used against it. Those that would wish the threat away by ignoring the existence of fundamentalist terrorists, or the participation of their state sponsors, are simply feeding it. For that reason, if no other, we need to develop a more profound understanding of this new face of warfare.

In Chapter 8, Group Captain MacFarling suggested that the Combined Bomber Offensive against Germany during World War II represented not only a war of attrition, but an asymmetric approach. His argument was based on the contention that all opposing forces are dissimilar. To accept this notion is to perpetuate the misapprehension that, in a globalised world, armed conflict is only an affair of states. World War II might have been metaphorically a struggle between apples and pears, which the pears with considerably inferior industrial power were doomed to lose. However, the adversaries, being Western states, at least belonged to the same genus. They had more in common than they had differences. It is not as if they were fighting a completely different type of organisation. What is more, Group Captain MacFarling pointed out that the allies were waging total war with the intention of bringing about unconditional surrender, not a political accommodation. In fact waging a war with the objective of bringing about the total surrender of the enemy represents the antithesis of asymmetric strategic objectives. As Colonels Qiao and Wang argue, the new objective of waging war is not just to use 'armed force to compel the enemy to submit to one's will'. Instead, they suggest it is 'using all means, including armed force or non-armed force, military and non-military, and lethal and non-lethal means to compel the enemy to accept one's interests'.[5] The point is that, in a complex and multilayered global society, battlefield success and a consequent political settlement no longer represent the sole definition of victory. For many antagonists it may be enough to assert their world view and to deter interference in their program. It may even be to promote a militant ideology or religious belief with no thought of achieving a political objective. Consequently, it is important to draw a distinction between the asymmetries of power that exist between all states and the application of asymmetric strategy in armed conflict. The use of violent strategies to achieve political or criminal ends is not confined to states. In the 21st century, the international community consists of a diverse collection of states, non-state actors, corporations and supranational social movements. Consequently, armies are going to have to contend with a potentially wider variety of opponents than ever before. Asymmetric warfare represents a completely different paradigm than state-on-state warfare.

Group Captain MacFarling's argument about asymmetric warfare relies on classical and medieval precedents to define the state and the part that it plays in conflict. Yet the system of states that we possess in the 21st century bears no resemblance to the states' system that existed even 100 years ago. Where once the sovereignty of the state was indefeasible, now states voluntarily forego or pool their authority in a great many areas. More significantly, there are so many different types of states, ranging from illegitimate 'rogue' states to a solitary superpower, that any attempt to discuss asymmetry as a matter for states only is nonsense. Group Captain MacFarling uses the example of the Melian dialogue to promote the notion that asymmetric strategies are natural. That conclusion is not supported by the end of the Melian affair. After some limited successes resisting the Athenian colossus in conventional fighting, the Melians were overrun; the Athenians killed all the men of military age, and sold the women and children into slavery.[6] An asymmetric power relationship was a fact, but it was not a strategy that this particular small state without allies was able to apply. While dissimilar power relationships exist between all states, conventional and legitimate states are limited in the types of asymmetric strategies that they can employ. On the other hand, an organisation without the responsibility of sovereignty and without the liabilities of land, kin and international legitimacy can apply asymmetric strategies effectively against a state made vulnerable by its very success.

Steven Metz and Douglas Johnson of the US Army's Strategic Studies Institute have proposed what is perhaps the most comprehensive definition of asymmetry yet devised. It is only one of many such definitions, but it has the distinct advantage of telling us what asymmetric strategy is *not*. It is not behaving in a similar way to an opponent, as occurred when the Allies matched German terror bombing with their own disproportionate response. Metz and Johnson argue that:

> [A]symmetry is acting, organizing, and thinking *differently* than opponents in order to maximise one's own advantages, exploit an opponent's weaknesses, attain the initiative, or gain greater freedom of action. It can be *political–strategic, military strategic, operational,* or a *combination* of these. It can entail different *methods, technologies, values, organizations, time perspectives* or some *combination* of these. It can be *short-term* or *long-term*. It can be *deliberate* or by *default*. It can be *discrete* or pursued in *conjunction* with symmetric approaches. It can have both *psychological* and *physical* dimensions.[7]

More tellingly, perhaps, they identify two types of strategic asymmetry: positive and negative. Positive asymmetry is what our side does—the use of differences to create an advantage. Our positive asymmetries are predominantly technological. The Australian Defence Force and its partners enjoy a proportionate advantage in firepower, battlefield surveillance, and command-and-control systems over most likely adversaries. We also enjoy an advantage in the training and educational standards that we bestow on our troops. These asymmetries are so obvious that we tend to take them for granted. Our comparative advantage is bought by investment of significant resources in both personnel and equipment. By comparison, negative asymmetry is the difference that an opponent will use to target our weaknesses and vulnerabilities. It may involve placing a bomb in a crowded bar full of holiday-makers. There is no intention of winning a conventional military victory, or even of achieving some political objective. The attacks in Bali in October 2002 and in Kenya the following month were merely demonstrations—pitting the terrorists' will against our own to demonstrate the supremacy of their world view. If we are to succeed in asymmetric conflict, we need to be aware of those points of weakness and use our strengths to compensate. There is little that the military can do in order to prevent an attack such as the one in Bali. However, military thinkers, together with other members of the security establishment, need to work in unison in order to build strategies that will help deter such outrages and root out concentrations of terrorists.

Asymmetric attack is not merely a terrorist technique, and armed forces cannot afford to ignore it. Being largely land-bound and man-power-intensive, armies are particularly vulnerable to this type of attack. Recent conflicts provide us with a range of examples of different asym-metric methods. At its crudest level, the use of cheap rocket-propelled grenades by the Somali militias against vulnerable, expensive helicopters in Mogadishu in 1993 was an example of exploiting technological differ-ences to achieve a significant cost–benefit outcome. This technique was also an example of a method being adopted that was beyond the intended use of the weapon, but one that was nonetheless effective. More fright-ening, though, was the use of asymmetries of will and of normative behaviour. Asymmetries of will occur where one party is fully committed to the struggle and the other is engaged in promoting less-than-vital inter-ests.[8] In Somalia the Habr Gidr clan was fighting for its political survival, whereas the United States was present in Somalia for humanitarian reasons. The Habr Gidr clan was willing to fight to the death and to act in a way that a professional military would not. By comparison with that level of commitment, Somalia was a zero-sum game for the United States. United States disengagement demonstrated that a committed fighter could beat a more powerful adversary in circumstances where the latter did not see its interests as being involved. In that instance, the Somali clansmen forced the United States, and ultimately the United Nations (UN), to accept their interests. It was a victory with a tragic legacy for their people, their country and the region, but as Ralph Peters argued in Chapter 1, rational objectives are not necessarily a part of contemporary conflict.

Closely associated with asymmetries of will are normative asymme-tries, which apply when the opposing parties do not share common behavioural or cultural norms. Eleven September 2001 was so shocking to Western sensibilities precisely because we were unable to understand what could cause the terrorists to immolate themselves. In the succeeding war in Afghanistan, we found it difficult to comprehend why Taliban warriors chose to fight to the death, content in the knowledge that at least they might have a chance of killing a few of their Western opponents. This sort of war should not come as a surprise—as an operational method it has been directed at Western troops for over twenty years. The first indication that fanatic asymmetry threatened Western military might occurred in Beirut in 1983 with the suicide bomb attack on the US Marines' barracks. In that incident, over 300 American and French troops died—victims not only of a fanatic ideology, but also Western inability to imagine that such an incident could take place.

The willingness of pre-modern warriors to use their women and children as shields, or to use swarm tactics against forces employing superior firepower, seems alien to us. Yet this is precisely what happened to the UN forces in Somalia, Russian troops in Chechnya and to the Israelis in the West Bank. It will happen again. Future armies will need to be prepared to fight opponents (state or non-state) that are willing and able to bring the battle to them on their terms.

Finally, asymmetric conflict has a psychological dimension that reaches into our societies and causes internal divisions quite different to those that exist in conventional warfare. Since September 2001 it has been made clear that postmodern adversaries are sometimes already present inside our borders and are willing to enlist any support that will damage our resolve to resist them. A terrorist organisation or rogue regime can effectively paralyse a modern plural democracy by sowing dissent. They can enlist an unlikely range of collaborators, not to support their cause, but to prevent an effective response. Unfortunately, we now see pacifist groups, church leaders, political figures, media personalities and entertainers routinely taking the part of rogue regimes and terrorist groups whose true nature they do not begin to understand. There is no military response to this internal dissent. Military forces will simply have to become accustomed to the fact that they may not have the total support of the societies that they protect.

Conclusion

If this book demonstrates one thing, it is that armed conflict remains with us. In the 21st century, it is still likely to involve low-tech adversaries who seek to impose their interests on others with the use of machetes, small arms and fertiliser bombs. We also possess an oversupply of aggressive totalitarian dictators who have the resources of a country at their disposal. The continued prevalence of violent conflict poses a substantial strategic challenge to those societies that consider themselves to have evolved beyond such antediluvian forms of social violence. Optimists thought that the end of the Cold War would usher in a new era of peace and global security; whereas, in fact, the opposite has occurred. Most alarmingly, we have witnessed strategic alliances between non-state groups and rogue states, some of which have access to advanced weapons of mass destruction.

Long-suppressed tensions and causes of conflict have surfaced to make ours a very insecure age. As Trotsky is credited with saying, 'you may not be interested in war, but war is interested in you'. For generations, technology has shielded Western society from the impact of war. Conflicts have been fought out in the Third World and nuclear stalemate has prevented the intrusion of unregulated violence into our own communities. The events of 11 September 2001 and the Bali bombing a year later put a dint in Western assurance. Violent conflict is still more likely to take place beyond our shores, but we have seen that we are no longer immune to its fallout. What is more, our vulnerability to certain forms of attack has been made manifest. Intercontinental ballistic missiles, stealth bombers and cruise missiles are of limited use against a shadowy warrior enemy who chooses not to be brought to battle on a conventional battlefield. In consequence, there remains a need for land forces that are creative and adaptive and who can take the battle to the enemy. What is more, the continued existence of armies, who alone can bring a decision and enforce security on land, provides the only definite guarantee that we can continue to engage our likely foes.

Warfare is always complex, and each generation must learn to overcome the fog and friction that is inherent in their own circumstances of conflict. As Clausewitz wrote: 'every war is rich in unique episodes. Each is an uncharted sea, full of reefs. The commander may suspect the reef's existence without ever having seen them; now he has to steer past them in the dark'.[9] In our own generation we need to confront the manifold uncertainties of unrestricted warfare. Once engaged in combat, Western armed forces can use information dominance to gain a comparative advantage over most likely adversaries, but it remains almost impossible to predict all the challenges ahead. In fact, it may even be folly to try. In his classic work, *Marching through Chaos: The Descent of Armies in Theory and Practice*, the Canadian military historian John English pointed out that a myriad of random factors made the course of war inherently unpredictable.[10] He was correct, of course, and so it is true that, despite our technological and social states of advancement, the problem of human conflict has yet to be resolved by peaceful or purely technological means. Now, and in the future, soldiers will be required to fight to protect the fragile illusion of civilisation. It is our responsibility to ensure that they are armed with the values, knowledge and tools with which to do so.

Notes

Introduction

1 The words are those of American radio broadcaster Herb Morrison who, in May 1937, described the explosion of the German commercial airship, the *Hindenburg*, as it landed near New York. See Herb Morrison, 'The burning of the Hindenburg,' in Richard Rhodes (ed.), *Visions of Technology: A Century of Vital Debate About Machines, Systems and the Human World*, Simon & Schuster, New York, 1999, p. 127.

2 Donald H. Rumsfeld, 'Transforming the military', *Foreign Affairs*, May/June 2002, vol. 81, no. 3, p. 23.

3 James F. Hoge Jr and Gideon Rose (eds), *How Did This Happen? Terrorism and the New War*, Public Affairs, New York, 2001.

4 Gore Vidal, 'Black Tuesday', in *The Last Empire: Essays 1992–2001*, Abacus, London, 2001, pp. 303–16.

5 United States Department of Defense, *Joint Vision 2020*, US Government Printing Office, Washington DC, June 2000.

6 John R. Galvin, 'Uncomfortable wars: towards a new paradigm', *Parameters: Journal of the US Army War College*, Winter 1986, vol. 16, no. 4, pp. 2–8. Galvin was then Commander-in-Chief, US Southern Command.

7 Max G. Mainwaring, 'An interview with General John R. Galvin, US Army (Retd), Dean, Fletcher School of Law and Diplomacy, 6 August 1997', *Small Wars and Insurgencies*, vol. 9, no. 1, Spring 1998, p. 9. For another, and more positive view, of the American experience of unconventional conflict see Max Boot, *The Savage Wars of Peace: Small Wars and the Rise of American Power*, Basic Books, New York, 2002.

8   John Carroll, *Terror: A Meditation on the Meaning of September 11*, Script Publications, Melbourne, 2002, pp. 7–8.

9   Michael Russell Rip and James M. Hasik, *The Precision Revolution: GPS and the Future of Aerial Warfare*, Naval Institute Press, Annapolis, MD, 2002, p. 426.

10 Francis Fukuyama, 'The end of history', *National Interest*, Spring 1989, vol. 15 and *The End of History and the Last Man*, The Free Press, New York, 1992.

11 Paul Johnson, *Modern Times: A History of the World from the 1920s to the 1990s*, Phoenix, London, 1992, Chapter 15.

12 Samuel P. Huntington, 'The clash of civilizations?', *Foreign Affairs*, Summer 1993, vol. 72, no. 3, pp. 22–49.

13 See Michael J. Hogan, *A Cross of Iron: Harry S. Truman and the Origins of the National Security State, 1945–1954*, Cambridge University Press, Cambridge, 1998.

14 President of the United States of America, *The National Security Strategy of the United States of America*, The White House, Washington DC, September 2002, p. 6.

15 John Lewis Gaddis, 'A grand strategy of transformation', *Foreign Policy*, November/December 2002, pp. 50–7.

16 ibid., p. 56.

17 Eric Hobsbawm, 'War and peace in the 20th Century', *London Review of Books*, 21 February 2002, pp. 16–18; Philip Bobbitt, *The Shield of Achilles: War, Peace and the Course of History*, Alfred A. Knopf, New York, 2002.

18 Hobsbawm, 'War and peace in the 20th Century', p. 17.

19 Bobbitt, *The Shield of Achilles*, p. 806.

20 Adda B. Bozeman, 'War and the clash of ideas', *Orbis: A Journal of World Affairs*, Spring 1976, vol. 20, no. 1, pp. 61–102.

21 John Keegan, *A History of Warfare*, Hutchinson, London, 1993; Samuel P. Huntington, *The Clash of Civilisations and The Remaking of World Order*, Simon & Schuster, New York, 1996; Martin van Creveld, *The Transformation of War*, The Free Press, New York, 1991 and *The Rise and Decline of the State*, Cambridge University Press, Cambridge, 1999.

22 Bozeman, 'War and the clash of ideas', pp. 62–3; 76–7.

23 ibid., pp. 64–8.

24 ibid., p. 73.

25 ibid.

26 ibid., p. 78.

27 ibid., p. 102.

28 ibid.

29 ibid., pp. 77–8.

30 ibid., p. 78.

31   ibid., p. 79.

32   ibid., pp. 79–102.

33   *The National Security Strategy of the United States of America*, especially pp. 1–7.

34   ibid., p. 31.

35   ibid., p. 3.

36   ibid., p. 31.

37   Rip and Hasik, *The Precision Revolution*, p. 427.

38   T. R. Fehrenbach, *This Kind of War: A Study in Unpreparedness*, Macmillan, New York, 1963, p. 427.

39   Samuel P. Huntington, *The Clash of Civilizations and the Remaking of World Order*, and Norman Cohn, *The Pursuit of the Millennium: Revolutionary Millenerians and Mystical Anarchists of the Middle Ages*, Secker & Warburg, London, 1957.

40   See Charles C. Moskos, John Allen Williams and David R. Segal (eds), *The Postmodern Military: Armed Forces after the Cold War*, Oxford University Press, New York, 2000, especially Chapters 1 and 14.

41   See Ulrich Beck, *Risk Society: Towards a New Modernity*, Sage Publications, London, 1992 and Anthony Giddens, *Runaway World: How Globalisation is Reshaping Our Lives*, Profile Books, London, 1999.

42   Giddens, *Runaway World*, p. 22.

43   This is a central theme in Christopher Coker, *Waging War Without Warriors? The Changing Culture of Military Conflict*, Lynne Rienner Publishers, Inc., Boulder, CO, 2002, especially Chapters 4–6.

44   See Michael Ignatieff, *Virtual War: Kosovo and Beyond*, Metropolitan Books, New York, 2000.

45   Quoted in Victor Davis Hanson, *The Wars of the Ancient Greeks*, Cassell, London, 1999, p. 18.

46   W. Somerset Maugham, 'The appointment in Samarra', preface in John O'Hara, *Appointment in Samarra*, Faber & Faber, London, 1933.

47   ibid.

Chapter 2

1   For a detailed analysis see Manuel Castells, *The Information Age: Economy, Society and Culture, Vol. 1, The Rise of the Network Society*, Blackwell Publishers, London, 1996, Chapters 5–7 and Philip Bobbitt, *The Shield of Achilles: War, Peace and the Course of History*, Alfred A. Knopf, New York, 2002, Chapters 10–12 and 24–26.

2 President Bill Clinton, 'Remarks by the President to American Society of Newspaper Editors', San Francisco, California, 15 April 1999, *Los Angeles Times*, 16 August 1999.

3 For a discussion of the bifurcation of the contemporary security environment see Richard H. Shultz Jr, Roy Godson and George H. Quester, 'Conclusion: policy implications', in Richard H. Shultz Jr, Roy Godson and George H. Quester (eds), *Security Studies for the 21st Century*, Brassey's, Washington DC, 1997, pp. 437–8 and Robert L. Pfaltzgraff Jr and Richard H. Shultz Jr 'Future actors in a changing security environment', in Robert L. Pfaltzgraff Jr. and Richard H. Shultz Jr (eds), *War in the Information Age: New Challenges for US Policy*, Brassey's, Washington DC, 1997, Chapter 1.

4 Jean-Marie Guéhenno, 'The impact of globalisation on strategy', *Survival*, Winter 1998–99, vol. 40, no. 4, pp. 5–19; David Held and Anthony McGrew, 'Globalisation and the prospects for world order', in Tim Dunne, Michael Cox and Ken Booth (eds), *The Eighty Years Crisis: International Relations 1919–99*, Cambridge University Press, Cambridge, 1999, pp. 219–43.

5 Francis Fukuyama, 'The end of history', *National Interest*, Spring 1989 and *The End of History and the Last Man*, The Free Press, New York, 1992.

6 See John M. Collins, *Military Geography for Professionals and the Public*, National Defense University Press, Washington DC, 1998 and the essays in Colin S. Gray and Geoffrey Sloan (eds), *Geopolitics, Geography and Strategy*, Frank Cass, London, 1999.

7 Bobbitt, *The Shield of Achilles*, p. 813.

8 Qiao Liang and Wang Xiangsui, *Unrestricted Warfare*, PLA Literature and Arts Publishing House, Beijing, 1999, p. 199.

9 For a useful discussion see Robert L. Pfaltzgraff Jr and Richard H. Shultz Jr, 'Future actors in a changing security environment', in Robert L. Pfaltzgraff Jr and Richard H. Schultz Jr (eds), *War in the Information Age: New Challenges for US Security Policy*, Chapter 1.

10 This typology is drawn from Robert Cooper's excellent essay on the fragmentation of the international system and the implications for global security. See Robert Cooper, *The Post-Modern State and the World Order*, Demos, London, 1996, especially pp. 38–47.

11 For views on the future of armed conflict see Makhmut Gareev, *If War Comes Tomorrow? The Contours of Future Armed Conflict*, Frank Cass, London, 1998; Mary Kaldor, *New & Old Wars: Organised Violence in a Global Era*, Polity Press, Cambridge, 1999; Gwyn Prins and Hylke Tromp (eds), *The Future of War*, Kluwer Law International, The Hague, 2000; Mark Duffield, *Global Governance and the New Wars: The Merging of Development and Security*, Zed Books, London, 2001; Robert

E. Harkavy and Stephanie G. Neuman, *Warfare and the Third World*, Palgrave, New York, 2001; Wesley K. Clark, *Waging Modern War: Bosnia, Kosovo and the Future of Combat*, Public Affairs, New York, 2001; Andrew J. Bacevich and Eliot A. Cohen (eds), *War Over Kosovo: Politics and Strategy in a Global Age*, Columbia University Press, New York, 2001; Christopher Coker, *Waging War Without Warriors? The Changing Culture of Military Conflict*, Lynne Rienner Publishers, Boulder, CO, 2002; William R. Schilling (ed.), *Nontraditional Warfare: Twenty-First Century Threats and Responses*, Brassey's Inc., Washington DC, 2002; and Colin S. Gray, *Strategy for Chaos: Revolutions in Military Affairs and The Evidence of History*, Frank Cass, London, 2002.

12 *New York Times*, 15 May 1999.

13 See Colonel Lloyd J. Matthews (ed.), *Challenging the United States Symmetrically and Asymmetrically: Can America be Defeated?*, US Army War College, Strategic Studies Institute, Carlisle Barracks, PA, July 1998, and Steven Metz and Douglas V. Johnson II, *Asymmetry and US Military Strategy: Definition, Background, and Strategic Concepts*, US Army War College, Strategic Studies Institute, Carlisle Barracks, PA, January 2001.

14 For a discussion see Coker, *Waging War Without Warriors? The Changing Culture of Military Conflict*, Chapter 7.

15 Pierre Hassner, 'Beyond war and totalitarianism: the new dynamics of violence', in Prins and Tromp, *The Future of War*, p. 205.

16 See Bernard Lewis, *What Went Wrong? The Clash Between Islam and Modernity in the Middle East*, Weidenfeld & Nicolson, London, 2002.

17 See Avi Kober, 'Low-intensity conflicts: why the gap between theory and practise?', *Defense & Security Analysis*, March 2002, vol. 18, no. 1, pp. 15–38, and Robert E. Harkavy and Stephanie G. Neuman, *Warfare and the Third World*, especially Chapter 5. See also Max G. Manwaring, *Internal Wars: Rethinking Problems and Responses*, US Army War College, Strategic Studies Institute, Carlisle Barracks, PA, September 2001, pp. 25–34.

18 John Mueller, *Retreat from Doomsday: The Obsolescence of Major War*, Basic Books, New York, 1989.

19 Martin van Creveld, *The Transformation of War*, The Free Press, New York, 1991.

20 Alvin Toffler and Heidi Toffler, *War and Anti-War: Survival at the Dawn of the 21st Century*, Little, Brown and Company, Boston, 1993.

21 Robert D. Kaplan, 'The coming anarchy', *Atlantic Journal*, February 1994 and *The Ends of the Earth: A Journey at the Dawn of the Twenty-First Century*, Random House, New York, 1996; Philip Cerny, 'Neomedievalism, civil war and the new security dilemma: globalisation as durable disorder', *Civil Wars*, Spring

1998, vol. I, no. I, pp. 36–64; Ralph Peters, *Fighting for the Future: Will America Triumph?*, Stackpole Books, Mechanicsburg, PA, 1999.

22 Samuel P. Huntington, *The Clash of Civilizations and the Remaking of World Order*, Simon and Schuster, New York, 1996.

23 Kaldor, *New and Old Wars: Organised Violence in a Global Era*, especially Chapters 4–6.

24 *New York Times*, 21 August 1998.

25 United States Commission on National Security/21st Century, *New World Coming: American Security in the 21st Century*, Supporting Research & Analysis, The Phase I Report on the Emerging Global Security Environment for the First Quarter of the 21st Century, US Commission on National Security/21st Century, Washington DC, 15 September 1999, p. 57. Emphasis added.

26 Donald H. Rumsfeld, 'Transforming the military', *Foreign Affairs*, May–June 2002, vol. 81, no. 3, p. 23.

27 The United States Commission on National Security/21st Century, *Seeking a National Strategy: A Concert for Preserving Security and Promoting Freedom*, The Phase II Report on a US National Security Strategy for the 21st Century, The Commission, Washington DC, 15 April 2000, p. 14.

28 Robert L. Pfaltzgraff Jr and Stephen E. Wright, 'The spectrum of conflict: symmetrical or asymmetrical challenge?', in Richard H. Shultz and Robert L. Pfaltzgraff Jr (eds), *The Role of Naval Forces in 21st-Century Operations*, Brassey's, Washington DC, 2000, pp. 9–28.

29 Michael Rose, 'The art of military intervention', in Prins and Tromp, *The Future of War*, pp. 241–50; Christopher Bellamy, *Spiral Through Time: Beyond 'Conflict Intensity'*, Strategic and Combat Studies Institute, The Occasional No. 35, Camberley, August 1998, pp. 15–38.

30 ibid.

31 See Huba Wass de Czege and Richard Hart Sinnreich, *Conceptual Foundations of a Transformed US Army*, Association of the United States Army, Institute for Land Warfare Paper No. 40, Washington DC, March 2002 and Bobbitt, *The Shield of Achilles*, Chapters 26–7.

32 For background see the stimulating essay by Eric Hobsbawm, 'War and peace in the 20th century', *London Review of Books*, 21 February 2002, pp. 16–18.

33 Carl von Clausewitz, *On War*, Michael Howard and Peter Paret (eds and trans.), Princeton University Press, Princeton, NJ, 1976, p. 89.

34 Gareev, *If War Comes Tomorrow? The Contours of Future Armed Conflict*, p. 94.

35 President George W. Bush, 'Remarks by the President at 2002 Graduation

Exercise of the United States Military Academy West Point New York', 1 June 2002.

36　De Czege and Sinnreich, *Conceptual Foundations of a Transformed US Army*, p. 6.

37　Huba Wass de Czege and Zbigniew M. Majchrzak, 'Enabling operational maneuver from strategic distances', *Military Review*, May–June 2002, vol. 82, no. 3, pp. 16–20. See also Huba Wass de Czege and Antulio J. Echevarria II, 'Insights for a power–projection army', *Military Review*, May–June 2000, vol. 80, no. 3, pp. 3–11.

38　See Brian Bond and Mungo Melvin (eds), *The Nature of Future Conflict: Implications for Force Development*, Strategic and Combat Studies Institute, The Occasional No. 36, Camberley, PA, September 1998 and Brigadier C. S. Grant, 'The 2015 battlefield', *The British Army Review*, Winter 2001–02, no. 128, pp. 5–13.

39　Brigadier General Loup Francart and Jean-Jacques Patry, 'Mastering violence: an option for operational military strategy', *Naval War College Review*, Summer 2000, vol. 53, no. 3, pp. 144–84. See also George A. Bloch, 'French military reform: lessons for America's army?', *Parameters: US Army War College Quarterly*, Summer 2000, vol. 30, no. 2, pp. 33–45.

40　Francart and Patry, 'Mastering violence', p. 145. Emphasis added.

41　General Wesley K. Clark, *Waging Modern War: Bosnia, Kosovo and the Future of Conflict*, Public Affairs, New York, 2001, pp. 10–11. For a recent discussion of civil–military relations see Eliot A. Cohen, *Supreme Command: Soldiers, Statesmen, and Leadership in Wartime*, The Free Press, New York, 2002.

42　For a discussion see Paul Bracken, 'The military crisis of the nation state: will Asia be different from Europe?', in John Dunn (ed.), *Contemporary Crisis of the Nation State?*, Blackwell, Oxford, 1995, pp. 97–114 and Jeffrey Record, 'Thinking about China and war', *Aerospace Power Journal*, Winter 2001, vol. 15, no. 4, pp. 69–80.

43　Lieutenant General Paul E. Funk, 'Battle space: a commander's tool on the future battlefield', *Military Review*, December 1993, vol. 73, no. 12, pp. 36–47; General Frederick M. Franks, 'Full-dimensional operations: a doctrine for an era of change', *Military Review*, December 1993, vol. 73, no. 12, pp. 5–10; and United States Army, *FM 3-0, Operations*, Department of the Army, Washington DC, June 2001, pp 4-20–4-21.

44　Michael Russell Rip and James M. Hasik, *The Precision Revolution: GPS and the Future of Aerial Warfare*, Naval Institute Press, Annapolis, MD, 2002, Chapters 11–13 and Ted Hooton, 'Naval firepower comes of age', *Jane's Defence Weekly*, 13 November 2002, vol. 38, no. 20, pp. 17–28.

45　Antulio J. Echevarria II, *Rapid Decisive Operations: An Assumptions-based Critique*,

US Army War College, Strategic Studies Institute, Carlisle Barracks, PA, November 2001, pp. 14–18.

46 Huba Wass de Czege, 'Maneuver in the information age', in Pfaltzgraff and Shultz (eds), *War in the Information Age*, pp. 203–24; Colonel Dick Applegate, 'Towards the future army', in Bond and Melvin, *The Nature of Future Conflict: Implications for Force Development*, pp. 77–91; and Grant, 'The 2015 battlefield', pp. 9–10.

47 See US Center for Army Lessons Learned (CALL), Fort Leavenworth, KS, 'Emerging lessons, insights and observations: operation enduring freedom', 1 August 2002. See also a useful summary of the report by Amy Svitak, 'US Army, Navy mull lessons learned in Afghanistan war', *Defense News*, 22–28 July, 2002. See also Stephen Biddle, *Afghanistan and the Future of Warfare: Implications for Army and Defense Policy*, Strategic Studies Institute, US Army War College, Carlisle Barracks, PA, November 2002, pp. 43–58.

48 For preliminary analysis of the fighting on the ground in the 2003 Iraqi War see Frank Tibani, 'US Army rethinks armor', *Defense News*, 7 April 2003; 'Interview: General Richard Myers', *Defense News*, 14 April 2003 and Richard T. Cooper and Peter Pae, 'Battle for the military's future unresolved', *Los Angeles Times*, 12 April 2003.

49 Bobbitt, *The Shield of Achilles*, p. xxi.

50 ibid., pp. 776–823. A view recently reinforced by Stephen E. Flynn et al., *America Still Unprepared—America Still in Danger: Report of an Independent Task Force Sponsored by the Council on Foreign Relations*, Council on Foreign Relations, New York, 2002.

51 Phillippe Delmas, *The Rosy Future of War*, The Free Press, New York, 1995, p. 213.

52 For discussions see Adam Paul Stoffa, 'Special forces, counterterrorism and the law of armed conflict', *Studies in Conflict and Terrorism*, June 1995, vol. 18, no. 1, pp. 47–66; Eric S. Krauss and Mike O. Lacey, 'Utilitarian vs. humanitarian: the battle over the law of war', *Parameters: US Army War College Quarterly*, Summer 2002, vol. 32, no. 2, pp. 73–84; and Bobbitt, *The Shield of Achilles*, Chapters 24–7.

53 Alastair Buchan, *War in Modern Society: An Introduction*, C. A. Watts & Co. Ltd., London, 1966, pp. 81–2.

Chapter 3

1 The author is indebted to Robert Worley, Fred Kagan, Steve Scroggs, VADM Arthur Cebrowski, USN (Retd), Steven Daskal, Michael Wood,

Price Bingham, David E. Johnson, and William R. Bode for their advice and suggestions during the preparation of this chapter.

2 Fred E. Saalfeld and John F. Petrik, 'Disruptive technologies: a concept for moving innovative military technologies rapidly to warfighters', *Armed Forces Journal International*, May 2001, p. 48.

3 Bill Gertz and Rowan Scarborough, 'Inside the ring', *Washington Times*, 17 August 2001, p. 7.

4 John T. Correll, 'Rumsfeld's review: the closed-door approach led to problems, and they are not over yet', *Air Force Magazine*, July 2001, p. 2.

5 Nicholas Lemann, 'Letter from Washington: dreaming about war', *New Yorker*, 16 July 2001, p. 32.

6 'Joint operations reality', *Defense News*, 9–15 July 2001, p. 10.

7 Title 10 of the United States Code comprises laws under which the US Congress assigns specific missions to each service. These laws are significant because they provide the basis for budget requests.

8 These core competencies include the Navy and Marine Corps' forward presence around the globe, the Air Force's global precision strike forces and the Army's capacity to seize and hold strategic territory. Elaine M. Grossman, 'DOD is shaping major review outcomes prior to releasing strategy', *Inside The Pentagon*, 14 June 2001, p. 1.

9 Thom Shanker, 'Defense chief will propose military change in course', *New York Times*, 15 June 2001, p. 2.

10 Kenneth Watman, 'Global 2000', *Naval War College Review*, vol. 54, no. 2, Spring 2001, p. 76.

11 Christian Lowe, 'Marine corps resurrects medium-weight force', *Defense Week*, 20 August 2001, p. 1.

12 Robert Holzer, 'Rumsfeld promises to shape-up Pentagon ways', *Defense News*, 4–10 June 2001, p. 6.

13 Kenneth Ray Young, *The General's General: The Life and Times of Arthur MacArthur*, Westview Press, Boulder, CO, 1994, pp. 305–6, 332.

Chapter 4

1 Captain A. T. Mahan, *The Influence of Sea Power upon History, 1660–1783*, Little Brown & Co., Boston, 1890.

2 Adi Ignatius and Tim McGirk, 'The Asian voyage', *Time*, 20 August 2001.

3 Richard Sisson and Leo Rose, *War and Secession*, University of California Press, Berkeley, CA, 1990.

4   K. C. Sagar, *The War of History of the Twins*, Northern Book Centre, New Delhi, 1997, Chapter V.

5   Francis Fukuyama, *The End of History and the Last Man*, The Free Press, New York, 1992, pp. 310–11.

6   US Navy, *From the Sea: Preparing the Naval Service for the 21st Century*, Washington DC, US Department of the Navy, 1992. The title first appeared in the US Navy's *The Maritime Strategy*, first published as a special supplement to the *Naval Institute Proceedings*, January 1986.

7   Ellery H. Clark Jr and Edwin M. Hall, 'Navies in transition 1815–1860', in *Sea Power: A Naval History*, R. B. Potter and Chester W. Nimitz (eds), Prentice Hall, Englewood Cliffs, NJ, 1960, pp. 225–32.

8   A good record of NATO naval strategy is contained in Sean M. Maloney, *Securing Command of the Sea, NATO Naval Planning 1948–1954*, Naval Institute Press, Annapolis, MD, 1995.

9   Richard Hallon, 'The future of air power', *RUSI Journal*, June 2001, p. 53.

10 Professor H. D. Kamradt and Dougie the Diver, 'Net centricity—seminal doctrine or just puff?', in *Naval Review*, January 2001, pp. 8–12.

11 Link 16 is a NATO-standardised communication link for the transmission of digital information. It is a secure, high-capacity, jam-resistant, nodeless data link. It is line of sight and carried on UHF or microwave channels. See Professor Henry Kamradt and Commander Douglas MacDonald RN, *The Implications of Network-centric Warfare for United States and Multinational Military Operations*, Occasional Paper 98-1, United States Naval War College, Newport, RI, 1998, pp. 7–8.

12 Hallon, 'The future of air power', p. 55.

13 Certainly six German and probably twelve to fourteen British submarines were involved in the Battle of Jutland. See Holloway Frost, *The Battle of Jutland*, United States Naval Institute, Annapolis, MD, 1936, pp. 118–27. Nineteen US and five Japanese submarines were deployed at Midway according to Samuel Morison, *History of the US Naval Operations in World War II*, vol. IV, Little Brown & Co., Boston, 1961, pp. 86–94.

14 Sir Arthur R. Hezlet, *The Submarine and Sea Power*, Stein & Day, New York, 1967.

15 Rear Admiral Raja Menon, *Maritime Strategy and Continental Wars*, Frank Cass, London, 1998, pp. 157; 204.

16 John Mearsheimer, 'The future of the American pacifier', *Foreign Affairs*, September–October 2001, pp. 46–60.

Chapter 5

1 The views expressed herein are the author's alone and should not be taken to represent the policies or official views of the United States Department of Defense or the Department of the Army. Much of this chapter is based on an earlier work, *Sharp Corners: Urban Operations at Century's End*, US Army Command and General Staff College Press, Fort Leavenworth, KS, 2001.

2 To this guidance I added one significant limitation of my own. I excluded consideration of all operations within the United States themselves on the grounds that constitutional, political and social factors combined to create such a unique set of operational questions as to require a separate study. I did not think that principles that might guide our operational considerations in a foreign theatre of war would suffice to guide domestic operations.

3 Steven Kull, I. M. Destler and Clay Ramsay, *The Foreign Policy Gap: How Policymakers Misread the Public*, Center for International and Security Studies, Baltimore, MD, 1997.

4 Gunther E. Rothenberg, 'Moltke, Schlieffen, and the doctrine of strategic envelopment', in Peter Paret (ed.), *Makers of Modern Strategy: From Machiavelli to the Nuclear Age*, Princeton University Press, Princeton, 1986, pp. 304–7.

5 Harry G. Summers Jr, *The Historical Atlas of the Vietnam War*, Houghton Mifflin, Boston, 1995, p. 130.

6 United Nations, *The World at Six Billion*, United Nations Population Division of the Department of Economic and Social Affairs, New York, 1999, pp. b-2, b-3. (Accessed on the Internet at <http://www.Popin.org/6billion>.)

7 Naturally, demographic projections disagree, mostly about the speed with which this point will be reached. A more recent report by the Central Intelligence Agency, published in July 2001, dates this point at 2015. United States Central Intelligence Agency, *Long-Term Global Demographic Trends: Reshaping the Geopolitical Landscape*, Langley VA, July 2001, p. 5. (Accessed on the Internet at <http://www.cia.gov>.)

8 *Sharp Corners*, pp. 10–12. See also Sir Peter Hall, *Cities in Civilization*, Pantheon, New York, 1998, p. 621; and Spiro Kostof, *The City Shaped: Urban Patterns and Meanings Through History*, Thames and Hudson, London, 1991, p. 37.

9 Robert B. Kent, 'Rio de Janeiro', *Microsoft Encarta Encyclopedia 99*, CD-ROM.

10 Hall, *Cities in Civilization*, pp. 611, 621, 627.

11 Stephen Halliday, *The Great Stink of London: Sir Joseph Bazalgette and the Cleansing of the Victorian Metropolis*, Sutton Publishing Limited, Sparkford, England, 1999, pp. 17–19.

12 Hall, *Cities in Civilization*, pp. 709, 753.

13 Robert Kaplan, *An Empire Wilderness*, Random House, New York, 1999, p. 37.

14 One need not be too precise about defining 'ordinary' in this instance. It could be the sort of life that one might live in Sydney or any other sizable Australian city.

15 Cornelius Ryan, *The Last Battle*, Simon and Schuster, New York, 1996, p. 458.

16 For an excellent comparative analysis of two fights for Grozny and a modern army's capacity (or incapacity) to learn even from its own operational mistakes, see Olga Oliker, *Russia's Chechen Wars 1994–2000: Lessons from Urban Combat*, RAND Corporation, Santa Monica, CA, 2001, especially p. xi.

Chapter 6

1 General Anthony C. Zinni, 'A military for the 21st Century: lessons from the recent past', *Strategic Forum*, no. 181, July 2001, p. 3.

2 Donald H. Rumsfeld, 'Transforming the military', *Foreign Affairs*, May/June 2002, p. 31.

3 The issue of the role that coalition forces play in providing legitimacy to military action is considered in greater detail in Alan Ryan, *From Desert Storm to East Timor: Australia, the Asia-Pacific and 'New Age' Coalition Operations*, Study Paper No. 302, Land Warfare Studies Centre, Duntroon, ACT, 2000, pp. 5–10.

4 Sir Shridath Ramphal, 'Our global neighbourhood—facing the 21st century', Fiftieth Anniversary Commemorative Lecture of the first Meeting of the United Nations General Assembly, Westminster Central Hall, London, 13 January 1996,< http://www.cgg.ch/unacgg.html> (downloaded 25 September 2001).

5 General Anthony C. Zinni, 'A military for the 21st century: lessons from the recent past', pp. 1–4.

6 Joint Publication 3-16, *Joint Doctrine for Multinational Operations*, Chairman, Joint Chiefs of Staff, Washington, 5 April 2000, p. GL-4.

7 Admiral Dennis C. Blair, USN, 'Change is possible and imperative', *Naval Institute Proceedings*, May 2001, vol. 127/5/1,179, <http://www.usni.org/Proceedings/Articles01/PROblair5.htm> (downloaded 6 September 2001).

8 American–British–Canadian–Australian Armies Program, *Coalition Operations Handbook*, Primary Standardization Office, Arlington, VA, May 1999, p. ix.

9   Trevor Findlay, *Cambodia: The Legacy and Lessons of UNTAC*, Stockholm International Peace Research Institute Research Report No. 9, Oxford University Press, 1995, pp. 27–8.

10   ibid., p. 139.

11   UN Newservice, 'Secretary-General thanks Australia for taking lead in helping East Timor', <http://www.un.org/News/dh/latest/page2.html#22>, 21 February 2000 (downloaded 23 February 2000); Lincoln Wright, 'Annan heaps praise on Howard, military', *The Canberra Times*, 22 February 2000, pp. 1–2.

12   Major General P. Cosgrove, The ANZAC Lecture at Georgetown University, 4 April 2000.

13   Tamara Duffey, 'Cultural issues in contemporary peacekeeping', in *Peacekeeping and Conflict Resolution*, Tom Woodhouse and Oliver Ramsbotham (eds), Frank Cass, London, 2000, p. 147.

14   Interview by author with Major General P. Cosgrove, Commander INTERFET at Headquarters INTERFET, Dili, 10 January 2000.

15   *Defence 2000: Our Future Defence Force*, Defence Publishing Service, Canberra, 2000, p. 10.

16   Lieutenant General Daniel W. Christman, 'Twenty-first century security challenges: the road to somewhere?', *National Security Studies Quarterly*, vol. VII, issue 2, Spring 2001, p. 130.

17   Conrad C. Crane, *Landpower and Crises: Army Roles and Missions in Smaller Scale Contingencies During the 1990s*, Strategic Studies Institute, US Army War College, Carlisle, PA, 2001, p. 6.

18   *Defence 2000: Our Future Defence Force*, p. 79.

19   General Robert W. RisCassi, 'Principles for coalition warfare', *Joint Forces Quarterly*, Summer 1993, p. 65.

20   Colonel Anthony J. Rice, 'Command and control: the essence of coalition warfare', *Parameters*, Spring 1997, p. 10 of 13, <http://carlisle www.army.mil/usawc/Parameters/97spring/rice.htm> (downloaded 15 June 1999).

21   Thomas Durrell-Young, 'Command in Coalition Operations', in *Problems and Solutions in Future Coalition Operations*, Thomas J. Marshall, Phillip Kaiser and Jon Kessmeire (eds), Strategic Studies Institute, Carlisle, PA, 1997, p. 30.

22   Captain Terry J. Pudas, USN, 'Preparing future coalition commanders', *Joint Forces Quarterly*, Winter 1993–94, p. 43.

23   Robert W. RisCassi, 'Principles for coalition warfare', *Joint Forces Quarterly*, Summer 1993, p. 71.

24 *Report of the Panel on United Nations Peace Operations* (The Brahimi Report), A/55/305–S/2000/809, 21 August 2000, pp. 16–20.

25 The author discovered this fact during interviews with a selection of New Zealand and Fijian officers in East Timor during July 2001.

26 *Coalition Military Operations: The Way Ahead Through Cooperability*, Report of a French–German–UK–US Working Group, US Center for Research and Education on Strategy and Technology, Arlington, VA, 2000, p. 65.

27 Michael Smith, 'Doctrine and training: The foundation of effective coalition operations', Chapter 4, in *Problems and Solutions in Future Coalition Operations*, Thomas J. Marshall, Phillip Kaiser and Jon Kessmeire (eds), Strategic Studies Institute, Carlisle, PA, 1997, p. 65.

28 B. Buzan and G. Segal, 'Rethinking East Asian security', Chapter 6 in *World Security: Challenges for a new Century* (3rd edn), M. Clare and I. Chandrani (eds), St Martin's Press, New York, 1998, pp. 99–100; *The Transformation of Security in the Asia/Pacific Region*, Desmond Ball (ed.), Frank Cass, London, 1996, pp. 10–11.

29 Nicola Baker and Leonard C. Sebastian, 'The problem with parachuting: strategic studies and security in the Asia/Pacific region', in Ball (ed.), *The Transformation of Security in the Asia/Pacific Region*, p. 27.

30 For further discussion of this point see Ryan, *From Desert Storm to East Timor*, pp. 27–33.

31 Bruce Gilley, 'The region takes sides', *Far Eastern Economic Review*, 27 September 2001, pp. 24–5.

32 Brian L. Job, 'Bilateralism and multilateralism: achieving the right balance in security relations', in F. Omori and M. Sommerville (eds), *Strength Through Cooperation: Military Forces in the Asia-Pacific Region*, Institute for National Strategic Studies, National Defense University Press, Washington DC, 1999, online edn <http://www.ndu.edu/inss/books/stccont.html> (downloaded 8 May 2001).

33 East Asian Strategy Report 1998, *The United States Security Strategy for the East Asia-Pacific Region*, Defense Department, Washington DC, 1998, pp. 42–3.

34 Karl W. Deutsch, *The Analysis of International Relations* (2nd edn), Prentice-Hall, Englewood Cliffs, NJ, 1978, p. 251.

35 Admiral Dennis C. Blair, Address to the Dean's Roundtable Breakfast, Graduate School of International Relations and Pacific Studies, University of California, San Diego, 13 April 2000, <http://www.pacom.mil/ref/2000/sst/SANDIEGO.htm> (downloaded 29 May 2000).

36 Andrew Scobell, *The U.S. Army and the Asia-Pacific*, Strategic Studies Institute, U.S. Army War College, Carlisle, PA, 2001, p. 2.

37 ibid., p. 30.

38 Michael Smith, 'Doctrine and training: the foundation of effective coalition operations', p. 73.

Chapter 8

1   Sun Tzu , 'The art of war', in *The Book of War*, Caleb Carr (ed.), The Modern Library, New York, 2000, p. 91.

2   Sigmund Freud, 'Letter to Einstein', in *The Standard Edition of the Complete Psychological Works*, James Strachey (ed.), Hogarth, London, 1964, p. 201.

3   Quincy Wright, *A Study of War*, University of Chicago Press Midway Reprint, Chicago, 1983, p. 7.

4   Samuel Finer, *The History of Government: Vol. 1: Ancient Monarchies and Empires*, Oxford University Press, Oxford, 1999, pp. 2–3.

5   Sun Tzu, 'The Art of War', in *Roots of Strategy*, vol. I, T. R. Phillips (ed.), Stackpole Books, Harrisburg, PA, 1985, p. 21.

6   Vegetius, 'De Re Militari' in *Roots of Strategy*, vol. I, p. 85.

7   ibid., p. 67.

8   William Shakespeare, *Henry V*, Act 4, Scene 1, lines 132–5.

9   Michael Walzer, *Just and Unjust Wars*, Basic Books, New York, 2000, p. 39.

10 Carl von Clausewitz, 'Principles of war', in *Roots of Strategy*, vol. 2, Stackpole Books, Mechanicsburg, PA, 1987, p. 310.

11 Walzer, *Just and Unjust Wars*, p. 5.

12 Vegetius, 'De Re Militari', in *Roots of Strategy*, vol. I, p. 97.

13 W. Shakespeare, *Henry IV*, Part I, Act 4, Scene 2 (Falstaff).

14 All of the comments relating to Sun Tzu's concepts are based on the text in Sun Tzu, 'The art of war', in *Roots of Strategy*, vol. I, T. R. Phillips (ed.).

15 All of the comments here on Vegetius's work are drawn from Vegetius, 'De Re Militari', in *Roots of Strategy*, Vol. I, T. R. Phillips (ed.).

16 The Einstein–Freud Correspondence (1931–32), <http://www.cis.vt. edn/modernworld/d/einsten.html>.

17 Elizabeth Barrett Browning, *Sonnets from the Portuguese 22*, 1850.

18 Walzer, *Just and Unjust Wars*, p. xvii.

19 ibid., p. 26.

20 Richard Overy, *Why the Allies Won*, Pimlico, London, 1995, p. 117.

21 House of Commons, 10 November 1932, Parliamentary Debates (H of C) Official Report, 5th Series, c632.

22 Richard Overy, *The Battle of Britain*, Penguin Books, London, 2000, particularly Chapter 4.

23 Churchill used the word 'exterminating' in his minute to Beaverbrook.

24 The statistics set out below are drawn from Martin Middlebrook and Chris Everitt, *The Bomber Command War Diaries: An Operational Reference Book 1939–1945*, Penguin, London, 1990, particularly pp. 707–8.

25 Professor John McCarthy notes that only 7.1 per cent of aircrew had a statistical chance of completing two operational tours against German targets during the period July 1943 to June 1944. John McCarthy, 'Did the bomber always get through?', in *The War in the Air 1914–1994*, Alan Stephens (ed.), RAAF Air Power Studies Centre, Canberra, 1994, p. 90. As an example, 460 Squadron—an Australian designated unit—was raised three times in four months because of the losses it sustained. While RAAF aircrew represented only 3 per cent of the total number of Australians enlisted during World War II, their losses over Germany represented almost 30 per cent of all Australian deaths in combat during that conflict.

26 Overy, *Why the Allies Won*, p. 131.

27 Samuel Stouffer et al., *Studies in Social Psychology, Volume 2, The American Soldier: Combat and its Aftermath*, Princeton University Press, Princeton, NJ, 1949, p. 407, Table 4.

28 Overy, *Why the Allies Won*, p. 132.

29 ibid., p. 131.

30 Richard Overy notes that the Germans deployed 75 per cent of their 88 mm guns as AAA defence weapons. See ibid., p. 129.

31 ibid., pp. 22, 309; and Geoffrey P. Megargee, *Inside Hitler's High Command*, Kansas University Press, Lawrence, KS, 2000, p. 220.

32 Goebbels' diary entry dated 1 March 1945, in Walzer, *Just and Unjust Wars*, p. 324.

33 For an entertaining and controversial version of the events surrounding Colonel Warden's dismissal see Richard T. Reynolds, *Heart of the Storm: The Genesis of the Air War against Iraq*, Air University Press, Montgomery, AL, 1995, pp. 128–9.

34 Edward C. Mann, *Thunder and Lightning: Desert Storm and the Air Power Debates*, Air University Press, Montgomery, AL, 1995, pp. 35–7.

35 Reynolds, *Heart of the Storm*, p. 72.

36 The data on Saddam's network is derived from the presentation by Major John Andreas Olsen, Royal Norwegian Air Force to the Royal Air Force History Conference at the RAF Museum, Hendon, England on 11 June 2001.

37 Phillip S. Meilinger, *10 Propositions Regarding Air Power*, Air University Press, Montgomery, AL, 1995, pp. 20–7.

38 *Editors' note.* What distinguished the highly successful ground–air campaign in 2003 was that the aerial targeting of Iraqi military power was accompanied by a ground offensive designed to occupy key locations and to physically remove the Ba'ath Regime from power. All the high explosives in the world, however intelligently delivered, will make no difference if the putative victors cannot impose their will on the defeated foe.

39 Walzer, *Just and Unjust Wars*, p. 297.

40 Michael Ignatieff, *The Warrior's Honor*, London, Vintage, 1999, p. 5.

Chapter 9

1   Michael Evans, 'Close combat—lessons from the cases of Albert Jacka and Audie Murphy', in M. Evans and A. Ryan (eds), *The Human Face of Warfare: Killing, Fear and Chaos in Battle*, Allen & Unwin, Sydney, 2000, p. 52.

2   ibid., p. 49.

3   ibid.

4   ibid., p. 50.

5   Russell Braddon, *The Naked Island*, Brown and Sons, London, 1952, p. 60.

6   Field Marshall Viscount Slim, *Defeat Into Victory*, Macmillan, London, 1972, p. 535.

7   Michael Evans, *Australia and the Revolution in Military Affairs*, Working Paper No. 115, Land Warfare Studies Centre, Canberra, August 2001, p. 54.

8   Gordon R. Sullivan and Michael V. Harper, *Hope is not a Method*, Doubleday, New York, 1996, pp. 84–5.

9   Jim Wallace, 'The ghost of Jomini: the effects of digitisation on commanders and the workings of headquarters', in M. Evans and A. Ryan (eds), *The Human Face of Warfare: Killing, Fear and Chaos in Battle*, p. 123.

10 James Adams, *The Next World War*, Hutchinson, London, p. 35.

11 ibid.

12 See Grant Johannsen, *The ABCA Program: Rhetoric to Reality*, ADSC Special Report No. 7, Australian Defence Studies Centre, Canberra, 2002.

13 *The Economist*, 'Why and when to go in: The principles that should govern military intervention abroad', 4 January 2001, p. 17.

14 Directorate of Public Affairs—Army, *The Australian Army in Profile—Centenary Edition*, Canberra, 2000, p. 24.

Chapter 10

1   'Protection of Civilian Persons and Populations in Time of War', Additional Protocol I, Part IV, Geneva Convention relative to the Protection of Civilian Persons in Time of War (Convention IV of 12 August 1949), Articles 49–52.

Chapter 11

1   Here the military profession refers to all those in uniform but especially those with responsibility for shaping the character of the profession. There is debate about whether the military actually constitute a profession. Cathy Downes, 'To be or not to be a profession: the military case', *Defense Analysis*, vol. I, no. 3, (1985). Writers also differ as to whether the term 'profession of arms' is more appropriate than 'military profession'—a debate that reflects the fundamental uncertainties about the military's role discussed in this chapter.

2   Charles C. Moskos, John Allen Williams, David R. Segal (eds), *The Postmodern Military: Armed Forces after the Cold War*, Oxford University Press, New York, 2000.

3   Hugh Smith, 'The changing political context of the laws of armed conflict', in H. Smith (ed.), *The Force of Law: International Law and the Land Commander*, Australian Defence Studies Centre, Canberra, 1994.

4   *Serving Australia: The Australian Defence Force in the Twenty First Century*, (Chair, Graham Glenn), Directorate of Publishing, Defence Centre, Canberra, 1995; *Report of the review into policies and practices to deal with sexual harassment and sexual offences*, (Chair, Bronwen Grey), Defence Personnel Executive, Canberra, June 1998; *Report of an Inquiry into Military Justice in the Australian Defence Force* (Investigating Officer: J. C. S. Burchett, QC), Department of Defence, Canberra, July 2001,<http://www.defence.gov.au/index.html>; *Review of Australian Defence Force Remuneration 2001*, (Chair, Major General Barry Nunn (retd)), Department of Defence, August 2001, <http://www.defence.gov.au/remuneration/>.

5   For example, *Australian Defence Force Reserves*, Audit Report No. 33, Canberra, 2001; *Causes and Consequences of Personnel Postings in the Australian Defence Force*, Audit Report No. 41, Canberra, 2001.

6   For recent studies see *Defence Personnel Environment Scan 2020*, (Author and

Researcher, Thomas Schindlmayr), Defence Personnel Executive, Canberra, August 2001; Commonwealth Parliament, *Recruitment and Retention of ADF Personnel*, Report of the Senate Foreign Affairs, Defence and Trade References Committee, October 2001.

7   *Defence Personnel Environment Scan*, p. 30.

8   ibid., Chapter 7.

9   *Report of the Committee of Inquiry into the Citizen Military Forces* (Chair: Dr T. B. Millar), Australian Government Publishing Service, Canberra, 1974, Chapter 3.

10   A related concern is that the profession may become divided between warfighters and the rest, as some elements, such as special forces, focus on combat, while others focus on operations other than war. As well as being divisive, this could encourage potential recruits to develop a preference for some elements and not others.

11   *Defence Personnel Environment Scan*, Chapter 8.

12   Cathy Downes, 'An ethos for an army in the twenty-first century' in Hugh Smith (ed.), *Preparing Future Leaders: Officer Education and Training for the Twenty-first Century*, Australian Defence Studies Centre, Canberra, 1998.

13   P. W. Singer, 'Corporate warriors: the rise of the privatized military industry and its ramifications for international security', *International Security*, vol. 26, no. 3, Winter 2001/02.

14   For the distinction between public perceptions of the individual soldier, the services, the military in general and defence, see Anthony Bergin, Hugh Smith, 'The public perceptions of the Army', in David Horner (ed.), *Reshaping the Australian Army: Challenges for the 1990s*, Canberra Papers on Strategy and Defence, No. 77, Strategic and Defence Studies Centre, ANU, Canberra, 1991.

15   On the *Collins* project and the dismissal of Paul Barrett, see Eric Andrews, *The Department of Defence,* vol. V, The Australian Centenary History of Defence, Oxford University Press, Melbourne, 2001, pp. 288–91.

16   For ideas on how to bring military professional expertise back into policy-making, see Lieutenant Colonel Neil James, *Reform of the Defence Management Paradigm: A Fresh View*, Working Paper No. 59, Australian Defence Studies Centre, Canberra, May 2000; also at <http://idun.itsc.adfa.edu.au/ADSC/wp59/wp59.html>.

17   Christopher Dandeker, 'The military in democratic societies: new times and new patterns of civil–military relations', in Jürgen Kuhlmann, Jean Callaghan (eds), *Military and Society in 21st Century Europe*, Transaction Publishers, Piscataway, NJ, 2000, p. 40.

18   James Thomson, *The Nexus between the Commercial Support Program and Members*

Required in Uniform, Working Paper No. 44, Australian Defence Studies Centre, Canberra, 1996, p. 2.

19 Hugh Smith, 'The use of armed forces in law enforcement: legal, constitutional and political issues in Australia', *Australian Journal of Political Science*, vol. 33, no. 2, July 1998.

20 *Defence Personnel Environment Scan*, p. 64.

21 Australian National Audit Office, *Australian Defence Force Reserves*, Audit Report No. 33, Canberra, 2001, p. 13.

22 *ADF Census 1999 Public Report*, Defence Personnel Executive, Department of Defence, Canberra, p. 27.

23 Australian National Audit Office, *Australian Defence Force Reserves*, Audit Report No. 33, Canberra, 2001, p. 12.

24 For details see Lieutenant General John Coates, Dr Hugh Smith, *Review of the Ready Reserve Scheme*, Report to the Parliamentary Secretary to the Minister for Defence, Unisearch, UNSW, 30 June 1995.

25 ibid., pp. 88–90.

26 Auditor-General, Australia's Army Reserve, Audit Report No. 3, 1990–91, Australian Government Publishing Service, Canberra, 1990, p. 42.

27 Directorate of Strategic Personnel Planning and Research, *2001 Australian Defence Force Reserves Survey Report*, Report 4/2001, Canberra, pp. 43–5.

28 See   <http://www.defencejobs.defence.gov.au/RAAFSEReserveFrame.html>.

29 Commonwealth of Australia, *From Phantom to Force: Towards a More Efficient and Effective Army*, August 2000, para. 7.68.

30 Defence Submission to the Senate Committee on Foreign Affairs Defence and Trade Inquiry into Recruitment and Retention, 24 May 2001, para 120, <http://www.aph.gov.au/senate/committee/fadt_ctte/adf_personnel/sublist.htm>.

31 Williamson Murray, 'Perspectives on policy and strategy', *Strategic Review*, vol. XXV, no. 3, Summer, p. 77.

32 Hugh Smith, 'The education of future military leaders', in Smith (ed.), *Preparing Future Leaders: Officer Education and Training for the Twenty-first Century*, Australian Defence Studies Centre, Canberra, 1998, pp. 155–58.

33 Hugh Smith, 'Educating the guardians: the Politics of the Australian Defence Force Academy', *Politics*, vol. 19, no. 1, May 1984.

34 Campbell Park being the site in Canberra where much of the Department of Defence's office space is located.

35 Submission no 109, Department of Defence, Inquiry into the Capacity of Public Universities to meet Australia's Higher Education Needs, Senate

Employment, Workplace Relations, Small Business and Education References Committee, 28 March 2001.

36   The Navy, however, plans to teach this topic as a summer course at the beginning of Year 3 at ADFA. This is inconsistent with the notion of a common body of knowledge essential for all officers.

37   Inquiry into the Capacity of Public Universities to meet Australia's Higher Education Needs, Submission no. 109, 29 March 2001, Part Two.

38   Ian Zimmer, Bruce McKern, *A Review into the Educational Services delivered through the Australian Defence Force Academy*, 2001, p. xii.

39   The enormous range of qualifications—from Graduate Diploma of Strategic Studies to Statement of Attainment towards Diploma of Hospitality (Management)—can be seen on the Defence website at <http://www.defence.gov.au/dpe/civilquals/>.

40   *The Training of Officers: From Military Professionalism to Irrelevance*, The Free Press, New York, 1990, Chapter 6.

41   Ronald G. Haycock, 'The labours of Athena and the Muses: historical and contemporary aspects of Canadian military education', *Canadian Military Journal*, vol. 2, no. 2, Summer 2001, p. 17.

42   Commonwealth of Australia, *Universities in Crisis*, Report of the Senate Employment, Work Relations, Small Business and Education References Committee, Canberra, 2001, pp. 263–4.

43   Inquiry into the Capacity of Public Universities to meet Australia's Higher Education Needs, Submission no. 109, 29 March 2001, para. 1.

44   *Joint Forces Quarterly*, 5th Anniversary Issue, no 19, Summer 1998.

45   Haycock, 'The labours of Athena and the Muses', p. 17.

46   See <http://www.usma.edu/cpme/welcome.htm and www.usna.edu/Ethics>.

47   See <http://www.usafa.af.mil/jscope/>.

48   Geoffrey Barker, 'Defence censorship absurd in peacetime', *Australian Financial Review*, 3 September 2001, p. 55; see also Geoffrey Barker, 'Censorship for defence news', ibid., p. 5.

49   Robert Garran, 'Recall for "critical" army paper', *The Australian*, 13 October 2000, p. 6.

Chapter 12

1   Mary Kaldor, 'Introduction', in *Restructuring the Global Military Sector: New Wars*, Mary Kaldor and Basker Vashee (eds), Pinter Press, London and

Washington, 1997, p. 5. For more on the relationship between war and the state, see Bruce D. Porter, *War and the Rise of the State: The Military Foundations of Modern Politics*, The Free Press, New York, 1994 and Kalevi J. Holsti, *The State, War, and the State of War*, Cambridge University Press, Cambridge, 1996.

2 Michael C. Desch, 'War and strong states, peace and weak states?', *International Organization*, 50(2), Spring 1996, pp. 237–68; David Campbell, *Writing Security: United States Foreign Policy and the Politics of Identity*, Manchester University Press, Manchester, 1992.

3 For an excellent discussion of the gendered nature of national military and social identities, see Cynthia Enloe, *Does Khaki Become You? The Militarization of Women's Lives*, Pluto Press, London, 1983.

4 Philip G. Cerny, 'What next for the state?', in *Globalization: Theory and Practice*, Eleonore Kofman and Gillian Youngs (eds), Pinter, London, 1996, pp. 123–37, at p. 132.

5 Tonny Brems Knudsen, 'Humanitarian intervention revisited: post-Cold War responses to classical problems', *International Peacekeeping*, 3(4), Winter 1996, pp. 146–65. Not everyone agrees with this view of course. Wheeler and Morris argue, for example, that the cases of Iraq, Rwanda and Somalia provide 'no more than the most tentative support for the descriptive claim that the concept of humanitarian intervention is now seen by the international community as legitimate'. In their view, the intervening states in these cases were compelled more by media and public pressure than by any ethical considerations. They also assert that the idea of humanitarian intervention may not be as attractive to non-Western governments such as China and Indonesia or to NGOs and the publics in these countries. Nicholas J. Wheeler and Justin Morris, 'Humanitarian intervention and state practice at the end of the Cold War', in *International Society after the Cold War: Anarchy and Order Reconsidered*, Rick Fawn and Jeremy Larkins (eds), Macmillan, London, 1996, pp. 135–71 at p. 160. See also Adam Roberts, 'Humanitarian war: military intervention and human rights', *International Affairs*, 69(3), 1993, pp. 429–49.

6 There is a huge literature on the emergence, characteristics and implications of this 'new' form of peacekeeping. Some examples include Donald C. Daniel and Brad C. Hayes (eds), *Beyond Traditional Peacekeeping*, Macmillan, London, 1995; Steven Ratner, *The New UN Peacekeeping*, Macmillan, London, 1995; S. Neil MacFarlane and Hans-George Ehrhart (eds), *Peacekeeping at a Crossroads*, The Canadian Peacekeeping Press, Clementsport, 1997; and John Mackinlay (ed.), *A Guide to Peace Support Operations*, Institute for International Studies, Brown University, Providence, RI, 1996.

7   Overviews of the potential links between resource depletion and environmental degradation and (largely interstate) conflict are contained in Jon Barnett and Stephen Dovers, 'Environmental security, sustainability and policy', *Pacifica Review*, 13(2), pp. 157–69, June 2001; Daniel Deudney and Richard Mathews (eds), *Contested Grounds: Security and Conflict in the New Environmental Politics*, State University of New York Press, Albany, 1999; and Lorraine Elliott, 'Environmental conflict: reviewing the arguments', *Journal of Environment and Development*, 5(2), June 1996, pp. 149–67.

8   Gary Smith and StJohn Kettle (eds), *Threats Without Enemies: Rethinking Australia's Security*, Pluto Press, Sydney, 1992: and Gwyn Prins (ed.), *Threats Without Enemies*, Earthscan, London, 1993.

9   Discussions of these are contained in Jon Barnett, *The Meaning of Environmental Security: Ecological Politics and Policy in the New Security Era*, Zed Books, London and New York, 2001; Barry Buzan, Ole Waever and Jaap de Wilde, *Security: A New Framework for Analysis*, Lynne Rienner, Boulder, CO, 1998; Keith Krause and Michael C. Williams (eds), *Critical Security Studies: Concepts and Cases*, University of Minnesota Press, Minneapolis, 1997; Ronnie Lipshutz (ed.), *On Security*, Columbia University Press, New York, 1995; and Terry Terriff, Stuart Croft, Lucy James and Patrick M. Morgan, *Security Studies Today*, Polity Press, Cambridge, 1999.

10   See Trevor Findlay, 'The new peacekeepers and the new peacekeeping', in Trevor Findlay (ed.), *Challenges for the New Peacekeepers*, SIPRI Research Report No. 12, Oxford University Press/SIPRI, Oxford, 1996, pp. 1–31.

11   Ministry of Defence, *The Strategic Review*, The Stationary Office, London, 1998, Ministry of Defence, *Supporting Essays*, The Stationary Office, London, 1998 and Department of Defence, *Defence 2000: Our Future Defence Force*, Defence Publishing Service, Canberra, 2000. For a more detailed description of these kinds of changes see Ian Wing, *Refocusing Concepts of Security: The Convergence of Military and Non-military Tasks*, Land Warfare Studies Centre Working Paper No. 111, Duntroon, November 2000.

12   Ian Malcolm, *Does the Blue Helmet Fit? The Canadian Forces and Peacekeeping*, The Norman Paterson School of International Affairs Occasional Paper No. 3, Carleton University, Ottowa, 1993. Malcolm noted that this view was maintained in spite of the recommendations contained in post-mission reports submitted by UN contingent commanders and those of two internal inquiries into peacekeeping—MR 1/90 and the so-called 'Douglas review'—for the Canadian Forces to adjust its command-and-control, training, logistics support and operational deployment procedures and structures to facilitate Canada's evolving peacekeeping activities. Discussions

of the Australian and US experiences is contained respectively in Graeme Cheeseman, 'Structuring the Australian Defence Force for United Nations operations: change and resistance', Tom Woodhouse, Robert Bruce and Malcolm Dando (eds), *Peacekeeping and Peacemaking: Towards Effective Intervention in Post-Cold War Conflicts*, Macmillan, Basingstoke, 1998, pp. 231–52; and Jennifer Morrison Taw, 'Planning for military operations other than war: the lessons from US Army efforts', in Desmond Ball (ed.), *Maintaining the Strategic Edge: The Defence of Australia in 2015*, Strategic and Defence Studies Centre, Australian National University, Canberra, 1999, pp. 207–28.

13 Charles C. Moskos, John Allen Williams and David R. Segal (eds), *The Postmodern Military: Armed Forces after the Cold War*, Oxford University Press, Oxford, 1999. See also Charles C. Moskos and James Burk, 'The Postmodern Military', in James Burk (ed.), *The Military in New Times: Adapting Armed Forces to a Turbulent World*, Westview Press, Boulder, CO, 1994, pp. 141–62.

14 Charles C. Moskos, John Allen Williams and David R. Segal, 'Armed Forces after the Cold War', in Moskos et al., *The Postmodern Military*, pp. 1–2. The emergence of postmodern militaries, they continue, is marked by five major organisational changes. 'One is the increasing interpenetrability of civilian and military spheres, both structurally and culturally. The second is the diminution of differences within the armed services based on branch of service, rank, and combat versus support roles. The third is the change in the military purpose from fighting wars to missions that would not be considered military in the traditional sense. The fourth change is that the military forces are used more in international missions authorized (or at least legitimated) by entities beyond the nation state. A final change is the internationalisation of military forces themselves.'

15 Mary Kaldor, 'Introduction', in Kaldor and Vashee, *Restructuring the Global Military Sector: New Wars*, p. 13. See also Doug Brooks, 'Messiahs or mercenaries? The future of private military services', *International Peacekeeping*, 7(4), Winter 2000, pp. 129–44.

16 See Michael Klare, 'An avalanche of guns: light weapons trafficking and armed conflict in the post-Cold War era', in Kaldor and Vashee, *Restructuring the Global Sector: New Wars*, pp. 55–77.

17 Ulrich Albrecht, Mary Kaldor and Genevieve Schmeder, 'Introduction', in Mary Kaldor, Ulrich Albrecht and Genevieve Schmeder (eds), *Restructuring the Global Military Sector: The End of Military Fordism*, Pinter/United Nations University, London and Washington, 1998, pp. 1–10, at p. 6.

18 Anthony Giddens, *Runaway World: How Globalisation is Reshaping Our Lives*,

Profile Books, London, 1999. Some useful treatments of the environmental problems currently confronting the world and their potential security implications are contained in Richard Falk, *This Endangered Planet: Prospects and Proposals for Human Survival*, Random House, New York, 1971; Jessica Tuchman Mathews, 'Redefining security', *Foreign Affairs*, 68, 1989, pp. 162–77; Norman Myers, *Ultimate Security: The Environmental Basis of Political Stability*, Norton, New York, 1993; Thomas F. Homer-Dixon, 'Global environmental change and international security', in David Dewitt, David Haglund and John Kirton (eds), *Building a New Global Order: Emerging Trends in International Security*, Oxford University Press, Toronto 1993, pp. 185–228; and Lorraine Elliott, *The Global Politics of the Environment*, Macmillan, Houndsmill and London, 1997.

19   The degree to which state sovereignty is being undermined by the twin forces of globalisation and fragmentation is subject to considerable debate. Some contending positions on the issue are contained in Richard Devetak and Richard Higgott, 'Justice unbound: globalization, states and the transformation of the social bond', *International Affairs*, 75(3), 1999, pp. 483–98; Michael Mann, 'Has globalization ended the rise and rise of the nation-state?', *Review of International Political Economy*, 4(3), 1997, pp. 472–96; and Linda Weiss, 'Globalization and the myth of the powerless state', *New Left Review*, 225, 1997, pp. 3–27.

20   See for example, John Gray, *False Dawn: The Delusion of Global Capitalism*, Granta, London, 1998 and Peter Botsman and Mark Latham (eds), *The Enabling State: People Before Bureaucracy*, Pluto Press, Annandale, NSW, 2001.

21   See K. J. Holsti, 'The coming chaos? Armed conflict in the world's periphery', in T. V. Paul and John A. Hall (eds), *International Order and the Future of World Politics*, Cambridge University Press, Cambridge, 1999, pp. 283–310.

22   See Andrew Linklater, 'What is a good international citizen?', in Paul Keal (ed.), *Ethics and Foreign Policy*, Allen & Unwin, St Leonards, 1992, pp. 21–43 and Bart van Steenbergen (ed.), *The Condition of Citizenship*, Sage Publications, London, 1994.

23   James Rosenau, 'Armed force and armed forces in a turbulent world', in Burk (ed.), *The Military in New Times*, pp. 25–62 and James N. Rosenau, *Along the Domestic-Foreign Frontier: Exploring Governance in a Turbulent World*, Cambridge University Press, Cambridge, 1997, Chapter 19.

24   These latter developments are thought to lessen the prospect of interstate wars by increasing the number of stakeholders in international disputes as well as the potential costs of military conflict, reducing the importance of territorial conquest in the calculation of national power, increasing the

incentives for institutional cooperation, and enhancing the view among state elites that war is no longer a rational way of achieving national political objectives. For contending views on the end of interstate war, see David A. Lake, 'Powerful pacifists: democratic states and war', *American Political Science Review*, 86(1), 1992, pp. 24–37; Bruce Russett, *Controlling the Sword: The democratic Convergence of National Security*, Harvard University Press, Cambridge, 1990; William R. Thompson, 'The future of transitional warfare', in Burk (ed.), *The Military in New Times*, pp 63–92; and Stephen Weart, *Never at War: Why Democracies Will Never Fight One Another*, Yale University Press, New Haven, 1998.

25 See, for example, David Callahan, *Unwinnable Wars: American Power and Ethnic Conflict*, Hill & Wang, New York, 1997; Laurence Freedman, 'The changing forms of military conflict', *Survival*, 40(4), 1998–99, pp. 39–56; Donald Snow, *Uncivil Wars: International Security and the New Internal Conflicts*, Lynne Rienner, Boulder, CO, 1996; and Martin van Creveld, *The Transformation of War*, The Free Press, New York, 1991.

26 Mary Kaldor, *New & Old Wars: Organized Violence in a Global Era*, Polity Press, Oxford, 1999.

27 Snow, *Uncivil Wars*, p. 7.

28 Carl H. Builder, *The Icarus Syndrome: The Role of Air Power Theory in the Evolution and Fate of the US Air Force*, Transaction Publishers, New Brunswick and London, 1994, p. 255.

29 Mary Kaldor, 'Introduction', in Mary Kaldor (ed.), *Global Insecurity*, Pinter Press, London and New York, 2000, pp. 3–4. This last view is echoed by Edward Luttwark who believes that America's political and military leaders need a 'post-Napoleonic and post-Clausewitzian concept of war' which borrows from 18th century experiences and norms. In addition to casualty avoidance, these invoke greater use of various non-military instruments and policies—such as trade embargoes and armed blockades—and place much less emphasis on the Napoleonic dictates of tempo and momentum. In the 21st century, Luttwak concludes, political and military leaders require 'not only a patient disposition, but also a modest one, so as to admit the desirability of partial results when to do more would be too costly in US lives, and to do nothing, too damaging to our self-respect and to world order'. See Edward Luttwak, 'The crisis of classic military power and the possible remedy of "post-heroic" intelligence based warfare', in Ryan Henry and Joseph S. Nye (eds), *The Information Revolution and International Security*, Center for Strategic and International Studies Press, Washington DC, 1998, p. 89.

30 Again the literature on appropriate concepts of security is large and growing.

Some examples include Simon Dalby, *Geopolitical Change and Contemporary Security Studies: Contextualising the Human Security Agenda*, Institute of International Relations Working Paper No 30, University of British Columbia, Vancouver, April 2000; Jessica Tuchman Mathews, 'Redefining security', *Foreign Affairs*, 68(2), 1989, pp. 162–77; J. Ann Tickner, 'Re-visioning security', in Ken Booth and Steve Smith (eds), *International Relations Theory Today*, Polity Press, Cambridge, 1995, Chapter 8; and R. B. J. Walker, 'The subject of security', in Krause and Williams, *Critical Security Studies*, pp. 61–82.

31   See, for example, Paul Bracken, 'The military after next', *The Washington Quarterly*, 16(4), 1993, pp. 157–74; Steven Metz, 'Which army after next? the strategic implications of alternative futures', *Parameters*, XXVII(3), 1997, pp. 15–26; Steven Metz, *Strategic Horizons: The Military Implications of Alternative Futures*, US Army War College, Strategic Studies Institute, Carlisle Barracks, PA, 1997 and Keith Thomas (ed.), *The Revolution in Military Affairs: Warfare in the Information Age*, Australian Defence Studies Centre, Australian Defence Force Academy, Canberra, 1997.

32   Yet it has been shown that there has in fact been a decline in the number of internal or other conflicts occurring throughout the world since the end of the Cold War. See for example, Peter Wallenstein and Margateta Sollenberg, 'Armed conflict and regional conflict complexes, 1989–97', *Journal of Peace Research*, 35(5), 1998, pp. 621–34.

33   See Graeme Cheeseman, 'Responding to "new times": securing Australia and Britain in a post-Cold War era', *Contemporary Security Policy*, 22(1), April 2001, pp. 107–36.

34   For general overviews of this issue, see Greg Fry and Jacinta O'Hagan (eds), *Contending Images of World Politics*, Macmillan, Basingstoke, 2000; Robert Harkavy, 'Images of the coming international system', *Orbis*, 41(4), Fall, 1997, pp. 569–90; R. B. J. Walker, *One World, Many Worlds: Struggles for a Just World Peace*, Lynne Rienner, Boulder, CO, 1988; and Stephen Walt, 'International relations: one world, many theories', *Foreign Policy*, Spring 1998, pp. 29–46.

35   Robert Kaplan, 'The coming anarchy', *The Atlantic Monthly*, 273(2), 1994, pp. 44–81.

36   See Rick Fawn and Jeremy Larkins (eds), *International Society After the Cold War: Anarchy and Order Reconsidered*, Macmillan, Houndsmills, 1996; Anne-Marie Slaughter, 'The real new world order', *Foreign Affairs*, 76(5), September/October 1997, pp. 183–97.

37   Samuel P. Huntington, *The Clash of Civilizations and the Remaking of World Order*, Simon & Schuster, New York, 1996 and Max Singer and Aaron Wildavsky,

The Real World Order: Zones of Peace/Zones of Turmoil, Chatham House, New Jersey, 1993.

38 These are detailed in Graeme Cheeseman, 'Military power and in/security', in Ken Booth (ed.), *Security, Community and Emancipation*, Lynne Rienner, Boulder, CO, forthcoming.

39 As Ken Booth argues, any such consideration of the future must include an appropriate 'ethicscape for the twenty-first century—the kinds of values and principles that should determine how we might organise our lives and experiences'. Booth's own preferred 'ethicscape' emphasises cosmopolitan over communitarian values, especially those concerning human rights and emancipation. It follows the tradition of those who conceive of humanity as a whole, and seeks to build on the 'variety of historical and contemporary theories' which already promote the ideals of world community, human needs and environmental sustainability (a position this writer broadly shares). Ken Booth, 'Human wrongs and international relations', *International Affairs*, 71(1), 1995, pp 103–26 at p. 111. See also Ken Booth, 'Security and emancipation', *Review of International Studies*, 17(4), 1991, pp. 313–26; and Ken Booth, 'Conclusion: security within global transformation?', in Ken Booth (ed.), *Statecraft and Security: The Cold War and Beyond*, Cambridge University Press, Cambridge, 1998, pp. 338–55. In this last work, Booth makes the powerful point that 'the main question ... is not "What will the twenty-first century be *like*?" but "Who will the twenty-first century be *for*?" ' (p. 346, emphasis in the original).

40 Harkavy, 'Images of the coming international system', p. 585. For discussions of such world orders, see Noam Chomsky, *World Orders, Old and New*, Pluto Press, London, 1994 and Richard Falk, *Predatory Globalisation: A Critique*, Polity Press, Cambridge, 1999.

41 Richard Falk, *On Humane Governance: Toward a New Global Politics*, Polity Press, Cambridge, 1995, p. 243.

42 Anthony McGrew, 'Globalisation and territorial democracy: an introduction', in Anthony McGrew (ed.), '*The transformation of Democracy?*, The Open University Press, Milton Keynes, 1997, p. 19.

43 Anthony McGrew, 'Democracy beyond borders? Globalisation and the reconstruction of democratic theory and practice', in McGrew, *The Transformation of Democracy*, p. 252.

44 Andrew Linklater, 'Cosmopolitan citizenship', *Citizenship Studies*, 2(1), 1998 pp. 23–41 at p. 26.

45 See Kaldor, *New and Old Wars*, p. 20.

46 Linklater, 'Cosmopolitan citizenship', pp. 26 and 28.

47   Andrew Linklater, *The Transformation of Political Community: Ethical Foundations of the Post-Westphalian Era*, Polity Press, Cambridge, 1998.

48   Daniele Archibugi, 'From the United Nations to cosmopolitan democracy', in Daniele Archibugi and David Held (eds), *Cosmopolitan Democracy: An Agenda for a New World Order*, Polity Press, Cambridge, 1995, p. 134. Archibugi goes on to say, at pp. 157–8, that such a change 'does not necessarily mean that there must be a substantial transfer of power from the states to the new institutions. Not only would this be unrealistic to expect this, but it would not be desirable either. The challenge of the cosmopolitan democracy model is not that of substituting one power with another, but in reducing the role of power in the political process while increasing the influence of procedures'. See also David Held, 'Globalization and cosmopolitan democracy', *Peace Review*, 9(3), 1997, pp. 309–14.

49   Linklater, 'Cosmopolitan citizenship', pp. 31–3. See also David Held, *Democracy and the Global Order: From the Modern State to Cosmopolitan Governance*, Stanford University Press, Stanford, 1995.

50   Daniele Archibugi, 'Immanuel Kant, cosmopolitan law and peace', *European Journal of International Relations*, 1(4), 1995, p. 430.

51   The importance of conceiving such concepts as global citizenship or cosmopolitan democracy in political as well as idealistic or aspirational terms is underscored by Richard Falk in 'The making of global citizenship', in van Steenbergan (ed.), *The Condition of Citizenship*, pp. 127–40.

52   Kaldor, *New & Old Wars*, p. 125.

53   Gustav Daniker, *The Guardian Soldier: On the Nature and Use of Future Armed Forces*, UN Institute for Disarmament Research, New York and Geneva, Research Paper No. 36, 1995, p. 93.

54   ibid., p. 95. 'In the long run', Daniker argues, 'today's enemies will be linked by common interests tomorrow. It is perhaps the most noble task of modern military leaders not to obstruct or delay this process while they are still engaged in an ongoing open conflict'.

55   This view is supported by, among others, John Mackinlay and Randolph Kent who suggest that rather than stabilising the military situation and then withdrawing, military forces will need to become the 'security guarantors' for the whole process of civil reconciliation and reconstruction in the affected areas, helping provide the time and space for a return to normalcy and 'encouraging and maintaining an environment in which each phase of post-conflict restoration can continue'. This requires, in turn, a more

holistic and longer-term planning perspective than is presently allowed by political and military leaders alike, one which recognises that military action is part of a much broader process, and accepts that other non-state actors and agencies have equally important roles to play in the management of complex emergencies and their aftermath. See John Mackinlay and Randolph Kent, 'A new approach to complex emergencies', *International Peacekeeping*, 4(4), Winter 1997, pp. 31–49 at p. 46.

56 Daniker, *The Guardian Soldier*, pp. 103–4.

57 Kaldor, *New & Old Wars*, p. 130.

58 Held, *Democracy and the Global Order*, p. 276.

59 David Held, 'Globalization and cosmopolitan democracy', p. 314.

60 Mel Gurtov, *Global Politics in the Human Interest* (4th edn), Lynne Rienner, Boulder, CO, 1999, pp. 268–9.

61 See, for example, Karl Kaysen and George W. Rathjens, 'Send in the troops: a UN Foreign Legion', *The Washington Quarterly*, 20(1), Winter 1997, pp. 207–28 and Sean D. Murphy, *Humanitarian Intervention: The United Nations in an Evolving World Order*, University of Philadelphia Press, Philadelphia, 1996.

62 Kaldor, *New & Old Wars*, p. 130.

63 ibid., p. 131. Gustav Daniker likewise sees that the soldier's mission in the 21st century will be increasingly oriented towards the task of securing a life worth living not just for his or her own country but for all nations. In Daniker's schema, 'protection' continues to include the 'classic defense mission against the attempt of an aggressor to seize a country and its population, [and] the establishment of a war-preventing effect like deterrence … or "dissuasion"'. But it 'also encompasses all the law enforcement functions against the use of force of strategic scope below the threshold of war, such as large-scale terrorism or gang warfare with which the police is unable to cope … [and] the battle against organised crime' (Daniker, *The Guardian Soldier*, p. 104).

64 This was a central message in *Our Global Neighbourhood: The Report of the Commission on Global Governance*, Oxford University Press, Oxford, 1995.

65 For an interesting discussion of the various political forces involved in this struggle, see Mary Kaldor, 'Cosmopolitanism and organised violence', paper presented to the Conference on *Conceiving Cosmopolitanism*, Warwick, 27–29 April 2000, <http://www.theglobalsite.ac.uk>.

66 Richard Falk, 'State of siege: will globalization win out?', *International Affairs*, 73(1), 1997, pp. 123–36 at p. 129.

Chapter 14

1 John Donne, 'Devotions upon emergent occasions', No. 17, 1624.

2 Dr Javier Solana, Secretary-General of NATO, Press Statement 040, 23 March 1999, <http://www.nato.int/docu/pr/1999/p99-040e.htm>, (downloaded 8 September 2002).

3 For a critical and alternative assessment see Ivo H. Daalder and Michael E. O'Hanlon, *Winning Ugly: NATO's War to Save Kosovo*, Brookings Institution Press, Washington DC, 2000, pp. 84–100, 198–200.

4 See General Wesley Clark, Press Conference Brussels, 27 April 1999, <http://www.freeserbia.net/Documents/Kosovo/NATO0427.html>, (downloaded 9 August 2002); House of Commons United Kingdom, Select Committee on Defence, *Lessons of Kosovo*, Fourteenth Report, 23 October 2000, para. 114. See also, the minutes of evidence given by General Sir Michael Jackson, the first commander of KFOR on 10 May 2000, questions 667–8, <http://www.publications.parliament.uk/pa/cm199900/cmselect/cmdfence/347/0051006.htm>.

5 B. H. Liddell Hart, *Strategy*, Praeger, New York, 1967, p. 335.

6 General Francis Briquemont, *Le Point*, 5 January 1994; *Le Figaro*, 18 September 1994.

7 Alfred Steinberg, *The Man from Missouri: Life and Times of Harry S. Truman*, Morrow, New York, 1973, p. 10.

Chapter 15

1 Forças Armadas da Libertação Nacional de Timor Leste (FRETILIN's armed forces).

2 General Sir Archibald Wavell, *Generals and Generalship*, Penguin Books, Harmondsworth, 1941, pp. 25–6.

Chapter 16

1 Ferdinand Foch, *The Principles of War*, J. de Morinni (trans.), H. K. Fly Company, New York, 1918, pp. 13, 48.

Conclusion

1 Edward N. Luttwak, *Strategy: The Logic of War and Peace* (rev. edn), The Belknap Press of Harvard University Press, Cambridge, MA, 2001, pp. 41–2, 264–5.

2 Qiao Liang and Wang Xiangsui, *Unrestricted Warfare*, PLA Literature and Arts Publishing House, 1999, <http://www.infowar.com.mil_c41/00/unre-strictedwarfare.pdf>, p. 48>.

3 See Martin Van Creveld, *The Transformation of War*, The Free Press, New York, 1991 and Ralph Peters, *Fighting for the Future*, Stackpole Books, Mechanisburg, PA, 1999.

4 Qiao and Wang, *Unrestricted Warfare*, p. 221.

5 ibid., p. 7.

6 Thucydides, *History of the Peloponnesian War*, Penguin Books, Harmondsworth, 1954, p. 408.

7 Steven Metz and Douglas V. Johnson II, *Asymmetry and U.S. Military Strategy: Definition, Background and Strategic Concepts*, Strategic Studies Institute, Carlisle, PA, January 2001, pp. 5–6. Emphasis in original.

8 ibid., p. 10.

9 Carl von Clausewitz, *On War*, in M. Howard and P. Paret (eds), Princeton University Press, Princeton, NJ, 1989, p. 120.

10 John A. English, *Marching through Chaos: The Descent of Armies in Theory and Practice*, Praeger, Westport, CT, 1996, p. 5.

Bibliography

Unpublished document

Cosgrove, Major General P., The ANZAC Lecture at Georgetown University, 4 April 2000.

Official sources

American–British–Canadian–Australian Armies Program, *Coalition Operations Handbook*, Primary Standardization Office, Arlington, VA, May 1999.

Auditor-General, *Australia's Army Reserve*, Audit Report No. 3, 1990–91, Australian Government Publishing Service, Canberra, 1990.

Australian National Audit Office, *Australian Defence Force Reserves*, Audit Report No. 33, Canberra, 2001.

——, *Causes and Consequences of Personnel Postings in the Australian Defence Force*, Audit Report No. 41, Canberra, 2001.

Coates, Lieutenant General John and Smith, Dr Hugh, *Review of the Ready Reserve Scheme*, Report to the Parliamentary Secretary to the Minister for Defence, Unisearch, UNSW, 30 June 1995.

Commonwealth of Australia, *From Phantom to Force: Towards a More Efficient and Effective Army*, Canberra, August 2000.

——, *Universities in Crisis*, Report of the Senate Employment, Work Relations, Small Business and Education References Committee, Canberra, 2001.

Commonwealth Parliament, *Recruitment and Retention of ADF Personnel*, Report of the Senate Foreign Affairs, Defence and Trade References Committee, October 2001.

CREST, *Coalition Military Operations: The Way Ahead Through Cooperability*, Report of a French–German–UK–US Working Group, US Center for Research and Education on Strategy and Technology, Arlington, VA, 2000.

Department of Defence, *Serving Australia: The Australian Defence Force in the Twenty First Century* (Chair: Graham Glenn), Directorate of Publishing, Defence Centre, Canberra, 1995.

——, *Report of the Review into Policies and Practices to Deal with Sexual Harassment and Sexual Offences* (Chair: Bronwen Grey), Defence Personnel Executive, Canberra, June 1998.

——, *ADF Census 1999 Public Report*, Defence Personnel Executive, Canberra, 1999.

——, *Defence 2000: Our Future Defence Force*, Defence Publishing Service, Canberra, 2000.

——, *Report of an Inquiry into Military Justice in the Australian Defence Force* (Investigating Officer: J. C. S. Burchett, QC), Department of Defence, Canberra, July 2001.

——, *Defence Personnel Environment Scan 2020* (Author and Researcher: Thomas Schindlmayr), Defence Personnel Executive, Canberra, August 2001.

——, *Review of Australian Defence Force Remuneration 2001* (Chair: Major General Barry Nunn (Retd.)), Department of Defence, August 2001.

Directorate of Public Affairs—Army, *The Australian Army in Profile—Centenary Edition*, Canberra, 2000.

Directorate of Strategic Personnel Planning and Research, *2001 Australian Defence Force Reserves Survey Report*, Report 4/2001, Canberra, 2001.

East Asian Strategy Report 1998, *The United States Security Strategy for the East Asia-Pacific Region*, Defense Department, Washington DC, 1998.

House of Commons United Kingdom, Select Committee on Defence, *Lessons of Kosovo*, Fourteenth Report, 23 October 2000.

Joint Publication 3–16, *Joint Doctrine for Multinational Operations*, Chairman, Joint Chiefs of Staff, Washington, 5 April 2000.

Ministry of Defence, *The Strategic Review*, The Stationary Office, London, 1998.

——, *Supporting Essays*, The Stationary Office, London, 1998.

President of the United States of America, *The National Security Strategy of the United States of America*, The White House, Washington DC, September 2002.

Report of the Panel on United Nations Peace Operations (The Brahimi Report), A/55/305—S/2000/809, The United Nations, New York, 21 August 2000.

Report of the Committee of Inquiry into the Citizen Military Forces (Chair: Dr T. B. Millar), Australian Government Publishing Service, Canberra, 1974.

United States Army, FM 3–0, *Operations*, Department of the Army, Washington, DC, June 2001.

United States Commission on National Security/21st Century, *New World Coming: American Security in the 21st Century, Supporting Research & Analysis*, The Phase I Report on the Emerging Global Security Environment for the First Quarter of the 21st Century, US Commission on National Security/21stCentury, Washington DC, 15 September 1999.

——, *Seeking a National Strategy: A Concert for Preserving Security and Promoting Freedom*, The Phase II Report on a US National Security Strategy for the 21st Century, The Commission, Washington DC, 15 April 2000.

United States Department of Defense, *Joint Vision 2020*, US Government Printing Office, Washington DC, June 2000.

United States Navy, *From the Sea: Preparing the Naval Service for the 21st Century*, Washington DC, US Department of the Navy, 1992.

Books and monographs

Adams, James, *The Next World War*, Hutchinson, London, 1998.

Andrews, Eric, *The Department of Defence, vol. V, The Australian Centenary History of Defence*, Oxford University Press, Melbourne, 2001.

Archibugi, Daniele, and Held, David (eds), *Cosmopolitan Democracy: An Agenda for a New World Order*, Polity Press, Cambridge, 1995, 'p. 134.

Bacevich, Andrew J. and Cohen, Eliot A. (eds), *War Over Kosovo; Politics and Strategy in a Global Age*, Columbia University Press, New York, 2001.

Ball, Desmond (ed.), *The Transformation of Security in the Asia/Pacific Region*, Frank Cass, London, 1996.

——, *Maintaining the Strategic Edge: The Defence of Australia in 2015*, Strategic and Defence Studies Centre, Australian National University, Canberra, 1999.

Barnett, Jon, *The Meaning of Environmental Security: Ecological Politics and Policy in the New Security Era*, Zed Books, London and New York, 2001.

Beck, Ulrich, *Risk Society: Towards a New Modernity*, Sage Publications, London, 1992.

Bellamy, Christopher, *Spiral Through Time: Beyond 'Conflict Intensity'*, Strategic and Combat Studies Institute, The Occasional No. 35, Camberley, August 1998.

Bobbitt, Philip, *The Shield of Achilles: War, Peace and the Course of History*, Alfred A. Knopf, New York, 2002.

Bond, Brian and Melvin, Mungo (eds), *The Nature of Future Conflict: Implications for Force Development*, Strategic and Combat Studies Institute, The Occasional No. 36, Camberley, September 1998.

Boot, Max, *The Savage Wars of Peace: Small Wars and the Rise of American Power*, Basic Books, New York, 2002.

Booth, Ken (ed.), *Statecraft and Security: The Cold War and Beyond*, Cambridge University Press, Cambridge, 1998.

Botsman, Peter and Latham, Mark (eds), *The Enabling State: People Before Bureaucracy*, Pluto Press, Annandale, NSW , 2001.

Braddon, Russell, *The Naked Island*, Brown and Sons, London, 1952.

Buchan, Alastair, *War in Modern Society: An Introduction*, C. A. Watts & Co. Ltd., London, 1966.

Builder, Carl H., *The Icarus Syndrome: The Role of Air Power Theory in the Evolution and Fate of the US Air Force*, Transaction Publishers, New Brunswick and London, 1994.

Burk, James (ed.), *The Military in New Times: Adapting Armed Forces to a Turbulent World*, Westview Press, Boulder, CO, 1994.

Buzan, Barry, Waever, Ole and de Wilde, Jaap, *Security: A New Framework for Analysis*, Lynne Rienner, Boulder, CO, 1998.

Callahan, David, *Unwinnable Wars: American Power and Ethnic Conflict*, Hill & Wang, New York, 1997.

Campbell, David, *Writing Security: United States Foreign Policy and the Politics of Identity*, Manchester University Press, Manchester, 1992.

Carroll, John, *Terror: A Meditation on the Meaning of September 11*, Script Publications, Melbourne, 2002.

Castells, Manuel, *The Information Age: Economy, Society and Culture, Vol. 1, The Rise of the Network Society*, Blackwell Publishers, London, 1996.

Chomsky, Noam, *World Orders, Old and New*, Pluto Press, London, 1994.

Clare, M. and Chandrani, I. (eds), *World Security: Challenges for a New Century* (3rd edn), St Martin's Press, New York, 1998.

Clark, General Wesley K., *Waging Modern War: Bosnia, Kosovo and the Future of Conflict*, Public Affairs, New York, 2001.

Cohen, Eliot A., *Supreme Command: Soldiers, Statesmen, and Leadership in Wartime*, The Free Press, New York, 2002.

Cohn, Norman, *The Pursuit of the Millennium: Revolutionary Millenerians and Mystical Anarchists of the Middle Ages*, Secker & Warburg, London, 1957.

Coker, Christopher, *Waging War Without Warriors? The Changing Culture of Military Conflict*, Lynne Rienner Publishers, Boulder, CO, 2002.

Collins, John M., *Military Geography for Professionals and the Public*, National Defense University Press, Washington DC, 1998.

Commission on Global Governance, *Our Global Neighbourhood: The Report of the Commission on Global Governance*, Oxford University Press, Oxford, 1995.

Cooper, Robert, *The Post-Modern State and the World Order*, Demos, London, 1996.

Crane, Conrad C., *Landpower and Crises: Army Roles and Missions in Smaller Scale Contingencies During the 1990s*, Strategic Studies Institute, US Army War College, Carlisle, PA, 2001.

Daalder, Ivo H. and O'Hanlon, Michael E., *Winning Ugly: NATO's War to Save Kosovo*, Brookings Institution Press, Washington DC, 2000.

Dalby, Simon, *Geopolitical Change and Contemporary Security Studies: Contextualising the Human Security Agenda*, Institute of International Relations Working Paper No 30, University of British Columbia, Vancouver, April 2000.

Daniel, Donald C. and Hayes, Brad C. (eds), *Beyond Traditional Peacekeeping*, Macmillan, London, 1995.

Daniker, Gustav, *The Guardian Soldier: On the Nature and Use of Future Armed Forces*, UN Institute for Disarmament Research, New York and Geneva, Research Paper No. 36, 1995.

Delmas, Phillippe, *The Rosy Future of War*, The Free Press, New York, 1995.

Deudney, Daniel and Mathews, Richard (eds), *Contested Grounds: Security and Conflict in the New Environmental Politics*, State University of New York Press, Albany, 1999.

Deutsch, Karl W., *The Analysis of International Relations* (2nd edn), Prentice-Hall, Englewood Cliffs, NJ, 1978.

Dewitt, David, Haglund, David and Kirton, John (eds), *Building a New Global Order: Emerging Trends in International Security*, Oxford University Press, Toronto 1993.

Duffield, Mark, *Global Governance and the New Wars: The Merging of Development and Security*, Zed Books, London, 2001.

Dunn, John (ed.), *Contemporary Crisis of the Nation State?*, Blackwell, Oxford, 1995.

Dunne, Tim, Cox, Michael and Booth, Ken (eds), *The Eighty Years Crisis: International Relations 1919–99*, Cambridge University Press, Cambridge, 1999.

Echevarria II, Antulio J., *Rapid Decisive Operations: An Assumptions-based Critique*, US Army War College, Strategic Studies Institute, Carlisle Barracks, PA, November 2001.

Elliott, Lorraine, *The Global Politics of the Environment*, Macmillan, Houndsmill and London, 1997.

English, John A., *Marching through Chaos: The Descent of Armies in Theory and Practice*, Praeger, Westport, CT, 1996.

Enloe, Cynthia, *Does Khaki Become You? The Militarization of Women's Lives*, Pluto Press, London, 1983.

Evans, Michael, *Australia and the Revolution in Military Affairs*, Working Paper No. 115, Land Warfare Studies Centre, Canberra, August 2001.

Evans, M. and Ryan, A. (eds), *The Human Face of Warfare: Killing, Fear and Chaos in Battle*, Allen & Unwin, Sydney, 2000.

Falk, Richard, *This Endangered Planet: Prospects and Proposals for Human Survival*, Random House, New York, 1971.

——*On Humane Governance: Toward a New Global Politics*, Polity Press, Cambridge, 1995.

——*Predatory Globalisation: A Critique*, Polity Press, Cambridge, 1999.

Fawn, Rick and Larkins, Jeremy (eds), *International Society after the Cold War: Anarchy and Order Reconsidered*, Macmillan, London, 1996.

Fehrenbach, T. R., *This Kind of War; A Study in Unpreparedness*, Macmillan, New York, 1963.

Findlay, Trevor, *Cambodia: The Legacy and Lessons of UNTAC*, Stockholm International Peace Research Institute Research Report No. 9, Oxford University Press, 1995.

—— (ed.), *Challenges for the New Peacekeepers*, SIPRI Research Report No. 12, Oxford University Press/SIPRI, Oxford, 1996.

Finer, Samuel, *The History of Government: Vol. 1: Ancient Monarchies and Empires*, Oxford University Press, Oxford, 1999.

Flynn, Stephen E. et al., *America Still Unprepared—America Still in Danger: Report of an Independent Task Force Sponsored by the Council on Foreign Relations*, Council on Foreign Relations, New York, 2002.

Foch, Ferdinand, *The Principles of War*, J. de Morinni (trans.), H. K. Fly Company, New York, 1918.

Frost, Holloway, *The Battle of Jutland*, United States Naval Institute, Annapolis, MD, 1936.

Fry, Greg and O'Hagan, Jacinta (eds), *Contending Images of World Politics*, Macmillan, Basingstoke, 2000.

Fukuyama, Francis, *The End of History and the Last Man*, The Free Press, New York, 1992.

Gareev, Makhmut, *If War Comes Tomorrow? The Contours of Future Armed Conflict*, Frank Cass, London, 1998.

Giddens, Anthony, *Runaway World: How Globalisation is Reshaping Our Lives*, Profile Books, London, 1999.

Gray, Colin S., *Strategy for Chaos: Revolutions in Military Affairs and The Evidence of History*, Frank Cass, London, 2002.

Gray, Colin S. and Sloan, Geoffrey (eds), *Geopolitics, Geography and Strategy*, Frank Cass, London, 1999.

Gray, John, *False Dawn: The Delusion of Global Capitalism*, Granta, London, 1998.

Gurtov, Mel, *Global Politics in the Human Interest* (4th edn), Lynne Rienner, Boulder, CO, 1999.

Hall, Sir Peter, *Cities in Civilization*, Pantheon, New York, 1998.

Halliday, Stephen, *The Great Stink of London: Sir Joseph Bazalgette and the Cleansing of the Victorian Metropolis*, Sutton Publishing Limited, Sparkford, England, 1999.

Hanson, Victor Davis, *The Wars of the Ancient Greeks*, Cassell, London, 1999.

Harkavy, Robert E. and Neuman, Stephanie G., *Warfare and the Third World*, Palgrave, New York, 2001.

Held, David, *Democracy and the Global Order: From the Modern State to Cosmopolitan Governance*, Stanford University Press, Stanford, 1995.

Henry, Ryan and Nye, Joseph S. (eds), *The Information Revolution and International Security*, Center for Strategic and International Studies Press, Washington DC, 1998.

Hezlet, Sir Arthur R., *The Submarine and Sea Power*, Stein & Day, New York, 1967.

Hogan, Michael J., *A Cross of Iron: Harry S. Truman and the Origins of the National Security State, 1945–1954*, Cambridge University Press, Cambridge, 1998.

Hoge Jr, James F. and Rose, Gideon (eds), *How Did This Happen? Terrorism and the New War*, Public Affairs, New York, 2001.

Holsti, Kalevi J., *The State, War, and the State of War*, Cambridge University Press, Cambridge, 1996.

Horner, David (ed.), *Reshaping the Australian Army: Challenges for the 1990s*, Canberra Papers on Strategy and Defence, No. 77, Strategic and Defence Studies Centre, ANU, Canberra, 1991.

Huntington, Samuel P., *The Clash of Civilizations and the Remaking of World Order*, Simon & Schuster, New York, 1996.

Ignatieff, Michael, *Virtual War: Kosovo and Beyond*, Metropolitan Books, New York, 2000.

James, Lieutenant Colonel Neil, *Reform of the Defence Management Paradigm: A Fresh View*, Working Paper No. 59, Australian Defence Studies Centre, Canberra, May 2000.

Johannsen, Grant, *The ABCA Program: Rhetoric to Reality*, Australian Defence Studies Centre, Canberra, 2002.

Johnson, Paul, *Modern Times: A History of the World from the 1920s to the 1990s*, Phoenix, London, 1992.

Kaldor, Mary, *New & Old Wars: Organized Violence in a Global Era*, Polity Press, Oxford, 1999.

Kaldor, Mary, Albrecht, Ulrich and Schmeder, Genevieve, *Restructuring the Global Military Sector: The End of Military Fordism*, Pinter/United Nations University, London and Washington, 1998.

Kaldor, Mary and Vashee, Basker (eds), *Restructuring the Global Military Sector: New Wars*, Pinter Press, London and Washington, 1997.

Kamradt, Professor Henry and MacDonald, Commander Douglas, *The Implications of Network-centric Warfare for United States and Multinational Military Operations*, Occasional Paper 98–1, United States Naval War College, Newport, RI, 1998.

Kaplan, Robert D., *The Ends of the Earth: A Journey at the Dawn of the Twenty-First Century*, Random House, New York, 1996.

——*An Empire Wilderness*, Random House, New York, 1999.

Keal, Paul (ed.), *Ethics and Foreign Policy*, Allen & Unwin, Sydney, 1992.

Keegan, John, *A History of Warfare*, Hutchinson, London, 1993.

Kofman, Eleonore and Youngs, Gillian (eds), *Globalization: Theory and Practice*, Pinter, London, 1996.

Kostof, Spiro, *The City Shaped: Urban Patterns and Meanings Through History*, Thames and Hudson, London, 1991.

Krause, Kieth and Williams, Michael C. (eds), *Critical Security Studies: Concepts and Cases*, University of Minnesota Press, Minneapolis, 1997.

Kuhlmann, Jürgen, Callaghan, Jean (eds), *Military and Society in 21st Century Europe*, Transaction Publishers, Piscataway, NJ, 2000.

Kull, Steven, Destler, I. M. and Ramsay, Clay, *The Foreign Policy Gap: How Policymakers Misread the Public*, Center for International and Security Studies, Baltimore, MD, 1997.

Lewis, Bernard, *What Went Wrong? The Clash Between Islam and Modernity in the Middle East*, Weidenfeld & Nicolson, London, 2002.

Liddell Hart, B. H., *Strategy*, Praeger, New York, 1967.

Linklater, Andrew, *The Transformation of Political Community: Ethical Foundations of the Post-Westphalian Era*, Polity Press, Cambridge, 1998.

Lipshutz, Ronnie (ed.), *On Security*, Columbia University Press, New York, 1995.

Luttwak, Edward N., *Strategy: The Logic of War and Peace* (rev. edn), The Belknap Press of Harvard University Press, Cambridge, MA, 2001.

MacFarlane, S. Neil and Ehrhart, Hans-George (eds), *Peacekeeping at a Crossroads*, The Canadian Peacekeeping Press, Clementsport, 1997.

McGrew, Anthony (ed.), *The Transformation of Democracy?*, The Open University Press, Milton Keynes, 1997.

Mackinlay, John (ed.), *A Guide to Peace Support Operations*, Institute for International Studies, Brown University, Providence, RI, 1996.

Machiavelli, Niccolo, *The Prince* (George Bull trans.), Penguin Books, Harmondsworth, 1961.

Mahan, Captain A. T., *The Influence of Sea Power upon History, 1660–1783*, Little Brown & Co., Boston, 1890.

Malcolm, Ian, *Does the Blue Helmet Fit? The Canadian Forces and Peacekeeping*, The Norman Paterson School of International Affairs Occasional Paper No. 3, Carleton University, Ottowa, 1993.

Maloney, Sean M., *Securing Command of the Sea, NATO Naval Planning 1948–1954*, Naval Institute Press, Annapolis, MD, 1995.

Mann, Edward C., *Thunder and Lightning: Desert Storm and the Air Power Debates*, Air University Press, Montgomery, AL, 1995.

Manwaring, Max G., *Internal Wars: Rethinking Problems and Responses*, US Army War College, Strategic Studies Institute, Carlisle Barracks, PA, September 2001.

Marshall, Thomas J., Kaiser, Phillip and Kessmeire, Jon (eds), *Problems and Solutions in Future Coalition Operations*, Strategic Studies Institute, Carlisle, PA, 1997.

Matthews, Colonel Lloyd J. (ed.), *Challenging the United States Symmetrically and Asymmetrically: Can America be Defeated?*, US Army War College, Strategic Studies Institute, Carlisle Barracks, PA, July 1998.

Megargee, Geoffrey P., *Inside Hitler's High Command*, Kansas University Press, Lawrence, KS, 2000.

Meilinger, Phillip S., *10 Propositions Regarding Air Power*, Air University Press, Montgomery, AL, 1995.

Metz, Steven, *Strategic Horizons: The Military Implications of Alternative Futures*, US Army War College, Strategic Studies Institute, Carlisle Barracks, PA, 1997.

Metz, Steven, and Johnson II, Douglas V., *Asymmetry and U.S. Military Strategy: Definition, Background and Strategic Concepts*, Strategic Studies Institute, Carlisle, PA, January 2001.

Middlebrook, Martin and Everitt, Chris, *The Bomber Command War Diaries: An Operational Reference Book 1939–1945*, Penguin, London, 1990.

Morison, Samuel, *History of the US Naval Operations in World War II*, vol. IV, Little Brown & Co., Boston, 1961.

Moskos, Charles C., Williams, John Allen and Segal, David R. (eds), *The Postmodern Military: Armed Forces after the Cold War*, Oxford University Press, Oxford, 1999.

Mueller, John, *Retreat from Doomsday: The Obsolescence of Major War*, Basic Books, New York, 1989.

Murphy, Sean D., *Humanitarian Intervention: The United Nations in an Evolving World Order*, University of Philadelphia Press, Philadelphia, 1996.

Myers, Norman, *Ultimate Security: The Environmental Basis of Political Stability*, Norton, New York, 1993.

O'Hara, John, *Appointment in Samarra*, Faber & Faber, London, 1933.

Oliker, Olga, *Russia's Chechen Wars 1994–2000: Lessons from Urban Combat*, RAND Corporation, Santa Monica, CA, 2001.

Omori, F. and Sommerville, M. (eds), *Strength Through Cooperation: Military Forces in the Asia-Pacific Region*, Institute for National Strategic Studies, National Defense University Press, Washington DC, 1999.

Overy, Richard, *The Battle of Britain*, Penguin Books, London, 2000.

Paret, Peter (ed.), *Makers of Modern Strategy: From Machiavelli to the Nuclear Age*, Princeton University Press, Princeton, 1986.

Paul, T. V. and Hall, John A. (eds), *International Order and the Future of World Politics*, Cambridge University Press, Cambridge, 1999.

Peters, Ralph, *Fighting for the Future*, Stackpole Books, Mechanicsburg, PA, 1999.

Pfaltzgraff Jr, Robert L. and Shultz Jr, Richard H. (eds), *War in the Information Age: New Challenges for US Policy*, Brassey's, Washington DC, 1997.

Porter, Bruce D., *War and the Rise of the State: The Military Foundations of Modern Politics*, The Free Press, New York, 1994

Potter, R. B. and Nimitz, Chester W. (eds), *Sea Power: A Naval History*, Prentice Hall, Englewood Cliffs, NJ, 1960.

Prins, Gwyn (ed.), *Threats Without Enemies*, Earthscan, London, 1993.

Prins, Gwyn and Tromp, Hylke (eds), *The Future of War*, Kluwer Law International, The Hague, 2000.

Ratner, Steven, *The New UN Peacekeeping*, Macmillan, London, 1995.

Reynolds, Richard T., *Heart of the Storm: The Genesis of the Air War against Iraq*, Air University Press, Montgomery, AL, 1995.

Rip, Michael Russell and Hasik, James M., *The Precision Revolution: GPS and the Future of Aerial Warfare*, Naval Institute Press, Annapolis, MD, 2002.

Rosenau, James N., *Along the Domestic-Foreign Frontier: Exploring Governance in a Turbulent World*, Cambridge University Press, Cambridge, 1997.

Russett, Bruce, *Controlling the Sword: The Democratic Convergence of National Security*, Harvard University Press, Cambridge, 1990.

Ryan, Cornelius, *The Last Battle*, Simon and Schuster, New York, 1966.

Sagar, K. C., *The War of History of the Twins*, Northern Book Centre, New Delhi, 1997.

Schilling, William R. (ed.), *Nontraditional Warfare: Twenty-First Century Threats and Responses*, Brassey's Inc, Washington DC, 2002.

Scobell, Andrew, *The U.S. Army and the Asia-Pacific*, Strategic Studies Institute, U.S. Army War College, Carlisle, PA, 2001.

Shultz, Richard H. and Pfaltzgraff Jr, Robert L . (eds), *The Role of Naval Forces in 21st Century Operations*, Brassey's, Washington DC, 2000.

Shultz, Richard H., Godson, Roy, and Quester, George H. (eds), *Security Studies for the 21st Century*, Brassey's, Washington DC, 1997.

Singer, Max and Wildavsky, Aaron, *The Real World Order: Zones of Peace/Zones of Turmoil*, Chatham House, New Jersey, 1993.

Sisson, Richard and Rose, Leo, *War and Secession*, University of California Press, Berkeley, CA, 1990.

Slim, Field Marshall Viscount, *Defeat Into Victory*, Macmillan, London, 1972.

Smith, Gary and Kettle, StJohn (eds), *Threats Without Enemies: Rethinking Australia's Security*, Pluto Press, Sydney, 1992.

Smith, Hugh (ed.), *Preparing Future Leaders: Officer Education and Training for the Twenty-first Century*, Australian Defence Studies Centre, Canberra, 1998.

———(ed.), *The Force of Law: International Law and the Land Commander*, Australian Defence Studies Centre, Canberra, 1994.

Snow, Donald, *Uncivil Wars: International Security and the New Internal Conflicts*, Lynne Rienner, Boulder, CO, 1996.

Spiller, Roger, *Sharp Corners: Urban Operations at Century's End*, US Army Command and General Staff College Press, Fort Leavenworth, KS, 2001.

Steinberg, Alfred, *The Man from Missouri: Life and Times of Harry S. Truman*, Morrow, New York, 1973.

Stephens, Alan (ed.), *The War in the Air 1914–1994*, RAAF Air Power Studies Centre, Canberra, 1994.

Stouffer, Samuel et al., *Studies in Social Psychology, Volume 2, The American Soldier: Combat and its Aftermath*, Princeton University Press, Princeton, NJ, 1949.

Strachey, James (ed.), *The Standard Edition of the Complete Psychological Works*, Hogarth, London, 1964.

Sullivan, Gordon R. and Harper, Michael V., *Hope is not a Method*, Doubleday, New York, 1996.

Summers Jr, Harry G., *The Historical Atlas of the Vietnam War*, Houghton Mifflin, Boston, 1995.

Terriff, Terry, Croft, Stuart, James, Lucy and Morgan, Patrick M., *Security Studies Today*, Polity Press, Cambridge, 1999.

Thomas, Keith (ed.), *The Revolution in Military Affairs: Warfare in the Information Age*, Australian Defence Studies Centre, Australian Defence Force Academy, Canberra, 1997.

Thomson, James, *The Nexus between the Commercial Support Program and Members Required in Uniform*, Working Paper No. 44, Australian Defence Studies Centre, Canberra, 1996.

Thucydides, *History of the Peloponnesian War*, Penguin Books, Harmondsworth, 1954.

Toffler, Alvin and Toffler, Heidi, *War and Anti-War: Survival at the Dawn of the 21st Century*, Little, Brown and Company, Boston, 1993.

van Creveld, Martin, *The Transformation of War*, The Free Press, New York, 1991.

——*The Rise and Decline of the State*, Cambridge University Press, Cambridge, 1999.

van Steenbergen, Bart (ed.), *The Condition of Citizenship*, Sage Publications, London, 1994.

Vidal, Gore, *The Last Empire: Essays 1992–2001*, Abacus, London, 2001.

von Clausewitz, Carl, *On War*, M. Howard and P. Paret (eds & trans.), Princeton University Press, Princeton, NJ, 1989.

Walker, R. B. J, *One World, Many Worlds: Struggles for a Just World Peace*, Lynne Rienner, Boulder, CO, 1988.

Walzer, Michael, *Just and Unjust Wars*, Basic Books, New York, 2000.

Wass de Czege, Huba, and Hart Sinnreich, Richard, *Conceptual Foundations of a Transformed US Army*, Association of the United States Army, Institute for Land Warfare Paper No. 40, Washington DC, March 2002.

Wavell, General Sir Archibald, *Generals and Generalship*, Penguin Books, Harmondsworth, 1941.

Wing, Ian, *Refocusing Concepts of Security: The Convergence of Military and Non-military Tasks*, Land Warfare Studies Centre Working Paper No. 111, Duntroon, ACT, November 2000.

Weart, Stephen, *Never at War: Why Democracies Will Never Fight One Another*, Yale University Press, New Haven, CT, 1998.

Woodhouse, Tom and Ramsbotham, Oliver (eds), *Peacekeeping and Conflict Resolution*, Frank Cass, London, 2000.

Woodhouse, Tom, Bruce, Robert and Dando, Malcolm, *Peacekeeping and Peacemaking: Towards Effective Intervention in Post-Cold War Conflicts*, Macmillan, Basingstoke, 1998.

Wright, Quincy, *A Study of War*, University of Chicago Press Midway Reprint, Chicago, 1983.

Articles

Archibugi, Daniele, 'Immanuel Kant, cosmopolitan law and peace', *European Journal of International Relations*, 1(4), 1995.

Barnett, Jon and Dovers, Stephen, 'Environmental security, sustainability and policy', *Pacifica Review*, 13(2), pp. 157–69.

Bloch, George A., 'French military reform: lessons for America's army?', *Parameters: US Army War College Quarterly*, Summer 2000, vol. 30, no. 2, pp. 33–45.

Booth, Ken 'Security and emancipation', *Review of International Studies*, 17(4), 1991, pp. 313–26.

———, 'Human wrongs and international relations', *International Affairs*, 71(1), 1995, pp. 103–26, at p. 111.

Bozeman, Adda B., 'War and the clash of ideas', *Orbis: A Journal of World Affairs*, Spring 1976, vol. 20, no. 1, pp. 61–102.

Bracken, Paul, 'The military after next', *The Washington Quarterly*, 16(4), 1993, pp. 157–74.

Brooks, Doug, 'Messiahs or mercenaries? The future of private military services', *International Peacekeeping*, 7(4), Winter 2000, pp. 129–44.

Cerny, Philip, 'Neomedievalism, civil war and the new security dilemma: globalisation as durable disorder', *Civil Wars*, Spring 1998, vol. 1, no. 1, pp. 36–64.

Cheeseman, Graeme, 'Responding to "new times": securing Australia and Britain in a post–Cold War era', *Contemporary Security Policy*, 22(1), April 2001, pp. 107–36.

Christman, Lieutenant General Daniel W., 'Twenty-first century security challenges: the road to somewhere?', *National Security Studies Quarterly*, vol. VII, Issue 2, Spring 2001.

Desch, Michael C., 'War and strong states, peace and weak states?', *International Organization*, 50(2), Spring 1996, pp. 237–68.

Devetak, Richard and Higgott, Richard, 'Justice unbound: globalization, states and the transformation of the social bond', *International Affairs*, 75(3), 1999, pp. 483–98.

Downes, Cathy, 'To be or not to be a profession: the military case', *Defense Analysis*, vol. 1, no. 3, 1985.

Elliott, Lorraine, 'Environmental conflict: reviewing the arguments', *Journal of Environment and Development*, 5(2), June 1996, pp. 149–67.

Falk, Richard, 'State of siege: will globalization win out?', *International Affairs*, 73(1), 1997, pp. 123–36.

Francart, Brigadier General Loup and Patry, Jean-Jacques, 'Mastering violence: an option for operational military strategy', *Naval War College Review*, Summer 2000, vol. 53, no. 3, pp. 144–84.

Franks, General Frederick M., 'Full-dimensional operations: a doctrine for an era of change', *Military Review*, December 1993, vol. 73, no. 12, pp. 5–10.

Freedman, Laurence, 'The changing forms of military conflict', *Survival*, 40(4), 1998–99, pp. 39–56.

Funk, Lieutenant General Paul E., 'Battle space: a commander's tool on the future battlefield', *Military Review*, December 1993, vol. 73, no. 12, pp. 36–47.

Gaddis, John Lewis, 'A grand strategy of transformation', *Foreign Policy*, November/December 2002, pp. 50–7.

Galvin, John R., 'Uncomfortable wars: towards a new paradigm', *Parameters: Journal of the US Army War College*, Winter 1986, vol. 16, no. 4, pp. 2–8.

Gilley, Bruce, 'The region takes sides', *Far Eastern Economic Review*, 27 September 2001, pp. 24–5.

Grant, Brigadier C. S., 'The 2015 battlefield', *The British Army Review*, Winter 2001–02, no. 128, pp. 5–13.

Guéhenno, Jean-Marie, 'The impact of globalisation on strategy', *Survival*, Winter 1998–99, vol. 40, no. 4, pp. 5–19.

Harkavy, Robert, 'Images of the coming international system', *Orbis*, 41(4), Fall 1997, pp. 569–90.

Haycock, Ronald G., 'The labours of Athena and the Muses: historical and contemporary aspects of Canadian military education', *Canadian Military Journal*, vol. 2, no. 2, Summer 2001.

Held, David, 'Globalization and cosmopolitan democracy', *Peace Review*, 9(3), 1997, pp. 309–14.

Hobsbawm, Eric, 'War and peace in the 20th century', *London Review of Books*, 21 February 2002, pp. 16–1.

Hooton, Ted, 'Naval firepower comes of age', *Jane's Defence Weekly*, 13 November 2002, vol. 38, no. 20, pp. 17–28.

Huntington, Samuel P., 'The clash of civilizations?', *Foreign Affairs*, Summer 1993, vol. 72, no. 3, pp. 22–49.

Ignatius, Adi and McGirk, Tim, 'The Asian voyage', *Time*, 20 August 2001.

Kamradt, Professor H. D. and Diver, Dougie the, 'Net centricity—seminal doctrine or just puff?', *Naval Review*, January 2001, pp. 8–12.

Kaplan, Robert, 'The coming anarchy', *The Atlantic Monthly*, 273(2), 1994, pp. 44–81.

Kaysen, Karl and Rathjens, George W., 'Send in the troops: a UN Foreign Legion', *The Washington Quarterly*, 20(1), Winter 1997, pp. 207–28.

Knudsen, Tonny Brems, 'Humanitarian intervention revisited: post-Cold War responses to classical problems', *International Peacekeeping*, 3(4), Winter 1996, pp. 146–65.

Kober, Avi, 'Low-intensity conflicts: why the gap between theory and practise?', *Defense & Security Analysis*, March 2002, vol. 18, no. 1, pp. 15–38.

Krauss, Eric S. and Lacey, Mike O., 'Utilitarian vs. humanitarian: the battle over the law of war', *Parameters: US Army War College Quarterly*, Summer 2002, vol. 32, no. 2, pp. 73–84.

Lake, David A., 'Powerful pacifists: democratic states and war', *American Political Science Review*, 86(1), 1992, pp. 24–37.

Linklater, Andrew, 'Cosmopolitan citizenship', *Citizenship Studies*, 2(1), 1998, pp. 23–41.

Mackinlay, John and Kent, Randolph, 'A new approach to complex emergencies', *International Peacekeeping*, 4(4), Winter 1997, pp. 31–49.

Mainwaring, Max G., 'An interview with General John R. Galvin, US Army (Retd), Dean, Fletcher School of Law and Diplomacy, 6 August 1997', *Small Wars and Insurgencies*, vol. 9, no. 1, Spring 1998.

Mann, Michael, 'Has globalization ended the rise and rise of the nation-state?', *Review of International Political Economy*, 4(3), 1997, pp. 472–96.

Mathews, Jessica Tuchman, 'Redefining security', *Foreign Affairs*, 68, 1989, pp. 162–77.

Mearsheimer, John, 'The future of the American pacifier', *Foreign Affairs*, September–October 2001, pp. 46–60.

Metz, Steven, 'Which army after next? The strategic implications of alternative futures', *Parameters*, XXVII (3), 1997, pp. 15–26.

Murray, Williamson, 'Perspectives on policy and strategy', *Strategic Review*, vol. XXV, no. 3, Summer, p. 77.

Pudas, Captain Terry J., 'Preparing future coalition commanders', *Joint Forces Quarterly*, Winter 1993–94.

Record, Jeffrey, 'Thinking about China and war', *Aerospace Power Journal*, Winter 2001, vol. 15, no. 4, pp. 69–80.

RisCassi, General Robert W., 'Principles for coalition warfare', *Joint Forces Quarterly*, Summer 1993.

Roberts, Adam, 'Humanitarian war: military intervention and human rights', *International Affairs*, 69(3), 1993, pp. 429–49.

Rumsfeld, Donald H., 'Transforming the military', *Foreign Affairs*, May/June 2002, pp. 20–32.

Singer, P. W., 'Corporate warriors: the rise of the privatized military industry and its ramifications for international security', *International Security*, vol. 26, no. 3, Winter 2001/02.

Smith, Hugh, 'Educating the guardians: the politics of the Australian Defence Force Academy', *Politics*, vol. 19, no. 1, May 1984.

——'The use of armed forces in law enforcement: legal, constitutional and political issues in Australia' , *Australian Journal of Political Science*, vol. 33, no. 2, July 1998.

Svitak, Amy, 'US Army, Navy mull lessons learned in Afghanistan war', *Defense News*, 22–28 July 2002.

Stoffa, Adam Paul, 'Special forces, counterterrorism and the law of armed conflict', *Studies in Conflict and Terrorism*, June 1995, vol. 18, no. 1, pp. 47–66.

The Economist, 'Why and when to go in: the principles that should govern military intervention abroad', 4 January 2001, pp. 17–19.

Wallenstein, Peter and Sollenberg, Margateta, 'Armed conflict and regional conflict complexes, 1989–97', *Journal of Peace Research*, 35(5), 1998, pp. 621–34.

Walt, Stephen, 'International relations: one world, many theories', *Foreign Policy*, Spring 1998, pp. 29–46.

Wass de Czege, Huba and Majchrzak, Zbigniew M., 'Enabling operational maneuver from strategic distances', *Military Review*, May–June 2002, vol. 82, no. 3, pp. 16–20.

Wass de Czege, Huba, and Echevarria II, Antulio J., 'Insights for a power-projection army', *Military Review*, May–June 2000, vol. 80, no. 3, pp. 3–11.

Weiss, Linda, 'Globalization and the myth of the powerless state', *New Left Review*, 225, 1997, pp. 3–27.

Slaughter, Anne-Marie, 'The real new world order', *Foreign Affairs*, 76(5), September/October 1997, pp. 183–97.

Zinni, General Anthony C., 'A military for the 21st century: lessons from the recent past', *Strategic Forum*, no. 181, July 2001.

Newspapers

Barker, Geoffrey, 'Defence censorship absurd in peacetime', *The Australian Financial Review*, 3 September 2001, p. 55.

Briquemont, General Francis, *Le Point*, 5 January 1994.

Briquemont, General Francis, *Le Figaro*, 18 September 1994.

Garran, Robert, 'Recall for "critical" army paper', *The Australian*, 13 October 2000, p. 6.

Wright, L., 'Annan heaps praise on Howard military', *The Canberra Times*, 22 February 2000, pp. 1–2.

Electronic sources

Blair, Admiral Dennis C., Address to the Dean's Roundtable Breakfast, Graduate School of International Relations and Pacific Studies, University of California,

San Diego, 13 April 2000, <http://www.pacom.mil/ref/2000/sst/SANDIEGO.htm> (downloaded 29 May 2000).

—— 'Change is possible and imperative', *Naval Institute Proceedings*, <http://www.usni.org/Proceedings/Articles01/PROblair5.htm> May 2001, vol. 127/5/1, 179 (downloaded 6 September 2001).

Clark, General Wesley, Press Conference Brussels 27 April 1999, <www.freeserbia.net/Documents/Kosovo/NATO0427.html> (downloaded 9 August 2002).

Department of Defence, *Defence Submission to the Senate Committee on Foreign Affairs Defence and Trade Inquiry into Recruitment and Retention*, 24 May 2001, para. 120, <http://www.aph.gov.au/senate/committee/fadt_ctte/adf_personnel/sublist.htm>.

Kaldor, Mary, 'Cosmopolitanism and organised violence', paper presented to the Conference on Conceiving Cosmopolitanism, Warwick, 27–29 April 2000, <http://www.theglobalsite.ac.uk>.

Qiao Liang and Wang Xiangsui, *Unrestricted Warfare*, PLA Literature and Arts Publishing House, 1999, <http://www.infowar.com.mil_c41/00/unrestrictedwarfare.pdf>.

Ramphal, Sir Shridath, 'Our global neighbourhood—facing the 21st century', Fiftieth Anniversary Commemorative Lecture of the first Meeting of the United Nations General Assembly, Westminster Central Hall, London, 13 January 1996, <http://www.cgg.ch/unacgg.html> (downloaded 25 September 2001).

Rice, Colonel Anthony J., 'Command and control: the essence of coalition warfare', *Parameters*, Spring 1997, p. 10 of 13, <http://carlisle www.army.mil/usawc/Parameters/97spring/rice.htm> (downloaded 15 June 1999).

Solana, Dr Javier, Secretary-General of NATO, Press Statement 040, 23 March 1999, <http://www.nato.int/docu/pr/1999/p99–040e.htm> (downloaded 8 September 2002).

The Einstein–Freud Correspondence (1931–32), <www.cis.vt.edn/modernworld/d/einstein.html>.

United Nations Newservice, 'Secretary-General thanks Australia for taking lead in helping East Timor', <http://www.un.org/News/dh/latest/page2.html#22>, 21 February 2000 (downloaded 23 February 2000).

United Nations, *The World at Six Billion*, United Nations Population Division of the Department of Economic and Social Affairs, New York, 1999, <http://www.Popin.org/6billion>.

United States Central Intelligence Agency, *Long-Term Global Demographic Trends: Reshaping the Geopolitical Landscape*, Langley VA, July 2001, <http://www.cia.gov>.

Index